DORA RUSSELL was born in 1894, the daughter of a distinguished civil servant. In 1912 she went to Girton College, Cambridge, where she obtained a first class degree. She visited Russia immediately after the 1917 Revolution, lived with Bertrand Russell in China in the 20s, married him, bore two of his children, and later founded with him their progressive school, Beacon Hill. Dora Russell was one of the first women to stand for Parliament, and she has always campaigned vigorously for birth control, maternity leave, sexual reform and world peace. Through her long public life of campaigning, travelling and writing she has retained a tireless idealism and integrity. In *Tamarisk Tree 3*, which spans the years between the 1940s and 80s, her unshakeable commitment to peace and particularly to improved relations between east and west, is portrayed in her work for the paper *British Ally*, hailed in Russia as a symbol of wartime alliance; her dismay at the burgeoning of Cold War politics toward the end of the 1940s, and her travels with the Women's Peace Caravan in the 50s and early 60s through Europe, India, China, East Berlin, Russia and the United States. Her involvement with the peace and women's movements has stretched into the 1980s.

Amongst Dora Russell's publications have been *Hypatia: or Women and Knowledge* (1925), *The Right to be Happy* (1927), attacking sexual taboos, *In Defence of Children* (1932), *The Religion of the Machine Age* (1983) and *The Dora Russell Reader: 57 Years of Writing and Journalism* (1984). Virago published her two earlier volumes of autobiography, *The Tamarisk Tree 1* in 1977, and *Volume 2* in 1981. Dora Russell settled in Cornwall many years ago: now in her nineties, she lives there still.

D1133771

THE
TAMARISK TREE
3
CHALLENGE TO THE COLD WAR

DORA RUSSELL

Published by VIRAGO PRESS Limited 1985
41 William IV Street, London WC2N 4DB

British Library Cataloguing in Publication Data

Russell, Dora
The tamarisk tree.
Vol. 3
1. Russell, Dora   2. Feminists – England –
Biography
I. Title
305.4'2'0924   HQ1595.R/

ISBN 0-86068-447-4
ISBN 0-86068-452-0 Pbk

Printed in Great Britain by
Anchor Brendon Ltd and
typeset by
Folio Photosetting, Bristol

To all those, men and women both sides of the Iron Curtain, with whose lives, work and faith my own life was entangled over many years in the effort to bring about understanding and peace between peoples and nations, I dedicate this record of our labours. I cannot name them all. Especially I pay tribute to those who faced war risks for the production of *British Ally*, among them the two Moscow editors – Horace White to whose story of the paper, *Experiment in Friendship*, I am greatly indebted, and Archie Johnstone, a man of principle to which he made his person sacrifice.

CONTENTS

Appendixes

PREFACE

I had undertaken to write the story of my life after the closing of my school and the end of the war. But what I had learned during the war, and from subsequent events, stirred my memory of a project that dated from far back in my first visit to the Soviet Union in 1920. I began to feel that my misgivings and prophecies about what I called *The Religion of the Machine Age* had begun to come true. So I wrote that book which was published in 1983.

When I began *Tamarisk Tree 3* there was a new rising tide of activity among women, feminism, consciousness raising, protests on nuclear war, disarmament and peace. Women who felt that there had been secrecy and misinformation wanted to know more about the immediate past. Quite a number of them kept coming to me to ask questions, and delayed my writing. But their coming was fruitful I believe, both for them and for me.

Writing the book was difficult enough in itself, hence this explanation. In addition to the personal story, what my family and I did or felt, there were matters of public service and public events in which, at times, both they and I were closely involved. I had therefore to write what in fact is a segment of little known political history. This is not based on my memory, but on actual, authentic documents, correspondence, records of journeys, which I have preserved in my 'archives'. I have tried to report what I knew personally of the activities of the women's movement from the 1940s onwards to the present day.

The second of my almost lifelong preoccupations, to mitigate and to challenge the Cold War between the West and the Soviet Union, finds a prominent place in this book because from 1943–1950 I worked in the Soviet Relations Department of the Ministry of Information and had considerable knowledge of the moods prevailing during those years both sides of the Iron Curtain.

This book, like my previous autobiographies, bears the title of the *Tamarisk Tree*. As a child I took that strange tree in my garden, with its feathery leaves and rare pink flowers, as a symbol of the fairy tale land of hopes and ideals. Today Utopia seems further off than ever; our vaunted progress a hollow sham; our science denuded of prestige and denigrated utterly to the service of war; humankind throughout the world increasingly in disunity, hatred and violence.

Yet dreams do not die, they recur, sleeping or waking they haunt us. Deep within us we know that our world could be redeemed from its present pitiful state and blossom forth to bring comfort, security and happiness to all humankind. So we labour on, whether alone or in communal association with one another. I hope this book may make a small contribution to our task. In this I am indebted and grateful for the constant help of my secretary Lally Henty, and Ruth Petrie for her careful reading and comment on a difficult text.

Dora Russell,
Carn Voel, Porthcurno,
January 1985

The very relevant film of the Women's Caravan of Peace can be obtained on videotape from Concord Films Council Limited, 201 Felixstowe Road, Ipswich, Suffolk, 1P3 9BJ.

PART ONE

1

I BECOME A
CIVIL SERVANT

Tamarisk Tree 2 was the story of what happened to my family and myself after Bertrand Russell had left me and I had fulfilled my undertaking to divorce him. The struggle to maintain Beacon Hill School, as I did for the next eleven years, up to the outbreak and during a part of the Second World War, is the main theme of the book. It ends with describing how, when I had been accepted for a post at the Ministry of Information, we moved furniture out of store in Penzance, to a house which my son John and I had found in Dartmouth Road, not far from Willesden Green station, in North West London. At that time there were many empty houses whose owners had moved away from the threat of the bombing in London.

My son John had returned from America to join the Navy. After his preliminary training, he was put on a course to learn Japanese at the Institute of Oriental Languages in London. He was allowed, during the course, to find himself lodgings; naturally he was glad at the thought of being able to live with my husband Pat and me. John's plans were what had finally clinched the decision on our part, to move. The school in the house in Cornwall could not expand; the work was exhausting and we could only barely survive financially. It was possible to make arrangements for the remaining boarding children to be placed safely elsewhere.

Our menagerie of cats, chickens and Rover the dog came too. The back garden became a poultry farm until we had eaten the birds. A large trunk contained tinned and packaged food from Cornwall to keep us going until such times as my salary began to come in. John's pay supplied the first three months' rent, to be repaid to him by his being fed for an appropriate period. My children Harriet and Roderick were with us. Looking back I note that it did not occur to any of us that they might remain in Cornwall like the evacuees. We took it for granted that we would not split up. Harriet, who had already attended secondary school in Penzance, did not find it too difficult to fit in with a similar school in North London. Roddy was a greater problem. He had, so far, not bothered much about academic subjects, nor was the atmosphere of the typical boys' school likely to be congenial to him. For a while he attended the Haberdashers' Aske School, where, for the first time, he became aware of the scholastic use made of the cane. I think it was here that, as a relief from the total change of atmosphere, he took to cricket, for which his love continued right up to when he became Captain of the young players at Lords and was on the point of embarking on a career as a professional cricketer. Cricket was all he ever learned in his short stay at this school. John often helped him with his homework in the evenings.

We had no shelter at this house, except for a very large, strong kitchen table. When a number of fire bombs began descending in our street (one in fact, made a hole in a bench on Willesden Green station and I was often amused to see the hole still there years after the war ended), Harriet and Roddy did not seem to be really afraid. I remember that Roddy rather wanted to run outside and watch them coming down. John and I had long hours of duty; Pat, now my husband, and released from the Army, turned his hand to anything and everything, but it was not really possible to care properly for the two children. For a time we sent them away, though they protested vigorously, to stay with Lily[1] and her people in Southport, Lancashire. Later on Curry, the Headmaster at Dartington, accepted them both, thus they were safely there in term time and in the holidays were able to be at Carn Voel, cared for by Ellery Fricker[2] with, I think, her daughter and others. I had begun earning a small salary and, as my status at the Ministry improved, so did my finances. Nonetheless, it was always very hard to find the money for the school fees.

The Ministry of Information, when I began to work there in 1943, was in the London University building behind the British Museum.

4

Universities and colleges had been evacuated to country areas and towns less likely to be exposed to attack from the air. Oddly enough, John came daily to his Japanese studies in the Oriental Languages section, just behind the main university building. Evidently it was thought that the teaching of the Navy might take place at greater risk than that of civilians.

My department in the Ministry was called the Reference Division. Its function was to follow the Press and other sources of information, and prepare periodical reports for other government departments, as well as any specially requested reports on some current topic or historical reference. I had enjoyed collecting information in libraries in my researches of postgraduate days. I was not a stranger to this kind of work, but I had done it on my own initiative. I had no idea what the life of a civil servant in a government department was like. But as I sat at a trestle table in that small back room, high up in the tall white building, facing the inevitable in- and out-trays I recalled my father's pride in the civil service. I felt some relief from the pioneering and responsibility of carrying on the school and from the long drain of trying to give out to the children the warmth and sense of security that they needed.

My colleague, facing me at the trestle table, was a very agreeable woman archaeologist, from New Zealand. According to its varied purposes, the Ministry recruited many types of intellectuals: academics, journalists, linguists, others conversant with Press photography and the film world. Many people, whose own work had been interrupted by the war, found in the Ministry occupations and opportunities of mutual benefit.

At first I missed the lively, warm companionship of the children. But no one with an enquiring mind and a passion for books and information is ever lonely. The lonely ones are those who feel that they do not belong because their ideals bring them into conflict with the tide of opinion and established institutions. This had been my experience on such issues as pacifism, birth control, women's rights, education. I could not help laughing that I should now find myself in government service and at the heart of the Established Order. Was this all right? Well, whatever the muddles and mistakes of our politicians, this war had now to be fought. I did find myself in accord with the present purposes of my fellow citizens.

Above all there came a great feeling of liberation. Released from the incessant coping with daily anxieties and domestic chores, I was able, as one individual, to use my mind and think freely and uninterrupted, as I had not done so for many years. So, in 1943, I began to read avidly everything that came my way in the In tray. There had been so little time, when running the school in its last home in Cornwall, to read the papers or even listen to the radio news. We had kept in touch only with the main events of the war.

Now I began to study both the reports of the fighting and the comments and opinions expressed in the daily Press.

The war had not been going well for the Allies. Though Churchill was respected, and felt to be the only possible leader, his prestige was greatly damaged by the fall of Tobruk in June 1942. Russia had been invaded on 22 June 1941 and the heroic resistance of her army and people to the German attacks caused considerable unrest and discontent in Britain at what was felt to be our failure of whole-hearted concentration on the war effort. There were persistent demands to know why the Second Front – by means of a landing in Brittany – had been so long delayed. In so far as I recollect what impressed me most of all in my first studies of the national Press, it was to find them discussing, with the war not yet won, what was to be the policy towards a defeated Germany.

It had, of course, never occurred to me that there would be any change in German frontiers when the war ended. I was surprised to read about plans to carve up Germany, and even of the section which each ally was to take over. It seems, I thought, that they intend that there shall be no Germany left. Then I read an article or letter by H.N. Brailsford, a journalist whom I knew personally and entirely trusted: he was protesting against these dismemberment proposals. My admiration for him soared. And my enthusiasm for collecting information greatly increased. I remember that, on the eve of Christmas, as I sat, alone at the time, oblivious to anything but reading documents, the Director of my division put his head round the door and remarked with surprise that I was still there, everyone having gone home sharp on time, or a trifle early, to celebrate the festive season. This is not to suggest that slackness was characteristic of my colleagues. On the contrary, we worked hard and long hours. The ministry was manned fully seven days, week-ends arranged by shifts.

Once or twice I was given the responsibility of producing the monthly report from the Division. The difficulty about this was, with so much material, what to leave out, as well as to avoid overlapping with other special sections, such as the information from French sources.

My most interesting and enlightening task was to start compiling a list of international organisations, of all types and purposes. I became fascinated by what I began to learn about the Pan-American Union.

The Pan-American Union interested me because it had obviously been started with the idea of bringing South America into relation with its highly-developed neighbour in the North. I thought this a good plan and in keeping with the Munro doctrine, which had been put forward as a means of preventing the old quarrels and sects of Europe repeating themselves in what was to be the new world of freedom and opportunity.

A Pan-American building in Washington symbolised the potential co-operation between the North and South. It seems that when it occurred to someone that it would be a good idea to plan a certain road, or rules about shipping in the southern continent, then the US Foreign Minister would approach the foreign ministers of the various countries and a meeting would take place. Next the chief businessmen of the Southern countries would be brought in, and presently an act of agreement on the topic under discussion would be drafted. Each country, in its turn, as it decided to ratify the agreement, would deposit the document of ratification in the Pan-American building in Washington.

Clearly all this was extremely useful for the separate governments and for their ambitious entrepreneurs, and developers. I was, of course, very ignorant about the politics of all these countries, and my task quite simply was to make notes and set down what the procedure was, and what had been accomplished and ratified. But I could not help reflecting that the people of these countries did not seem to have been consulted, and that there was but little element of democracy in the whole process. It was not my business to comment, but to record.

When, however, the war ended, and the Allies met together for the purpose of founding the United Nations, somehow my memory recalled this small piece of research. And as I listened to the trumpeting voices from California proclaiming 'We the Peoples' I thought to myself, how much do they really care about the peoples? It is the governments and statesmen who are setting up this organisation; quite on the model of the Pan-American Union. At that time also United

Nations' Associations within the member countries were made up of people nominated by certain of their own State Departments. In England, Ellen Wilkinson, then at the Ministry of Education, took an active part in this local aspect.

Of course, in time, the United Nations Association within countries extended into membership and democratic procedure; a great variety of associations sought, and acquired, what was called 'non-governmental consultative status' (the NGOs) and were able to bring the issues with which they were concerned to various sectors and sessions at the United Nations. The voice of the people, if only in the lobbies or occasionally on the floor in debate, began to be heard. I was present with a group of English feminists, including Mrs Pethick Lawrence, when, in London, we met and asked the President of the Economic and Social Council of the UN (at that date an Indian gentleman) to give us a Status of Women Committee. We got it, with results for women's status that have been world-wide, if not yet achieving all that must be done both by and for women.

I remember one entertaining small incident in the Reference Division, when a colleague came to me saying, 'You have been in America, what do the letters GOP stand for in American politics?' In those days, of course, we had not yet arrived at the present abominable practice of designating groups and organisations by their acronyms. I confessed my ignorance about GOP. Presently my colleague returned, 'You'll never believe it,' she said, 'it means Grand Old Party – the Republicans.' At this, with some merriment, we decided that perhaps the last letter might well have been 'D'. In their box-like abodes civil servants do not have much to amuse them except the jokes they make for themselves.

I was of course not a permanent, but merely temporary civil servant; the exact grade at which I began I cannot now remember, but my salary, then not large, was by present standards abysmally small. However, any civil servant has opportunities for advancement and promotion. Presently I found that several posts, some of them newly created, were available in other departments of the Ministry and were to be found listed on notice boards.

I applied for one in what was described as the Soviet Relations Branch, was interviewed and accepted. I did not know what my work might be. For the first time I learned of the existence of *British Ally*,

Britansky Soyuznik, a paper which the British government was actually publishing in Moscow and which I was to have the pleasure of serving for the next six years.

Notes

1. Lily had been matron at Beacon Hill, my school.
2. Mrs Fricker's daughter had been a pupil at the school.

2

BRITISH ALLY

When I came into the Soviet Relations Branch, *British Ally* had been in existence for nearly two years, since August 1942. Although this was before I joined the staff of the paper, it seems the moment to record the history of its birth. Communication with the Soviet Union had not been easy, or amicable, because the war had begun with the assumption that Russia would be neutral or, potentially, on the German side. When the Germans invaded and penetrated even further into Russian territory, came the need to try and help the Russians with war supplies. At the same time came the feeling that there ought to be closer cultural relations and understanding between ourselves and our new ally. Peter Smollett, Head of Soviet Relations Branch, already had direct relations with the Soviet Embassy in London because the Ministry of Information was concerned with the supply of paper for the weekly bulletin of *Soviet War News*, published by the Soviet Embassy.

Already in October 1941, Smollett had tentatively discussed with Mr Zinchenco, First Secretary of the Soviet Embassy, the possibility of publishing a similar weekly bulletin of British War News via His Majesty's Embassy in Moscow. The idea had been favourably received and accompanied by suggested offers of help from Pravda of translators and staff, as well as distribution. Accordingly, a telegram asking the British Ambassador in Moscow to make a definite request for such a paper to Mr Molotov, People's Commissioner for Foreign Affairs, was sent on 29 March 1942. Molotov's reply on 5 April to the British

Ambassador was favourable but indefinite. However, definite permission came through from the Soviet Embassy by 11 April and on the following day Mr Smollett applied for the first financial sanction permitting the cabling of material for such a paper.

Meantime it seems that even from the Bank of England a suggestion had come, via Sir John Russell, FRS (adviser to Soviet Relations Branch) that some means of acquainting the Russians with British news and views was desirable, if Soviet permission could be obtained. British moves were tentative, no doubt in view of pre-war diplomatic tension, and the known hostility of the Russians to what they considered propaganda from Western sources. There were also the sheer physical difficulties and risks of travel. The Soviet Government was in retreat from Moscow to Kuibishev. Nonetheless, with a view to establishing Anglo–Soviet cultural relations, John Lawrence of the BBC European Service and George Reavey, an Irish poet and translator of some Russian work, left England by ship in March 1942 to act as Press Attaché and Assistant Press Attaché; with them also was Barry Cornwall, who had journalistic experience. They carried a mass of material – photographs, films, articles, books. A few days out from Murmansk, their ship was attacked by air and sunk. They survived, but all their baggage was lost; they reached Kuibishev in June 1942 with no resources at all. It is said that two women secretaries were flown out to reach Kuibishev in the bomb racks of planes. The Soviet authorities offered a nucleus of Russian staff, printing facilities and paper.

In London discussions were taking place about the layout, size and style of the paper, as well as editorship and preparation of material. The idea was an eight page paper with a centre spread, which could be posted up in clubs where many more than the subscribers might read it. The number of copies was limited by the issue of paper; the agreement was for 50,000 copies, the exact number of *Soviet War News*.

Paper supplies did vary, and at times some paper was sent from Britain. It must be remembered what communication was like under war conditions in 1942. Even air flights by statesmen between Russia and Britain could be highly dangerous. All important material for the paper had to be cabled, about 5,000 miles, via Cairo and Teheran, and photographs were wired. The technical and editorial staff on the paper were half in London, half in Kuibishev, and later in Moscow, to which, as the Russians held their ground at and after Stalingrad, the central direction of Government and attendant activities returned.

Russian co-operation was willingly given and this new enterprise began to mean much to all concerned. The name *British War News* was never used for the paper, it became *Britansky Soyuznik/British Ally* from the start and soon carried a masthead showing a British and Russian soldier side by side with their flags. The paper was never once censored in all the eight years of its existence. That the first issue of *British Ally* appeared little more than a year after it was first thought of must be regarded as an honour to all those who, in war-time danger and frustration, managed to achieve its publication.

Relations between the two governments were improving; Churchill visited Stalin and, despite Stalin's pressure for a second war front, their conversations were amicable. Molotov came to England, and in May 1942, a treaty between him and the then Foreign Secretary, Anthony Eden, pledged the two countries to work together in Europe for common aims for the next twenty years.

On 16 August 1942 the first issue of *British Ally* was published in an edition of 15,000 with eight pages. It carried a portrait of Churchill on the front page and warm messages from Anthony Eden and Brendan Bracken, who was then Minister of Information.

Anthony Eden wrote of Molotov's visit and the pact. Brendan Bracken stressed the British war effort, not only by the armed forces, but by the civilians in factories, workshops and mines. He looked forward to understanding and co-operation between Russia and Britain in post-war reconstruction. Other messages in this issue came from the First Sea Lord, Chief of Naval Staff Admiral of the Fleet Sir Dudley Pound and from the Commander-in-Chief, Air Chief Marshal Sir Arthur Harris.

The paper received a warm welcome, for it supplied a long-felt want. M. Vyshinsky thanked H.M. Ambassador 'from the heart' for a copy of the first issue. Russians had felt themselves cut off from the outside world. Letters and subscriptions flooded in. Horace White, from the *Daily Herald*, who became editor in Russia in January 1943 and continued until 1946, has described how the paper would be resold at ten and twenty times its published price. He also notes the comment of readers that the paper gave the news 'without political propaganda'.

In Kuibishev the staff endured much hardship, inadequate heating in the cold winter, frequent breakdowns of electric fires and phones. The

London staff, by contrast, worked in comparative comfort, though exposed to enemy action. We did not retire into shelters but were instructed just to keep away from windows when bombs fell.

As is usual, there were editorial meetings to which it was hoped that we would all come with bright ideas. At that time the average person in Britain knew, or cared, very little about the Soviet Union, unless he or she were a member of the Communist Party, whom the Government were naturally reluctant to employ. There was for a long time a general impression that the extreme right or extreme left must be excluded on security grounds. Most of us owed our jobs to our useful background experience, knowledge of languages, travels, journalistic ability. What did emerge, as I soon felt, was the sense among us all that it was worthwhile to work for the success of this paper. War had brought us an ally gallant in battle and of superhuman endurance, to whom we owed something in return. For me personally it meant more. I had visited Russia twice since the revolution, but each time without any political commitment. I had loved the kind of people I had met there from our very first acquaintance.

When I came into Soviet Relations Branch I felt at first both diffident and inadequate. I had never been in a job like this, I wondered what use I would be to those who employed me or to the Russians who would read our paper. Here in this pleasant office I met my colleagues, who were, I felt sure, more competent than I. They were a small group, an assorted variety of people.

Peter Smollett, at the head, was of Hungarian origin; he consulted frequently the Honourable Richard Hare, who was fluent in Russian, with a Russian wife. There was Marris Murray, an agreeable woman journalist, who I believe hailed from South Africa; A.L. (Bert) Lloyd, mostly famous later for his brilliance in folksong, was a journalist of varied experience, including working on whaling ships; Lena Chivers, permanent civil servant, had been seconded from Inland Revenue, I think, because she had sent in some articles likely to be of interest to young people. (Lena is now Baroness Jeger.) Rose Kosky acted in a very competent secretarial capacity. Maurice Lovell, it appeared to me, was the editor in the sense that he indicated to us what were the regular features of the paper and what each of us should contribute.

At that time, of course, I did not know the earlier history of the venture, nor about all that went into continuous maintenance of contact,

13

and despatch of material: a savage war on land, sea and air was being waged while we merely sat at our desks getting ideas, making suggestions and giving orders – a prevailing attitude characteristic of all Whitehall, against which all civil servants should be on their guard.

Maurice Lovell explained to us the general layout of the paper: it gave news of the war effort, projected Britain's countryside and towns and way of life. One feature was comment from the British Press which did not confine itself to right-wing views, but even included extracts from the *Daily Worker*.

My first task was to produce a short article to celebrate Churchill's seventieth birthday. I began to look for something complimentary that Churchill might have said about Soviet Russia. Apart from his assurance of whole-hearted support when Germany attacked, there was absolutely nothing. Since the war much has been said about Stalin's disregard of warnings from British intelligence but the Russians may have felt that, based on previous experience, they had little reason to trust such a source. Churchill does, in fact, stand out as the one Western statesman who had, all along, envisaged the probability that Russia would become a great military power. This, their potential power and not their system of government to which he was bitterly opposed, was what concerned him in the international diplomatic balance. I wrote my piece with tact and care, making what I could of Churchill's present pledges of support and friendship, and of what his leadership meant to our people at home.

The daily and weekly Press, journals of all kinds, came into our office and were distributed to the appropriate recipients to give information and inspire ideas. One morning at the editorial conference there was some discussion about a message received from our office in Russia, saying that there was a demand for coverage of science in the paper. Here I must explain that, in 1943, science had not permeated the popular press or popular consciousness to the extent which it has today.

The findings of science, results of research by scientists, were almost exclusively to be found in their separate journals which covered medicine, engineering, biology and so on in infinite succession. The journal *Nature* attempted a general survey; its very title indicates that the ultimate basis of science was man's curiosity about the natural world. So convinced had I become that science was exercising an increasing influence on human life and behaviour that in my own researches I had been puzzled by the fact that, so far, no one seemed to have written a history of science. Nor, as I recall, were there any journals which attempted to explain various disciplines of science to ordinary people in popular terms, and there seemed to be no journalists to supply copy for such journals if they were to exist.

There were blank faces at our editorial meeting when 'covering science' in *British Ally* was discussed. Journalists were not scientists; scientists, who write in their own jargon, were not journalists. I had been looking over some of the journals which had found their way into my In tray. I made a rash offer. I said that my knowledge of science extended to having passed Higher School Certificate Chemistry with distinction, but that I would be delighted to receive the science periodicals and see whether I could do anything useful in that field. So, unless and until a professional scientist might be acquired, I found a place on the editorial team which did not clash with the topics covered by others, and which afforded me several years of delighted discovery and learning about science itself, as well as its relations to the interests of our Russian readers. What is more, I become fully aware of the fact that scientific discovery and invention are regarded by men of science as the one real link which surpasses political or nationalist feeling in uniting human intelligence. Scientists did seek, or professed to seek, fundamental realities that thinking men the world over might accept as truths.

The procedure for obtaining material for *British Ally* was elastic and gave room for individual initiative. Each of us could suggest a topic on which an article might be commissioned, or else select one from a periodical. The 'second rights' of such an article were then purchased and the article was sent to the office in Russia for translation and publication. This dispatch of an article implied the consent of the London editorial office, and nothing was of course sent which was not sanctioned in London. The Russian editorial end could ask for material, make suggestions and objections, but had no authority to initiate publication of material other than what was sent and sanctioned from London.

One of my first discoveries was the non-existence of popular science journalists in Britain. Ritchie Calder (who later became a Peer) was beginning to be known; there was also Edward Goldsmith. Ritchie

Calder, who died recently, is still insufficiently appreciated for his services to human understanding and popular causes for human welfare and survival; he is a very great loss. He began professional life as a crime reporter, frequenting magistrates' courts. There he must have become acquainted with the seamy side of human relations, problems of human welfare and human ignorance. He became interested in science and in offering popular articles. While I was on *British Ally*, when I came across some topic on which a specialist was not available or not suitable, I often picked up the telephone and contacted Ritchie Calder. I could count not only on an immediate response, but on an article delivered promptly of appropriate content and length.

As I browsed, day after day, in so many journals, my absorption in the work gradually inspired greater self-confidence. In *Nature* I came across a letter from a Swiss scientist about a new insecticide for which great claims were being made. I hesitated and then asked for an article by him on this subject. My choice met a query from my chiefs; why should an insecticide be of special interest to *British Ally*? I replied that, melancholy though it might seem, in my experience in the Soviet Union the topic might be of considerable relevance. It so happened that, at that juncture, the British Army authorities in Naples were dealing with a threatened epidemic of typhus by spraying the troops with this very insecticide, DDT. Not only that, but Churchill, in the House of Commons, made a speech expounding the wonders of science and how they were contributing to the war effort, and he actually said, 'We have the wonderful DDT.'

The article went to Moscow and carried a headline of Churchill's words. This greatly contributed to my reputation as a science editor. Among the constant flow of fan mail from all over the Soviet Union a considerable amount began to come to my contributions on science. It is a fact, I believe, that the Russians' first knowledge of the Rhesus blood factor came to them through me and *British Ally*. The extent to which the war, and before that the cold war, had isolated them, had not been imagined.

Another item which I considered to be one of my successes was not scientific, but a piece which I concocted out of all the Press reports when the flying bombs began coming over. They did rather terrify, with a horrible rattling like a worn-out engine, then a breathless silence, while you wondered just where the beastly thing was finally going to drop.

'Old motorbikes', or 'flying bedsteads' and other comical names were given to them with admirable levity by our Press. My summary, I heard, was appreciated by our Russian readers as evidence of our national courage under bombardment. The V2 rockets, which came later, were really worse; they simply stole in silently and landed. One blew out all the windows in our house – and embedded itself several yards along the road in the embankment of the District line. My husband Pat and our dog happened, at the time, to be alone in the house; Pat was thrown out of bed but uninjured. In the beds, which might otherwise have been occupied, great spokes of broken glass stood up like spears.

An autobiography of events during a war signifies nothing. At such times a personal life is meaningless, bound up as it is with what is happening to the community as a whole, and conditioned, day by day, by rules necessarily imposed by authority about food rations, movement, military duty, civilian work-loads, not to mention the additional disruption of life by day, and sleep by night, from enemy action.

In retrospect the whole period becomes a never-ending nightmare in which dates, sequences, even relevance are in wild confusion.

For instance, on the night when the V2 visited our road, John and Kate and I were spending a weekend in the Isle of Wight. It was fairly late on in the war. My daughter Kate, having finished her university course in America had decided, war or no war, to join her brother while he was not yet on active duty. Naturally she was with us, and I found that the Reference Division at the Ministry was quite pleased to employ her. I was too busy to be much of a companion, but one or two of John's Naval friends came to our house. My twin nephews, whose mother had died of TB during the war, were both now in the armed services. One, Harold, in the RAF; the other, Fisher, in the Army. Occasionally, on coming into my kitchen in the morning I would find one of them sitting asleep with arms on the table – the back door was never locked. Harold, like many young RAF men, soon went away for training in Rhodesia. Fisher continued in the Army.

Once as I served the Sunday joint I remarked that we must cut no more but put it away for another time. Kate asked why. This was one of her first experiences of the severity of war-time rationing. I could see that London at war was very different from what Kate had left behind. There were people who managed some social life, frequenting theatres and cinemas and night clubs, but we were not among them. I had enough with office and home; and Pat's continued bronchitic cough worried me. Nor had I entirely recovered from the long strain of holding on to the school. When I saw a doctor who had known me previously about my health, he said, 'You will be all right, but you are a very tired lady.'

For fun I said we would take a weekend off; where, was my secret, but it would be 'out of England'. So over the water we went, on an absurd trip to my beloved Isle of Wight; only, in phoning Pat, I got the message 'Ellen right' (our code indicating that there had been an 'incident') and hence, on our return, had to sweep up more broken glass.

Kate presently found that she could obtain a post-graduate grant at her college in the States and, feeling that she was not able to contribute much to the war effort, went back to America. I do not blame her. One could hardly say that we had much home life. For a time, Ady, mother of Wynne Henderson, who had cooked for us briefly in Cornwall, was with us, but left London when the incendiaries began to fall.

There was a considerable period when John, Pat and I, at the sound of an alert in the late evening, would go by tube to St John's Wood, and there share the platforms with other weary citizens. There was an old empty shop on the corner, where we kept our sleeping bags and old blankets. John was sometimes out of London at weekends to visit a school friend whom I hoped he was going to marry.

We had gradually eaten our chicken and ducks; it became very difficult to get a bird for Christmas dinner, but about such matters Pat always proved resourceful. At home we still had one or two cats, but Rover, our dog, developed an internal growth and had to be put down. John and I were at work; Pat was not, and in his isolation, the loss of his dog affected him very deeply. After John got his sailing orders I persuaded Pat to go down to Cornwall for fresh air and at least the company of one or two old friends.

For a while I was alone all night in the house at Dartmouth Road except for the cats. I must confess that I was horribly scared. I fed the cats, but all my own meals I took in the Ministry canteen or in cafés. There were no more casual visitors. My nephew Fisher took part in the D-Day landings, during which he suffered a head wound, which involved considerable hospital care and time. Harold was fortunate in that the war ended before he was on active service. John's sailing orders, which he was not allowed to divulge, took him back to the United States where his war, in Washington, was to translate Japanese messages and cables.

In those years we all learned the true meaning of those fatal words 'total war'. A personal life became a part of the war, or it meant nothing. I was fortunate in that, whatever the harassment, my life was filled with thinking and doing of deep interest to me and what I felt to be a real service to peace and the good and creative in human life.

No doubt there are thousands of people in the upper ranks of bureaucracy and government who feel that they are spending their lives in the service of humanity. For the most part they are actuated by the need to earn their living, as I was, but also by personal ambition and a delight in the possession, not only of power over others, but of secrets and inside information that is carefully withheld from the people as a whole. Secrecy in wartime is unavoidable; the trouble is that, as mankind insists on maintaining a state of war in what they call peace, secrecy remains and widely extends as an essential function of government. If only the people who hold power, and access to vital and important knowledge and information, really did use it for the purpose of caring for and informing the general public, how different would be the world in which we live.

The hours and days in the Ministry became my whole life, a life of communication with the minds of others, whether far off, or beside me on the printed pages, or in the voices which I called to my phone. As we built up the circulation of *British Ally*, I felt to the full that beguiling sense of power and purpose which nowadays, with the immense spread of all kinds of electronic communication in the hands of those who rule over us, we have come to fear. By chance, I was also immersed in the waters of the source which presently flooded such communications – the discoveries of science. Reviewing those years, my conscience tells me that I did not misuse what little either of power or of purpose I possessed.

Apart from my own contributions, I knew only part of the rest of the paper. With Lena Chivers, who dealt with education, as well as so many other aspects in the 'projection' of Britain, I formed a friendship which has lasted over all the years. Some of the time we faced each other across desks in the same room. For a short period Lena enjoyed a visit to the office in Moscow, and communicated with me from there.

Younger than I, she contributed a great deal to encouraging me by her lively initiatives. Frequently I remarked that she would certainly take to politics. After the ending of *British Ally*, her marriage to Dr Jeger, MP was what one might have expected. When my husband Pat died they both helped, with their sympathy, inviting me to stay at their cottage in Essex. Tragically, Dr Jeger died not long after, as a result of injuries from a bomb 'incident' during the war. Lena was adopted as candidate in his constituency and endured the strain of an election in addition to that of his death. I have continued to follow Lena's career in politics, right up to her chairmanship of the Labour Party and elevation to the Lords. She is one of those people who has consistently done what she feels to be right, a path which does not, and did not, in her case, through many years, lead to office. Whether or not one approves of the House of Lords or life peers, Baroness Jeger is one of those whose true people's (not public) service is far more deserving of that honour than so many to whom it has been given. When, bearing in mind so much of our odd joint past, I wrote to congratulate her I said that I could not help laughing, which did not offend her.

In those early days in the office I had no other real friendships, but cordial relations with my colleagues. However, I did begin to enjoy the practices of Ministry life: the writing of minutes to one another which were carried about by the Government messengers, upstairs and downstairs, to In trays and Out trays, and on which we added queries and observations, at times witty, and relevant to an imminent decision or proposal. I thought minutes were quite fun and presently dared to set some moving myself.

Apart from the brief editorial meetings, and occasional discussions with a colleague, I knew very little of the content of the paper other than in my own sphere. But we had lists of thousands of the distinguished men and women in all spheres, literature, science, the arts, politics, the armed forces, who in the years from 1942–1946 appeared in the pages of *British Ally* either through special messages and articles or reprints of their work published at home. (These contributors are listed in Appendix 1.) We had learned of the Russian enthusiasm for football and horse racing, so we had a regular Sports Page with a sports contributor. We also covered chess.

Our circulation was determined, to a large extent, by the paper supply. Nor was it easy to estimate sales at kiosks, or the extent to which the paper passed from hand to hand, or was posted up in some meeting place or club. We did have lists of subscribers, institutions and academies as well as individuals, and the regions of the Soviet Union to which our paper carried its messages, information and news.

Applications for subscriptions began to come in from the beginning and were stimulated by the experimental – and, in effect, tragic – landing by the Allies in France in 1942, two days after our first number appeared. They rose steadily and began to reach a peak, flooding in after the invasion of 1944 and up to 1945–46. By then we had reached our quota, an issue of 50,000, and were quite unable to meet all the demands from would-be readers. We had 22,000 postal subscribers, and a mailing to a large and impressive number of learned institutes.

Britansky Soyuznik was circulating from Archangel in the north, to the shores of the Black Sea in the south, east to the Urals and Siberia, west to Latvia, Estonia and Lithuania. Georgia, Armenia, the Ukraine, and the romantic names of Uzbekistan, Samarkand, Azerbaijan, Turkmenistan, figured in our lists; excluding Moscow and district, no fewer than 155 regions were covered. (See Appendix 2.) It became distressing to be unable to respond to the urgent requests for the paper.

In June 1944, in a debate in the House of Commons, Brendan Bracken paid a very warm tribute to the success of *British Ally*:

> The Ministry's work in the immense territories of our great ally, Russia, has presented us with an entirely different set of tasks . . . I am not making an exaggerated claim when I describe the Ministry's staff in Russia as real pioneers. Nobody, private or official, has ever before had this chance of telling the people of Russia about life in Britain and British achievements.
>
> Our Press department has been greatly encouraged by the intense Soviet interest, I might call it curiosity about Britain. Our weekly paper, *British Ally*, grows in popularity and it is estimated that it has twelve readers for each copy. It is the most dog-eared paper in the world. Its editor receives a large and appreciative post-bag, which would rejoice the heart of many an editor in England.

He concluded that, in three years' work, though it could not be claimed that the misunderstandings of a generation had been undone, a highly praiseworthy beginning had been made by the paper's staff.

Very many letters that we received complained bitterly if the paper arrived late, still more so when a request for a postal subscription had not received a favourable response. Choices had to be made with regard to those likely to be most effective in spreading the news and content of the journal. These pages could be filled by quoting from notes I made of our fan mail from individuals and institutions: there was the veteran of the 1905 abortive revolution, over seventy, living on a pension; army officers; soldiers writing in eagerly from an army post office; hospitals; a medical officer of health in the Stalino region of the Donbass finds it 'simply unbearable' that *Britansky Soyuznik* arrives irregularly; factories; engineers; chemists; collective farmers. From a woman working on a state farm: 'I am writing to you from remote Kazakstan, be so kind as to let me know how I can subscribe to your interesting paper.' One factory in remote Stalinsk was aggrieved:

> In a very short time your paper has become very popular. In the offices that are receiving it the paper is being read with increasing interest. Unfortunately the greatest industrial factory in the USSR (that is our factory) is not receiving your paper. Less important factories are getting your paper and we thus consider there has been a misunderstanding. We should be quite satisfied if you can send us two or three copies.

> The first-class cinema in Moscow, which accommodates up to 150,000 spectators a month, has a well equipped reading room and gets many requests from spectators for the chance of reading your paper. Please send us two copies.

> Five thousand students and over 400 members of the teaching staff of an industrial institute in the Urals are interested in the life and struggle of the friendly British people and obtain from your journal most valuable information about the fighting day-to-day life of the glorious British soldiers, sailors, and workers.

Boys' schools, sporting interests, local communist groups all commend the content, lay-out, pictures of the paper. 'Please do not refuse in your kindness to send your paper to the Consulate of the Chinese Republic in Andijan Uzbekistan.'

All of our would-be, and actual, readers show that naïveté; that eagerness for knowledge; that sense of loyalty to comrades; that open, hospitable welcome to any who come as friends which I had come to associate with my experience of the Russian character. In addition, there was evidence of a growing conviction that the pact signed by Eden and Molotov in London meant a fruitful collaboration between our two countries when the war was over. Even at a distance, and personally unknown to each other, these who worked on *British Ally* felt that they were united in a great and just common cause.

My own function absorbed me more than ever, providing opportunites for learning in unfamiliar and fascinating subjects. Of course I did not rely on my own judgement; I could always obtain information and counsel from scientists and their departments, with whom I had built up some telephonic friendships. Once, when I rang up the Coal Board on some point, I was answered by Dr Bronowski, who, on learning my name, expressed surprise that I sounded so young. I was not, after all, I told him, as old as my former distinguished husband. I had the entry to many scientific meetings and conferences, where, quietly in a back row, I could listen to discussions by eminent members of the Royal Society.

There were other benefits and pleasures of inside knowledge, not related to my own special work. I had nothing to do with the political side; nonetheless, the news from the Yalta Conference on which the Ministry, and our Section, were putting out information, was of great interest and importance. It also afforded us excellent pictures of the 'great three' in conference: Churchill, Roosevelt, Stalin. Some of the indications of their convivial enjoyment we did not release to the public.

Professor Joseph Needham, arriving in London from his mission in Chung King, to study events in China, gave us a talk from which we must have been among the first to learn how the advance of the communists, under Mao Tse Tung, was forcing the retreat, to and over the Yangtze River, of Chiang Kai Shek and his Kuomintang.

There was a cinema in the university building in which we were shown some special films of unusual interest. I saw one of pre-war Germany called *Die Ferien Vom Ich* (*Holidays from the Self*): it

23

showed an intense neurosis of staff and bosses in offices, being retired to rest homes, and may well have illustrated something of the German state of mind on the eve of the Nazis' coming to power and the war. There was a very moving Russian film of a village in which some youths who had been shot by the Germans lay buried in hard frozen snow close to their homes. Unable to bear parting from them, their women folk came regularly to visit them so long as the hard frost endured.

Some films were shot of Churchill's visits to Russia: in one from 1944, in which Stalin was seeing him on to his plane, I noted on Stalin's face a glow of what seemed to me unmistakably a genuine, comradely affection. The two old warlords were in their element in a joint enterprise that, for both, fulfilled their nature and ambition. So long as we consent to war, such steely realists will always be there in the background, determining the fate of people and nations.

One film made about the battle and sinking of the *Rawalpindi*, her captain still erect with one arm shot away, struck nearer home for me. It was just after John had received his secret sailing orders. Sharing our joint home, we had been enjoying each other's company, learning Russian together in the intervals of his Japanese studies. I feared that he, small and dark, might be bound for the Pacific and under-cover commando activities. Gasping 'Oh John,' I dashed out of the cinema. And after all, John turned up in Washington, decoding cables!

I had been parted from my other two, Harriet and Roderick, for the first time when they went to Dartington School. We had kept in touch by letter for what was not much longer than a year. As the war ended, in 1945, they would at least have their holidays at home. I looked forward to those times, and to the work which I hoped and expected to continue in the Soviet Relations Department of the Ministry of Information.

3

SCIENCE,
SECRECY AND WAR

———————

Though the year 1945 was to see the end of the war, many events which took place in its early months were already determining the fate of the post-war world.

During the conference at Yalta from 4–11 February, though the British and American forces were still stuck west of the Rhine, and in Italy, and the Russians were straining every nerve, crossing their rivers in their bid to be the first to reach Berlin, all three statesmen, Churchill, Roosevelt and Stalin, were concerned with what they held to be the vital future interests of their nations.

Stalin, who felt that he had little reason to trust his new-found allies, aimed to establish a barrier to shield his country from yet another attack from Europe. Roosevelt, though now a tired and ailing man, was sympathetic to the Soviet fears, and still somewhat animated by traditional American suspicion of British imperialism; he wanted to ensure that American power would give his country a clear voice in post-war decisions. Churchill wanted a free hand in the East Mediterranean; he was inclined also to favour establishing states in East Europe which, in his view, would be independent of Russia. By the decisions that were taken, ultimately the status of East Germany, Poland, Czechoslovakia, Bulgaria and Rumania was settled, while Stalin, in return, virtually betrayed the Greek communists to British diplomacy and aggression (as he had already betrayed the Chinese communists to Chiang Kai Shek and the Kuomintang).

At home in Britain, scientists and highly skilled industrial workers of all political persuasions – from right to extreme left – had been helping the strategists of the armed forces, for the assault on the western front in 1944, with all sorts of inventions and devices which were only to be revealed when the war ended. Meanwhile, at Los Alamos, in the American west, a group of American, British and European scientists were racing against time with their consultations and calculations, in the endeavour to use the knowledge obtained by splitting the atom in order to create an atomic bomb. This famous story has now been told endlessly: accused, attacked, defended in argument in print and on television screens.

The first hint of success came to Churchill in London in March 1945. The bomb was feasible, was ready. Should it be used? At the Conference in Quebec in 1943, agreement had been reached that it should not be used except with the consent of Britain and America.

The closing events of the war now began to follow in rapid succession. One such tragic event was the death of President Roosevelt on 11 April. This death, though not on the battlefield, may well have been of far greater significance than those of the millions who died fighting. Roosevelt lived to see the probable coming of victory, but his wisdom and statesmanship were not there to influence the final decision about the bomb.

On 29 April, Italy surrendered; on 30 April Hitler was dead; the Russians were in Berlin and the final surrender of Germany to Field Marshal Montgomery on 4 May was ratified by Zhukov for the Russians at their Berlin headquarters at 11.30 p.m. on 8 May.

On that same day London went nearly crazy celebrating victory; Russia did likewise, possibly with less massive exuberance, on 9 May.

During the war, as co-operation and a sense of fellowship between the Allies increased, President Roosevelt referred to them as the United Nations. Victory days in the West and in the Soviet Union stimulated a resolve to cement this alliance. Somewhat surprisingly, this was carried into immediate action during that very month of May by the meeting of the Allied Powers in San Francisco and the founding of the United Nations in substance and in fact and law. Germany and Japan were excluded; provision was made for a General Assembly and the Council of the five powers – the United States, United Kingdom, France,

United Socialist Soviet Republics and China – with a rule of unanimity agreement, but rights of veto.

Amid a plethora of emotional and congratulatory speeches the statesmen issued the famous declaration, which opens with the words, 'We the Peoples . . .'

At that time my work kept me too busy for much reflection on this great event. But it was not long before, at odd moments, it evoked in my mind my study of the shaping of the Pan-American Union, on which, I became convinced, this new organisation basically was modelled. Rather than 'We the Peoples . . .' should it not read 'We the Governments – or the Great Powers'? Provision was made, it is true, for 'status' to be allowed to 'non-governmental bodies' deemed fit for acceptance; later this did lead to some popular access and influence.

Coupled with my misgivings about the intentions of the Great Powers in their moment of success, was the realisation that the victors were in truth carrying out their purpose, which I had viewed with horror – the dismemberment of Germany.

The Russians lost no time in following up the friendship and alliance established with Great Britain. On 19 May came an invitation from Russian scientists to their British colleagues to visit Moscow on 18 June, to celebrate the 220th anniversary of the Russian Academy of Sciences. Through their Ambassador in London, the Soviet Government issued personal invitations to forty-four British scientists. Numerous scientific bodies were also invited.

The occasion was international, some 146 individual scientists from other countries and fifty-five scientific societies from outside the USSR received invitations. The war had isolated Russian scientists from communication with colleagues in other lands, especially with those cut off by the Cold War. The Russians hoped by this means to restore contact and exchanges, in accord with the traditional understanding of the universal nature of scientific information and discovery. For their part, the English and American men of science also looked forward to a visit from which they could learn more about the effect of the war on the state of Soviet science, as well as the trends of Soviet thought in their special fields. The British delegation, which covered a very wide field, was the largest, the American the second largest.

Soviet Relations Division at the Ministry were not officially informed of this invitation, but, very naturally, we became interested in the publicity which we might give to it through *British Ally*. Most of the work inevitably fell to me. From the list of those who were expected to go, I began, by phone and letters, to seek help in obtaining biographical material, photographs and Press notices, for the earliest possible dispatch to our office in Moscow. A Soviet plane was to transport the British delegation. (See Appendix 3 for a list of delegates.) I urged on my colleagues that the Press should be alerted to photograph their departure, but, in spite of my plea as to the immense importance of science and such exchanges, their general feeling was that this would attach too much weight to a mere meeting of scientists to celebrate their achievements and history.

The Royal Society, together with the Soviet Embassy, was responsible for all the arrangements of the journey. Within the month all those who had accepted the invitation had made their personal arrangements for absence from work, and had had such inoculations as were necessary for their health. We had done our best to support their publicity; all was in readiness. Among the scientists who were to attend the ceremonies, Professor Joseph Needham travelled specially from China. J.B.S. Haldane, in spite of his sympathies with the Soviet Union, declined the invitation. On 14 June the Royal Society gave a party in its own rooms to wish success for their colleagues' mission and adventure. Peter Smollett, as Chief of Soviet Relations Division, was invited by the Royal Society to attend this function. He very kindly asked me, in view of the amount of work I had done, if I would like to accompany him.

Among all these eminent persons I felt somewhat lost, though there were one or two whom I knew personally, such as Professor Blackett, Julian Huxley and Desmond Bernal. Suddenly, in the midst of all the lively and cheerful conversation and the imbibing of cocktails, a disturbance became evident. One group was discussing something obviously serious and with agitation. Then I found Professor Norrish beside me, quite clearly very angry. He told me that, at the very last moment, several of these scientists had been forbidden by the British authorities to go to Russia. Since I represented *British Ally* and my department, he wished to give me, in strict confidence, a list of the eight names. I was, very naturally, shocked, and queried as to what anyone could do about this. I understood that some of the delegation had gone down to Parliament to try and find out what had happened, and to see if it might not still be possible for the group to go. Peter Smollett was at that moment somewhere else among the crowd; I supposed that he would, in any case, learn the news. I went home, feeling disappointment and some anger.

Next morning at our editorial conference, Peter Smollett said he had heard the rumour about the ban, but did not know to whom it was applied and why. Had I any information? I was in some doubt as to what to say. The names had been given to me in confidence, but there was no doubt that all the delegates and the Royal Society must know all about it. It was unlikely that it would remain secret. So I told my colleagues that, although I knew nothing about the reasons, I had in confidence been given a list of the names, by one of those forbidden to go. These were Professor Bernal, Professor P.M.S. Blackett, Sir Charles Darwin, Professors P.A.M. Dirac, E.A. Milne, N.F. Mott, R.G.W. Norrish and E.K. Rideal. They were all not only extremely distinguished but all Fellows of the Royal Society.

Meantime rumours were spreading; I was rung up at home by, I think, the *Daily Express*, asking if I had any information. To which I replied, like a correct civil servant, that I had not! Then Tom Driberg, Labour MP, that same day of 15 June put down a question in the Commons, asking about the refusal of permits for eight members of a party of eminent British scientists who were to leave on a visit to Russia. He understood that permission had been refused on security grounds, and he asked what security was involved.

Mr Churchill replied that

the Soviet Government were good enough to issue invitations to some forty distinguished men of science in the United Kingdom to attend the celebration in Moscow and Leningrad of the two hundred and twentieth Jubilee of the Soviet Academy of Scientists. The Royal Society, and some fifteen other scientific institutions of Great Britain, were also invited to send representatives.

The Soviet Ambassador informed the Foreign Secretary on 22 May of the issue of these invitations and the Foreign Secretary replied welcoming the very courteous action of the Soviet Government and expressing the hope that as many as possible of those invited would be able to go.

As the Soviet Ambassador was informed yesterday, His Majesty's Government are happy to know that it has been possible for twenty-one of the scientists invited from this country to undertake the visit.

It is true that, in the case of eight other scientists who had accepted, His Majesty's Government did not feel able to authorise the granting of facilities for the journey. His Majesty's Government, on consideration, found it impossible to spare from the United Kingdom, at this stage of the war against Japan, so many eminent scientists whose services they might wish to employ on services of war and other operations. He was confident that the Soviet Union would understand the preoccupations in this respect of HM Government in view of the fact that this country is still engaged in a deadly war against a formidable enemy.

Mr Driberg then insisted that the scientists who had been refused permission included world famous men like Sir Charles Darwin and Professor Bernal. These scientists had been told by the Ministry of Information, which arranged the visit, that it was only the last minute insistence of the military security authority which prevented their departure.

Mr Churchill then said that it was not a question of security but of getting work done here for the purpose of the Japanese war.

When this report appeared in the *Daily Telegraph* (15 June 1945), it became necessary for me to address a minute to my superiors and via them to Government officials and the Press, pointing out that we had not been responsible for the arrangements concerning the delegation, since these were in the hands of the Royal Society and the Soviet Embassy. That we had been sending appropriate biographical and photographic material was well known to the Press as to the many delegates themselves.

As to which arm of the government had imposed the ban and why, we were as ignorant as anyone else. But a storm of protests broke loose in the next few days, expressive of the reactions of different cultural and political views. *Reynolds News* (the Sunday paper) on 17 June had a heavy headline, 'Tory Gestapo put gag on Leading Scientists' based on an interview with Tom Driberg in which he insisted that Mr Churchill's reply to him had concealed the facts.

The visit to Russia had been planned for a month with full Government approval. At the last moment the military security authorities had stepped in because these scientists knew secrets of our war production and defences which had not yet been released, and that if they were entertained too lavishly by the Russians they might talk indiscreetly. He added that he could imagine no action more calculated to impair the good relations between Britain and the Soviet Union than to make it clear in this heavy-handed way that neither do we trust our own world famous men of science, nor do we trust our Allies. Before Mr Churchill wished hypothetical Gestapos on his political opponents, he should start keeping his own Gestapo in order.

The Sunday Express's 'That Visit to Russia, Fear of Banquets, A Socialist Allegation', was in similar vein. It added the statement of the Association of Scientific Workers that: 'if the Government used its powers to prevent any of these scientists from making contact with their colleagues abroad, the whole future freedom of international science is gravely threatened.'

The evening papers and some provincial papers carried the story; *The Times* and *Sunday Times* gave the facts, but did not add comment.

The liberal Press, the *Manchester Guardian* and *News Chronicle* were highly critical of the imposition of the ban, but were more thoughtful and temperate in comment.

The *Manchester Guardian* (18 June) gave the news, described as a 'Home Office Ban', from a scientific correspondent, as causing widespread regret in scientific quarters. He continued:

It seems incredible that these scientists should not have been told at an earlier stage that they could not go to the anniversary celebration, and it seems particularly unfortunate that such an incident should have occurred on the first post-war occasion on which the Soviet scientists have made a major gesture towards the resumption of normal scientific relations, which have been interrupted by the general state of affairs in Europe during the last ten years.

It would have seemed impossible that the British peoples could afford to forego the most perfect acceptance of such an opportunity for improving relations between themselves and the people of the Soviet Union. The incident and the circumstances connected with it clearly raise general questions concerning the liberty of the subject at the present time. A thorough investigation of the matter from every angle seems essential.

The *Guardian*'s leading article of the same day headed 'The British Scientists' carried political punches:

The prohibition of the visit of certain British scientists to Moscow is a strange business. The more that is known of it the more it seems to be a pure piece of totalitarianism. The closest parallel is with the Russian and German restrictions on the movements of their scientists before the war. We shall expect to hear the voices of Lord Beaverbrook and Mr Bracken raised in horror against this 'control' over the liberty of Englishmen. And, if rumour is right in attributing the decision to one of these mysterious Security branches that still lurk in dark corners in Whitehall, we shall expect to hear the Prime Minister fulminating against this Gestapo in our midst. Altogether it is a poor advertisement for the new freedom that the 'National' Government promises us. But dictatorial methods apart, what is the reason behind the prohibition? That the scientists are engaged on work for the Japanese war is neither here nor there. Are they not permitted to have a few days' intermission or is it supposed that being only 'backroom boys' they will work the better for being snubbed? Is it feared that our good friends the Russians will kidnap them or that when the vodka is flowing the scientists' heads will prove too weak to prevent their pencils from working out formulae on the tablecloths? One guess seems as good as another. The safest is that the affair will cost the Government a few votes.

The anonymous reporter of the *News Chronicle* almost certainly must have been one of the guests of the Royal Society on the evening of 14 June, for it carried, next day, not only a full story and comments by some of the scientists, but a very pleasing photo of Professor J.D. Bernal as he left the party the previous night. None of the eight who had been banned would discuss politics.

Asked if there was any truth in suggestions that political motives were behind the ban, the scientists said that they could not tell – most of them preferred to put it down to mismanagement. Professors Bernal and Norrish 'did not quite understand what it was all about', but Professor Haldane remarked, 'Of course, there's been some interference. There's some political motive somewhere.'

Most of the eight scientists were not now, it seemed, concentrating their full energy on scientific problems of war. 'We had all been inoculated and were fully prepared to go, the Government had agreed to our going over a month ago and the last minute cancellation is a mystery to all of us,' complained Professor Mott. 'I am going back to-night to Bristol, to carry on with my ordinary work and give lectures.'

Professor Milne said:

I know nothing beyond what I have been told, that my services are still required in this country. That fact was conveyed to me in a most complimentary letter. I am still serving on some Government Committees and I do not quarrel with the decision that some of us cannot go to Russia. But I do regret the discourtesy to our Russian hosts by having to withdraw at such short notice.

Sir Charles Darwin stated: 'I am still in the Government Service, and presumably I cannot be spared. I am not a politician and there is no reason to think my views have been held against me.' The Secretary of the Physical Laboratory added that Sir Charles had been engaged on highly secret work throughout the war.

That Tom Driberg had caused some alarm was shown by the steps taken a few days later by the *Express* to counteract his allegations: the paper obtained further statements from three of the eight scientists. Sir Charles Darwin asserted that Mr Churchill gave the true story; he was 'quite satisfied' that the ban on their visit was proper and necessary. Professor Rideal, denying that left-wing views had anything to do with the ban, remarked that at least three of the eight were Conservatives. He himself was still engaged on important war research. Professor Milne, who also said that he was still serving on government committees 'very much concerned' with the prosecution of the war, added that Mr Driberg's statements

33

were 'very highly coloured'.

Most of these Fellows of the famous Royal Society were, however, troubled by the wider implications for science beyond the immediate prosecution of the war. Bernal shared the attitude of the Association of Scientific Workers: 'There is a danger of getting ourselves boxed in. Science is international and relies on the free exchange of ideas.'

Professor A.V. Hill, Secretary of the Royal Society, in a letter to the journal, *Nature*, on 23 June, which was extensively copied in the national Press, spoke in language at once dignified and, alas, old-fashioned, of the pride and faith that lie at the heart of the scientist:

Many readers of *Nature* will have been astonished and repelled by the studied discourtesy with which eight of the intending guests of the Soviet Academy of Sciences were prevented by His Majesty's Government last week from going to Moscow. Not only were they put to gross inconvenience and annoyance by the refusal, without warning and at the last moment, of permission to travel, but also the explanation given was as incredible as the real reason was insulting.

In this prohibited group were those whose talents and devotion have rendered priceless service to the nation during the War. But let us remember the words of the 'Preacher': 'There was a little city and few men within it; and there came a great king against it and besieged it and built great bulwarks against it:

'Now there was found in it a poor wise man and he by his wisdom delivered the city: yet no man remembered that same poor man.

'Then said I, Wisdom is better than strength: nevertheless the poor man's wisdom is despised, and his words are not heard.'

The offensive treatment of our scientific colleagues, inconceivable towards members of most other professions, is a sufficient comment on the patronizing Ministerial praise with which science and scientific men are occasionally favoured. When they, and others, are offered reparation later on in 'awards' or 'honours', let them recall the words of T.H. Huxley: 'The sole order of nobility which, in my judgment, becomes a philosopher, is the rank which he holds in the estimation of his fellow-workers, who are the only competent judges in such matters.'

Soon the cloud of gloom cast by this incident on Soviet Relations Division, more especially on myself, began to be dispelled by the glowing and ecstatic reports of the Conference of Scientists in Moscow that were coming over the Moscow radio and flooding our office with Soviet news releases. These, however, received only modest paragraphs in our Press.

The Russians described how the 'brocaded curtain of the Bolshoi rose to reveal, on the stage, some of the world's most eminent men of science and their Soviet hosts'. The British, and no doubt others, in their ornate academic robes, to celebrate, in a great gala occasion (such as the Russians love), 'the liberation of science for international collaboration, that was consequent on the victory achieved over Nazi aggression in Europe'. This sixteenth of June, 1945, they said

would stand out as a red letter day, a historic occasion, when presidents and members of Institutes and Academies throughout the Soviet Union were uniting with 150 foreign scientists from seventeen countries. The hall and boxes were packed with military and scientific heroes of the war, resplendent in uniforms and medals. Opening the session, the Veteran Scientist President Vladimir Komarov, greeting those present, noted that never before in the history of science had there been, in one gathering, such a galaxy of brilliant thinkers in various fields of knowledge, who were also united by a common interest. Never had men of science assembled at such an important moment in history, when the greatest war ever known by humanity had ended and now a period of peaceful and constructive work could begin in which science could play a prominent role. The opening session was followed by a banquet with a thousand guests and a dance.

In the British Press, the *Scotsman* reported that the welcome in Moscow had been broadcast over the radio, when the cheers of the crowd almost drowned the voice of the commentator and one of the British scientists who spoke was Julian Huxley. The *Manchester*

Guardian (23 June) gave news of a week spent by the guests visiting laboratories:

> The Russians have delighted everybody by their lack of reserve in disclosing the progress made in the field of research and applied science, and any idea that the visiting scientists brought with them that they would find their hosts tongue-tied or inhibited by an exaggerated respect for security was quite dispelled.
>
> The visitors are impressed by the freedom with which the Soviet scientists were able to reveal processes which in other lands would be kept secret from respect for patent rights. As one British scientist put it, the Russians told us they have nothing to buy or sell and were interested only in the pooling of knowledge beneficial to the community.
>
> One Oxford member of the British delegation scored a great success by delivering an address in Russian.

The *Yorkshire Post* had the good fortune to have a correspondent in Moscow. Surprisingly she was a woman, Iris Morley, of whom I have no further information beyond her dispatch, which her paper printed on 19 June:

> Had Peter the Great seen the Academy open its 1945 session at the Bolshoi theatre, he would certainly have realised that his ambitious dreams had been fulfilled.
>
> In the first great international congress since the war began, scientists of all Allied countries, and from all Republics of the Soviet Union, filled the Bolshoi, which seats 3,000 people, and heard addresses from rows of Academicians seated on the stage before a bank of brilliant flowers surrounding the bust of Lenin and a huge portrait of Stalin.
>
> Although the combined talent and ingenuity of Russian scientists has provided the Red Army with weapons with which to wage triumphantly the greatest war in history, the appearance of the most distinguished of the scientists attending is oddly at variance with their achievements. Flowing beards and hair, such as were popular with the intelligentsia of 1870, frame faces which would have been suitable subjects for the Russian painter,

Repin. They are faces totally different from the type usually seen among the present generation. The playing of Tchaikovsky's 1812 Overture, which brought the meeting to a close, seemed an excellent way of emphasising the picturesque atmosphere.

However, the content of the speeches was in every sense up to the minute. President Komarov's speech as well as that of Academician Volgins, emphasised the close connection of Soviet science with the people and the Red Army, and paid tribute to Stalin as a 'genius scientist' who had developed the theories of Marxism and Leninism, and created Socialism in one-sixth of the world.

A graceful compliment was paid to England. 'Russian science,' it was explained, 'has historical ties with English science. The works of Darwin met in Russia a tremendous scientific and social response, Darwin himself followed the first steps of the galaxy of Russian Darwinists with interest. In fact, Russia can claim to be the second fatherland of Darwinism.'

The speeches were enthusiastically received by the audience, which included members of the Diplomatic Corps, among whom I saw President Beirut, of Poland, and Premier Osubkamoravsky. A crowd had collected outside the Bolshoi to see the eminent persons leave, and everyone was interested in the English delegation who looked rather self-conscious in their gowns, and in Madame Joliot-Curie, in a white blouse and socks, looking very much like pictures of her famous mother.

In fact, brilliant men of science are two-a-penny in Moscow this week. Bus loads of astro-physicists are driven about the streets without anyone glancing at them twice.

Regular surveys of the Soviet Press came into our office from Moscow; they covered many topics, but not always as much about science as I would have liked. I was able to learn, however, much about the names of the scientists attending the celebrations and the countries from which they came. Most of the Soviet Press gave the occasion extensive coverage, especially of the Soviet speeches. Academician Komarov, while offering compliments to his guests, remarked how satisfactory it now was for the Russians that their students could study at home and no longer needed, as under the

Tsarist regime, to flee abroad for their scientific education. There had been an unfortunate pro-German bias in science, coming from the West, which had neglected the achievements of some great nineteenth-century Russian men of science, such as Mendelev, Mechnikov and others.

Churchill's reply to Tom Driberg's question received a paragraph, without comment. On other political matters at this date, President Truman's Press conference had been fully reported, stating that he had sent Mr Hopkins to Moscow and Mr Davies to London to facilitate exchange of views about a projected meeting of the Big Three powers. Uneasiness was already apparent about the Polish situation and the types of Germans who were being allowed by the Allies to administer the reconstruction of social and economic life in their sections of Germany.

When the scientists returned from Moscow a Press conference was held on the afternoon of 9 July, in the large hall at the University (then Ministry) buildings. Letters of invitation, which I wrote and signed, went to the eight who had been unable to go, as well as to the others. Many individuals and nearly thirty scientific journals and institutions received invitations. A full list of the scientists who had visited the celebrations was circulated widely to the Press.

Sir Robert Robinson, as the Vice-President of the Royal Society, opened the proceedings, followed by the Astronomer Royal, Sir Harold Spencer Jones, and then Professor E.N. da C. Andrade.

Any questions asked were to be referred to the appropriate specialist if he were present; if anyone could not be there, we would be glad (indeed, in any case) to receive written reports. We did receive some, one of special interest from Sir Thomas Holland, President of the Geological Society, in which he surveyed what was known, over the years, about the mineral resources of Russia, America and the Commonwealth. He was impressed by the number of Russians, and the large funds, devoted to geological research.

The Russians realised in good time that no five-year plan of industrial development could work unless based on mineral resources; and having realised this truth, they acted. But their work is not limited to applied science, fundamental problems are supported on a lavish scale unthought of in this country or in any part of the British Empire.

He went on to remark that Britain had painful lessons to learn, not only in this respect, but in 'the unrestricted access to the Russians' stock of information and ideas', and in the 'example of good manners set to our politicians, by their Ambassador, who had personally attended at the aerodrome the early morning departure of the British scientists, as well as to welcome them back on the first of July.' It appeared to him that 'the Russians give more attention to science than our people do to dog-racing, to judge by the space given to it in their press.'

Our Press conference rewarded us with reports in the varied specialist journals of the scientists, from engineering to medicine. Although there were leading articles, the signed and unsigned individual impressions were the most interesting. *Chemical Age* had already pointed out in a leading article (23 June) that two of the eight refused permission to travel by an 'extraordinary instance of official maladroitness' were distinguished chemists. Now (14 July) they devoted a whole page to 'Scientists in the USSR: Achievements in Adversity', and the following number to aspects of internationalism in science in various countries, more especially the contributions made by Britain in that sphere. They stressed that Soviet scientists were 'hungry for international co-operation' at the same time expressing admiration for their 'magnificently equipped laboratories'; the social status of Soviet scientists; their pay; the care of their health; their disposal of large funds for research. 'When Professor Kapitza was erecting a new large scale laboratory, he was asked by M. Molotov why he did not ask for more funds (sic). Our readers are now left to muse on what science in Britain could achieve had it similar facilities at its disposal.'

Some particulars were given of Professor Kapitza's work on liquid helium and his attempts to obtain aluminium from clay by the use of oxygen. Professor F.C. Donhan referred to his meetings with Academician Frunkin and Professor Semenov in Moscow, and Academician Joffé in Leningrad.

The *Lancet* (14 July) had an encouraging report by Professor

Arnold Sorsby about the training of medical students, both as to methods and numbers, indicating the very great increase in medical and health facilities during and since the war years. In later issues its 'Running commentary by Peripatetic Correspondents' revealed that the doctors had encountered some shocks. Whilst admitting the need for statistics, the correspondent confessed to bewilderment at the Russians' apparent obsession with these and the multiplicity which they offered. Continuing in a light vein, the correspondent informs us that the Soviet medical profession is 'the handsomest in the world' – it consists entirely of women. A question as to the actual proportion of women among Russian doctors elicited only the reply that 'they were not interested in that sort of statistics'. However, during a morning spent attending the oral examination for the qualifying examination in medicine, the correspondent not only discovered that such Soviet occasions – unlike the British – are not solemn, but cheerful and encouraging, but also that the percentage graduating that day consisted of men 0.0 per cent and women 100 per cent. He remarks with approval the Soviet plan of small fraternities of doctors who work together, supplementing each other's degree of skill. He continues in a whimsical and half serious mood:

Your correspondent, starved for feminine charm during his visits in London medical schools, and yet fearful that in Moscow the 'monstrous regiment of women' had captured the time-honoured masculine stronghold of medicine, pursued his insistent inquiries on the position of mere man in Soviet medicine. It may relieve readers to know that of late years the social embargo on men students that seems to have been operative appears to have lifted. Soviet engineering no longer exercises an irresistible magnetic pull on the men of the Soviet Union, and it appears that in the years immediately preceding the war young men have not shown quite the same contempt for medicine as formerly. From 1936 to 1941 there appears to have been quite an influx of men into the medical schools. A strange thing is that your correspondent's Russian informant could only recollect this under persistent questioning. It does not appear to have bothered anyone, neither the teachers, nor the 'monstrous regiment' – perhaps them least of all.

Recalling his own student days, your correspondent was somewhat shocked to find that not only are students expected to work at their study, but that the community at large regarded their study as work to be remunerated as all useful things are. The remuneration of the Soviet student is admittedly not high, but increases with each year of study. Apparently the Soviet student is not expected to produce crews that paddle wooden contraptions in water, but has to discipline himself as a member of an order of service. When he has finished his studies his first service consists of three years work wherever the need may be greatest. There appears to be no shortage of candidates for the most exacting tasks. Having thus graduated into his Order the young Soviet doctor is now expected to 'improve his qualifications', an attitude that prevails apparently throughout all Soviet life. He is free to take up specialisation at the expense of the State and so satisfy his individual urges as well as increasing his value to the community. The first three years of service need not necessarily be arduous work in some remote part of the Union. The State may require the newly-qualified physician to devote himself immediately to some specialised training, and this requirement will be exacted from those who as students have shown special aptitudes for some particular work, whether in the clinical field or in research. It seems to be the belief of Soviet educationists that for a flower to blush unseen, and waste its sweetness on the desert air, is shocking social extravagance.

The repercussions of this visit were, of course, of deep interest to me, and also, though probably less so, to my department, whose relations with British Ally were not solely to do with science. Nor was the enthusiasm of the visitors from Britain solely due to the generous hospitality, which is so much a part of the Russian character. Our scientists were surprised at the expansion of Soviet science both in spite of, and in part, due to the war; what is more, the political hostility between the two nations had done much to impede the communication of knowledge. Our scientists must have been impressed by the evidence that the Soviet government and people took science very seriously. Consequently, they were glad, for themselves, to receive recognition which they felt neither government nor people accorded them at home. What is more, our Royal Society and other institutions must have been increasingly aware (as our politicians and people were not, being less well informed and educated in such matters) of the part which science and technology would in future play in our lives.

As I sat at my desk, day after day, reading their scientific journals, not comprehending all the details, but the implications of what I read, I also became imbued with some intuitive presage of what this powerful force was to mean to human life. At the same time, the contrasts between the English and Russian temperaments intrigued me. Exalted with the end of the war and the opening of frontiers, and proud of their achievements, these Soviet men and women were naïvely prepared to display and share these with their colleagues; while those from the West were more sceptical, more aware of discords, hiding their sense of their own shortcomings, their lack of warmth and open-heartedness with turns of wit that their hosts would not easily understand.

Of course Press cuttings of all sorts came to my desk for information, and not necessarily for transmission to *British Ally*. I used notes from some of them in articles that I now sometimes wrote for *British Ally*. For instance, I reported, in less than a thousand words, a pleasant, informal meeting at the House for Visiting Scientists in London, attended by men and women from Canada, Australia, the United States, and members of the French Scientific Mission to Britain, as well as others in Britain who had not been part of the recent delegation. Amongst them were Sir Henry Dale, President of the Royal Society, Mrs Lonsdale, one of the first women to be entitled FRS, and M. Karavaev, First Secretary of the Soviet Embassy: through him, a message of thanks was given to the Soviet Ambassador, M. Gusev, and Madame Gusev, for their care and interest. Among subjects raised was a tribute by Julian Huxley to the heroism of the people of Leningrad in the state of siege that they had suffered.

The House for Visiting Scientists, mainly sponsored by the British Council, was like a club, with a comfortable lounge, refectory, a bar, and some residential accommodation. It planned also to organise lectures. Its membership, of 500, came already from thirty-nine countries.

The Royal Society was meditating on the type and scale of the invitation it should extend to its Soviet colleagues for a reciprocal visit to Britain. In the meantime a delegation of Soviet men and women of different skills and professions visited Britain at the invitation of the Society for Friendly Relations with the USSR. Their tour was extensive and included Scotland, where in the Labour movement, sympathy with Russia was strong.

This was a voluntary effort in which we had no part, though we naturally took note of the reports in the Press. The sports clubs became active and the famous Soviet soccer team Dynamo came over to play Chelsea. It seems incredible to me that this was in the spring (though it must have been, since it was in the period when M. Karavaev and I were frequently colleagues in cultural matters, though mainly by phone) because the match was played in a complete pea-soup fog, so thick that the ball was scarcely visible. The score was two all. As a matter of courtesy, or personal interest, I called at the entrance of the Café Royal, where the teams were dining, to pay my compliments to M. Karavaev at this fraternisation and hope that they were enjoying themselves. With what I felt to be diplomatic tact, I remarked that the result of the match had been good. Drawing himself up with dignity and in a tone which spoke enigmatic volumes, M. Karavaev replied: 'Very good – for Chelsea.'

The impulse to restore contact with other peoples was very natural after the tensions and claustrophobia of the war. A special enthusiasm for Russia, born of the story of Stalingrad, was felt by large numbers of the general public. There was, as yet, not much they could do for relations with the European countries over which the war had been waged.

It must be recalled that the British had more on their minds at this time than festive occasions. The war with Japan was not over; their American allies were, with justification, pressing for support and help. Moreover, our statesmen faced many uncertainties; very little was yet known about the character and policies of President Truman, now at the head of the American nation.

With the end of the European war, the Labour Party in Britain was calling for an end to the coalition government. Churchill was anxious to continue the coalition until Japan was defeated. British troops were making progress in Burma against the enemy. Stalin had promised advance through Manchuria, which in fact, he kept. But America wanted an invasion of Japan itself.

Britain had depended on lend-lease for its finances; with the end of the war, the country was virtually bankrupt. In the final campaign, the British armed forces were placed under the sole direction of the American Chiefs of Staff.

Churchill resigned on 23 May 1945 to open a General Election campaign; meantime he carried on with an interim caretaker government, mostly Conservative and Liberal. There was thus, both in military and civil administration, an interregnum in which, unhappily, some fatal decisions took place.

Polling day was 5 July, four days after the return of the scientists from Moscow. But the result could not be known until 26 July, when the votes of the Armed Forces had come in. The Potsdam Conference of the Big Three, Churchill, Stalin and now Truman, began on 17 July and continued until 2 August.

In the meantime Truman, who became famous in history as the President who placed over his desk the motto 'The buck stops here', had decided that the atomic bomb, which he knew to be in readiness, should be used against Japan. By the decision of the Quebec conference, he had no authority to use it without British consent. In the midst of this virtual suspension of both civil and military authority in Britain, consent to use the bomb was given without hearing any arguments about it or even how it was to be used. According to A.J.P. Taylor, the agreement took place between Truman and Churchill, without reference to the British Chiefs of Staff, or the temporary War Cabinet.[1] 'The British,' he says, 'issued a blank cheque which they could not refuse, and the Americans accepted the cheque without attaching any value to it.'

The date was 2 July. On 5 July, it became clear that Churchill had lost the election, though it was not until the 26th that he resigned. Labour came into power, with a full majority, for the first time since 1931. Attlee became Prime Minister and Ernest Bevin Foreign Secretary. Attlee now took the place of Churchill at the deliberations of Potsdam.

Relevant to these crucial moments in the history of the world is what the unseen but dominating actors in the drama – the world scientists – were doing at this time.

The Royal Society, untroubled by election fever, or diplomatic events, realising that the tercentenary of their greatest, Isaac Newton, had fallen in the year 1942 when the war prevented its due celebration, decided that immediate preparations should be put in hand for a world jamboree of scientists in his honour, in Britain. This was scheduled for July 1946.

I looked forward to being involved in some of the publicity in *British Ally* for this event. On 6 and 9 August 1945 the bombs fell on Hiroshima and Nagasaki, dropped, as it were casually, by two warlord politicians, one of them parochial and inexperienced, the other no longer strictly in power with right to decide; both supremely ignorant and incapable of understanding the meaning and power of science. The shock of that catastrophic explosion has reverberated through world politics and world science ever since. I wondered how many of those brilliant men whose careers I had been studying with fascination, had been in possession of this dread secret all the time.

Some of these scientists had, of course, been involved in the preparation of the bomb. They knew well enough the reason for Churchill's misgivings about the visit of that delegation to Moscow. Some of the scientists concerned had already tried to influence the American government against the use of the bomb.

The general public, by now accustomed to the threat and experience of destruction of house, home and families from the air, did not really take in the full impact of this appalling new weapon. They had the natural reaction of effectively getting back at an enemy, but much greater was the relief that this meant the end of the war and hence the saving of lives of British and American soldiers, sailors and airmen.

Many scientists may have felt the same way, but presently dawned on them the stark truth that attends every effective new invention of science – once there, it does not, like live things in nature, simply die and go away. The conscience of scientists was deeply disturbed.

One of their highest achievements, on which men from several countries had worked in unity, and could rejoice and congratulate one another, had resulted in creating this monstrous instrument of destruction, which could not, in effect, itself be destroyed. Its birth and development, under war conditions, had imposed the utmost secrecy. What was now to become of that international fellowship, that common language of understanding, which was the pride of scientists, its

45

interchange the true source of the very growth of science itself? That scientific knowledge should be free and open to all had been, since its foundation, the creed of the Royal Society of Britain. Sir Henry Dale, its president, now angrily proclaimed that there must be no more secrecy. Perhaps this is why the society pressed forward resolutely with their large-scale Newton Tercentenary celebrations. However that may be, Sir Henry's voice was soon lost in the raucous hubbub of dispute, dismay, anxiety, and anger which broke out between the people versus the scientists and/or the government; individual governments and intelligence services versus one another and the subversives; recalcitrant students versus scientific education, which began with the fatal date 6 August 1945 and since then has never ceased.

In those few years, the scientists who were troubled by conscience already began defending themselves by blaming the politicians and the electorate for the misuse of science. On one occasion, in spite of my position as a civil servant, I could not help adding my voice to this argument. During a session of the British Association for the Advancement of Science, Sir Edward Appleton, FRS, who was at the head of the government Scientific Research Department, insisted that scientists were not responsible for the results outside their laboratories for what went on within them. I stood up and said angrily that, as a teacher of many years standing, I would be ashamed of not admitting responsibility, in some part, for the results outside my classroom of what had been taught within it. There was quite some applause. A woman seated behind me tapped my shoulder and said, 'Bravo'. This turned out to be Annabel Williams-Ellis[2] – I had not known she was there. A woman in front of me looked round approvingly. This turned out to be Freda Grimble, who became very active with International Women's Day and later the National Assembly of Women, which, owing to this encounter, I later joined when I was free of government service.

If the scientists were conscience-striken, no such remorse afflicted the politicians and the popular Press. My In tray became flooded with the journalists' stories of 'now it can be told' – the magnificent contribution made by science to victory. Military strategies and devices preserve their secrecy by odd names or acronyms. So now we learned about PLUTO – pipe line under the ocean – by which petrol had flowed from England to France; and Mulberry, the artificial harbour specially constructed for the ships that supported the landings of 1944; of the close attention given by scientific experts to the soil of the Normandy beaches, to make sure that landing craft and tanks would not be bogged down while under enemy fire.

The marvels of Dr Watson Watt's invention, radar, in detecting approaching planes in flight, were written up with gusto; the famous Spitfire was extolled, and the story of the Mosquito, invented and built out of wood, because of shortage of metal, was told; while, for the first time, appeared a full account of Frank Whittle's jet engine, which had been manufactured in time to intercept flying bombs and was now transforming flight.

By a binding agreement all intelligence and scientific information was communicated by Britain to the United States: it was withheld from the Soviet Union. With its greater size and consequent larger technological capacity, as well as immunity from air strikes, America acquired considerable advantages. Inventions, to which wartime Britain could not devote factory space and machinery, thus came to be developed in America. A dismantled jet engine was flown over during the war for such development and production. In the medical sphere there still lingers in my mind a certain resentment that, because of the war, Fleming's great discovery of penicillin was handed over to America for production; Britain even had to pay later for the rights to produce its own doctor's brilliant discovery.

Most of these stories of our prowess in science and invention were transmitted to *British Ally* for publication. Here was evidence that, as an ally, Britain had fully pulled her weight in the struggle against Hitler, and was a well-advanced, modern industrial nation. Victory inevitably brings a flush of pride and triumph. It seems to me that this was the moment when science and technology, for peace as for war, began to make that impression on the minds of our people, which was to assume near dominance in the prosperous post-war years and beyond.

Watching the intake of comment from Soviet radio and press, I was less happy about the effects of all this self-advertisement on Anglo–Soviet relations. Those joint celebrations of the common cause of science had been, in Moscow, all sweetness and light. But now there were already signs of Soviet suspicion about the policies of the Allies in Europe. Of course the Russians must have felt it was right that those British scientists had rallied, as had their Soviet comrades, to the help of their nation. But what about that treaty signed between Britain and

Russia for twenty years post-war co-operation in Europe? Suppose Britain were to tear it up? Then, what Eisenhower was before long to call the 'military industrial complex', in British hands, aimed not against Germany but against Russia, could be a formidable antagonist. Above all there loomed over the two nations a haunting spectre, not that declared in Marx's *Manifesto*, of communism, but of the undivulged, uncommunicated secret of the Atomic Bomb.

I was happier in sending out the stories that were less closely associated with fighting, but I myself was not unaffected by some of the marvels now revealed. I went to look at the Aircraft Exhibition, set up jointly by the Ministries of Information and Aircraft Production, sponsored and opened by Lord Beaverbrook, on a bomb site in Oxford Street where it would be visited by shopping crowds. I found there material for an article which told something about the feats of design and engineering of our people, as well as popular reaction to it. For myself it was the huge, intricate, shining aeroplane engines that intrigued me most. I stood long by these, gazing at the elaborate workmanship, the innumerable intricate leads and connections. I thought of the astounding ingenuity of man, and then of the colossal waste of war; how many, how many of these splendid tributes to his skill now lay rusting at the bottom of the sea, together with the very gallant young men who had operated them.

Here are a few extracts from the article:

At the entrance to the Exhibition the up-ended wing of a Wellington bomber, painted sky-blue with part of its aluminium skeleton uncovered, towers like a monument against the high jagged walls, which, to use Lord Beaverbrook's words on the opening day, 'speak of nights of terror and endurance, the worst of which was averted by those instruments of power and speed which have here been collected for our admiration . . .'

Since the opening day, to judge by the crowds to be met there, the workers have made the Exhibition a holiday outing for themselves and their families, or part of a shopping expedition. Toddling children are held up to pat the sides of the Mosquito, or finger the ten-ton bomb; small boys and girls run in and out under the great wings of the Halifax or stand beneath the Lancaster gazing up at the wax model of an airman peering down at them from its transparent nose. One has no need to wonder if people are air-minded when a fifteen-year-old schoolgirl confides, as with obvious intelligence she studies the propellers and radio equipment, that she hopes that she may one day pilot 'one of those little two-seaters' herself . . . As the voice of a loudspeaker announcer, calling two small boys by name, informs them that their mother is waiting at the entrance, one cheerful looking woman remarks to another, 'I bet they'll keep Mum waiting a long time now that they know where she is.'

The interest shown by elderly women in the Exhibition is surprising, until it is remembered that large numbers of them have also been working on aviation and radio parts during the war, or at the very least serving in the canteens for the workers. The new-found technical skill of their sons and daughters has also been for them a cause for pride . . .

The length of time allotted for the Exhibition has had to be doubled, from six weeks to twelve.

Another story which I sent out at that time had a touch of light entertainment. It was about women's war on rats. Post-war Italy was threatened by the dread bubonic plague, due to a rat infestation of stores. The rats had become wary of the usual poisoned foodstuffs offered them. Women from the registers of the highly educated, with university degrees, were called upon and accepted the challenge to become, not rat killers, Oh no, we now described them as 'rodent operatives'. Very cunningly, they enticed the rats by judicious feeding on delights in the end to deceive them by the fatal dose.

The year 1946, after the advent of the Labour government, was to see many changes in social and economic life.

For instance, International Women's Day, then acknowledged and respected almost world-wide, was celebrated in Britain in many towns with the theme of promoting peace, and in London by a well-attended conference, to which Mrs Attlee, wife of the Prime Minister, sent a message, while Leah Manning, a much respected Labour MP took the chair. Delegates came from the newly founded organisations of women in France and Italy. The rights of women, in general, but specially at work, were emphasised. My article about this went out, not only to *British Ally*, but in the general release of Overseas Features: some notes of it I still possess.

That year was also to see many changes in our work at the Ministry. The University buildings, of course, had to be vacated; our section was moved to some flats in and around Baker Street, where, I think, some of the Secret Operations for France had been.

To our regret we were being demoted from the status of a Ministry, with a minister to defend us in Parliament, to a Central Office of Information, which was to serve the needs of various departments under their direction. We now came under the Foreign Office. It was rumoured that Ernest Bevin, Foreign Secretary, was most anxious to continue the work of *British Ally* and also to expand our services in other parts of Eastern Europe. During this year, Horace White, to whose work and enthusiasm *British Ally* had owed so much, felt that he needed a rest and change.

The Ministry had absorbed almost my entire life and time. This was possible because our beloved Lil had been able to come back and live with us. Till war ended, both she and her husband Walter had been roped in for some sort of national service, but they finally escaped. Lil told me that she was not going to go on counting b---screws any longer than she could help. Both, as I have told, had been the mainstay of the school in its hard war years, till it closed. Neither had ever been needed for or adapted to factory life.

Lil just took charge of my entire household. Harriet and Roderick were there only in the holidays; there were spare rooms, one of which we let to a colleague of mine at the Ministry and her husband, an artist, who was employed elsewhere. Our little circle now existed by serving the Ministry; Walter was able to get a job as one of the messengers, Pat to do sums in the Accounts department. This was not a matter of nepotism, good service of this kind was required. Walter became so well esteemed that he was offered the Head Messenger post, but a shy and retiring man, he would not take it. Both Pat and Walter were still in their jobs when they died.

Our little community faced one problem. The landlord, anxious to return from the country to which he had retreated, requested me to give up the house. Fortunately for us, such occupation was protected by law; we could not be turned out except for sound reasons. However, I was obliged to get counsel and face an action in court. The landlord's solicitor pointed out that I let rooms and part-boarded my lodgers. Evidence as to how they were fed and its cost proved that I made no profit. But the strongest card in my pack was that my eldest son, demobilised from the Navy, was about to return from Washington with a wife and one adopted and one yet-to-be-born, or new-born child. The landlord lost his case. John and family returned the following year.

In my office preparations for the Newton Tercentenary occupied much of my time, though the work was not so heavy as it had been for the celebrations in Russia. I kept note of any reference to the preparations that appeared in the Press, or came into our office from organisations. To publicise our scientists was very much the business of such institutions and of the Royal Society itself, as well as our national Press. As to foreign guests, we could not know very much until they arrived. My chief duty was to follow events and produce a report to send to *British Ally*.

My position enabled me to attend many kinds of scientific meetings; the exchanges between highly qualified men, as well as their personalities, were to me a constant fascination. I was fortunate in being present at most of the important occasions of the celebration; not, of course, the Royal Garden Party, the Reception by the Lord Mayor and Corporation of London or the ballet at Covent Garden. This last had been specially arranged at the request of Maynard Keynes, who was chairman of the Covent Garden Trust. He had married the famous Russian ballerina Lydia Lopokova. I had predicted this surprising marriage to Bertie Russell after we dined with Keynes on one occasion in Bloomsbury, but Russell had not believed me. Keynes had recently died and Lopokova was appearing for the first time since his death.

I was at the reception of the Royal Society and at the absorbing lectures at the Royal Institution, as well as at Trinity College for the Cambridge visit. Some extracts from the article which I wrote and sent to *British Ally* will tell part of that story.

At the Royal Society's premises the atmosphere of a real peacetime great occasion prevailed. An awning at the entrance, carpets of rich scarlet, bright English flowers, soft concealed

51

lighting throwing into relief those white classical columns which seem always to be associated with the austere clarity of thought, gave appropriate welcome to all these guests who, in honouring Newton, were themselves also worthy of much honour. The mace of the Royal Society, shining with gold, a gift of King Charles II, was borne before the President, Sir Robert Robinson, as he came to the library to open the proceedings.

Sir Robert announced that a modern Isaac Newton Observatory was to be established in Great Britain to honour the Tercentenary. There followed presentation of guests and by them their illuminated addresses and gifts. Among these were Newton's works translated into Russian and bound in scarlet leather with the head of Newton embossed in gold, presented by the Soviet Academy of Science. Addresses from scientists of many countries were then spoken.

At the Royal Institution in the afternoon, Professor Andrade delivered the first of the lectures commemorating Newton. He drew an absorbing picture of Newton against the background of his contemporaries' view of him: sensitive, conscious of his own genius but dreading controversy, yet a man 'capable of greater sustained mental effort than any man before or since'. With extracts of noble seventeenth-century prose, as with his own wit and poetic feeling, Professor Andrade moved his hearers to applause such as men of science seldom indulge in, and, in fact, broke the rules of the Royal Institution which by custom requires that scientific lectures be received in respectful silence.

At Cambridge, after visiting the Cavendish Laboratory, the scientists drove to Trinity College to be received by the Master of Trinity, the famous historian, Dr G.M. Trevelyan O.M. and to lunch with the Fellows of Trinity in the Great Hall where Newton had served as a poor scholar and where he later dined. As the Master spoke of this festival organised by the Royal Society as a 'ray of sunlight breaking through the clouds of the greatest war the modern world had endured', in the appropriate setting of the dark panelled, high raftered medieval hall, with its long refectory tables, a sudden summer storm broke, thunder rolled, flashes of lightning illuminated the scarlet robes of some present, till, as if to give point to the Master's words, the sun again streamed through the high windows.

Mr Geoffrey Keynes, a famous member of Cambridge University, Senior Surgeon of St Bartholomew's Hospital, London, and Consultant to the Royal Air Force, read to the assembly some of the work which his brother, John Maynard, Lord Keynes, had done on the little-known manuscripts of Newton. These displayed him against the true background of his age, as a man with one foot in the world of alchemy, magic, theology, as well as rising science – tormented near to madness by his own disbelief, taking refuge ultimately as a corpulent idol of London society.

Like an answering phrase in a musical symphony to Keynes' presentation came the paper on Newton's Atomism, sent by the Academician Sergei Vavilov, Present of the Academy of Sciences USSR, and read by Sir Henry Dale at the Royal Institution. Vavilov implied that Newton in his chemical studies had come near to conjecturing the atomic nucleus. Substances, Newton said, porous bodies, had been composed by God in hard primitive particles which man had no power to divide, but which, should the particles break away or change the substances composed of them could change. The models made by modern scientists of the atomic structure of elements were in accord with Newton's scheme. Here was no mere alchemist's dream, but a mind reaching far into atomic theory.

The Royal Society was charged to write and thank Vavilov for this paper on so great an occasion, and for its 'perfect English text'.

Among the list of delegates to the celebrations which, as I received it, is in Appendix 4, I found the name of Yuen Ren Chao from China, who had been the interpreter for Russell and me in China in 1920.

After the lapse of so many years I want to record here my very clear memory of the rapt attention with which I listened to the reading of Academician Sergei Vavilov's then unpublished paper on Newton's Atomism. I was almost glued to my seat as my mind followed the tracing of this subtle link between medieval alchemy, Newton, Rutherford and atomic splitting. It has even more meaning today for me after some of my recent researches into our twelfth-century monastic devotees of science. The type of interest shown by Keynes was also remarkable, as were two quotations from Newton himself given by Professor Andrade to illustrate the mystical element in Newton's nature. In 1676, in a letter, Newton referred to the transmutation of metals, when he was mostly concerned with chemical operations. 'I cannot hope to convince the sceptical that Newton had some power of prophecy or special vision, had some inkling of atomic power,' said Professor Andrade, 'but I do say that they do not read to me as if all he meant was that the manufacture of gold would upset world trade.'

The first quotation reads:

Because the way by which mercury may be so impregnated has been thought to be concealed by others that have known it, and therefore may possibly be an inlet to something more noble, not to be communicated without immense danger to the world, if there should be any verity in hermetic writers.

And further on: 'There be other things besides the transmutation of metals (if those great pretenders brag not [pretenders was not then derogatory]) which none but they understand.'

'A remarkable passage in view of what has happened recently,' commented Professor Andrade and he went on: 'I feel that Newton derived his knowledge by something more like direct contact with the unknown sources that surround us, with the world of mystery, than has been vouchsafed to any other man of science.'

The Newton Tercentenary Celebrations, except for the omission of Germany and Japan, were, both in intention and in fact, a world gathering of men of science. Those who organised this event did so with dignity and some splendour, in the true spirit and tradition of the Royal Society of Great Britain and other similar academies, which is that 'the new philosophy' – that is, science – by its very nature, and speaking in its own terms of language, is such that it can be understood by serious students throughout the world, and that the knowledge it imparts belongs by right to all men and should be communicated to them.

Apart from the efforts, from time to time, of men of good will, to restore internationalism to science, the Tercentenary of Isaac

Newton on 15–19 July 1946 was the very last occasion on which the command implicit in this great total of human achievement, this gift to mankind, was duly honoured and upheld.

Notes

1. A.J.P. Taylor, *English History, 1914–1945*, Penguin, p. 725
2. Lady Williams-Ellis was a prolific writer and the widow of Clough Williams-Ellis of Portmeirion, North Wales.

4

THE GREAT PRETENDERS:
THEIR BOMB
AND TOTAL WAR

From the year 1946 onwards, as the (now) Central Office of Information settled into its new quarters, working no longer under war conditions and with a new government and a different status and directives, there were bound to be many changes. Of the editorial staff of Soviet Relations none remained but Lena Chivers and myself. Maurice Lovell moved to Overseas Press Services, though he was still available for consultation and advice. With a view to establishing journals in Poland and possibly in Czechoslovakia, an overall director for such papers, Mr Keith Fowler, was appointed. Mr Wright Miller came in as editor of *British Ally*; on which Lena continued her admirable 'projection of Britain' as it was called; and science remained my special preserve. Before long, because I might have to service more than one paper, I was given an assistant, Lydia Oshinsky. She was of Russian emigré origin: her father, a medical doctor, had left Bolshevik Russia with her mother for Germany and then, when Hitler came to power, they had fled to Britain. Lydia had never lived in Russia, nonetheless I recognised in her much of the Russian temperament. She was invaluable, and for years during and after our work together we were fast friends, until her sad early death.

Our *British Ally* editorial conferences, at which we could all give an opinion, were continued, and to these came periodically Ian Gray and his colleague Joe Dobbs, two young men newly appointed at the Foreign Office, both, I think, from the Navy. Their job was to take

British Ally under their wing, get to know about our work, make suggestions and also inform us as to political directives. Before long, Joe Dobbs disappeared to join the Press attaché's department in Moscow. From time to time we were briefly introduced to other men appointed at Press attaché level, passing through the office en route for Moscow. I did not pay much attention to these senior persons, who would be closeted with Keith Fowler to discuss policy. In my own mind I felt convinced that they none of them really knew what they were doing or – if they did – how to set about it.

The most important appointment was that of the new editor for the Moscow end, to replace Horace White: this was not easy. Horace White had come from his work on the *Daily Herald*, a Labour and Trade Union paper. After some delay we were introduced to our new colleague, Archie Johnstone, an experienced working journalist, who had been, for a time, on the liberal *News Chronicle*. We met Archie over lunch to make his acquaintance and wish him the best of luck. To my amazement, Archie greeted me with the remark that he knew me already, having reviewed my book, *The Right to be Happy*, published as far back as 1927. Naturally, I was pleased to find someone to work with who, apparently, respected my ability. As I remember, we chaffed him a bit about being vetted for his politics (what is now and was, I suppose even then, in the inner circles, styled 'security').

Ernest Bevin, our Foreign Secretary, had looked forward to a Labour victory in the election, more especially hoping this would mean establishing relations with the Soviet Union which was, after all, a declared communist State with power in the hands of the workers. It had been Bevin's own trade union, the dockers, who had refused to load munitions for Churchill's war against the Bolsheviks in 1918. Now the Russians had shown themselves, as allies, fighters of amazing tenacity and courage. British Labour was certainly not communist, but Bevin had once said that, in talking to Russia, 'like would be speaking to like'. Unfortunately, owing to Hitler, Stalin, Churchill and Truman, it did not turn out quite that way.

The post-war mood of the Western Allies and that of the Soviet Union differed widely. This was bound to happen, but neither side had sufficient imagination to understand this, or the foresight and inclination to maintain their wartime alliance and co-operation. The Soviet Zone in Germany gave Russia an added border state. For these countries Churchill and Roosevelt had envisaged free elections which would keep them within western ideology. Stalin, on the contrary, was determined that, for Soviet protection, they must be, and remain, loyally communist.

In both the East and West, the peoples of Europe and their territories were exhausted by the war; food and reconstruction were imperative. In this respect, the Russians, with a large hinterland to draw upon, had some advantage. But they were greatly worried lest it prove impossible to restore to cultivation the shallow soils of the steppes in the west, churned up by the tanks: they sought advice about this from soil experts in Britain. Despite all their losses the people were not despondent; on the contrary, virile and resilient, they were proud of their valour in the 'great patriotic war' and looked forward to a great future.

France, Britain and America were not joyful. In addition to the urgent economic reconstruction and sheer hunger of the people in their occupied zones of Germany, they faced the task of re-educating these people out of Hitler totalitarian domination into democratic procedures, as well as the identification and trial of war criminals, great and small.

France and Britain were also virtually bankrupt and had to reconstruct their devastated areas. A bitter pill for Britain was that the Labour government were actually forced by circumstances to ration bread for a time. Urgent revival of trade was essential.

I remember Stafford Cripps' slogan, put out, I believe, by our Central Office – 'Britain's bread hangs by Lancashire's thread' – and how indignant I felt about it at the time. It seemed to me that we should rather help ourselves, that, setting aside all rules and regulations the able-bodied should at once start clearing the rubble of our cities and rebuild as the Poles were already doing. I felt sure that our youth would respond to such an appeal. However, there was no such revolutionary fervour in our staid Labour and trade union leaders. What is more, all the land in the heart of our cities was private property, whereas, in communist countries, it belonged to the people.

Among the peoples, especially women, there were already movements for unity and peace. A new worldwide women's organisation to combat fascism, the Women's International Democratic Federation (WIDF), had been set up in Paris in 1945 and to this had come women from many countries, including Americans, some of whom were already members of the existing Women's International League for Peace and Freedom (WILPF), started as far back as 1915. Parallel with the women's moves, a World Peace Council was being born. Such movements had promise, but no political power. But at the very top levels, where decisions are made, the intentions of the statesmen were quite otherwise.

No one, at any level, had as yet fully understood the fatal legacies of Hitler's total war and the bomb. War was no longer an enterprise conducted solely by persons allocated to the 'armed forces', backed by efforts from the civil population to supply them. War was now total: it aimed at civil and military persons alike, it demanded the allegiance and services of the entire population, including those of the very best brains of the men of science. This meant that in the eyes of authority it was now dangerous and subversive for individuals, nations and peoples to get to like one another and make friends. The bomb, if put in production, could, as was now evident, make its contribution to the totalitarian chorus as the instrument of total destruction.

The modern alchemists, those Great Pretenders, had built it and held its secrets, this thing more powerful than gold; but gold in plenty was already in their hands. Both gold and bomb were very real; the one could revive active life; the other, no mere spectre now, but a sword of Damocles poised overhead, spelt death. President Truman, supreme of Great Pretenders, gold in one hand, bomb in the other, now set out to impose his doctrine on Western Europe – the Marshall Plan, ultimately accepted by the war-torn countries, and by Ernest Bevin for Britain. For a time it seemed as if the Russians might come into the scheme, but finally they stayed out. After all, the plan was a capitalist one and 'aid' meant conditions, 'strings' as they came to be called. There was a comedian at the Windmill theatre in London at the time, who gave great joy by his witty monologue about money with strings attached. Quite a number of people in Britain were also highly suspicious of 'strings'. For the Russians, the existence of the bomb and the secrecy surrounding it, together with the Allies' procedure in post-war Germany, evoked a loss of trust and cautious withdrawal.

This guilty secret and its relation to all power politics bulked larger than economics in the minds of intellectuals on both sides. In our division of the Central Office of Information, we were still custodians of the cultural relations of our country with Russia and Eastern Europe.

Editors and editorial material for *Glos Anglii*, the Polish paper, and *Britsky Magazin* for Czechoslovakia, were going ahead. In Russia we had also a monthly called *British Chronicle* which carried serious articles of some length. Bertha Malnick, its editor, had left when our status changed; the journal was now included in the work of myself and Lydia Oshinsky. Radio Broadcasts to Russia had been agreed by the Russians and we had reports of transmissions that came from them.

All through the next years our department lived in the constant cross-fire of contending ideologies. Propaganda material from both sides flooded our In trays, disturbing our minds, either more or less according to whether we really cared, or saw it all as no more than a job to earn prestige or bread and butter. Those years, when I sat day after day at my desk, a witness and also a part of a tragic struggle in which I had no power to determine the outcome, made an indelible impression on me. In a way it was like being an observer from Mars, or even God himself, hoping against hope that humankind would not do evil, but follow the paths of righteousness. We peoples had come so near to a longed-for reconciliation and peace, if only our statesmen would implement our desires. I was no stranger to the argument as to what ethic should govern industrial civilisation, but the bomb was a powerful new factor. At the heart of it all was science. As I considered the daily Press and looked over the journals that lay in my In tray, I was surprised that the consequences of Hiroshima were so little understood. The making of the bomb was hailed as a great scientific achievement, which, having regard to the brilliance of the physicists who split the atom, and those who carried that work further, it certainly was. They had not foreseen the consequences nor the popular outburst of glorification associated with the bomb and now also revealing, for the first time, all the other new weapons and inventions – radar, Whittle's jet engine, the bomb that could skip across the water surface, the ten-ton bomb, the deadly napalm. All these were glorified, as were the weeks and hours devoted by scientists to winning the war, without any compunction for this insidious prostitution of the highest powers of the human intellect to the lowest of human activities – killing fellow men and women in war.

Sir Henry Dale's bold call to men of science to risk persecution, as Giordano Bruno and Galileo had done, in a campaign against secrecy in science, was answered by only two men, Klaus Fuchs and Nun May, both of whom suffered long terms in prison for enabling Russia to obtain the coveted secret of the bomb. Whatever may have been the judgement of their contemporaries, they were true to the doctrine of the universality of science. Sir Henry himself later upheld scientific devotion to truth when he resigned from the Soviet Academy of Science because it upheld Lysenko's belief in the inheritance of acquired characteristics, rejected and refuted by most biologists, many of whom in Russia were being persecuted for opposition to Lysenko. Under Stalin, Soviet scientists allowed political considerations to overrule the objectivity of science. But no more was heard from Sir Henry about the increasing subservience of scientists to politics in the West.

This issue was troubling the best among our scientists, as I found when I went as an observer to a meeting of the Association of Scientific Workers. Its members were discussing how far they would remain in various aspects of government service, as they had done during the war. Watson Watt, inventor of radar, was disinclined; Max Nicholson was quite certain that he wanted to return to purely civilian life. He later wrote an impressive book called *The System* against the bureaucracy of the Establishment. They talked about the newly formed United Nations and what might be its influence. The question of the power to veto resolutions in the UN Council came up. Some thought that the procedure should allow a democratic decision by vote. But Professor Blackett, the association's president, maintained, to the surprise of some, that to allow a veto was right. Julian Huxley was one of those taking part in that discussion. All were deeply concerned about the responsibility of scientists for the bomb and its relation to politics. Freeman Dyson, in his very remarkable book *Disturbing the Universe*,[1] mentions how a sense of guilt, as well as pride in the achievements of the physicists and mathematicians, drove them all to research into how nuclear power could be turned to peaceful uses.

At the meeting of the British Association in 1947 Professor Cockcroft presided over a discussion on atomic energy to which 300 papers had been contributed. There was also a World Power Conference at The Hague where Professor Cockcroft spoke on the same subject. The Association of Scientific Workers issued a statement which was reproduced in full in *Pravda* in September 1947. We at *British Ally* had been instructed to refrain from any mention of atomic energy in our pages. It seemed to me a mistaken policy to avoid mentioning matters of extreme topical interest that were, in any case, well known to the public and to our Russian readers. I did, I remember, protest to my superiors to that effect. The Russians were taking care not to miss anything, spoken or written, that had any bearing on their own anxieties and purposes.

I felt frustrated as I reviewed the state of what had been defined as our purpose, to foster cultural relations with Russia and her border countries and peoples. Of course, I continued routine selection of interesting scientific and technical material, such as my superiors deemed 'harmless'. But I looked for some international theme, and presently found one among film makers who held a congress in Paris in October 1947, convened jointly by the Scientific Film Association in London and the Institute of Scientific Cinematography in Paris. As a result, an International Scientific Films Association was set up. Twenty-two countries provisionally joined it, among them Poland, Czechoslovakia and Yugoslavia. The president was a Pole but the vice-president was none other than Mr J. Maddison of Great Britain of the Films Division of the Central Office of Information. Mr Maddison was asked to do an article for *British Ally*. This put Mr Maddison and myself in contact with one another, and for some time I was much interested in what our film people hoped to do, in Africa among other places. I still remember a good film they did about the work of a District Commissioner in an African village to build and establish a maternity centre. All that now belongs to the colonial past.

I did a short article on the political sessions sponsored by the UN for our schoolchildren in the Christmas holidays, at which young people heard eminent lecturers and were given the opportunity for asking questions and having discussions in groups.

The UN and its offshoot UNESCO, which was growing in importance, offered some hope of constructive action. UNESCO, as an integral part of the United Nations, had been constituted in November 1945 at a meeting in London in which forty-four nations took part. Formal ratification from the governments concerned, as well as an agreement prepared with the UN, was to define the relations between the two organisations. In July 1946 the last meeting of the Preparatory Commission took place in London. There is no doubt that the British government which, in effect, meant Ernest Bevin and Ellen Wilkinson, played a very significant part in the launching of this cultural effort which was to wield considerable influence in many future world affairs.

At the July conference Ellen Wilkinson, as the Minister of Education, was in the chair. There were 150 delegates, all prominent figures in science and the arts. All members of the UN Council were represented with the exception of the USSR, for whom a seat on the UNESCO council was reserved, if and when Russia decided to take part. Most of the South American republics were there; Greece, Iraq, Iran, Saudi Arabia and other Middle Eastern states; and Yugoslavia, Poland and Czechoslovakia from those European states not members of the UN Council.

Julian Huxley, who maintained an interest in the political aspects of science, more especially in promoting international understanding, had accepted the secretaryship of the Preliminary Commission. He made his report to this meeting, which was to be the last before the work of the full body began.

I was, naturally, anxious that the USSR should participate, so I took pains in my report for *British Ally* to clarify those points which might encourage – or antagonise – their eminent men and women in science and the arts. For instance, the first article in UNESCO's constitution stated as its aim 'to contribute to peace and security by promoting collaboration among the nations through education, science and culture'. It meant effective *international* collaboration, with no intention of internal interference. It desired to act with existing international organisations within its sphere, but with no intent of absorbing them. From the start, a clear distinction was made between science and the arts. Whereas science did aim at uniformity of opinion as to what was factual truth in nature, in the arts imagination had play: greater variety and diversity, unfettered, could minister to the enjoyment of all.

Julian Huxley and his colleagues, during those preliminary commissions, were full of enthusiasm and great ideals; they made plans and set up many committees. They were doomed to disappointment in some of their more ambitious hopes but, in the end, the work of the pioneers bore fruit. It was expected that Huxley would be appointed as the first director of the organisation when it met in Paris in November 1946.

I was able to attend both the London and Paris meetings. As I walked into the London meeting to join the groups just assembling, the first people I saw were my old friends Iuen Ren Chao and Hu Shih, who had been almost my daily companions twenty-six years ago in Peking. They had been regarded then, and were still, among the outstanding intellectuals in contemporary China. Mr Chao, with his wife and growing family, had moved to and fro between China and America. With Hu Shih he had an honourable place as a leader in cultural understanding and contact with the West. Three years after this meeting, the communist take-over in China led to Mr Chao and his family returning to live permanently in America, where he had, in fact, spent the greater part of his education and working life. But, at least for some time under the Mao Tse Tung regime they had been able to pay return visits.

In Paris, the British delegation included J.B. Priestley, whose broadcasts during the war had impressed listeners overseas as well as at home. Priestley was among those intellectuals, shocked by the Hiroshima bomb, who were not slow in realising what it might mean for the future. He was anxious to foster cultural contacts for international understanding. There was also Ronald Gould, General Secretary of the National Union of Teachers (NUT), and, as Press officer, John Maud, a civil servant from the Department of Education. (Both these men were later knighted.)

In greeting some members of the Press, John Maud made the point that this new organisation was an adventurous departure. He was there to discuss and answer any questions. His fellow delegates from Britain had come with open minds, hoping that subjects might be dealt with in themselves and not in narrow national terms. His manner appeared to me that of the good clubbable Englishman.

When later it came to decisions on resolutions I thought the British delegation over-cautious, and am sure that I was not wrong in detecting phone communication for advice from our Foreign or Education offices. No doubt all the other 'open-minded' representatives from their countries did likewise. But something of what this conference meant to those at the grassroots came to me when a young Chinese teacher approached me in great distress because he could not understand why the English delegation seemed unwilling to accept proposals that school history and geography text books should be altered in order to give a fairer presentation of what had actually taken place. I ventured to ask Ronald Gould about this. Striding up and down the corridor, he explained to me that this proposal was really futile in the face of the vast propaganda that was now prevalent through the many new means of communication – cinema, radio, television – mostly under the direction of governments. I thought then, and still do, that Gould's attitude was mistaken and short-sighted. The written word and libraries have a permanence for research which radio, television and the daily Press do not offer to the general public. The printed word provides opportunity for reflection over the opinions and events reported; what comes to the ear by radio, and to the eye and ear in television, may or may not linger in the memory.

At the time when I had this brief conversation with Ronald Gould, I had already been learning something from my colleagues at the COI, who were interested in films for Africa, about how well-meaning teachers in the schools there taught the history of England as I had been taught, in a succession of Kings and Queens. English history be it noted – the pupils' own country, designated as savage, clearly had no history worth considering.

To do Ronald Gould justice, I must here digress further to 1960. In that year he showed that he and his trade union were deeply sincere in their concern about the effects of new aspects of communication. They were responsible for that amazing and comprehensive congress, entitled Popular Culture and Personal Responsibility, held at Church House, Westminster. Its massive verbatim report, compiled by its conference secretary, Fred Jarvis, is treasured among the books on my shelves.

As was expected, Julian Huxley became the first Director of UNESCO. He was a good choice. He had an established reputation as a scientist, but he had more than this, a genuine desire to bring nations and peoples together to understand one another. He had visited the Soviet Union, respected the work of their scientists and hoped that the Russians would soon be taking part in UNESCO and other efforts at co-operation in the cultural world. As a biologist and humanist, who accepted the theory of evolution, Julian did also have some hope and faith that the human species might, given favourable conditions, evolve even further in knowledge and creative purpose. His brother, Aldous Huxley, author of the famous, satirical book *Brave New World*, was of a very different turn of mind.

It seems to me that Julian, like vast numbers of people who think rationally and are disposed to living in peace with their neighbours, cherished his hope that UNESCO, with world-wide influence, might establish a humane – humanist – tolerance and conciliation that would be assisted and supported by the common aims of scientists in pursuit of their discoveries. Like all such well-meaning and well-disposed people, he reckoned without the believers in 'revealed' religions, dogmatists, power-seekers and bureaucrats. The Catholic Church had long aimed at the establishment of a universal, institutional Christianity, whilst the disciples of Karl Marx now had a not dissimilar purpose.

The United Nations and UNESCO are still with us today, but the nations have not yet accepted, from the UN, a rule of law, nor, from UNESCO, a universal humanist tolerance. Nonetheless, in no more than forty years of their existence, both these institutions have found many tasks, beneficial to all peoples, to which to put their hand.

As this book was going to press came the information that the United States' government has given notice of withdrawal of support and funds from UNESCO. Criticism is expressed of many of its undertakings, as well as of extravagance. The British government appears likely to join with the United States in withdrawal. This decision will almost certainly meet with very considerable protest from other member countries of the United Nations. The Prime Minister of Australia has already given his view that the world cannot do without services rendered by UNESCO, chiefly, it would seem, in the less developed nations. I am not familiar with recent developments at this excellent institution set up with such enthusiasm in 1946. But for me these events are a sign of the tendency of the great powers to insist on the dominance of their style of culture, and of a tragic growing indifference to the arts and any sciences not directed to technology or military research.

This is perhaps the moment to pause and say something of what was happening to my family and myself. John was still away in the United States, in Washington, where he had been spending his war decoding and translating Japanese. He had considered himself more or less engaged to a school friend whom he had wanted to get out from England. But now he had fallen in love with Susan, the daughter of the American poet Vachel Lindsay. The whole affair was complicated. Susan was separated from her husband, by whom she had a daughter, and was getting a divorce. John, meantime, was about to be demobilised, which meant he was out of a job, but could not come home until these personal affairs were settled. He wanted not only to marry

Susan, but to adopt her small daughter. This is one of the occasions in my life when I acted out of an intuition (what some would call extrasensory perception). With John's worried letter in my hand, I felt impelled to get up from my desk in the office, to go down to the Baker Street Post Office, and telegraph to John, 'If in trouble consult . . .' and gave the name and address of Ted Lloyd, a distinguished civil servant, who was then working with the newly established Food and Agricultural Organisation in Washington – an address that I had obtained for possible prospects for myself.

The message came to John in the night over the phone, as he said, like the voice of God, at the moment when Susan was in hospital giving birth to her second child, their daughter. Oddly enough, no confirmation copy of this message ever came. But there it was, written down in the night hours. It enabled John to have a job in the rural section of FAO, which relieved him of immediate anxiety and was also stimulating. In 1947, John and Susan and the two daughters came to join us in the house in Dartmouth Road, which I had gone to law to retain.

Kate continued in America on her post-graduate course. My Harriet, now growing up, wanted to join her half-sister and go to college in America. The two girls were always good friends; besides Harriet had already been to America as a small child and felt that half of her belonged there. There were opportunities and grants for English students. Bill Curry at Dartington undertook to coach Harriet in the necessary subjects, one of which, mathematics as he woefully said, cost him great effort. On the salary I now had, though it was scarcely affluent, I felt that I could manage what I would have to contribute.

Roderick was continuing at Dartington, chiefly engaged in developing and promoting his passion for cricket, organising it in a school which, of course, did not go in for compulsory games! Meantime the father of these two, Griffin Barry, had now crossed the Atlantic, to see his children; but also with a project and a publisher's support to go to Ireland and write a book about it. He was, of course, an Irish-American. Harriet and Roddy were invited to visit him in Dublin during part of their summer holidays. For this I had to go to the Passport Office and see to visas for their passports. A stern official informed me that these children could not leave the country without their father's permission. Somewhat to his dismay I replied quite loudly and in the presence of other applicants, 'Oh, but these children are illegitimate and are going to visit their father.'

I have photos, August 1946, of the two handsome teenagers, Roddy plus cricket bat, with his father, and also with Harriet. On the back Harriet wrote that she did not much like the one of herself, but she noted that Daddy was standing on an edge of fence 'so as not to appear shorter than his fourteen-year-old son, which of course he is!'

For me there was no question of a holiday at that time. To go abroad was out of the question, unless on appointment to one of the Allied Commissions that were being formed. Nor was it easy to take money abroad. In fact a year or so later, when Harriet was in college in America, the embargo on the export of money made it impossible for me to continue my contribution. She had some help at first from John and Kate, but thereafter had, like other American students, to work her own way through college. She did excellently and acquired a poise and independence which, when she came home, made me say once that I stood in awe of my own daughter.

Pat and I continued in our labours at the Ministry; he doing sums in the accounts department, happy in the thought, as he said, that 'like your father' he was now also a civil servant. In his work he made one or two friends with whom to snatch a midday sandwich and a drink. I was intensely worried about his bronchitic cough.

While doing what I could for the family, my real concern was the political situation in Europe. Pat shared my anxiety about the vicissitudes of the renewing Cold War. There were many Europeans, like Julian Huxley, as well as Americans, who, in those fateful years 1945–50, still hoped to preserve some vestige of the wartime alliance with Russia, symbolised in the treaty by which our two countries were to co-operate in Europe for twenty years after the war.

Many aspects of the relation between our countries were known to me in the course of my work. But there was much happening in the Press and broadcasting that I had no time or opportunity to observe. In addition, some events of the period have only recently come to light, whose relevance I must also take into account.

Some awareness of the Foreign Office views percolated through to me, since our department was under their direction. A bankrupt British government, under pressure of the Truman doctrine and the Marshall economic plan, was being forced simply to ignore the treaty with Russia.

Ernest Bevin, Labour's Foreign Minister, was perhaps the most harassed statesman in all Europe. The Allies owed him a debt for the vital part he had played, through his trade union reputation, in managing the problem of manpower for forces and factories in wartime Britain. True to his working-class origins and sympathies, and his consequent desire to maintain good Anglo–Soviet relations, he, more than other members of the Cabinet, felt angry and humiliated by dependence on America's economic help and by the harsh terms on which it had been given. Not only had our American holdings been sacrificed in Lend Lease, but we were bound by treaty to share all scientific and security information with the USA.

Churchill, now in Parliamentary opposition, was supporting the American contention that the true enemy, all along, had been the Soviet Union. Stalin, as Warlord, had been welcomed at the top table by diplomats in warlike mood, but now he began to be anathematised as a totalitarian dictator, enemy of democracy. The true 'crime' of Soviet Russia had, of course, from the beginning really been their opposition to capitalist profit and exploitation. Now the current popular trend of the West was to explain and defend its truly Christian and democratic civilisation, at the same time exposing and containing the highly dangerous ideology of Marxist–Leninist communism in the East.

The communist parties of Europe, justifiably proud of the Soviet achievements in war, continued in their loyalty to Stalin's leadership, and had accepted his version of the treachery of Russian Party members who had been tried and executed. They were, so far, unaware of the extent to which he had become the oppressor of his people.

Stalin himself, of whom the desperate battles of the war had taken their toll, was feeling his age, as he watched the Allied manoeuvres to exclude his country from participation in power and influence. Inevitably, in these few vital years, he became ever more obsessed with the paranoiac defence of his frontiers and the principles of the revolution by which he had shaped his own and his people's lives. Democracy did have *one* merit, that it enabled the British to depose their Warlord –however ungratefully – when no longer in need of him, whereas the Russians had to wait to be free of theirs until his death in 1953. Stalin's position in history remains to be fully evaluated: here I will recall only a remark from Isaac Deutscher's obituary in the *Manchester Guardian*, 6 March 1953: 'Stalin found Russia working with a

69

wooden plough and left her equipped with atomic piles.'

The Cold War debate proceeded increasingly by means of broadcasting, as Ronald Gould of the National Union of Teachers had predicted. J.B. Priestley, whose wartime broadcasts had been popular, now seemed to be no longer in favour with the policy makers. Bertrand Russell had returned from America and before long he became the authoritative voice broadcast by the BBC both from and within Britain, and thus, to a large extent, from Western Europe.

He and his wife and younger son were in Cambridge, where Trinity College were offering him a post. He had broken all contact with me, so that I knew little of what he was doing or the views that he expressed. It is not surprising, however, that I did not know of the speech on Hiroshima and the atom bomb that he delivered in the House of Lords on Wednesday 28 November 1945, since he himself later asserted that it never appeared anywhere except in Hansard. Again not surprising, since the Allies still cherished the hope that the secret of manufacturing the bomb might be kept from the Russians.

Russell had agreed with Einstein in not opposing the manufacture of the bomb. But when Russell made his speech he was not yet aware of the Franck Report, a statement which seven of the most eminent nuclear scientists presented to the British Secretary for War in June 1945, urging the use of the bomb in a desert space to demonstrate its appalling effect if used in war. There had been, in addition, a desperate appeal from Niels Bohr to Churchill and Roosevelt – which lay unopened on Roosevelt's desk when he died.

This speech, not four months after Hiroshima, was the first by an eminent informed individual on that tragic event. With both scientific knowledge and foresight, it summed up all the issues. Russell saw that this discovery involved world-wide responsibility and advocated sharing both secrets and responsibility with the Russians.

Here is the speech as delivered, enriched with my italics.

My Lords, it is with very great diffidence that I rise to address you, both because I have only once before addressed your Lordships' House and because, after listening to the debate yesterday and today, I feel that other speakers have ten times the political knowledge and twenty times the experience that has fallen to my lot, and that it is an impertinence for me to say anything at all. At the same time, the subject to which I wish to confine my remarks – namely, the atomic bomb and its bearing on policy – is so important and weighs so heavily upon my mind that I feel almost bound to say something about what it means for the future of mankind.

I should like to begin with just a few technical points which I think are familiar to everybody. The first is that the atomic bomb is, of course, in its infancy, and is quite certain very quickly to become both much more destructive and very much cheaper to produce. Both these points I think we may take as certain. Then there is another point which was raised by Professor Oliphant, and that is that it will be not very difficult to spray a countryside with radio-active products which will kill every living thing throughout a wide area, not only human beings but every insect, every sort of thing that lives. And there is a further point which perhaps relates to the somewhat more distant future. As your Lordships know, there are in theory two ways of tapping nuclear energy. One is the way which has now been made practicable, by breaking up a heavy nucleus into nuclei of medium weight. The other is the way which has not yet been made practicable, but which, I think, will be in time, namely, the synthesizing of hydrogen atoms to make heavier atoms, helium atoms or perhaps, in the first instance, nitrogen atoms. In the course of that synthesis, if it can be effected, there will be a very much greater release of energy than there is in the disintegration of uranium atoms. At present this process has never been observed but it is held that it occurs in the sun and in the interior of other stars. It only occurs in nature at temperatures comparable to those you get in the inside of the sun. The present atomic bomb, in exploding, produces temperatures which are thought to be about those in the inside of the sun. It is therefore possible that some mechanism analogous to the present atomic bomb, could be used to set off this much more violent explosion which would be obtained if one could synthesize heavier elements out of hydrogen.

All that must take place if our scientific civilisation goes on, if it does not bring itself to destruction; all that is bound to happen. We do not want to look at this thing simply from the point of view of the

71

next few years; we want to look at it from the point of view of the future of mankind. *The question is a simple one: is it possible for a scientific society to continue to exist, or must such a society inevitably bring itself to destruction?* It is a simple question but a very vital one. *I do not think it is possible to exaggerate the gravity of the possibilities of evil that lie in the utilisation of atomic energy.* As I go about the streets and see St Paul's, the British Museum, the Houses of Parliament and the other monuments of our civilisation, in my mind's eye I see a nightmare vision of those buildings as heaps of rubble with corpses all round them. That is a thing we have got to face, not only in our own country and cities, but throughout the civilised world as a real probability unless the world will agree to find a way of abolishing war. It is not enough to make war rare; great and serious war has got to be abolished, because otherwise these things will happen.

To abolish war is, of course, a very difficult problem. I have no desire to find fault with those who are trying to tackle that problem; I am quite sure I could not do any better. I simply feel that this is a problem that man has got to solve; otherwise man will drop out and the planet will perhaps be happier without us, although we cannot be expected to share that view. I think we have got to find a way of dealing with this. As everybody is aware, the immediate difficulty is to find a way of co-operating with Russia in dealing with it. I think that what the Prime Minister achieved in Washington was probably as much as could, at that time, be achieved. I do not suppose he could have done any better at that time. I am not one of those who favour the unconditional and immediate revelation to Russia of the exact processes by which the bomb is manufactured. *I think it is right that conditions should be attached to that revelation, but I make the proviso that the conditions must be solely those which will facilitate international co-operation; they must have no national object of any sort or kind. Neither we nor America must seek any advantage for ourselves, but if we are to give the secret to the Russians, it must be on the basis that they are willing to co-operate.* On that basis, I think, it would be right to let them know all about it as soon as possible, partly, of course, on the grounds that the secret is a short-term one. Within a few years the Russians will no doubt have bombs every bit as good as those which are at present being made in the United States; so it is only a question of a very short time during which we have this bargaining point, if it is one. The men of science, as your Lordships know, who have been concerned with the work are all extremely anxious to have the process revealed at once. I do not altogether agree with that, for the reasons I have stated, but I think it can be used as a means of getting a more sincere and a more thorough-going co-operation between ourselves and Russia. I find myself a whole-hearted supporter of the Foreign Secretary in the speeches he has made. I do not believe that the way to secure Russian co-operation is merely to express a desire for it. I think it is absolutely necessary to be firm on what we consider to be vital interests. I think it is more likely that you will get genuine co-operation from a certain firmness rather than merely going to them and begging them to co-operate. I agree entirely with the tone the Foreign Secretary has adopted on those matters.

We must, I think, hope – and I do not think this is a chimerical hope – that the Russian government can be made to see that the utilisation of this means of warfare would mean destruction to themselves as well as to everybody else. We must hope that they can be made to see that this is a universal human interest and not one on which countries are divided. I cannot really doubt that if that were put to them in a convincing manner they would see it. It is not a very difficult thing to see, and I cannot help thinking that they have enough intelligence to see it, provided it is separated from politics and from competition. There is, as everybody repeats, an attitude of suspicion. That attitude of suspicion can only be got over by complete and utter frankness, by stating, 'There are these things which we consider vital, but on other points we are quite willing that you should stand up for the things you consider vital. If there is any point which we both consider vital, let us try to find a compromise rather than that each side should annihilate the other, which would not be for the good of anybody.' I cannot help thinking that if that were put in a perfectly frank and unpolitical manner to the Russians they would be as capable of seeing it as we are – at least I hope so.

I think one could make some use of the scientists in this matter. They themselves are extremely uneasy, with a very bad conscience about what they have done. They know they had to do it but they do not like it. *They would be very thankful if some task could be assigned to them which would somewhat mitigate the disaster that threatens mankind.* I think they might be perhaps better able to persuade the Russians than those of us who are more in the game; they could, at any rate, confer with Russian scientists and perhaps get an entry that way towards genuine co-operation. We have, I think, some time ahead of us. The world at the moment is in a war-weary mood, and I do not think it is unduly optimistic to suppose there will not be a great war within the next ten years. Therefore we have some time during which we can generate the necessary genuine mutual understanding.

There is one difficulty that I think is not always sufficiently understood on our side, and that is that the Russians always feel —and feel, as it appears, rightly — that in any conflict of interests there will be Russians on one side and everybody else on the other. They felt that over the Big Three versus the Big Five question; it was Russia on one side and either two or four on the other. When people have that feeling, you have, I suppose, to be somewhat tender in bargaining with them and certainly not expect them to submit to a majority. You cannot expect that, when they feel that it is themselves against the field. There will no doubt have to be a good deal of tact employed during the coming years to bring about continuing international co-operation.

I do not see any alternative to the proposal which is before the world of making the United Nations the repository. I do not think that there is very much hope in that, because the United Nations, at any rate at present, are not a strong military body, capable of waging war against a great Power; and whoever is ultimately to be the possessor of the atomic bomb will have to be strong enough to fight a great Power. Until you can create an international organisation of that sort, you will not be secure. I do not think that there is any use whatever in paper prohibitions, either of the use or of the manufacture of bombs, because you cannot enforce them, and the penalty for obeying such a prohibition is greater than the penalty for infringing it, if you are really thinking of war. I do not think, therefore, that these paper arrangements have any force in them at all.

You have first to create the will to have international control over this weapon, and, when that exists, it will be easy to manufacture the machinery. Moreover, once that machinery exists, once you have an international body which is strong and which is the sole repository of the use of atomic energy, that will be a self-perpetuating system. It will really prevent great wars. Habits of political action will grow up about it, and we may seriously hope that war will disappear from the world. That is, of course, a very large order; but this is what we all have to face: either war stops or else the whole of civilised mankind stops and you are left with mere remnants, a few people in outlying districts, too unscientific to manufacture these instruments of destruction. The only people who will be too unscientific to do that will be people who have lost all the traditions of civilisation; and that is a disaster so grave that I think that all the civilised nations of the world ought to realise it. I think they probably can be brought to realise it before it is too late. At any rate I most profoundly hope so.

Very remarkable facts emerge from this speech: first Russell's assertion that the scientists who made the bomb wished to make its secrets widely known. This was in the true tradition of science as defined by the English Royal Society. What is more, the bomb could not have been made without the discoveries and work of the scientists from Europe, to which Britain had made no small contribution. The second point is that Russell, who above all cherished science, should have seen so clearly that science itself could now bring about world destruction.

How different were the minds of politicians is shown by what took place in the British inner Cabinet only a year later in 1946. This story has just been revealed by the BBC in its programme 'Time Watch' and written up in *The Listener* on 7 October 1982. Prime Minister Attlee, Dalton and Sir Stafford Cripps were discussing whether the British should make their own bomb. Sir Michael Perrin, then Assistant to the Atomic Energy Chief, Lord Portal, recalled that these members were opposed to what they felt to be a waste of materials and money. Lord Portal was instrumental in prolonging the discussion until Ernest Bevin arrived, late, coming from a meeting with American diplomats. As Attlee retailed the details about expense and lack of materials, Bevin turned to him and said: 'Oh no, Prime Minister, that won't do at all, we've got to have this. Quite bluntly,' he continued, 'I don't care for myself, but I don't want any other Foreign Secretary of this country to be talked at or to by the Secretary of State in the United States as I have just been in my discussions with Mr Byrnes. We've got to have this thing over here, whatever it costs.' And, Sir Michael Perrin added, 'I think I am right in remembering that he ended with "We've got to have a bloody Union Jack flying on top of it".'

So, without knowledge of the full Cabinet, Parliament or people, (and to the delight of Churchill, after he defeated Labour and took power again in 1951) the bomb was made. Its first test explosion took place at Monto Bello Lagoon, off the North-west of Australia in 1952.

Bevin's desperation and anger are explicable, though not entirely to be excused. It may be that the Americans had been complaining of lax British security over secrets, in the case of Nun May. But, had he wished, Bevin had a right to fend off American interference on the strength of the treaty which Anthony Eden and Molotov had signed.

As things stood, the United Nations, set up with so much eagerness in San Francisco, were already at loggerheads. No decision could be reached about a united policy over defeated Germany. Appeals by Bevin to the Russians to put their cards on the table were met and every constructive proposal countered by the famous Molotov NO. The American conviction that the Russians would move to take over Europe with the help of revolt by the Communist parties gave rise to the suggestion that possibly the best thing would be a 'preventive war', dropping the atomic bomb on Russia before they had one of their own. This was the great Truman bluff, for he only had about seven bombs, their pieces not yet put together for action.

Bevin, on the contrary, never believed that Russia would attempt invasion. Unlike the Americans, he had before his eyes the condition of destruction and hunger of nations and peoples consequent on war. Russian secretiveness and pride, Western indifference and hostility to them, meant, as usual, that Russia was better informed about the state of

Europe than their former Allies were about them. The stark fact was that the peoples of all Europe, Russia included, could do little to help one another to recovery.

I am convinced that Bevin had set his sights on a united Europe with Soviet co-operation. If it could have been realised, this would have been the best solution, not only for Europe, but for most other peoples of the world. The stony Soviet response to all the feelers Bevin put out brought bitter frustration. Yet the pro-communist workers in Europe, especially in France, had been the most active and devoted of the underground resistance during the war: their sympathy with Russia remained strong.

But the leaders of the Labour government in Britain had not come to power in a revolutionary mood. Their war years had been spent in coalition government, during which the Liberal Beveridge had been preparing his plan for the Welfare State, while the Tory Education Minister, Rab Butler, had, in 1944, got through his reforming Education Act. Nor was it easy now to be rude to American allies, who had fought in the war, but still remained affluent and untouched at home.

There has never been a Labour government in Britain who understood fully the meaning of taking power and were prepared to risk hardship for their people by acting rigidly on principle. According to how you look at it, temporising, or compromise, is a virtue or a vice. In 1947, unavoidable bread rationing in Britain and a very cold, bitter winter, brought a state of crisis.

The Americans had the money that could start the process of European rehabilitation. Bevin called a conference of European countries in Paris to set up OEEC – Organisation for European Economic Co-operation – to accept the Marshall plan. I well remember that winter, how I walked down from Willesden, through the deep snow, to my office in Baker Street, to work which was to become as disheartening in the world of ideas and human understanding as was the economic state of Europe. Whoever took the hand of hostile America could not expect a friendly gesture from Stalin, the warlord.

In 1948, in reply to the Allies' change in the German currency which adversely affected dealings with the Russian sector of Berlin, Stalin made his mistaken move to take over the whole city. He was defeated by the Berlin airlift, which took nearly a year.

There was no German peace treaty; Germany was, and remains, divided.

In the eyes of 'democrats' of Europe and America, the Soviet Union, from then on, was regarded as the example and shocking warning of a totalitarian dictatorship, similar to that of Hitler's, against which they had all united to fight.

What none of them realised was that they had now all become, in essence, totalitarians, in that they had been fighting a total war that involved entire populations, but a war that was completely *non* human – a totalitarian, technological, machine war based on their industrial development and strength. What is more, they had deliberately drawn into this struggle all that was most advanced in their science and the finest scientific brains of their peoples, who had responded with the gift of the bomb. All these events would, in future, determine their entire concept of government, and every detail of policy and administration.

Soon, only the very few would remember that it is not in their technology, but in their poetry, that the heart of a people resides.

Notes

1. Harper and Row, 1979.

5

THE WAR
OF IDEOLOGIES

Though 1948 may be marked as the year when the fear of renewed war in Europe revived, but was allayed by the Berlin airlift, it had also ended the hope of a united Europe. The Russians now had the secret of manufacturing the bomb; rearmament, embattled positions for defence, even more than peaceful reconstruction, seemed indicated for both sides.

Whatever the governments might decide, the voices of the people in argument or agreement were continuously to be heard so that even the governments felt constrained to defend their ideologies, not only by diplomacy, but on the air. As a consequence of their genuine interest in *British Ally*, the Russians had agreed to receive British broadcasting to Russia.

Our enlarged office and staff were still very busy, pursuing the hope of the journals in Poland and Czechoslovakia; my work with varied scientific material went on. But some of the old enthusiasm and intimacy of the war years had departed; we were more organised, officialdom and bureaucracy increased. I recall sending an indignant minute to my boss (I had become highly efficient about minutes) complaining at the number of hands through which material now had to go before it finally got on its way to Moscow.

From the moment an article had been received or selected there were no less than fifteen stages in processing until it finally went on its way to Moscow, Warsaw or Prague. This was not necessarily censorship; much of it was typing, negotiating rights – all that has to be done to produce a periodical.

Lydia and I worked happily together in our corner; it was the appreciation and exchanges that came to us from Moscow that gave us a feeling of friendly contact. The new editor, Archie Johnstone, had been there since early in 1947; Lena Chivers had gone over to help and get to know the people at that end. There was a new Press attaché, Mr R. Poston. With one of the staff returned from Moscow, George Graham, Pat and I were on friendly terms, and George often described his pleasure in the friendships with Russians which he had been able to make in Moscow.

Unhappily the pleasure that we derived from the news that not only our own editor and staff in Moscow, but also our readers appreciated our efforts to entertain and inform them, was ruined by something far more serious than our irritation at the official tone of our department.

This was the new directive given to us that, in future, our paper must aim at counteracting Soviet propaganda by answering back and 'getting under the Russians skin'. So far, whatever was appearing in the Soviet Press or put out on the air was not directed against our paper. Two criticisms of it in a Soviet internal journal, *Culture and Life*, had apparently *pleased* some of our diplomatic sponsors as a sample of 'getting under the Russians' skin'.

Evidently, during 1947, a change of policy had already been under consideration by our diplomats in Moscow and their opposite numbers at home. The Central Office of Information (COI) directors were disturbed. Though obliged to accept that the purpose and policy of *British Ally* were matters for the Foreign Office and were interpreted by the embassy in Moscow, those responsible at home had noticed to what extent the paper had recently been used to counter current Soviet propaganda; such use had its dangers, and was a matter for careful consideration. Clearly they were worried and, while admitting the need to answer back when required, they hoped to be able to continue the constructive line which had hitherto usually inspired the material sent from Newspapers Section.

All through 1947 the Moscow staff found themselves contending with an apparent decrease in the popularity of the paper. An organisation called Soyuspechat, consulting with them, dealt with the commercial side, such as the subscription list and sales in bookshops and kiosks. The subscription list was evidence of continuing interest; it also afforded contact with libraries, institutes and other bodies. This list at the beginning of the year stood at the high point of 45,000. Soyuspechat now decided that it was reduced to 15,000, the remainder of the copies, 30,000 to be distributed for public sale.

Our people did not believe that such a limited number of subscriptions was justified, but were assured from the Soviet Foreign Ministry that this was a commercial matter, which now applied to Soviet papers as well to save manpower and costs of distribution.

To meet wider popular distribution, and the loss of subscriptions, steps were taken through 1947 to 1948 to make a more popular appeal by lighter material, more pictures, attractive layout and arresting front page picture.

But all this time the East European Information Department at the Foreign Office was requiring publication of speeches in their entirety by the Foreign Minister at the UN. The review of our Press which previously had total coverage now omitted left-wing papers; also any event showing Anglo–Soviet cultural relations did not appear in the paper. The paper was no longer promoting friendship, but becoming an instrument of political warfare.

When, in February 1948, *British Ally* published a long statement by Mr Bevin in the Commons about problems affecting Western Europe, and the front page of the paper in heavy type informed its readers of the now joint Anglo-American organisation of their zones in Western Germany, there were at least six immediate cancellations of subscriptions or repudiations objecting quite definitely to its political line.

A Mr Pudalov said uncompromisingly:

your paper is becoming less and less an organ for informing the Soviet reader about England and more and more a vehicle for attacking the USSR. I already receive sufficient information in the Soviet Press concerning the Anti-Soviet policy of His Majesty's Government, and stand in no need of further information of this sort from *British Ally*. In view of this, the continued delivery of your paper has become superfluous.

In reviewing the fortunes of our paper at this time, it must not be forgotten that 1948 was the year of the Berlin airlift.

It was really remarkable in these circumstances that Joe Dobbs was able in the autumn to report from Moscow that the sales of the paper had been 45,000 a week, that it had been noticed in libraries in Astrakhan, was well known to Russians in Stalingrad, that people had been observed reading the paper in the intervals at a Leningrad theatre. Soviet pilots flying to Stockholm also had the paper.

In March our Head of Section, Mr Keith Fowler, had been in Moscow for consultation. Further consultation together with HM Ambassador took place in October. The London editor, Wright Miller, had been writing to his opposite number, Archie Johnstone, in Moscow, pointing out that while we were obliged, on the insistence of East European Information (EEID) at the Foreign Office, to carry their controversial material, there was much in the lives of the peoples that was of interest to both sides and its communication could be felt as a real need by the Russians who had been receiving the journal. It must be both possible and right for *British Ally* to continue conveying the British scene and way of life. This Anglo–Soviet communication did provide the kind of news that had been given and for which our readers still wanted the paper. I personally was well aware of this from the multiple requests for information that reached me, mostly on medical subjects, to which replies might be given in articles that divulged no secrets and could do no possible harm.

Those of us at both ends, who had been working for *British Ally*, had much greater knowledge of how far and wide our paper was distributed, of the place it had begun to establish, one might say, in the hearts of its readers, than the diplomats who wanted to convey little more than the voice of the British government

On the eve of Christmas 1948 those of us working on *British Ally* received a minute from our chief, Keith Fowler, offering about fifteen points as suggestions for improvement of the paper, on which we were to reflect. A longer document embodying the discussions which had taken place in Moscow and in London, and representing the point of view of COI on editorial and policy changes that might arrest the decline in circulation (which appeared as the main point of concern), was appended and sent to staff at both ends for consideration.

It was at last admitted, both in Moscow and London, that 'The main cause of the decline in circulation was the worsening of relations between the British and Soviet governments and the unfriendly attitude in the Soviet Union towards anything British that has resulted.'

Strictly editorial action might help but could do little to affect the situation in the absence of any modification of policy. With these melancholy admonishments we were to go home for our Christmas dinner.

What can civil servants, who have been specially recruited to foster friendship with another nation, do when ordered to turn the vehicle of their labours into an instrument of political warfare? This was, in effect, the position in which our superiors had placed us all.

In the war some of our company had faced considerable risks; we had all worked indefatigably and long hours, applying our minds with pleasure to what seemed a constructive task. In its steady growth our paper had succeeded, not so much by any ability on our part to understand and meet our readers' needs, as by the welcome given our efforts through that almost naïve, open-hearted, friendly temperament of the Russians, so different from the character ascribed to them by their opponents in the West. But the welcome of open arms turns in a moment to menacing fists when any deceit or ulterior motive is discerned.

The success of our original purpose had also resulted in the direct broadcasting service to Russia as well as our journal. We realised that this channel was open now for use by anyone whom those responsible for foreign policy might appoint.

I was deeply troubled that, while all the talk about the problems facing the paper had been under consideration, we had been so little informed or consulted, and treated as mere recipients of orders. I had known that none of the higher-ups really had any knowledge as to what Russians were like, and how best to approach and make friends with them. But now I began to believe that this had never been the aim from the start.

As we talked, we found our friend George Graham in some distress because it seemed that he had been asked to deliver in Russian some broadcasts on the Russian service. His friends over there, he felt sure, would recognise his voice and accent. He had no wish to be associated in their minds with the content of what he was likely to be asked to put out. He said he would have to 'go sick'. 'You can't go sick forever, George,' we told him. 'It's no good going sick, this is policy.' I believe that in the end he resolved his difficulty by getting transferred to the BBC listening end at Reading.

I began to seek opportunities of doing some constructive 'projects of Britain' scripts that might mitigate what would be sent to criticise and annoy. The tale of our redistribution of our milk service with the setting up of the Milk Marketing Board, which I wrote, was used, among others, for the service.

I vaguely considered resigning – but dismissed the thought, intending to stay by a paper for which I now had so great an attachment as long as I could.

However, circumstances in my life ruled that I might even then have soon left the Ministry. I must here digress to give some account of what was happening to my family, and presently, with grief, to myself.

My daughters Kate and Harriet were in America, but John and his wife and two small daughters had come to stay in our Dartmouth Road house. Knowing that 'our Lil' was with us, John, I think, may have felt that a home with the two of us might provide understanding help for his young wife and two babes. He was being considered for a post at the Treasury. For Lil, it was second nature to do all that she could for the young, but she had to run the household and I was tied, day after day, at my office. It seemed that Susan would prefer to be on her own. But it was extremely difficult to get anywhere to live in London; huge premiums and compulsory purchase of furniture and fittings were demanded for flats and houses. They found a place in St John's Wood where a family could be boarded and where a nurse was in residence to help with the children. This seemed to them a novel, enterprising and excellent solution. Now that none of the family were there I began to feel that we might as well let the landlord have his house back as and when Lil and Walter, and Pat and I, could find modest places on our own. The employment of Walter, Pat and myself at the Central Office of Information seemed likely to continue. Giving up the house was a foolish idea because, though I did not take proper account of it, we were protected from eviction by the new law which had created sitting – 'statuary' – tenants, whose rights continued to be sustained for years and years, causing rage and agony to landlords and property developers.

By chance, I came across a notice of a ground floor flat at Richmond, in a cul de sac, with a narrow gate straight into Richmond Park. The premium was far more than Pat and I could afford, but John and Susan's arrangements had come unstuck, perhaps because they cost too much. In any case, John with his gratuity could afford to take the flat and the nurse, an agreeable Frenchwoman, agreed to go with them. It was an ideal place for such young children, and an easy journey from Richmond to London. As private secretary to Sir Edwin Plowden at the Treasury, John seemed to have prospects of a settled life. When, for some reason, they parted with the nurse, Lil was constantly on her way to Richmond to 'give Susan a hand'.

It must have been some time in 1948 that the conversion of a house at 72 Gloucester Place, near the Central Office of Information, offered us the possibility of acquiring a flat. Pat and I moved there; Lily and Walter, with some difficulty, found themselves a home in North London.

We had room for Roddy in the holidays in our flat; he had become restless, felt he was doing nothing at school and wanted to leave and take up cricket as a professional. We came to terms about this. I agreed to pay for some cricket practice lessons for him during the winter, whilst, in the summer, as was the practice for young aspirants, he joined the group at Lords who helped in many ways and got some payment. Whether Roddy would, in the end, go on to study some subject at a Polytechnic was, for the time, left open.

The move to 72 Gloucester Place was, for both Pat and me, a tragic mistake. I do not think that it made any difference as to what actually happened, but if we four, Lil, Walter, Pat and I, who had weathered so much together, had not separated, it would all have been somewhat easier to bear. The winter brought choking pea soup fog which was not good for Pat's bronchial troubles. We got a new doctor from nearby in to see him. Then, for the first time, we understood that he suffered from emphysema and that his lungs were very badly affected. He had already been given an inhaler to help, as he had thought, just for bronchitis. He suddenly had a very bad attack and was rushed to University College Hospital in Gower Street and put on oxygen. I then understood that, above all, he ought to be in a dry, warm climate. I did not see any way of getting him to the Riviera, or to a hospital abroad. He went for a time to one of the convalescent health centres at Hastings to recuperate. A doctor from UCH came to examine him, and afterwards, with me, he shook his head gravely. It was evident that he did not think Pat's chances very good. (Strangely enough, this doctor reminded me then that we already knew each other. He had been a medical student when, in 1919, we acted together in plays that I helped to produce at University College.)

Seeking a dry climate, I heard that there were opportunities in Africa. Through the Commonwealth Office I made contact with an official from Lusaka who was looking for someone to help with simple books to educate people in English. I spoke of this to Pat. His view was that, yes, we might go, but we must make sure that we could take Roddy with us. I was not certain how Roddy would react to this proposal, so I did not discuss it with him until it seemed more likely that I would get the job.

Just as it began to seem likely that we might go to Lusaka, one morning Pat had a severe attack; University College Hospital, for some reason, could not take him in immediately. He was rushed by ambulance to another hospital. I was with him. But he barely recovered consciousness and, by the evening, he was dead. There had not even been time for words of farewell between us.

I went through the cremation ceremony at Golders Green in a dazed condition, astonished, and rather overwhelmed, by the sympathy shown by my colleagues, the many wreaths that they sent, the warm friendly words spoken. What heartened me most was that some of them, whom I scarcely knew, came up and told me – what I had also not known – of the many kindnesses that Pat had done to them. I liked to hear that his worth had been known and valued.

What Pat meant to me I may speak of later. Here, at the moment, I was shaken and bereft at the loss of my comrade-in-arms. Barely a week or so before his death, we had gone, in a taxi because of his state of health, to see together once again a film that we both loved – the friendly and amusing Soviet story of how Makarenko had rescued and educated boys orphaned by the civil war. Now this was to stay in my memory as one of the last happy moments we had spent together, sharing something dear to the hearts of both – the care of children, the promise and hope of socialism one day for all peoples. The last stanzas of 'Ich hat einen Kamaraden' kept sounding in my ears.

Eine Kugel kam geflogen
Gilt sie mir oder gilt sie dir . . . ?

Will mir die Hand noch reichen
Derweil ich eben lad . . .
Kann dir die Hand nicht geben . . .
Bleib Du imewigen Leben
Mein guter Kamerad.[1]

Lena, now Mrs Jeger, and her husband brought some comfort by their invitation for a weekend at their cottage. I took some leave. An impulse which even now I do not fully understand led me to go with Roddy to Wales, to meet and talk with Bertie Russell. He managed to come for a brief afternoon visit to the hotel where Roddy and I stayed. I was not seeking a reunion. Perhaps it was the momentary comfort of a father figure that I needed, or the reassurance that my first comrade-in-arms in the political struggle was still there and might well be in action. In actual fact, our talk was not about politics, but about our son and daughter and the loss of my husband. I also much wanted Bertie to meet Roddy.

To my desk at one centre of that political conflict I now returned, summoning what courage I could, of heart and mind, to carry on alone.

Notes

1. I had a comrade.
   A shot came flying
   Is it for me or thee?

   He seeks to reach my hand
   But I am loading my gun
   Cannot give thee my hand . . .
   Rest in eternity
   My good comrade.

6

THE IDEOLOGICAL WAR
INTENSIFIES:
CAN WE SAVE *BRITISH ALLY*?

We civil servants now, in 1949, returned to a not-so-very Happy New Year – the year which brought for me the tragic loss which I have just related.

Turning ourselves into a Think Tank, we began to go over every detail of the production of *British Ally*, as also of *Glos Anglii*, which was appearing in Poland. To do them justice, our superiors contributed all that they could, applying the methods, and using the experience, of public relations men and women, editors, and journalists. At top level, the department defended our Section and did not hesitate to point out the extent to which we were hampered by the material which policy required us to carry. It was easy to talk about a 'popular' paper, attractive in content, good pictures, entertaining feature articles, non-political news, short stories, a serial perhaps. Such a recipe would work for the home market. But what sort of stories or serial would appeal to Russian or Polish readers? The Poles would perhaps be easier to please, but the Russians had usually, in their comments, presented themselves as extremely serious-minded. There had never been any trouble about sport; the back page carried quantities of this, especially football and horse racing news. Monica Foster, who was then working on *Glos Anglii*, was asked to undertake the difficult task of finding suitable serials; we were all urged to help if we could, especially by suggesting short stories. The Russians at least resembled us in a taste for detective yarns; some of those by G.K. Chesterton were published, also an article by Dorothy Sayers. One of our readers did comment on her work, and that of Agatha Christie, to the effect that they tended to cause their criminals to collapse or be too easily found out at the end. As regards catering for the Russian taste, at some point it had been remarked that the Russians admired Byron. So some literary man had been asked to write an article about him, which evidently contained the usual 'Anglo-Saxon attitude' of mild qualified approval. The result was a furore of enthusiastic protest from a teenage Russian girl about the denigration of her hero. Of course the Russians loved Byron, but whoever wrote the article had not known just how passionately and how much.

I made one small contribution to the literary output: a folk tale of my grandmother's, 'The Three Silly People', which was, I thought, in the Russian folk tale genre. Illustrated with drawings, it was a success, I was told. But I did not offer more, in part because, while still dealing with *British Chronicle*, which, together with *Ally* and *Glos Anglii*, I had to service on the science and technology side (and this consumed a considerable amount of time in reading), I did not have much confidence in an imitation of the illustrated popular weeklies of our home media. In fact, several of us argued that *British Ally* had been most highly praised by our readers when it had been the reverse of 'popular'. The plain fact was that our Russian readers liked and wanted the paper simply because it had been bringing them some contact and information about people and places from whom they had for so many years been cut off.

That I fared well in comment on my work, both in Moscow and, it seemed, at home, was due less to merit on my part, than to the fact that the Russians had an omnivorous hunger for absolutely all aspects of science; engineering, technology, medicine, nutrition, public health. I have a note which says that the USSR Scientific and Technical Council was itself complaining that while in Russia there was still not enough paper available, apparently, for science, there was plenty for political propaganda. They pointed out to their own people that the British, with only one paper in the Soviet Union, were 'politically clever' in that they realised that publicity for science was much better propaganda in the long run than mere politics. Our British comment continues: 'This illustrates the popularity of the scientific material published during the past eight or nine months in *Britanski Soyuznik*, and gives some indication of the status our paper has won in scientific circles, who are, apart from officials, the most influential section of the community in Russia today.'

Of course, nothing was sent to the paper which was not openly and fully known and published in Britain, but there were some subjects, though publicly known, which my superiors felt too delicate to handle. Though it might be tactless to report open discussion about the atom bomb, no objection was made by EEID to sending any published scientific material that might interest the Russians. But now in our time the very great advances made in technology and the development of nuclear weapons have actually led to increased suspicion and secrecy. The Americans object to the dispatch to Russia of any gadgets whatever that might be useful for manufacturing weapons, or indeed assist serious scientific progress. An embargo is placed even on sending the computers made for children. There was also an embargo on the help being given by a British firm in the construction of the pipeline bringing supplies of Russian gas that might have benefited Europe.

I remember one of my own mistakes in the selection of material. It was a brief article publicising fluorescent lighting, which was then new. I did not know that lighting of this kind was already used with great artistic taste in the now famous Moscow Underground. Nor had our staff and diplomats known about this since they were not in the habit of travelling by metro.

My two science 'pieces', a page and a half, continued up to the end of the paper and, incidentally, in one of the last issues, which I possess, is a full centre spread of pictures and an account of the London underground, pleasant and efficient, but not grand and glamorous like the Russian one.

Though I had not discussed politics with Bertie Russell at our very brief meeting, he had become deeply involved in the ideological war and his presence was now very much in evidence in my work.

Starting with what must have been a New Year message, 'Where Do We Go Now', on 8 January 1945, from then onwards until April 1952, either for home or overseas, Bertie Russell made no fewer than seventy-eight broadcasts on an immense variety of subjects. These included the first Reith Lectures, which he broadcast in December 1948 and on into 1949 on the subject of Authority and the Individual. The dates of some of these broadcasts coincide with the Berlin airlift (1948–49) and the centenary of the Communist Manifesto, on which Russell did broadcast on 4 May 1948. It was also in about 1948 that Russia had obtained the secret of the manufacture of the atomic bomb.

The BBC Archives have records of these scripts and of Russell's correspondence showing their close association with him which existed during this period. I was not aware of all this at the time, nor was it a part of my work to know about it in detail. Transmissions came to me only in fragments, echoing the excitable dialogue that went on between the intellectuals of the West and those of the Soviet Union. Russell's Reith Lectures began with this statement: 'The fundamental problem I propose to consider in these lectures is this: how can we combine that degree of individual initiative which is necessary for progress with the degree of social cohesion that is necessary for survival.'

There is nothing in these lectures which could be construed as a definite attack on communist ideology or totalitarianism. Russell did deal with the difficulties of an individual in relation to the bureaucracy of a civil service, as well as to large-scale industrial organisations, whether capitalist or socialist. He does indicate a need for devolution of power and is concerned that the State should be sufficiently liberal to ensure certain human rights. His statement, in Lecture V on Control and Initiative, 'It is only in the West that this liberty and these rights have been assured', may well provoke dissent. Russell does, however, write as a socialist, intent on economic justice which can only be secured by the State and a considerable degree of centralisation.

Favoured though he might have been by the BBC and the public who listened to him, Russell was no favourite of the Tory Press, who took pains to distort these lectures by emphasising those passages which were critical of State control.

As far as the Russians were concerned however, it would seem that it was not philosophic argument, but rather Russell's habit of lacing his comments with wit that caused the trouble. He spoke of men's obsession with war; of the Papuan head-hunters' intense passion for collecting human skulls; of the dangers of fanaticism. Madame Borisova, unable to see the jokes, used these comments as the peg on which to hang a blast of rhetoric.

A direct reference to Bertrand Russell's BBC broadcasts was made by Borisova in a commentary which said that, in inviting this 'fashionable English philosopher' to the microphone, the BBC had furnished listeners with a 'complete illusion of the jungle'. She continued:

I am ready to wager that if a wolf could speak English and express his wolfish views more or less fluently, he would be delighted to repeat the aphorisms of this English philosopher who claims that life would lose all its attractions if there were no one to hate, that life is futile in a world where everyone loves everybody or, finally, that the thirst to kill is a normal instinct. Even Rudyard Kipling, that bard of imperialism, in extolling the law of the jungle, didn't glorify cruelty. Kipling's hero, the boy Mowgli reared by a pack of wolves, had something like a human soul. But in Bertrand Russell's hero, the present-day imperialist, there is nothing human left with the exception of his speech and his pseudo-scientific terminology.

Hitler's ideologies, Borisova went on,

have found worthy successors in England. Bertrand Russell urges the atom-bombing of the Soviet Union. This is only natural, for he hates socialism: under socialism life would lose all its attractions for him, for there would be no one to hate, no one to kill.

This howling wolf, shamelessly broadcast by the BBC, serves as a striking illustration of present-day capitalist civilisation. Such are the philosophy, religion, ethics, law – the law of the capitalist jungle – which Bertrand Russell and others like him are trying to force upon mankind.

It was no wonder, said Borisova, that guided by such ethics, politicians in Britain and the USA were 'reinstating German war criminals and reviving fascism on the territory under their occupation'. Bertrand Russell had drawn a parallel between the present-day businessman and the Papuan head-hunters who lost all interest in life when forbidden to collect skulls. The prospect of a triumph over this world by the forces of democracy and progress caused him to 'become melancholy and to lose interest in life despite the fact that the world he lives in is still ruled by the law of the capitalists, so dear to his heart, and that the British Labour leaders are much too humane to go so far as to drive head-hunters to the point of a nervous breakdown'. The US monopolies were trying hard 'to skin the European nations alive' and the British fascists 'to crack the skulls of the supporters of peace and democracy', and 'even the bona fide head-hunters have been taken care of by the humane Labourite administrators who have sent savage Dyaks to Malaya and permitted them to collect as many Malayan skulls as they please'. Dreaming of 'a world blood bath', Bertrand Russell had recently addressed an audience of British teachers in Westminster Abbey, and in this spirit, 'with the help of the British radio run by Labourites', he was now 'instructing the rest of the world'.

This was the civilisation, said Borisova, in the name of which the Soviet proposals to cut armaments were rejected, this was what had been called 'culture' and 'a human ethical code'. Fortunately, however, humankind was not compelled to take 'the path of degeneration along which fascist creatures like Bertrand Russell are leading it'. There was a different path, a different world, the world of socialism.

> But how can philosophising cannibals understand this new civilisation of great socialist culture? True, they don't eat human flesh – they use the radio: they sometimes have Labour Party membership cards in their pockets. But in ethics and culture even the Papuan head-hunter stands head and shoulders above them. The Papuans at least didn't demand remuneration for killing. These get paid in dollars.[1]

It is unlikely that the Soviet propagandists were unaware of Russell's serious analysis of the problem of human rivalries and hatred. At this time his belief was that probably nothing but a world government could end wars. It is significant that his broadcasts up to 1948 were on such topics as John Stuart Mill on the idea of liberty; science and democracy; the relation of the artist to the State; on great men such as Einstein.

But from 1949 onwards the broadcasts relate much more to actual problems of the time: the Impact of America upon European Culture; International Control of Atomic Energy, Taking Stock; Some Problems of the Atomic Bomb. By 1950 he is asking, What Will Future Ages Think about Our Own? And by 1951, Could We Do More to Secure Human Rights? and Why Defend the Free World?

The Moscow commentators, knowing well the extent to which American influence was becoming dominant among the Allies, and that in the USA communists were being put on trial, concentrated their attacks on the British intellectuals and the BBC.

Gerald Barry, Vernon Bartlett and Kingsley Martin come under fire as 'trying to apply Bertrand Russell's anti-Soviet theories to world affairs'.

Russell's philosophic observation that wars may actually prove instruments of progress evoked furious anger in Moscow. I cannot help wondering if it was because he had spent the war in the USA that Russell did not realise what a provocation such an observation would be to allies who had fought and suffered bombing and devastation.

Gerald Barry (a lively journalist who had started the *Week End Review*, a rival to the *New Statesman*) must have perceived this, for in a broadcast on the BBC Pacific Service he tried to explain that Russell's suggestion that 'progress had always been the result of fear and war' was very involved and comprehensible only to philosophers dwelling in ivory towers.

Professor Boris Isakov, in a broadcast in English from Moscow,[2] takes this up: 'the fact is, that this utterly false theory has much more to do with politics than philosophy – in the language of politics it is called war propaganda. Hitler and Goebbels had tried to justify war in this way.'

Isakov goes on to complain of the duplicity of British commentators in Russian who talk about 'sympathy with the Russian people' while the BBC broadcasts in English are 'unbridled war propaganda in the spirit of Bertrand Russell or Gerald Barry'. He adds that Vernon Bartlett (also in the Pacific Service) had 'spoken in a most vicious manner of the Soviet Union' and claimed that affairs in Czechoslovakia were in such a bad way that 'the Czechs are fleeing abroad in droves'. Isakov is well informed. Referring to the betrayal of the Czechs at Munich, he states that Lord Halifax, one of those directly involved in that event, is now President of the Advisory Committee of the BBC.

Kingsley Martin, editor of the *New Statesman*, had been to Wroclaw to seek some information as to Soviet views. I seem to remember that he was distressed because all Western politicians, including Labour, were being called 'capitalist hyenas'.

Kingsley, who felt himself to be deeply sincere, as indeed did his fellow intellectuals under attack, broadcast on the BBC service to Russia, in which he explained that he and the Labour Party had long been working for Anglo–Soviet friendship. Now on the question of the Marshall Aid plan for Europe, supported by all parties in Britain and accepted by the Labour government, he was, like many other individuals, uneasy and divided in mind. He mentioned the Tory Lord Beaverbrook's continuous opposition to dependence on the USA through their economic aid.

On this issue Martin was under attack both from Boris Zvavich in an English broadcast, and from Viktorov in a *Pravda* review. Viktorov writes, 'Kingsley Martin [is] shedding crocodile tears about the split between East and West and declaring that he accepted neither western capitalism's accusation against the USSR for having caused this split, nor the USSR's charges against western capitalism.'

Viktorov claims that the preliminary report of the Organisation for European Economic Co-operation (OEEC) showed the pitiful results and proposals of the Marshall Plan. The right-wing socialists were being compelled to resort to 'the meanest swindling tricks', the latest of which consisted in asserting that the poverty of the Marshall Plan was due not to those who participated in it, but to those who abstained. This truth had been proclaimed 'with unwonted irritation by Mr Attlee in his speech of January 11' and the argument had been developed in an international review by Mr Kingsley Martin . . . Avoiding all details, Kingsley Martin had tried to prove that the main cause was the failure of the USSR and the peoples' democracies to join the Marshall Plan. He had said that the Communists objected not to dollars but to the political strings attached to them, but that the Communists and any sensible man well knew that any loan invariably had strings attached to it. In this he had revealed his 'lackey mentality' and he could not fail to admit that these strings had now proved to be 'heavy chains of dollar bondage', had proved in fact to be 'a noose which is gripping and choking the Western European countries, which are losing more and more of their political and economic independence'. He had to admit further that the Marshall Plan had a military aim, and that US help to Western Europe was 'openly directed against the USSR'. Whose fault was this, enquired the commentator, adding that in answering this question Mr Kingsley Martin 'turns a somersault, revealing a political swindle to which he and his high patrons are having recourse.'[3]

The reply by Boris Zvavich to Kingsley Martin was a direct broadcast in English from Moscow to the United Kingdom. He speaks rather as one socialist deploring betrayal of the cause by another. He recalls recent history and makes the Soviet case. I quote this from the BBC's account of the broadcast exactly as received on my desk in my office:

The editor of the *New Statesman* had claimed that he and his Labour Party friends had long been working for Anglo–Soviet friendship, but, while the Russian people would never forget 'the friendly feeling expressed for our Socialist country by the British working class, we have learned to draw the line between workers and the plain people and those Labour and Conservative politicians who claim to be real socialists.' Zvavich recalled that in 1939, at the time of the Finnish war, the *New Statesman and Nation* had published an article by Eileen Power concerning the expulsion of the USSR from the League of Nations. Today, Mr Kingsley Martin was 'claiming credit' for the fact that Britain was at war before the USSR, although he 'clearly knew' that before and after September 1939 British and French reactionary circles had done 'everything in their power to provoke a war between the USSR and Germany in order that Britain and France could stand by and watch it'. Moreover, added Zvavich, 'you forget, and you would like to make others forget, that at that very time the Anglo–French imperialists were equipping an expeditionary corps to aid Finland against the USSR.'

After Dunkirk, Zvavich continued, friendship with the USSR had become Mr Kingsley Martin's 'anchor of salvation and hope', but he had 'forgotten how negligible was the assistance rendered by Britain to the anti-fascists of Europe compared with the Soviet people's enormous contribution', and, although criticising Mr Churchill 'slightly' he had 'called him an incomparable Prime Minister'. The British Labour leaders' support of friendship for the USSR, Zvavich continued, had been a 'historical necessity', but it had not lasted long with the Labour Party's right wing.

Zvavich continued that Mr Kingsley Martin was now feeling that the time had come to explain his 'turn to the right'. A 'subtle division of labour' existed between Mr Kingsley Martin and the right-wing Labour leaders: 'they act, you justify their actions'. Mr Martin had described USSR policy as 'inconsistent', but it was an open secret that the right-wing Labour leaders were 'repudiating British signatures on wartime political treaties and agreements', and now Mr Martin had 'taken the warpath against the Soviet Union, and especially against Soviet culture'. Zvavich said in conclusion:

It may be that you are annoyed with me for having tried to give something of a pen-portrait of you at the very moment when you are about to change to your right-hand chair. It is your own fault, Mr Martin. At Wroclaw you shifted your centre of gravity somewhat ungracefully. Artists like Max Beerbohm or David Low would have been delighted by your pose and made much of it.

These broadcasts from Moscow differ greatly in tone from those of 1948 of which I also have some records.

In one of these Boris Zvavich described at length the agreeable life and education of his son under the Soviet regime: 'The Rights of a Young Soviet Man'.[4] In another, long and detailed and of the same date, Thomas Murray, Secretary General of the Scotland–USSR Friendship Association describes how he found conditions and people on his visit to their country. He speaks of the spirit of reconstruction being applied to a new five-year plan and concludes:

Given the blessings of lasting peace and a triumphant over-fulfilment of the postwar Five-Year Plan, this will indeed be a land flowing with milk and honey and all the joyful experiences of a happy fraternity of peoples. What they can have, so also we can have in Scotland, England, Wales and Ireland. But the condition must be honest friendship and co-operation with the peoples of USSR; there is absolutely no other alternative for the people of Britain.[5]

So, unhappily, the clever people on both sides were unable, or unwilling, to understand one another and the gulf between Western Europe and the Soviet Union widened. The tragic continuing dilemma of the West was the necessity to reconcile, or accommodate so many different nations and cultures. The voices that came from Moscow, whatever may have been the condition of the country and people, sent forth a message of a united nation. And, while it had been possible in the 1920's for a Russia torn by civil war to accept the succour that came from the Nansen project, or other compassionate aid, an established Communist state that could now well defend its borders, could not possibly risk opening its gates to the forces of American capitalist enterprise.

The only hope would have been in a British government courageous and revolutionary enough to stand by the wartime Eden and Molotov Treaty.

Had the Attlee government so decided, and thus Europe, like Russia, recovered its strength by its own efforts, there might not today be American bases in Europe and its people would now live free of the agony of the nuclear threat.

In 1949 the American forces engaged on German rehabilitation would have withdrawn. In time, friendly relations between the two continents would have been negotiated.

It is true that anti-Communism was being zealously fostered by the American government, but there were also very many in America, as in Britain, who, like Kingsley Martin, were uneasy about the politics pursued in Western Europe. Cedric Belfrage, an English journalist who had long lived in America, was one of those sent by the American government to replace Nazism in Germany by establishing and fostering newspapers and journals that would restore democratic habits and ways of thought; so shocked was he by the attitude prevailing among his superiors and his colleagues that he resigned. He felt that his work was being sabotaged from the start. He was then given a fellowship by the John Simon Guggenheim Foundation to write a book on the subject. But he was summoned by Senator McCarthy to answer charges that amounted to an accusation that he was a Russian agent. He was arrested and held on Ellis Island, subject to deportation; publication of his book was refused. In 1954, under the title *Seeds of Destruction, the Truth about the US Occupation of Germany*, it finally appeared.

It so happens that Bruce Belfrage, a well-known and admired BBC newsreader, was Cedric's brother, though how far they agreed on politics is unknown to me.

In our department at the Central Office we received periodically from our office in Moscow typed scripts of extracts from the Soviet press. These, sent also to the Foreign Office, were read by those responsible for contact with us as producers of material for our journals in Eastern Europe. No doubt it was quite a good idea to obtain the information provided by such a review. But inevitably, scanning the Soviet journals, our Moscow staff would pick out and record any critical comment, though it might only be a very small part of the total volume of the Soviet papers scanned. The result was what appeared to be a constant hostile barrage, some of it policy, but some trivial carping, just done to annoy. I imagine that the Soviet Embassy in London may have been sending similar provocative missives, cullings from our Press, to its comrades in Moscow. Such is probably the traditional method used by all embassies to promote the amity of nations.

By now all events had combined to put the Powers that Be into a very bad temper. It can hardly have been a coincidence that April 1949 saw the birth of NATO; it was shortly followed by the Warsaw Pact.

The hostile exchanges on the air were, as already explained, distinct from our work on *British Ally* and not under our control. What began to give me trouble were these internal scanning reports which put ideas into the heads of our Foreign Office advisors. In one very comical incident the Russians came out with a story that finely ground flour, fed to dogs in Great Britain, caused the animals to become hysterical. The inference was that our people partook of a similar diet. 'Should we not answer back?' came the query. 'Certainly not' was my reply. In the first place we were not in the habit of rearing our dogs on fine white flour, secondly this was not a bad example of Russian humour. By phone I sought information about milling and so forth, from the experts. In fact, the origin of the story could probably be traced to efforts and experiments made during the war for practical and health reasons, to induce the British public to eat more coarsely ground wholemeal bread.

My more serious trouble was with Lysenko and his theories and so-called experiments on the inheritance of acquired characteristics. Every topic, no matter what, was subject to Stalin's diktat: he supported Lysenko. Biologists everywhere were convinced that Lysenko was wrong. And in Russia they were persecuted for this disagreement. One of our foremost biologists, J.B.S. Haldane, faced a dilemma. He shared his colleagues' views in not accepting Lysenko. But he himself was a member of the Communist Party and wrote regular science articles in the *Daily Worker*.

I was being pressed to print anti-Lysenko articles in my science pages. I knew that this meant the use of science as a political ploy, and suggested that, as this was simply a dispute about a science between scientists, it was best avoided. However, there was to be a Home Service broadcast on the matter by Haldane and other biologists. If it proved to be genuinely about science I would use it. As might be expected, it turned out to be equivocal in both senses. Next day I rang my mentors at EEID. To my relief they did agree that the treatment of the subject had proved 'hardly suitable' for *British Ally*.

In my disillusion with government policy and helplessness to stem the war of words, I was intensely lonely. I was taking steps to move from the flat which Pat and I had not really liked. But, for a time, it had one feature which helped to provide solace. It was possible to get out on to the flat roof. There, lying out on calm warm nights there was nothing between me and 'those infinite spaces', the 'steadfast stars', the 'pale stars and the wandering moon' of the poets and dreamers. I felt that I knew why humans had invented god for the sake of a peace that their own world of strife could never give. I sought no god, only peace within my own conscience and purpose.

As far as time allowed, I turned to interests outside my work, the feminist Six Point Group, of which I was a member. My friend Roxane Arnold, an able barrister, was chairman. I also came in contact with the Married Women's Association, a body that had been started to deal with the many inequalities about finance between husbands and wives. It was non-party; I followed the Conservative Lady Nutting as chairman.

One event that now gave me unalloyed pleasure, was that China had 'stood up' under the lead of Mao Tse Tung and had, to my relief, been recognised by our government. I cherished a special delight in this because of my association with China, and because of my 'inside knowledge' of the chances of Mao coming to power which we had learned of from Dr Joseph Needham's visit to us in Soviet Relations Section during the war. China's arrival on the international scene soon stirred up trouble; her claims for new China to take her place at the United Nations were linked, I believe, with the temporary withdrawal of the Soviet Union from the UN Council.

Now there were signs of unrest in our own small circle. In Moscow from the beginning, the Russian staff had co-operated with pleasure. But now one day, when the offprint of the first page of *Ally* was brought to Archie Johnstone, he noticed that the masthead presented two soldiers in tin hats, instead of the two bareheaded strong-armed workers, each carrying his country's flag, which we had substituted when the war ended. As he pointed to the mistake, the editor received the reply, 'Oh, we thought you had gone back to war and this would be more appropriate.'

Subscriptions were falling off and some time in April 1949 there was a meeting between COI and EEID from which a long minute on policy emerged. I do not know if Archie was aware of its contents. However that may be, on 24 April, while the pen of the editor lay on his desk, its owner did not appear and nobody knew of his whereabouts.

Presently a letter appeared in the Soviet press, and one also in the *Daily Worker*, to the effect that Archie could no longer concur with the policy of the British government towards the Soviet Union, and if there were to be atom bombs, he preferred to be at the receiving rather than the delivering end. The embassy was quite unable to find out where Archie was – all sorts of rumours began to circulate; he had taken to drink, he had been kidnapped.

British Ally carried these remarks:

> It has always been the editorial policy of *British Ally* to serve the cause of peace by making known to the Soviet people the policy of His Majesty's Government and the views of the British people. The paper will continue to follow this policy faithfully. While the resignation of the editor is naturally regretted he has done no more than exercise the right to express his own opinion, to change his nationality and his place of domicile, which are the rights of all British citizens.

After some delay, Mr R. Jones replaced Archie Johnstone as editor. In the meantime, it appeared that the London editor, Mr Wright Miller, had now moved to another post in COI. Lena Jeger became acting editor and Mr F. Cox moved from *Glos Anglii* to be editor in London.

In spite of Archie Johnstone's disappearance, *British Ally* continued to sell well. Both in Moscow and in London all those still concerned with the paper made strenuous efforts in its defence.

Joe Dobbs, now Press attache, continued, I am sure, to believe in its importance. He kept a careful watch on the records of sales in 1949 as compared with 1948. Soyuspechat, the distributing agent, also paid over the proceeds of sales. The total issue of the paper was still 50,000. Calculating on averages of sales per week, it seemed that in 1948 up to 47,000 were sold, whilst in 1949 the number fell to 43,000. The significant difference was in the fall of subscriptions, which were practically halved. Kiosk sales, on the other hand, had risen. Payment for the whole issue was made by Soyuspechat. On the face of it, it seemed that popular sales were holding their ground.

The COI was very naturally anxious to defend the soundness of its advice about the conduct of the paper. Taking a number of issues in the latter period of 1949, Mr Cox surveyed them to find out the relation between their contents and the sales figures given by the distributors. Early in the new year Mr Cox, supported by Mr Hadfield, COI Overseas Controller, reported their joint conclusion that the fall off in sales was definitely caused by the provocative nature of the contents, either due to the reaction of the readers, or possibly that of the distributors.

Further meetings with the Foreign Office were proposed in the vain hope that they might agree to reduce the provocation. A definite policy decision to use the paper for an attack on Soviet institutions and way of life had been taken and would not be changed. Indeed, during May, it had been intimated to Mr Keith Fowler that the Under-Secretary for Foreign Affairs, Mr, now Lord Mayhew, considered the paper still far too weak in presenting the British case, and that its publicity value was not worth its financial cost. In fact, at that date, *British Ally* was making a profit over and above our Moscow expenses.

The paper outlining the policy defined by the EEID of the Foreign Office on periodicals published in Eastern Europe, together with the minutes of the meeting between that department and COI, now arrived in my In tray.

As I read these documents, I reflected on the power of a couple of men in what we call our democracy, to take decisions that affect the lives of millions; also the obligation, in our system, of public servants to obey orders. And then I thought of all those far-flung borders that were reached by *British Ally*; I heard the voices that had come to us, during the war-torn years, from factory, farm and battlefield – from 'far-off people

102

of whom we know very little and care less' – in the language of our diplomats. Those people had bought *British Ally*, passed it from hand to hand, pasted it on the walls of club and factory. To them it had come as a sign of the peace and fellowship that were to be once the war was won.

True, those who ruled them, and their intellectuals, like their counterparts in Britain, had taken their part in the ideological war. But the mass of their peoples, with us as we with them, would have hailed with delight the end of that fruitless and, it seems, never-ending contest.

Once, as I recall, I did ask the young men from the Foreign Office: 'If you were running this paper in a Roman Catholic country, would you be doing your best to undermine the people's religion? Then why are you doing it to the faith of the Russians in communism?'

I thought of those whom they served, the supercilious, patronising, cunning, destructive statesmen and politicians. On 27 May 1949, I wrote my opinion of those documents to my chief, Keith Fowler. Because this statement embodies my own feeling as to the proper duties of a Public Relations Officer, but, what is more, it carries my long-standing objection, over more than sixty-five years, to the utterly mistaken policy of Britain's official hostility to the Soviet Union, I have placed it in full in Appendix 5.

Here I include part of the memorandum and my comments as I then wrote them.

To Mr Keith Fowler.
I have been reading carefully the paper prepared by EEID, FO on the subject of periodicals published in Eastern Europe, together with the minutes of the joint meeting between EEID and COI. Certain aspects of this statement of policy seem to me to require analysis and comment.

Though the memorandum contains directives as to what type of material should be used in the papers in question, it still does not make clear what is the underlying policy and ultimate objective of these papers. *British Ally* and the *Voice of England* are paid for by their subscribers and readers in the Soviet Union and in Poland, and by the British tax-payers. Is it not important that this fact should be borne in mind in assessing what the effects of these papers may be on the lives of those people who are paying for them?

One might suppose that the primary object of publications financed in this manner would be to promote better understanding of British life among their readers and to evoke mutual good will. If this is not the primary object, one must ask oneself why such papers should be published at all?

Those people in Eastern Europe who buy the papers surely must do so out of a genuine interest in Great Britain – her life, her art, her scientific achievements. The average Briton, on the other hand, speaking through journals with such names as the *Voice of England* and *British Ally* must wish to have his country presented in a straightforward and favourable light, with a view to gaining him friends and good will in Eastern Europe. Such a presentation of Great Britain and her Commonwealth is not only vitally important but far from difficult.

Britain has played and is playing a great creative role in the world: her culture is rich, her achievements magnificent. There is no need for apology, humility, or undue self-critical analysis, though modesty is not out of place. It seems to me that belief in our Country and the positive achievements and greatness of our people suffices as a fundamental directive to those who serve the British public.

Yet this quality is, on the whole, absent from the *Voice of England* and *British Ally*. On the other hand, it is amply apparent in such papers as *Soviet Weekly*, however crude its approach. Though I wish to make quite clear that I in no way suggest *Soviet Weekly* as a model, it is instructive to consider why our papers lack the 'punch' which *Soviet Weekly* undoubtedly possesses.

I believe the reason for lack of 'punch' to be that these papers are no longer projecting Britain and the British people as a whole, but have become bogged down in the directives of government departments with their own axes to grind, and more especially in the confused animosities of diplomacy. Diplomacy and the projection of Britain through information services are very distinct activities and have little in common either in method or ultimate aim. Nor does the fact that the FO is the department ultimately responsible for overseas publicity invalidate this contention.

The EEID memorandum goes on to suggest that the main purpose of *British Ally* is to 'publish official statements of British policy in relation to the Eastern bloc', 'as a channel for the new anti-communist line of publicity adopted in 1948', 'to foment the uneasiness of Soviet intellectuals'. It suggests 'projecting Britain's military and economic strength' and 'in the absence of untoward results' every occasion should be seized to level criticism of Soviet institutions and their conduct, if this can be done 'under the pretext of an expression of British and Western opinion'. I replied:

In my view the policy suggested by these statements oversteps the legitimate bounds of information services to countries which extend them hospitality and enters the field of political warfare, which is neither morally justifiable nor politically effective in publications whose apparent aim is something quite different. Further, it is a negative and destructive policy in a situation which calls above all things for a creative purpose.

I think that the tempers of those responsible for the publication of British papers may be too much affected by the volume of Soviet propaganda which they read in the course of official duty. A similar study of the British and American press for home consumption and of the radio broadcast reveals an equal volume of criticism and abuse on the other side. This, no doubt, has its effect in goading the Soviet propagandists to still more extravagant efforts. This virulent propaganda ends in stalemate, as possibly those responsible on both sides may ultimately realise.

For all these reasons the new policy would appear to have little strategical value. It is unlikely to produce disaffection in the countries concerned, it can only produce resentment and ill will towards this country and bring discredit upon us. Even on the assumption that we regard the Eastern bloc as an enemy, these methods are likely to strengthen the 'enemy's' resolution and solidarity. I can, in fact, see no purpose which this policy serves other than emotional satisfaction to those who promote it.
27 May 1949

The Foreign Office attitude was still that an aggressive policy should continue (so long as it did not cost too much), until the Soviet government took steps to stop the paper. They appeared to believe that among Soviet intellectuals there existed a scepticism about their government's propaganda, an uneasiness which *British Ally* could be used to foment. At the same time, they also believed that Soyuspechat was not distributing the paper whilst paying us for it in full.

At the beginning of 1950 there was some kind of crisis when Mr Dobbs asked for a full consideration of the 1949 sales. He was then told that there was a remainder of about 50,000, and that, in future, unsold copies would be returned and no payment made for them. The attitude of the Soviet authorities was obviously hardening, but it is noteworthy that they still did not ban the paper. It was evident, however, in London, that the Foreign Office were preparing to bring its publication to an end.

A last attempt to avert this was made by Sir Robert Fraser, Head of COI, in a reasoned appeal. He intimated that it had been proven that a journal describing life in Britain had flourished and even been encouraged by the Russian authorities. Surely this was worthwhile, even if it was necessary to forgo criticising the Russians?

The reply of the Foreign Office was curious. Suggesting that it would now be impossible after the fall in circulation to revive the paper, they evaded their own responsibility for that fall. They said also that to revert to the old style would be difficult to defend in Parliament. That might well have been true, since the Cold War was now, more than ever, in full spate. In March 1950, Herbert Morrison was delivering impassioned speeches entirely devoted to the necessity of purging the trade unions of communist influence. As is usual in such purges, communists were accused of being a conspiracy rather than a party.

In July it was intimated to the COI that *British Ally* would probably close in October. In August press rumours of its imminent demise were denied by the Foreign Office, also by COI. But on Thursday 31 August, when the London editor, Mr Cox, telephoned to Mr Ian Gray at EEID, Foreign Office about despatching some material, he was informed that the paper had closed down. The last issue was that of 21 August; of the two subsequent issues prepared, one was not delivered and the second never printed.

With the closing of *British Ally* came that of *British Chronicle* and *Glos*

Anglii. This meant unemployment for very many of the newspaper section staff. But before I deal with the personal aspect I want to say something about the political situation.

The Foreign Office attitude clearly indicated that the Labour government had committed itself completely to the prosecution of the renewed Cold War. But at this time there was something like Cold War within the United Nations itself – that body established with such pride only five years before. Mao Tse Tung's China was the bone of contention. The Security Council and, in consequence, the various organs and committees of the UN, were split in half on the issue of the admission of the new China to replace that of Chiang Kai Shek. In May 1950, Trygve Lie, the Secretary General of the UN, visited Moscow to talk with Stalin. Dean Acheson came from the United States to consult with its European allies, notably with Ernest Bevin, and Mr Schumann, Foreign Ministers of Britain and France. Dean Acheson impressed on his colleagues that the Cold War would last at least a generation and that the United States would expect its allies in Europe to maintain their support of a long continuing antagonism between the Western Powers and the Russian groups. The Europeans replied that, if the United States wanted such support to be maintained, it would have to increase the strength of its own armies in Europe.

Some of the English Press, anxious about this crisis, hoped above all that the Cold War would end; but they laid the blame on the Russians and urged them to stop denouncing the Western countries as a camp of imperialists and warmongers. At the same time, the Press supported proposals made by the Tories to the effect that they should work with the remnant of the Liberals to defeat the socialist government!

I seem to remember a meeting in Trafalgar Square at about this time, at which Ilya Ehrenburg, then a well-known Russian writer, spoke. It must have been before the left groups' plan for an International Peace Conference, to take place in Sheffield. The Sheffield meeting was switched, at twenty-four hours' notice, to Warsaw, because the Labour government refused visas to East European delegates, among them Ehrenburg. Burgess and Maclean (subsequently denounced as Soviet agents within our Foreign Service), realised that this was the moment to depart. They made their escape in 1951.

Since all this history has been revived recently by the accusations of other agents and the insinuation that there may, at that date, have been even more agents involved, to me it is important to examine the reason for the tendency in those times to what is commonly reviled as treason to State and people. It has been correctly referred back to the 1930s, when many young men – and not only those at Cambridge University – were inclined to join the Communist Party because there seemed no other place for those of left-wing views to go. Ramsay MacDonald had sold out: in the 1931 election the Labour Party had to fight as a shadow of itself. In my book *Tamarisk Tree 1*, I pointed to the political polarisation that took place, how even the Independent Labour Party, of which I was a member, very nearly, in despair, thought of joining the Third International; and some members did join the communists. Our women's delegation from the ILP, in 1932, walked out of the Labour Women's conference, because the platform would not allow us to move our amendments. Subsequently the ILP split from the main party. Then came divided allegiances over the Spanish Civil War; finally, during the war against Hitler, under the coalition government, though fascist sympathisers and aliens from enemy countries were interned, it was evident that left wingers and communists were regarded as the true subversives; left-wing aliens, many actually refugees from Hitler, also got interned.

Only after the war, when the first meetings of the New Left began, were tongues loosed and voices heard in open discussion; only then did the fighting spirit of the left wing of the Labour movement revive. At these meetings I heard a variety of left-wing voices, Richard Hoggart I think, Isaac Deutcher and that of Paul Johnson, who alas, has sadly fallen from grace. Unhappily the imprint of anti-communism had now gone so deep, that the reconciliation with Russia which ought to have been possible, did not occur.

I have often wondered, did those young men of the thirties in the Communist Party immediately become involved as spies, or when and how did that decision take place? Russian heroism during the war, especially in Stalingrad, held the imagination of so many people in the West who were far from communist that this feeling for the people of Soviet Russia continued to exist. What I am saying is that young men of the thirties who had obtained posts in government service, if they were not already agents for Soviet Russia, might well have felt inclined to become so or to defect after observing the political actions and intentions of their superiors towards that country.

In the 1950s the British Press was complaining of the dark mystery that surrounded what was happening behind the Iron Curtain, whilst the British government was virtually forbidding the exchange of visits and communication that could enable people to find out. Admittedly the Russians themselves now took steps to block the intake of all sorts of publications, as well as jamming broadcasts which they did not like. Since one of these sent out was Orwell's *Animal Farm*, this is scarcely surprising. I have never been able to fathom the folly of people so obsessed with profit and competitive economics, as not to realise or care about the variety with which the human mind and imagination express themselves, from country to country, from one race or people to another.

Our human species, so far, has only one world on which we live and move and have our being, and which, by reason of our superior intelligence and skills, we may lay claim to possess. Why then do we the mass of the peoples allow half the world to be shut out of our lives, to be treated with contempt and enmity, at the bidding of a mere handful of individuals among us who just want to be powerful and rich?

To return to the disillusioned few who had suffered from such a division. For most of the staff of COI Newspaper Section, the closure of their journals did mean the loss of a job. We were temporary, not permanent, civil servants. However, the Central Office was in the process of itself becoming a permanency, and there were opportunities in its other departments. Some of our section remained and are still there, among them Monica Foster, in Overseas Press Services, who did such able work on *Glos Anglii*.

So far as I was concerned, I had to earn money and would have accepted any routine job which did not mean political involvement. I had acquired considerable knowledge of publishing scientific and technical material, for which there was a growing demand in the publishing world. But, as I was now fifty-six, prospective employers found me too old to fit in to their pension schemes, though I might not be too old for the job. Annoyed at any such suggestions about my age, I shocked the office one day by walking in with my hair dyed. This was not then such a common occurrence as it is now.

Fortunately, a good friend of the family, Eric Estorick, who had helped John in some of his dilemmas when in Washington, was now in London and in the Public Relations department of Marks & Spencer.

Knowing my predicament, he assured me that he would find me a job. It seemed that the firm were in process of considering writing their history. I came on the payroll to help with this project. It might only be temporary, but it was work that did not involve a daily office routine, but could in large part be done at home. This was a great relief to me because, though they were aware of my ability, it was clear that COI would be unlikely to offer me anything. At the same time, my seven years in their service had cut me off from writing books or articles on my own. Civil servants cannot do this without permission, on account of possible political implications. Then there was the added difficulty that, if I began to write about matters in which Russell and I had been involved together, it could be only too easy for the Press to stir up stories of hostility and difference of opinion between us.

On the day of my departure, my chief made me a pleasant speech, the Foreign Office sent letters thanking me for my valuable services! My colleagues gave me a fine briefcase. Thanking them all very much, I then told them that I had joined a rival firm just across the way. Marks & Spencer's main office was then in Baker Street, almost directly opposite our Section of the Central Office.

I was really glad to be free of the shackles imposed by Public Service employment; I was very angry with my government. I was glad too, that I could earn my bread by work which left me liberty and some time to spend with women friends and colleagues in organisations for women's rights of which I was a member, and for whose causes there was still so much to be done.

Notes

1. Moscow in English for UK, 20.30, 17.1.49; also in German, Turkish, Arabic and very many other foreign languages.
2. Moscow to United Kingdom in English, 14 January 1949.
3. Moscow, 16 January 1949.
4. Moscow, 5 December 1948.
5. Moscow, 5 December 1948.

PART TWO

'Something women had to say was being left out of
everything in the world.'

7

ON THE
HOME FRONT

After the death of my husband, Pat, I had, in spite of my job, spent much of my free time in the evenings on committees of women's organisations. These were many, and for the most part, non-party, with aims which, although political, consisted in demands, or protests against injustice to women on the home front.

Labour's accession to power in 1945 breathed a new life into groups and societies that had had little opportunity for action in the war years. The Labour government set up Royal Commissions on such matters as injustices to women in the marriage laws, taxes, share of property as well as grounds for divorce. There was also a commission on the question of equal pay for women, who were, during and since the war, entering more and more into the wage market.

The Married Women's Association, in addition to its attitude on the usual injustices to women, took, as a central position, a demand that income, whether earned or inherited, ought to be shared equally between husband and wife.

The Six Point Group, on the other hand, was more concerned with the rights of women as individuals and wage earners, though their Six Points did cover practically the whole field. The Six Point Group's demands were as follows: Economic Equality; Legal Equality; Moral Equality; Social Equality; Occupational Equality; Political Equality.

The group had been in existence since 1921 when it was founded by Lady Rhondda, who also for some time ran the feminist weekly magazine, *Time and Tide*.

Other women's groups were: The Women's Freedom League; The International Women's Day Committee; Women's Peace Movement; Equal Pay Campaign Committee; Liaison with Indian Women; Status of Women Committee.

This last committee related to the Status of Women Committee of the United Nations. When the United Nations was founded a group of feminists had gone to meet the chairman of the United Nations Economic and Social Council when he was in London, and asked that a special Women's Committee should be set up. Among them were Mrs Pethick Lawrence and Monica Whately and I was able to attend and hear the consent given for what became a very important instrument of the United Nations.

Very prominent in the work of the Six Point Group had been Dorothy Evans, who had recently died, and Sybil Morrison, who, as an uncompromising pacifist, was detained during the war. She was prominent in the Peace Pledge Union, and it was at their offices in Endsleigh Street, Bloomsbury, that the Six Point Group met after it got itself together again in 1947, when Dr Edith Summerskill agreed to become president and Roxanne Arnold was chairman. The Group had worked together with Women for Westminster during the election campaign.

One of the first tasks was to deal with a government that, after two years of a Royal Commission that came up in favour of equal pay, still refused to grant this to women, on the excuse that the country could not afford it, and it would cause inflation. A pamphlet, in a series named for Dorothy Evans, strenuously argued the case for equal pay and was issued in December 1948.

In 1949 I was fairly constant in my attendance at the committee, which met monthly and became very active. Its members were women well known and distinguished for ability and political work. Roxanne Arnold was herself a barrister; Hazel Hunkins Hallinan, an American journalist and staunch feminist, long resident in England; Charlotte (Charlie) Marsh, a militant suffragette. (The Executive Committee members are listed in Appendix 6.)

These Committee members were from all three political parties. Ambrose Appelbe, a distinguished lawyer, one of the few men who supported women's demands with enthusiasm, had been a member of the committee, but was now too busy, though always willing to advise. In addition to women's groups we kept in touch with the Council for Civil Liberties and other organisations with relevance to women's affairs. Though nominally not an international organisation, the Six Point Group was appealed to by women in other countries for help. In addition to the Indian women, women in Cyprus asked for our support in their demands for the vote.

The committee members of the Six Point Group were hard workers, taking an active part in the sub-committees formed and as liaison members of other groups. Some of them were active in local council work, as for instance, Lyndal Evans, or as prospective candidates for Parliament like Myrtle Solomon.

In relating the end of *British Ally* I have explained that I was anxious to find work which did not involve me in controversial international relations. But controversy at home on women's rights was a different matter, and I entered into it with all my heart.

We had a government which should have taken steps to give women equal status, yet we were having constantly to lobby and protest. Women MPs were not playing their part to help. Women were still being dismissed from their posts on marriage. Lloyds Bank removed the ban on married women employees. A letter of congratulation was sent to Lord Balfour, Chairman of the bank.

To increase the number of women in Parliament the idea of the coupled vote was considered and a pamphlet prepared. The coupled vote proposal was that in every constituency parties should put up a man and a woman, for both of whom electors would be required to vote.

A weekend conference was planned and took place at Elfinswood, Haywards Heath from Saturday 29 October to Monday 31 October 1949. The Six Point Group had four Vice-Presidents, Miss Vera Brittain, Lady Megan Lloyd George, Miss Clemence Dane, and Storm Jameson. They were invited to come and speak on any topic of their own within the framework of 'Is there a Women's Point of View?'

The choice of this theme for the conference has a special interest in view of the changes in women's, and especially feminist, attitudes which have taken place. Today, after the era of 'consciousness raising' I doubt whether this question would even be put, so convinced are women that they certainly have a point of view which men do not, but must be obliged, to understand.

When women first had the vote, the general idea was that electors, male or female, were persons who calmly and with reason duly considered political issues and party programmes and then voted according to their choice. Sex and a possible difference of sexual nature and attitude between men and women was not seen as a factor in politics. This was why, when we raised the issue of birth control, we were told not to drag sex into politics. There were, however, some of us in the feminist movement who could perceive that men and women think with their sex as well as with their reason. I myself had long been concerned that, in spite of the sentiment about maternity, mothers were politically both neglected and oppressed.

Invitations to the Conference in 1949 were sent to the Married Women's Association and to the National Union of Women Teachers for both delegates and speakers.

Four sessions, Education; Industry and the Professions; Marriage and the Home; Politics, were proposed. The hopes for speakers were disappointed. Among those approached were Mary Stocks, Dr Kathleen Lonsdale (scientist), Professor Ethel Taylor (geographer), Lady Violet Bonham Carter and Mrs Mallilieu. Ambrose Appelbe was invited to take the chair at one session. Male friends who were supporters or members of the Group were welcome.

Regrettably I do not have a report or full memory of that conference, except that Mrs Olwen Campbell was booked to speak on education, and that Sybil Morrison and I myself did speak. What I do recall is an atmosphere of comradeship and lively discussion and that Juanita Frances, who was the original founder of the Married Women's Association, was present, as well as David Burke, an argumentative and irrepressible Irishman, who was later to play a part in political enterprises in which we were both concerned. I left the conference on Sunday evening because I was still in my post at the Central Office of Information.

Among the occasions at which the energetic Six Point members were officially present was the Suffragette Fellowship's celebration of Mrs Pankhurst's birthday, which, very appropriately, falls on 14 July. We visited her statue near the Houses of Parliament with flowers. There was also a meeting, chaired by 'Charlie' Marsh. At this a Conservative woman MP spoke of how, by their great victory in winning the vote, the

Suffrage pioneers had opened the door to a vital, important career for women. In contrast came Mrs Pethick Lawrence's speech which made an impression on me that lasted the rest of my life. Mrs 'Peth', with her husband, was closely involved with the liberation of India. She said that for her the liberation of women was part and parcel of the struggle for the rights and liberties of all the oppressed people of the world.

The appeal of many international causes tugged at our time and energy, could divert us from the tasks on the home front. There was International Women's Day, the International Day for Children. International Women's Day originated, I believe, in America, and had been regarded as non-party. But already, inspired by government attitudes, were hints that its organising committee in Britain was too left-wing or communist. Above all was the greatest issue, that of world peace, shadowed by the spectre of Hiroshima – another occasion that we were under obligation to commemorate. Mrs Leah Manning, a Labour MP, took a prominent part in the 8 March International Day celebrations and she is remembered in history for a speech on peace in Parliament which, in the conventional phrase, literally brought down the house. The issue of world peace should rightly hold a central place in politics.

In the two feminist groups, the Six Point Group and the Married Women's Association, in which I took some part, and which certainly had their hands full, lobbying and working for their own concerns, opinion became divided on the issue of home front versus world peace, a dilemma which, in our time, many have not yet resolved.

Although I had sought some respite from the distress over the world peace issue occasioned by what had happened to *British Ally*, I saw that no individual of active mind and heart could escape. I found myself accepting an appointment to the Six Point International committee whose convener was Miss Elsie Maitland, who already kindly acted as our very efficient minute secretary, and, as proved important, was not Labour but Conservative.

Like all who could realise its implications, we could not escape the shock of Hiroshima. We drafted a leaflet, '2000 AD and the Six Point Group' (see Appendix 7), in which we asked what hope the human race and our civilisation now had of surviving the next fifty years. We put forward a new Six Points, which, while covering all the old ones, added others. This effort for peace was well meant and honourable, but can

117

hardly be called successful. Members began to resign because of our divergence from the original Six Point Group aims.

I had made my own decision. While in no way departing from the human rights which feminism demanded, for me the struggle of the women's movement for peace was first on the agenda. At the same time I recognised that the group might well desire to keep strictly to the aims for which it had been founded. Sybil Morrison, as I remember, once remarked to me that we might have known what would happen if we dared to mention peace. Nonetheless, Sybil was with us in the Six Point Group in our action over the Korean war, an involved story which must be reserved for the next chapter.

In the course of time the Six Point Group presently and rightly returned to its excellent activities in and out of Parliament, on the home front.

Although I was engaged in many other activities I did not sever my connection with the Six Point Group. I have the programme of a conference held by them on 9–11 March 1962, again at Elfinswood, which reveals them as now duly returned to their proper feminist functions. The original Six Points head the letter paper, together with the name of the then president, Mrs Mary Stocks BSc, LLD, Litt D, and Mrs Hazel Hunkins Hallinan in the chair. The champions of the cause are there in full force and ready for battle. Mrs Leah Manning, Vera Brittain, Mrs Corbett Ashby, Dr Doris Odlum (psychiatrist), Dr Esther Hodge (*Open Door Column* and *Women Speaking*), and there are newcomers. A note at the bottom of the page says: 'Dear Dora, it would be nice to have you here.' The initials are Hazel's, H.H.H. But I was now in Cornwall and no longer had my flat in London, which had been so near to hers. Just before she died in 1982, she hoped to come to the private showing of the film *Reds*, at which I was hostess, but she felt too unwell. Dale Spender obtained what must have been the last interview with Hazel, published in Dale's book, *There's Always Been a Women's Movement this Century*;[1] the interview is a clear and remarkable statement of the feminist position, and the story of a devoted, single-minded campaigner, who was a link with the women's movement in the United States and herself a lovable, complete human being. She was critical of women's failure to unite and to be aware of the great power which they possess and could use in the realities of day-to-day politics.

Hazel Hunkins Hallinan died in London which she had made her home and the centre of her life. She closed the books of her beloved Six Point Group in 1981, and gave its archives to the Fawcett Library.

Before leaving the feminist arena, something must be said about the Married Women's Association, which faced some divided loyalties similar to those of the Six Point women.

The Married Women's Association had existed since 1938, when it was started by Juanita Frances as an offshoot of one of the committees of the Six Point Group. She had the determination and single-mindedness required to make this kind of organisation succeed.

In 1949, when I first became a member of its committee, it had impressive sponsorship as well as a good informative journal, *Wife and Citizen*. The President was Dr Edith Summerskill, MP; Founder and Editor: Juanita Frances; Vice-Presidents: Ambrose Appelbe, MA, LLB, Mrs Billington-Greig, Mrs Corbett-Ashby, LLD, Constance Colwill, LLB, Laurence Housman, Lady Pethick-Lawrence, Lady Rhys-Williams, Dr Eustace Chesser; Chairman: Lady Helen Nutting; Hon Sec: Vera Westerland; Hon Organising Secretary: Mrs H. Drew; Hon Treasurer: Mrs E. Hamilton.

Best known for its demand for equal sharing of the family income, it also campaigned for equality between husband and wife in respect of guardianship of children, to ensure the rights of women as to domicile and/or the marital home. It supported family allowances for children, and the right of non-gainfully employed married women to national insurance and pension schemes.

The members of the association were all middle-class women, whose action was directed not so much towards a large membership, as to bringing pressure to bear on Parliament, or otherwise on influential institutions or persons. It did have thirteen local branches.

It was non-party, but its chairman in 1949, Lady Helen Nutting, was Conservative; she had succeeded in spreading its influence considerably, even in the daily Press. Dr Eustace Chesser was a Harley Street specialist, who was also interested in the sex education of adolescents, for whom he wrote a book.

Wife and Citizen was an interesting journal, well edited by Juanita. An attempt was made to persuade other women's groups to support this journal, as a vehicle for publicity for the many urgent women's needs and requests. Each group would have space for its own material. Political, but non-party, it could have a wide circulation and influence.

Developed as a women's newspaper, it could be read by the wife at the breakfast table while her husband perused his masculine news and policy sheet.

The paper would not provide cooking recipes; 'women were in a desperate need of interests beyond the kitchen stove and those magazines already providing gooey trivialities'. Contributions might be invited from correspondents on women's position overseas.

The standard of contributions in the few issues of *Wife and Citizen* which I still possess illustrate how unfortunate it was that the plan for its development, carefully drawn up and considered by an able committee, did not succeed.

The December 1948 issue contains an excellent article by Claire Madden on the coupled vote. She quotes Bernard Shaw's contention that the 'great extension of the activities' of modern governments required that 'detailed criticism by women has become indispensable in Cabinets'. Claire Madden goes beyond the purely political factors by insisting on biological differences between men and women, in terms that differ from those of some recent advocates of Women's Liberation. She is in no doubt that there *does* exist a 'women's point of view'. She says:

It follows that we must discard the old idea that equality of status lies along the road of sameness, of adopting men's standards and values as the human norm, or marching to their slogans under their banners, of trying to modify ourselves to fit into a world made by men for men instead of modifying that ill-balanced masculine society to suit ourselves. At the beginning of the women's movement we had perforce to accept their codes and standards. They had written the books all down the centuries, they had invented all the world religions, they had built up all the impressive edifices of civilisation's philosophical and ethical systems.

But the time has now come when we must realise that we have a contribution to make to human welfare which cannot be made by men. If we are content merely to do as they do, think as they think, if we imagine that *they* can do *our* job as well as their own, we shall be betraying not merely ourselves but mankind. We have for too long fought merely for equality within the framework of socio-political systems designed to suit purely masculine needs. We must now insist on the modification of this framework if experience shows that it does not allow us scope to make our specific contribution in public life to the welfare of the race . . .

Let us abandon once and for all that out-of-date feminist slogan that it is the person and not the sex that matters. It is a half-truth but it is far from being the whole truth. It is true in relation to mathematics, the exact sciences, and also of automatic routine functions which are performed with a fraction of the personality. But it is not true in relation to art, the social sciences, politics, or any of the activities concerned with living beings or involving the total personality.

There is no such thing as abstract mental ability. Mental ability, human nature, do not exist at all apart from sex. They are always incarnated in a particular man or woman; that is the only form under which we know them. And because they never exist apart from sex differences they can never exist unmodified by sex. The thought that we call rational has its basis in the physical and emotional make-up of an individual; it can never be uncoloured by that individual's sex.

A paragraph in the issue of January 1949 in support of the coupled vote by Lady Helen Nutting is remarkable.

Congratulations to Claire Madden on her clear exposition of the necessity for the reform of the Coupled Vote. This is the only logical answer to the vexed question of adequate feminine representation in Parliament. I have always been as much in favour of Equal Partnership and Equal Responsibility in the sphere of government as I have been for Equality in the home. *The single vote, male or female, destroys a fundamental world rhythm which safeguards the smooth working of the complementary function of the sexes, without which the future holds nothing but anarchy and chaos.* (My italics)

In the same issue Juanita Frances emphasises the fact that the only way a woman has of obtaining any allowance by law from her husband is to leave him. Husbands are under no obligation to give to wives anything more than bed and board.

In March 1949, *Wife and Citizen* notes that after ten years of campaigning, Parliament is at last proposing to increase the payment to a deserted wife from two to five pounds a week, and for children from ten to twenty pounds. In the same issue there are comments on the fact that women are still not allowed to speak at the Cambridge Union debates; on sex education in schools; on the fact that though wages are up, men are not giving more housekeeping money to their wives. There is a passionate plea about International Action for Peace by Ruth Flint – 'men are still slaughtering the children women bear'.

In 1950 I became Chairman of the Married Women's Association; Ms Doreen Gorsky and Hilda Misselbrook were Vice-Chairmen.

A document planning evidence on the Proposed Royal Commission on Divorce was drawn up and carries my signature. It pleads for a much wider consideration of marital problems than the mere question of divorce. The proposals drawn up by the M.W.A. Committee were carefully considered and sound in their wide approach. Their intention was to go before the commission and give evidence. Helena Normanton, a barrister, was chosen to draw up the legal points to be stressed. Unfortunately, disagreement arose as to her statements and the organisation fell into a serious quarrel and disarray.

Harmony was finally restored and in 1953 evidence was presented at the Royal Commission on the terms required. The occasion brought a larger number than usual to the visitors' galleries. With all of this quarrel I was not involved. I had resigned earlier when objection was raised to my concern about the Korean War and other aspects of East-West Cold War politics.

Almost immediately after the Soviet government obtained the secret of the atom bomb (in 1948–49), and presumably began preparations to make it themselves, they also started a world-wide Peace Petition and began to set up a World Council for Peace, open to all anywhere to sign and support.

The Labour government, which had refused visas for communist delegates to the proposed conference in Sheffield, now denounced the Peace Petition and Peace Council as communist propaganda.

The Western Cold War warriors went into vigorous action to prevent the growth of a movement for signing the petition or attending peace conferences.

It so happened that the Married Women's Association was organising one of its entertaining and successful garden parties in Juanita Frances' large garden in Hampstead. There were stalls and raffles of home-made goods. We all attended, very ladylike in our summertime best, especially donning stylish and decorative hats. In considering side shows, the committee wanted to have coconut shies. Should we ask David Burke, as a supporter, to undertake this? He was delighted to oblige, but only on one condition, that we should have the Peace Petition in a modest corner, open for signatures. This was agreed and David was on the spot contributing much to the life of the occasion by his frequent exhortations and announcements on a megaphone.

At one such garden party when I was asked to draw the winning raffle ticket for a cake and David announced 'the high integrity of your chairman for such a purpose', I put in my hand and immediately chanced on my own raffle ticket!

Edith Summerskill, our President, honoured us with her presence. Suddenly she became aware of that noxious petition. 'Either it leaves the garden party or I do', she exclaimed. The chairman was sought for complaint but oddly enough was not in evidence. The distinguished Privy Councillor and member of the Labour Cabinet departed in high dudgeon. Hard grind though left-wing politics might be, it always had one attractive aspect – it was much more fun than being pompous.

While even the narrower feminist sections of the women's movement on the home front found themselves unable to preserve their parochial attitude, there were other sections openly crusading on international questions. I continued to be active with the women of the Independent Labour Party. I also became associated with the Assembly of Women, which arose at first out of International Women's Day.

The idea was to bring women together in conference, on their own, and not as sections of the men's political parties. I was on the Conference Arrangements Committee of the first of these, held at what was the St Pancras Town Hall. Women from all over the country, from the Welsh valleys and industrial areas, came on the platform and spoke for the first time in their lives. Monica Felton, I think, was chairman.

The new peace movement was vocal. The Conference Arrangements Committee agreed that at the end of the conference a woman from the London Peace Committee should put to the conference her suggestion for a march to the Cenotaph with a wreath as a demonstration for peace, not war. The entire conference rose as one and each section carried the stick with the label of the area it came from. Outside was the 'band' which David Burke got together for demonstrations. I had advised him that this event might take place. Although there were May Day marches, it might surprise women today to know that there were some who thought our demonstration on that day was 'unladylike'.

The Assembly of Women continued as a body, but was not able to stage more than two such conferences. As usual, it was smeared with the communist label and it must be said that the *Daily Worker* of the day hindered rather than helped by writing of it with enthusiasm as if it were (which it was *not*) the women's conference of the British Communist Party. The Assembly of Women did stage the first women's conference against the bomb and another on youth and education.

I could not accept that the World Peace Council and Peace Petitions were insincere and so much propaganda. Call these efforts propaganda if you like – they still stood there as efforts for peace, open for anyone in the world to take part. Why, just as they had the secret of the bomb, should the Soviet government suddenly launch peace proposals? If this was not sincere, what was the point of it?

The attempt at a peace conference in the West, in Sheffield, had been frustrated by the refusal of visas. My own experience in the Soviet Relations Division on *British Ally*, had given me an insight into the Soviet attitude which the average person could not obtain and was, in fact, being prevented from obtaining.

To discern and try to understand the Soviet direction of policy and the feeling of her people seemed to me very important. New factors had rendered the international situation more complex. The response of groups and individuals on both sides can only be understood if I first attempt some explanation of these events.

Notes

1. Pandora Press, 1983.

8

THE SOVIET
PEACE INITIATIVE

This chapter must begin by recalling events as far back as 1917, when no sooner had the Bolsheviks taken power in Russia than Winston Churchill despatched Colonel Josiah Wedgwood, MP to the Far East in the hope of promoting belligerent opposition to Russia from Siberia.

From 1920, when I first visited the Soviet Union, right up until this very day, that country and people, at every one of their wide borders, have been encircled by enemy forces and hostile propaganda.

That Russia has never attacked Britain, but has been our ally in two wars against German aggression, must also not be forgotten.

Stalin had negotiated with Roosevelt and Churchill at their Yalta conference, with a view to keeping the countries bordering Russia in Europe as a protective barrier against any further attack on his country from the West. When, after the war ended in 1945, he saw the treaty he had made with Britain, which promised post-war mutual co-operation, virtually treated with contempt, he had made the mistake of attempting to include in East Germany the whole of Berlin. The Berlin airlift of 1948 had resulted – as had also the first stationing of American B29 bombers (in July, 1948) in East Anglia in Britain. With Truman as President, and James Forrestal as Defence Secretary, the Americans were already in full cry against their former ally, now their arch enemy.

It has recently been revealed that, already in 1945, the Pentagon had been considering a first strike with the atom bomb on Russia, and therefore it was vital to have the B29s, capable of carrying nuclear bombs, stationed near enough to the Soviet Union for attack.[1]

When the planes arrived, the Labour lawyer, John Platts Mills, MP, appears to have been the only one to ask questions. He was told the planes were there on a 'temporary mission for goodwill and training'. Whereas James Forrestal wrote in his diary, 'We have the opportunity *now* of sending these planes, and once sent, they would become something of an accepted fixture.' James Forrestal, as is well known, was so afflicted with paranoia and sheer terror of the Russians, that he presently threw himself out of a window to his death.

In 1949 a new character had come on the scene. In China, Mao Tse Tung's forces drove those of Chiang Kai Shek over the Yangtze into final defeat. China had, as Chairman Mao announced, 'stood up'. I was not surprised by this news, after what Dr Needham had told us about China's growing power when he visited Soviet Relations Division.

Soviet Russia, making advances into Manchuria against Japan, as Stalin had promised his Western Allies, now had a communist neighbour prepared to open relations with foreign countries, and to claim the seat occupied by China in the United Nations.

This event was a severe blow to United States policy which had looked upon China as an opening for trade and almost for colonisation. America had supported Chiang Kai Shek and his wife with money and ostentatious friendship. Americans felt, and even wrote, that the communists had succeeded in 'stealing' China from them.

They refused to recognise Mao's government or to accept his representative at the United Nations. Chiang Kai Shek moved to Taiwan, then recognised and still supported by America, whilst Ernest Bevin, at the British Foreign Office, recognised Mao, but with little welcoming warmth.

Because I loved China I was relieved that we had recognised Mao's government. From the year I spent in China with Bertie Russell, I had known that some form of communism was the likely outcome. I heard that a British–China Friendship Society was starting. Looking for it, I mounted to the top of a dilapidated building near Paddington Station and found there the lone figure of Jack Dribbon, its secretary. As I recall, I tried to give some help in the intervals of my own work, by bringing food for him or taking him out for lunch. In time, of course the society grew. I was able to be on the committee and Jim Mortimer, until recently Secretary of the Labour Party, was there also as a trade union representative.

In 1949 came a delegation from China, whom I went to meet at the airport. But on the way my taxi collided with another car and I had a slight gash on the eyebrow, which needed medical attention. However, I got to the celebration in the evening with a suitable plaster. I was delighted to meet there a middle-aged woman, now a Minister, who had known me when she was a student in Peking.

We held a public meeting, but it was difficult, in the strained political atmosphere, to persuade Labour people to meet and support a delegation of declared communists, although they represented their government. The Chinese, on the other hand, were also choosy. They wanted to meet fellow communists, or those who at least were on their side. What is more, the Labour government made no gesture of a reception for them. Joseph Needham was at the meeting and he came straight to me, shook hands and remarked, 'I am glad to see you here.' I had tried, without success, to persuade several other people to come. I do not now recall exactly who was there.

The wrangle about China's seat at the United Nations went on. The Soviet Union, in support, refused for a time to attend the Security Council. This, in my view, provided the opportunity for the Korean war, though who began it still remains a mystery which I hope will one day be revealed. I remain convinced that what evidence there is points to its origin in United States policy. Had Russia been at the Security Council of the United Nations she would certainly have used her veto to prevent it. As it was, there was a very hasty meeting early in the day, at which a vote was obtained for a war by the United Nations against North Korea as the aggressor. This was extremely serious, since it meant that Britain, and all other nations supporting the United Nations, were required to send troops in aid of the South.

In Britain no one understood what it was all about. Amid considerable anxiety a debate was to take place in Parliament. Fenner Brockway hoped to speak. He asked me, if I could find the time, to go to the office of the *New York Times* in Fleet Street to look out some articles which had come from its American correspondents in South Korea. I was able to do this. I found that the point was that the South Korean government had been receiving considerable financial aid from the United States, but its conduct had been such that, according to these despatches, the aid was likely to be withdrawn. Many foreign affairs observers at the time thought that South Korea had engineered the war in order to make sure that support and cash from the United States would be maintained. The date for the end of United States aid to South Korea was June 1950. The war started on 25 June.

I was afraid that China would presently be involved. As one individual I went straight to the House of Commons to lobby. Meeting me there, Lena Jeger's husband, Dr Jeger, sat down beside me in the corridor and asked me to tell him what this war was all about. Fenner did not get into the debate, but the extracts which I got for him proved useful to the Council for Civil Liberties.

I come now to the part played by the Six Point Group in what was a very complex international situation, and one which was to play a serious, long lasting part in national politics, bringing disruption and tragedy not only to those who fought in the war, but to many individual civilians on whom it cast its shadow.

I have been able to obtain by courtesy of the Archives of the Six Point Group copies both of the minutes of the session on 10 July 1950 at 6 Endsleigh Street, and the decisions taken and documents drafted and sent. Sybil Morrison was in the chair; present were the following members of all parties: Mrs Hunkins Hallinan, Miss Charlotte Marsh, Miss Harriet Campbell, Mrs Margery Nicholson, Mrs Dora Russell, Miss Lyndal Evans and Miss Elsie Maitland.

A resolution which I drafted was sent to the Prime Minister, the Foreign Secretary and Mr Gladwin Jebb at the United Nations. It said:

> The Six Point Group, who hold that World Peace must be one of the first concerns of all women, call upon the British government to support their own recognition of the Chinese government by urging the United States government to take similar action and to receive the accredited representatives of the Chinese People's Republic as members of the United Nations; thus making it possible for the full Security Council to operate and bring about peace in the Far East.

I drafted also a letter which was then amended by the committee, and we agreed unanimously to send it to every Member of Parliament. Elsie Maitland, who was secretary at that date, and who undertook the dispatch of the 600 missives, was in fact a Conservative.

THE SIX POINT GROUP

FOR

POLITICAL EQUALITY, OCCUPATIONAL EQUALITY, MORAL EQUALITY
SOCIAL EQUALITY, ECONOMIC EQUALITY AND LEGAL EQUALITY.

National President:
The Right Hon. Dr. Edith Summerskill, M.P.

6, Endsleigh Street,
W.C.1.

Dear Sir or Madam,

The Six Point Group who hold that World Peace must be one of the first concerns of all women, are far from satisfied at the action taken by the Government and the House of Commons about Korea and Formosa.

We would point out that, whatever the position about Korea, the defence of Formosa, taken by the United States, is directed against a Government which the British Government has recognised. Further, that, in view of the treaty between China and the Soviet Union of February, 1950, in which each undertakes to support the other, if attacked, this action in Formosa can, even now, be construed as such an attack, and may involve the United States and Great Britain at any moment in a war with both these powers.

We believe further that it would have been possible to persuade the United States Government at an earlier stage to recognise the Chinese People's Republic and to support their right to send delegates to the United Nations. Had this been done, it is probable that the War in Korea would have been averted.

It does not appear to be generally known that, when the United States Government proposed aid to S. Korea early in this year, President Truman was unable to get the bill passed without including in it aid to Chiang Kai Shek on Formosa. Recognition of the Chinese Republic would have ruled out the possibility of such aid and prevented the present situation regarding Formosa, which has not been the subject of United Nations' decision and is solely a United States' act.

We would add that the date for the end of United States aid to S. Korea was June 1950. The war started on June 25th. We hold that the sequence of events leading up to the outbreak of hostilities in Korea is extremely obscure. We urge that, even at this late date, the recognition of the Chinese Republic, and their entry into the United Nations, and the submission of the dispute in Korea and the action in Formosa to arbitration by the Hague Court or a reconstituted United Nations may still avert World catastrophe, and bring about peace in the Far East.

Yours faithfully,
Sybil Morrison,
(Chairman of Executive Committee)

Notably, we did not say that we opposed the United Nations war but simply that it might lead to the involvement of China and world conflict. I am amused to find at the end of the minutes a note that the letter, though duly authorised and signed, should not be sent 'on our special notepaper'. This must have been disregarded, for it evidently went out with the heading which included the name of our President, the Rt. Hon. Dr Edith Summerskill, who had words to say on the subject in Parliament, and accused me of pulling communist wool over the Six Point members' eyes. I believe we were the only national organisation to make that wholesale appeal to Parliament. And we were not wrong. It was not long before everyone was anxiously watching Clement Attlee, the Prime Minister, en route for Washington to avert General McArthur dropping the atomic bomb on the Chinese. Attlee was aware, as we were not, of those B29 American bombers that had been poised, alert, prepared on our East Anglian coast since 1948.

The purpose of the Russians in starting the Peace Petition and seeking a Peace Conference in Sheffield had now become clearer.

They had good reason to be alarmed at a war that threatened the new China under Mao Tse Tung, and eventually, possibly themselves. In the West, communists and others on the left, though confused, were equally alarmed.

Chief organisers of the Sheffield effort were Ivor Montagu and Desmond Bernal. Both were communists but also intellectuals of good standing; Bernal was one of our most distinguished scientists, and, with others, had been one of the 'backroom boys' scientists whose knowledge had helped in the war against Hitler.

The ambitious intention of such a congress was to be world-wide, but obviously its main contributors at that post-war stage would come from Europe. Supported by the Cabinet, Chuter Ede, Home Secretary, made a show of tolerance in not refusing visas to all the delegates, but only to a large and selected list of those evidently considered most dangerous. Of special interest is the refusal to the Russians; to the religious Metropolitan Nicolaii Krutitsky, the composer Shostakovitch and the writers Ehrenburg, Fadeyev, Korneichuk and Tikhonov. The refusal to Shostakovitch and Ehrenburg was the most unfortunate since they were strongly in favour of cultural exchanges between nations and both spoke to that effect in the congress. Ehrenburg had lived much in Paris; Shostakovitch, as is now known, had barely survived the appalling wartime blockade and starvation in ice-bound Leningrad. Both were not entirely happy under Stalin's claim to dictate absolutely everything cultural and scientific.

Delegates from countries not requiring visas, such as France, were stopped from entry at the port. Among them was Joliot-Curie, designated president of the congress, one of France's most distinguished scientists who had helped in the making of the atom bomb, mainly through facilitating the supply of heavy water. But he had been dismissed from his post as head of France's atomic research because he was a communist.

In England, as in America and France, the drive against communists was severe. Herbert Morrison was calling for their expulsion from membership of trade unions.

Public opinion was uneasy at the visa refusals. In November 1950, when the matter was raised in Parliament, Attlee defended the government's action, declaring that Britain is a free society in which, so long as the law is not broken, all people enjoy the right of free assembly

131

and free speech, no matter how misguided they are. British communists enjoyed this freedom together with other citizens. But the government examined each foreign application on its merits and reserved the right to refuse those undesirable. The fear of propaganda by communist visitors was evident; Attlee accused them of 'calling us cannibals and warmongers'. In view of the remarks being made at the time both by Britons and Americans about their Soviet allies, the pot was in effect, calling the kettle black – or red. What about Truman's projected preventive war, the dropping of the atom bomb and those B29 bombers?

Questions began to be asked in Parliament. The Home Secretary, Chuter Ede, repeated Attlee's assertion and argued that, in spite of the refusal of entry to about half the applicants, a good-sized congress could nonetheless have been held. An Independent member, Blackburn, suggested that the congress should have been left to the 'tolerant ridicule' of the British people. Lord Hinchingbroke, Conservative, felt that the 'natural robustness and integrity' of British citizens would prevent them from being suborned or seduced by statements made at Sheffield. Labour member, Emrys Hughes, suggested that the Home Secretary was imitating the methods of a communist police state. Whilst Ian Mikardo, Labour, thought we could have found a better way of 'showing our detestation of totalitarian regimes than by imitating their practice'. The Labour MP, Sidney Silverman, not satisfied with the government's replies, raised the matter again. A very humane man (who happens to have been responsible for getting Parliament to abolish the death penalty for murder), he urged that the rights of free speech, free assembly, the right to know, to argue freely, which are the very basis of a free society, were under fire all over the world, and must be defended. He added that this was not a democratic congress as we understand it. Chuter Ede replied that neither was it properly speaking a 'peace' congress. Ede made clear that the Labour government, as a democracy, opposed attempts at subversion by communist ideology, to which it held that it had 'both the answer and the practice'.

Bernal and Montagu had hoped for a conference of *discussion* and consultation for peace. The transfer of the congress to Warsaw led to the views of the Soviet Union and its close allies becoming more prominent.

The conference put forward a plea to governments for an end to the

Korean war and for a mutual halt to rearmament. From this, it would appear that the Soviet bloc regarded South Korea as the aggressor.

In Britain, on the assumption that the North was the aggressor, an odd hypothetical question was put to Ivor Montagu at a Press conference: would the Soviet Union, for instance, grant visas to delegates from Western countries to whom it occurred to hold a conference in Russia – at Khaborosk or Vladivostok – to demand that the Soviet Union use its influence to ask the North Korean aggressor to stop bloodshed? This would certainly have been in the interests of peace? (In actual fact, such conferences for peace open to all nationalities have subsequently been held, with government approval, in Moscow and other cities behind the Iron Curtain.) This incident was reported by the BBC in its Russian service.[2] One wonders what did the BBC, at that date, actually know or believe about the origin of the Korean war?

In the conference itself Joliot-Curie made an ambiguous statement to the effect that this was a tragic conflict on which there existed numerous contradictory interpretations.

> Even if there were people among us who held different views on the circumstances connected with the origin of the war, we should, all the same concern ourselves with supporting any initiative which could be undertaken for the purpose of putting an end to the conflict.
>
> The Security Council of the United Nations had not given a hearing to both sides [i.e. Korea], two great powers, neighbours of Korea [USSR and China] were not represented. Then foreign intervention began.

The BBC broadcasts to Russia, from start to finish of the Warsaw conference, were one long saga of vituperation. Whatever the Russians did, or said, must, by definition, be wrong or of hostile intent.

In October 1950, on the eve of the peace conference, the BBC 'observed' the setting up of a peace committee by the Soviet government.[3] It notes that on the committee the direct Communist Party interest is represented only through the Secretary Mikhail Ivanovitch Kotov, head of the propaganda department of the communist youth league; whereas the rest of the membership is wide and 'of an all-national character'. The committee comprises as many prominent scientists, artists and writers as possible, the Soviet intelligentsia forming the majority of the 110 members, with only a token representation of workers and peasants. The BBC observer goes on to notice 'the total absence of high Soviet bureaucracy' as well as of 'officials and chiefs of the dominating group in the newly elected Soviet Parliament'.

An unprejudiced observer might see in this absence of control by higher authority a sign of sincerity in shaping a national committee to act for peace. On the contrary, the BBC insists that this is no more than a 'facade' to deceive the gullible. It goes on to maintain that, in any case, under the repressive Soviet government, no member of the committee would dare refuse nomination. And then it explains the inclusion of Church representatives from Georgia, Armenia, Tashkent and a Lutheran from Latvia, as proof that the Soviets have had to 'accept the failure of their anti-religious propaganda'.

There follow details of the nomination of poets, writers, and agriculturalists from regions such as Byelorussia and Turkmenia, who had been exiled or out of favour with Stalin but were now apparently forgiven and included.

From these facts, as recorded, it would seem that a government reviled as totalitarian had not done badly in setting up a committee which, by its nature and purpose, would have a considerable independent voice. No proof is offered of the assertion that its individuals had to accept nomination under duress. This is a typical fiction of the consistenly hostile imagination of the West.

From 31 October to 26 November 1950, in more than fifteen broadcasts, the BBC Russian or European service harps on the theme that conferences for peace are nothing but a smokescreen for the build-up of armaments for war. At a meeting in London called to promote peace I tried to alert the audience to the nature of our anti-Soviet propaganda: it was not secret and could be listened to. Many would not believe what I said about the dear BBC.

It was evident that the Labour government was extremely anxious to prevent the spread of communism, either at home or abroad. Yet while they insisted on the peaceful intentions of the western democracies, the B29 bombers stood there on British soil, ready for Truman's preventive war by means of the atom bomb.

At the Warsaw conference Shostakovich said:[4]

Defence of culture does not lie in isolation or in closing the frontiers to culture and truth, its faithfully ally, but in opening the door before them. The more books, written in various countries, a man will read, the more symphonies he will hear, the more pictures and films he will see, the more clearly will he understand the value of culture, and the more criminal will appear to him any attempt against culture or against the lives of all men, near and far. We must ensure a cultural exchange between various countries, we must make use of everything that can contribute to bringing people nearer to each other instead of pushing them apart, we must contribute to mutual understanding, not to the fanning of hatred.

Ilya Ehrenburg developed the same theme:

One must cease to develop in the growing generation disrespect for other peoples and hostility to them. The development of human culture is incompatible with isolation, with the creation of artificial barriers or with mass attacks against culture and the way of life of other peoples. The exchange of material and spiritual values is essential for the development of mankind. This exchange is at present disrupted, and all peoples suffer equally from artificial barriers.

To do the broadcaster from England justice, these speeches are reported and described as 'absolutely correct and wonderfully expressed', but he rightly points out that these speeches are contrary to the policy of the Soviet government, which, in fact, operates a policy of cultural isolation for its own people: 'Such speeches to the congress must have been authorised for propaganda purposes, and merely demonstrate the insincerity of the so-called peace movement.'

At this late date one can only grieve at the spectacle of the endeavours of a great musician and eminent writer on the one side, and a brilliant scientist and other thoughtful men and women on the other, being frustrated by short-sighted politicians, whose only values lay in power. That the gifts of the human mind, heart and imagination should be indivisible, universal, and belong to the whole world, remains still a truth that must constantly be spoken until, at long last, perhaps it will be understood.

The Soviet Union made another attempt to breach the barrier of the Cold War by the Festival of Youth in 1951 in Berlin. It was obstructed by the Labour government as communist propaganda, which, no doubt, in part it was. But, what was consistently not understood or misrepresented was that the intention of these moves was to seek peace, not a drive by the military for war.

Many young left wingers from Britain wanted to attend this meeting. They found themselves obstructed over visas by the Foreign Office under Herbert Morrison, refused aid by British consuls, even faced with violence from American troops in Europe.

A group of these, many young students, were stopped in Austria by American troops, bundled into trucks and detained. Among them was Colin Sweet, a student at the London School of Economics, who was hit with a rifle butt by an American officer. A report, with a photo of his bandaged head, appeared in the *Daily Worker* of 15 August 1951. My younger son, Roderick, and I shared left-wing views (though I was not and never have been a member of the Communist Party). Roderick set off for Berlin and found himself in difficulties in Austria, in Innsbruck, I believe, where he was seen sitting on the railway line playing his guitar, awaiting help, which he and others presently got from the Austrian railway workers, to continue their journey. Meanwhile at home, I was on the phone to the private secretary of Herbert Morrison, demanding why my son and others were not being duly helped, as their passports stated, by the British consular service. The Foreign Secretary I was informed, does not agree with this journey. I retorted that the Foreign Secretary's view was neither here nor there, if my son wished to travel to Berlin with valid visa and passport, he should pass in accord with the regulations 'without let or hindrance'. I suggested that the private secretary should convey to Mr Morrison (whom I knew very well) what was the view not only of myself but of many others at this interference with freedom.

After the event the Council for Civil Liberties staged an enquiry at which various people described their experiences. The object was to expose and ridicule the folly and danger of a persistent Cold War anti-Soviet stance.

I was now invited to go with a delegation of women who were preparing to visit their opposite numbers in the Soviet Union. I had at the time no obligation to work or family that would prevent my accepting the offer. Above all, I wanted once more to meet and talk with Russians, to find out the state of their country and learn what the Russian women felt and had to say. On 10 August our delegation, consisting of twenty women, from various parts of the country and representing all types of women's activities, left for Moscow. It was led by myself and Mollie Mandell as members of the International Women's Day Committee. Nancy Silverman (wife of the MP, Sidney Silverman) was a delegate. A full list of delegates is in Appendix 8. The list of names alone shows that we represented a considerable spectrum of British women's outlook.

In Moscow we were received by our hostesses, the Soviet Anti-Fascist Women's Committee, whose chairman was Madame Parfenova. We had a busy period in Moscow, which included visits to a watch factory where we were able to observe women at their delicate work, and hear about the special care given to their eyesight; to a clothing factory; to the Lenin Library, especially the department of rare books; to the special House for Children's books, to see not only the literature provided but meet some of the young readers. We visited also a senior girls' school and saw their reading room. We could not see any schools in operation, because of the summer holidays. We did, however, visit a children's pioneer summer camp – and, as regards adult education, we were able to see the plans and meet the architect of the new Lenin University which was being built.

But it was not only in education that the cultural needs of the people were served. A feature of Soviet organisation are the adjuncts to the factories, available for all kinds of leisure pursuits; not to mention also creches for the babies of nursing mothers.

We were greatly impressed with the progress in public health only six years after the war ended. On this visit I obtained a booklet in English, which I still have. Well produced and with good photographs, it gives an account by N.A. Vinogradov, of public health in the Soviet Union.

After the time in Moscow we went to Stalingrad. Here are some extracts from an article I wrote in Russia, which was published in a

Soviet journal but never saw light in the British press:

The plane touched down on the sunbaked brown earth in the heat of the midday sun. Twenty average women from Britain, somewhat stiff and weary, stepped out. Our first impression was the comfortable presence and smiling faces of the Soviet women who were our hosts, the next the clean white building of the airport. As our bus moved off we passed alongside one of the newly planted shelter belts of shrubs and trees; later we were to see how innumerable trees had been planted everywhere – in squares, gardens, and along the roads. Our eyes fell upon dugout houses, roofs level with the soil, made during the siege and still homes for some people. Contrasting with these, two smart new cars, admirably sprung, speeded along the dusty road. As we neared the town itself, the bronze figure of a soldier, sword held high, on top of a column in a commanding position, expressed indomitable courage.

Two days of vivid experience followed. We listened to the chief architect of new Stalingrad explaining the plans for the city. New building was obvious all around. As we were able to see from a model in the Stalin museum next day, nothing whatever had remained of Stalingrad but a few fantastic ruins. Some of these still stand, between them are spaces cleared of rubble, but on these are rapidly rising Stalingrad's new palaces. I use this word advisedly, size, dignity, light, space are the keynote of all construction, while large squares and broad avenues with trees and flowers, leading down to the river front esplanade, will give the fine buildings the setting which they deserve.

A cinema with a Greek portico – though most of the architecture is not Greek – contains not only the film projection hall, but also an auditorium of considerable size where actors and singers entertain the audience while waiting. Upstairs an even larger hall with comfortable settees and tables placed around the walls, offers ice cream and cool drinks in place of the queue in the hot street. Adjoining this hall is a library of periodicals.

Residential and school building in new Stalingrad is four to five stories high. There is ample space and taller buildings are not needed. Anything approaching pokiness is abhorred. It is characteristic of the Russians to live in the grand manner. And fine things there are not for ornament but for use. A pleasant fountain basin in the courtyard of blocks of new flats was full of sun tanned children bathing; the palaces of culture are well frequented by active young people.

As the heat abated we drove out to the tractor plant, which is some distance from the town proper. The road led between the river Volga and the famous hill Mamai Kurgan. A mass grave and a small scarlet obelisk by the road side, commemorate the struggle, momentous for all Europe, which was concentrated in these few square miles. It doesn't look much; railway tracks, a tree-lined road, a fairly high bank sloping to the river; beyond the railway a bare green hill, high only in contrast to the flat surrounding country – a strategic hill, fought over, once blood-soaked. You cannot look at this scene without strange and deep emotion. Here is where the Germans were really held and the place itself tells the strategic story. A bare thousand yards from the hill is the river bank, in which for a time the Soviet headquarters was embedded. Beyond lay access to that vital crossing of the river which the Germans never made. Here later the Russian reinforcements poured over to surround Paulus's army. The beloved river and the great cause of liberty were saved by superhuman sacrifice.

Rows upon rows of Stalingrad's caterpillar tractors greet you as you approach the plant, whose interior on a hot day is, for a novice, almost an inferno. But we saw it all, from the blast furnaces to the finished articles, which as we stood there, were coming off the assembly line every five minutes. This plant does not make tanks, it has never made them. A nucleus of workers who stayed there during the battle did tank repairs.

Not far from the tractor plant is the palace of culture for its workers. It is correctly named. In a series of spacious rooms, young people, mostly in their early twenties or younger, who had been working in the heat, noise and oily grime of the factory were taking ballet and singing lessons, painting or modelling, practising in an orchestra, or reading in a well-stocked library which contained translations of many English classics. No one was organising or managing them. The large windows of the rooms looked out on to a terraced garden which extended to the river, which on this night was lit by a full moon.

An impromptu concert was given for us in the large concert hall by these amateurs. Young women, prettily dressed, and with really good well-trained voices, sang to full orchestral accompaniment without the slightest trace of nerves. Both young men and young women performed Russian dances.

The lighting of these new buildings is extremely brilliant and beautiful. It is impossible to describe adequately the great chandeliers sparkling with glass and crystal, and all the other devices of lighting which, as in the Moscow Metro, betray the artist's hand.

At the end of the concert I had the pleasure of thanking our young entertainers on behalf of our delegation and I said to them from my heart that we women in England also had sons and daughters and we wanted to see them dancing and singing too and not marching with the weapons of war in their hands. Our young Soviet friends replied, and there was among us a deep feeling of unity in our need for peace.

The next day we were able to see the history of heroic Stalingrad in the Stalin Museum. We saw there the sword which was sent from our country, and we decided to write in the book of the museum that we hoped to see our countries united in the future, not through a sword, but through the bonds of peace and social construction. As we came out of the museum a crowd of school children who had come from Saratov to see the exhibits, crowded round us and questioned us eagerly, telling us that they wanted peace and friendship, and, as we left they sang for us the song of the Youth.

Next, our women friends took us on the Volga, and we bathed and swam together stripped to our panties. To me, this simple pleasure meant as much as any of the other things that we did. These women whose personal sufferings had been so great were full of life and hope, and such good companions.

140

They organised our evening meal and we danced together. I remember thinking that women at home would have felt that such an occasion was flat without the presence of men. But these women were self-sufficient, self-confident, conducting their evening as any club men might. At table they followed the Russian custom of taking turns in offering toasts. As I lifted my glass I said that in my country we had a saying that when we were friends we 'let down our hair together', and hinting at but not mentioning our bathe, I went on, 'but we have taken down much more than our hair as a sign of friendship and trust'. I drank to these women who have proved that out of their disasters they can create happiness and life.

Our next visit after Stalingrad was to Armenia, on whose frontier with Turkey stands a dominant snow-white landmark, Mount Ararat, where, according to Holy Writ, Noah came to rest with his ark. I remember very vividly our descent in the plane to Erevan. The dashing young Armenian pilot wanted to display his skills. We dipped, slid sideways, alarmingly, high over the waters of the Lake Sevan, in which I began to fear that we would end our days.

Safe at the airport, as we went towards the women who were advancing with flowers to greet us, suddenly I realised that they were speaking and I could not hear a word. I gave my head a shake, my ears 'popped', overcoming the effect of that descent. I was able just in time to hear and respond to the greeting with words of friendship.

Lake Seven, high in the mountains, was part of the programme arranged for us; later we enjoyed a trip on its waters by launch; subsequently, we were deep under the earth in the power station which drew upon those waters and was, as I recall, lofty, clean and a bit like a palace with artistic coloured fluorescent lights.

Armenia is agriculturally rich. We talked with women in the fields picking cotton; we visited the vineyards and drank the excellent local wine. In Erevan, the chief city, the central square was being developed on a special design. As building material they have what is, I think, a limestone, which comes in colours, varying from a soft yellow to pink or mauve. In these varied hues rose buildings, all of them resting on arcades, whose graceful arches afforded shade for walking and shopping precincts.

The architect of the new plan accompanied us on our visits, as well as on the lake excursion. He talked enthusiastically of his work. When we went also to watch the weaving of fine tapestries and rugs, I remarked to him that no doubt, on our next visit, we would find the whole central square carpeted with these beautiful works of art. He enjoyed the joke and laughed heartily. He was a most charming man; so, we were given to understand by our hostesses (who themselves did not lack charm), are most of his sex in Armenia, including no doubt their saucy and intrepid pilots. The Armenians are a warm and hospitable people.

On our next visit, which was to one of the establishments on the Black Sea for rest and recuperation, as well as for holiday pleasures, we were refreshed by an excursion in a fast motor boat.

Back in Moscow we had a lively Press conference –I possess the text of our joint views. In Moscow, whether then or at the first visit, we were taken to the Bolshoi theatre. Of course our hostesses chose for us the night when the ballet Swan Lake was being performed.

Here I digress in order to relate what was for me one of the most entertaining, though in its significance, heartbreaking events of my visit. On the very first day of my arrival at my hotel in Moscow, the telephone went. I picked up the receiver a bit nervously, because of my very limited Russian. But the voice which spoke was English – none other than that of the long-lost editor of *British Ally* – Archie Johnstone. No one, I had always understood had been able to 'find Archie'. But I did, first thing. He would not miss greeting an old colleague. He now had a Russian wife and was settled doing translation and literary work. I was able to meet him and his wife in a restaurant for a talk late at night. This was only the first of several reunions which we had when I came again through Moscow. At times, with visitors from Britain, we discussed the political situation. Once, after the revelations following Stalin's death, when the visitors included some disillusioned British communists, our talk became rather intense. I did not love Stalin, but neither did I love Churchill. For me, Stalin was not the Russian people, any more than Churchill was the people of my own country. Both were men who liked power, played politics against their rivals but were the warlords their peoples needed in desperate times of war. I could not understand either, why communists in Britain had not realised that the Soviet Union, if constantly subject to ostracism, abuse and war, must inevitably arm in order to become a great power like all the rest. The prime enemy of humanity is, quite simply, war itself.

Archie and I corresponded; we exchanged gifts. I have still Russian tea glasses and a Russian folktale picture done on wood in poker work which he took from his kitchen wall. It is dated 16 August 1951 and an inscription on the back is now very hard to decipher. It says:

> To Dora
>   with love from the kitchen
>   in the USSR Moscow.
> And, at your next spring cleaning when you dust the back of this picture I hope you will say to yourself there is not really an excuse for not writing to me.
> This is my address in Russian.
> You can also put my address in English
> AR Johnstone   St No 21.   Flat 20   Moscow, USSR

I cherish it in honour of a man of principle who condemned himself to abuse and isolation for what he believed to be right. To return to England would have done no good and only meant prosecution. I think, as time went on, his flat became a rendezvous for talk by people who cared about Russia and peace.

We came back to England on the eve of a general election which was to see the defeat of the Attlee government. We had discussed this possibility with our Russian women friends, who asked us what might be the result if Churchill were returned to power. When we said that we supposed his government would undo all that the Labour party had fought for, they laughed and suggested that, after all, might not a one-party state be simpler and achieve more benefit to the people – a dilemma about consensus politics that still haunts democracies, ourselves included.

In our visit of a whole month our delegation had ample opportunity to make copious notes and to observe the pervasive mood of peaceful friendship, hope and work for the future that prevailed among the people. We knew it would be hard to persuade our own people out of their hostility. But we were all active, speaking at local meetings, getting letters into the local Press. I spoke at a meeting of writers for peace, another of teachers for peace. Those who had access to technical journals fared best. Dr Mary Barber achieved an article of 4,000 words in the *Lancet*. Messages came in of thirty-two requests to Mollie Evans for meetings in Bristol, of many to Mrs Chappell in Cardiff and to

Rose Hayes in Leeds. The Press were interested enough to spend time on a three-hour conference, but did not print what we said. Even the *New Statesman*, like other journals, did not print the letters I sent. I tried the BBC and women's journals in vain. Election meetings gave opportunities for raising the issue, but the tide was turning in favour of the Tories. We delayed publication of our booklet till election fever died down.

I wrote a warm personal letter to Madam Parfenova, thanking her and her committee for their hospitality and reported our, as we felt, small successes. With Nadia Chimach and her family I had formed a real friendship. In a letter to her in October, hoping she will enjoy the 7 November celebrations, I tell her how I had taken some pretty Soviet china cups and some nylon-made stockings to meetings as evidence of Soviet civilised life.

> I show the Russian label and say, 'You see, Soviet women wear nylons too.' Of course this is silly nonsense, and what we have to say about you and the Soviet Union is much more interesting and important than nylons, but it is a way of making people laugh, and also see that their values in life are not really as good as yours.

Nylons at that time were a new feature of Western feminine civilisation -- agreeable, but to me trivial, beside the issues with which I could not help being concerned.

While our delegation were away in Russia, another action, brave and dangerous, had been taken by women for the sake of peace. The Women's International Democratic Federation (WIDF), learning from women in Korea about the horrors of that war, had assembled a group of twenty women and one observer to go to Korea and themselves find out what was happening. The chairman of the delegation was Nora K. Rodd, a Canadian, the vice-chairmen were from China and Denmark. Delegates came from Holland, West Germany, Czechoslovakia, China and other countries, making it almost world-wide. Three of the women were lawyers.

Monica Felton, then chairman of the Stevenage new town development under the Labour government, was invited to go. In the pamphlet *What I Saw in Korea*, published immediately on her return, she says:

My own invitation to join the commission came to me from the committee of the Women's International Democratic Federation in this country. Although this was an organisation with which I had never been connected, it seemed to me that, as a life-long member of the Labour Party, I would be doing a service to the Labour Movement as a whole – and too, following in some of the Labour Party's finest traditions – by accepting. Since the Korean war broke out, on June 25, 1950, the people of this country had had no first-hand account of what was happening in North Korea, and even reports from South Korea had become, since last autumn, more and more heavily censored. On the other hand, the great strength of the Labour Movement in this country has always sprung from the eagerness of the rank and file to understand world events, and to base their opinions on facts. In going to Korea I had one aim, and one aim only: to discover the truth and, having discovered it, to make it known.

After travelling by air to Mukden in North China, they had to continue their journey by train and by night, because of the bombing of North-east China by United States aircraft. They arrived at the border town of An'tung, and from there crossed the river Yalu to the Korean city of Sinyju. Visiting as many cities as possible, including Pyongyang, Sinyju, Anak, Nampho, Wonsan, Kaichen, they found complete devastation by bombing. Clambering over the rubble, they talked with survivors who were seeking no more than holes in which to exist. Slaughter had been indiscriminate, open graves revealed bodies bound hand and foot or burned by napalm. As I write I am turning the pages, with illustrations, of Monica's appalling eye-witness report. She issues a warning:

> Korea today is a ruin so absolute that no one can see it without getting the most clear and terrible warning of what a third world war would inevitably mean.

The delegation sought to go to South Korea but this proved impossible. Their talk with American prisoners in the North brought about the SOS – Save Our Sons –movement in the USA which helped to end the war. Members of their delegation, however, suffered in some countries on their return home. The German woman went to prison.

In England some of the war correspondents began to be horrified at what was going on. James Cameron, among them, lost his job on *Picture Post*, which refused to print his report. Monica Felton lost her job under the Labour government. I found myself, when she was ill, addressing meetings on her behalf, at which noisy audiences shouted that she should be hanged as a traitor. Flaming with anger on one occasion at least, I talked them into silence, shouting, 'Shut up, I shall tell you what this Korean war is really about.' I learned that I did convince some of the audience. Friends also at times served Monica as a bodyguard in case of attack.

The war was brought to an inconclusive end in 1953 – but there has never been a peace treaty between North and South. The South, under United States' domination, now undercuts our car, shoe-making and other industries by means of the kind of wages that, no doubt, our own capitalists would like to impose on our people. The North, under a much-vaunted leader, Kim Il Sung, has developed along its own communist lines to what looks like considerable prosperity There are people on both sides who, as in all countries artificially divided by great power politics, would like to achieve reunion.

Turning now to my own family fortunes, back from the Soviet visit, I had been able to look forward to a happy Christmas with my younger daughter and son. Harriet had returned from four years' education in America, a very capable and self-reliant person. Roddy got back from his adventures at the Berlin Festival only just in time to start term at the polytechnic to study economics. Ingeborg and Jack Flugel invited us all to enjoy Christmas dinner and festivity with them – one of those happiest days that stay in the memory, of time spent in the company and mutual affection of real friends. Presently Harriet, through her United States experience, obtained a job with the United Nations organisation dealing with the youth section. She had become used to independence and went to share a flat with another girl. Roddy, at the polytechnic, was with me. I kept going on my small alimony and some ghost writing which I was doing on a novel with Eric Estorick; it was quite a good thriller and I regret to say, owing to his acquiring other interests such as art, it has never been published.

Roddy and I were deeply absorbed in politics in which we saw almost eye to eye. Harriet was not hostile, merely her interests were otherwise. She and her brother had to get to know each other after four years' separation. This went well, because both really valued the brother-sister relation. I wanted only to help if and when I could, but to let them take their own road in life. It was hard to meet Roddy's fees, but we managed, and in the latter part of the time he studied at night while acting in a not too arduous night watchman's job. I had to come to his rescue once, when he was about to be turned out of the poly for not studying. I faced one of the toughest tasks in my life. I went to see the Heads of Department and sat there simply refusing to go away unless Roddy were reprieved. I insisted that his intelligence made him well worth education and asked them had they taken note of what he did when attending the institution, if he did not work? They could not tell me. I explained that he spent much time and energy on student organisation in which he was passionately interested because, above all, he liked people. In the end I won. It is true that at that time he made friendships among fellow students who valued him, which lasted to the end of his life. He qualified in economics and, looking with characteristic modesty at the lowest list, was amazed to find himself higher up, with a second-class degree.

Before long we found ourselves celebrating Roddy's twenty-first birthday. We discussed how best to do this. With his characteristic independence he had in mind a lively evening with his contemporaries. I pointed out that usually young persons coming of age received compliments from their elders. The upshot was a family luncheon party given by me at the Café Royal, which included my mother and sister, while Roddy had his own celebration, as and when he pleased. Since Roddy was the youngest of my family, raising my glass in a toast I said that I wished on this great occasion to celebrate my emancipation from the duties of parenthood. How wrong I was. Very shortly after this event family problems arose which were to produce anxieties and inescapable burdens for the rest of my life. Even at that date there was little in political or personal life to offer happiness or encouragement.

Selected by a Hampstead Peace Committee to go as their delegate,

I had to attend a Peace Congress in Vienna to which a sizeable group from Britain was sent. This involved much organisation, lists and allocation to plane flights. I must have been tired by whatever labours had been involved in packing and preparing, for, on the day of departure I was awakened by a phone call from the organiser to say that my plane was just leaving. But all was not lost. So long as I was coming, I could be put on the next flight.

Such world congresses for peace as that which I attended in Vienna in 1952, which are organised by the communist powers, continue to be the target of hostile propaganda, and their countries threatened by war from those capitalist powers which like to consider themselves as democracies in opposition to totalitarian regimes. To attend such a conference in good faith is a revealing experience.

In Vienna at the height of the Korean war I met Chinese delegates, as well as people from all over the world. A point was made, as is usual, to have there priests of all religions, and from many countries groups of scientists, writers, artists, teachers, doctors, trade unionists. It was wonderful to make the acquaintance of people in one's own field of work, of whom one had heard, to meet others of interest and value whom one had not known, and then, for me, some people from India, including Muk Raj Anand, who had actually read my books. It was a great meeting of world-wide fellowship for all.

The main speeches of the congress were delivered in a large theatre, in a more or less continuing session. Of these my abiding memory is one by Jean-Paul Sartre.

> The statesmen of the world when they meet together, are concerned with their differences, their objections, the demands which they make upon other nations. We are met here to find out in what it is that we can agree.

The message was so simple, why had one never seen it just that way oneself?

Congress divided into commissions in search of some of that agreement on various topics. These were thoroughly democratic, somewhat like a Quaker meeting. With someone chosen to preside, be the rapporteur, then anyone could suggest a statement of policy on education, relations between workers and employer, human rights, the use of science, or whatever seemed important. All suggestions were adopted, unless some members of the commission had objections that they could state. The document produced in the end was, as it were, the consensus of the meeting. I remember the commission in which I was involved, which had as rapporteur Desmond Bernal, whom I greatly admired. Somewhere near 3 a.m. we were locked in the agony of trying to reconcile the views of the Chinese delegates, who were sure that the Americans were experimenting with germ warfare in Korea, and those of some British scientists who refused to believe this allegation. There was no enmity, and somehow we all found ourselves baring our souls in these efforts at communication and understanding one another. Professor Joseph Needham and Dr Andrea Andreen had signed a massive Chinese statement (which I possess) in their belief that some such attempt based on information obtained from Japanese experiments had really been made, though Needham thought it amateur and clumsy. He had himself, while in China during the war, obtained some information about such Japanese activity on which he informed the Foreign Office. Recently, BBC television's 'Horizon' contacted him on this subject for their programme on bacterial warfare. I wrote to him also then about the discussions in Vienna in 1952 when the young scientists from Britain would not agree that such acts by America were possible. Similarly, it took a long time to convince public opinion about the devastation of crops and vegetation chemically engineered by America in the Vietnam war. Throughout the congress the Chinese showed themselves as remarkable conciliators, seeking always some statement with which all could agree. On the Korean war, full agreement, as I remember, was not quite possible, so two statements on the subject were allowed to appear in the final report.

It was customary at the congress for delegations to invite one another for a 'get together' over an evening meal – and also for the agenda of speech making to be so arranged that it would not require a speaker who was at some special evening social. One evening our British delegation were being entertained by the comrades from the Soviet Union. We were a very mixed group. I do not now recall the delegates' names, but there were quite a few not used to such excursions abroad. All was going well except that vodka, in glass decanters, was deceptively like water. Suddenly a message came through from the theatre that the agenda had reached the speeches of religious contributors. A young Church of England clergyman, a canon, was being called for. I do not suggest that he was inebriated, but like the rest of us, he was in a convivial mood and exalted. In fact he made one of the best speeches of the congress, which I listened to, exalted myself, from a seat in an upper circle. We had, of course, all thanked our Soviet hosts and adjourned with our colleagues to the theatre. The churchman was among those who were continuously striving for peace.

The delegations at Vienna from Western Europe comprised about 200 from Italy, nearly that number from France and 160 or more from Britain. I firmly believe that the strength of those numbers helped to avert the preventive war whose threat still haunted the conflict in Korea. All British Labour members who were present were expelled from the party.

A similar, almost forgotten peace conference of the Asian and Pacific regions took place in Peking from 2–12 October 1952, instigated by the Mao Tse Tung government, and led by the remarkable woman, Soong Ching Ling, sister, though opponent, of Madame Chiang Kai Shek. There were 367 delegates and thirty-seven observers representing thirty-seven countries in Asia, Australasia and the Americas on the Pacific Coast. There were a large number of specially invited guests, among them nine international organisations.

The conference claimed to represent 1,600 million people for peace in the Asian and Pacific regions. It issued an Appeal to the Peoples of the World and an Address to the United Nations. It put forward nine resolutions on: Japan; Korea; National Independence; Cultural Exchange; Economic Relations; The Campaign for a Five Power Peace Pact; Women's Rights and Child Welfare; Support for a Convocation of the Congress of Peoples for Peace; and establishing a Peace Liaison Committee for Asian and Pacific Regions.

Among well-known names of that committee appear James G. Endicott (Canada), Paul Robeson (USA) and Pablo Neruda (Chile). The conference report carries messages from Joliot-Curie, among others, Pablo Neruda and Paul Robeson.

I returned from Vienna to report to the Hampstead peace committee, and to continue other efforts to alleviate the Cold War. Antagonism to communism, or anything approaching sympathy and friendship with communist countries, frustrated every effort to rouse people at home to the imperative need for greater international understanding.

I continued to work with the Assembly of Women and to earn what I could to supplement my modest alimony.

The Labour government had nationalised coal and transport; it built up the Welfare State, made progress in education, and established the National Health Service – all regarded as great achievements. The Welfare State, however, was founded on the work of Beveridge during the war, while Butler's Education Act of 1944 had already opened doors in education. Labour leaders had become accustomed to working in coalition with those who were their natural political opponents. For me, there was still something lacking in all this apparent progress. Somehow it fell short of what I had looked for as socialism. Even the *New Statesman*, whose editor was Kingsley Martin, would not print my protest against this type of welfare to which I objected not only because it had the odour of charity, but because the regulations were too complex for the semi-literate, not used to official forms, to understand, and thus they would not obtain benefits.

My experience while working on *British Ally*, and what I knew now of the Communist peace initiatives both from the Soviet Union and China in the Far East, convinced me that here was something on which our socialists were turning their backs in peril for the future. The Tories, now in power, began to dismantle the transport services, and to stimulate free enterprise and profit. They were aware of the present advantages of retaining the Welfare State to preserve contentment among the people. Soon, however, new inventions, production of goods, hire purchase, were able to offer something more – the 'I'm all right, Jack', and 'You never had it so good' of the consumer bonanza.

Now, early in 1954, that peace initiative from the East again began to enter my personal life. I became involved in a further contribution to events caused by the Korean war. At the United Nations, the United States, supported by the United Kingdom and influencing other governments, had mounted an attack on the Women's International Democratic Federation (WIDF) to deprive it of 'consultative status' at the United Nations. In February 1954, an abrupt letter had been received by its secretary, Marie Claude Vaillant Couturier, at the office in East Berlin, announcing that it would lose its status when the Economic and Social Council and the Status of Women Commission met in New York early in March. No reason was given. But it was obvious that the action of WIDF in organising the women's delegation during the war in Korea was almost certainly the cause. WIDF, as one of the 'non-governmental' organisations (NGOs), had received and held consultative status since the UN was founded in 1945. In common with delegates from communist countries to the Status of Women Commission at the UN, it was having difficulty in obtaining visas to go to the meetings in New York. This was contrary to the pledge, given by the United States government when the UN centre was established in New York, that visas for those with business at the UN would never be refused. WIDF was world-wide and in 1953 had just had an impressive conference in Copenhagen. Someone was needed to go to New York in WIDF's defence.

I was not a member or associated with this body, but, like Monica Felton, I felt an obligation to women who were clearly striving for peace and more friendly international relations. Friends suggested that with Soviet visas on my passport I too would be unlikely to get in. But at the Passport Office there was no difficulty. They took it for granted that a new passport, unsullied by these prejudicial blemishes, was needed. I took the opportunity on my new passport of ceasing to be described as the Rt. Hon. Countess Russell and became the technically correct Mrs D.W. Grace. Later on this proved somewhat of a nuisance. I should then have established my pen name, Dora Russell, by which everyone continued to call me.

The next few days were hectic. With passport in order, on 15 March I went by air to Berlin. Thence, by continuing in the Strassenbahn, I entered East Berlin for the first time, to consult with WIDF, whose office, due to exclusion from the West, was now established there. The Berlin Wall did not yet exist. Passengers on the Strassenbahn were informed at one point that they were now about to enter the Russian sector and should therefore get out. If not doing so, one needed to have either East German currency or friends to meet one on arrival.

At WIDF I was impressed by the well-informed women; secretaries from Italy, America, Britain, France and the Soviet Union informed me as to the case which they thought I should put to the UN. We also discussed brief statements, one about China, which I might put to the Status of Women Commission if its chairman gave permission for a WIDF representative to speak.

I was back in London by the afternoon of 17 March. At 9.15 a.m. on

18 March I went to the United States Embassy to ask for the visa. While waiting there I phoned my daughter Harriet, who was still at the United Nations Association office. I phoned also the UN Information Service because I knew that Dag Hammarskjöld, the UN Secretary General, was in London and was to speak there at a meeting. At the US Embassy I was called for a special interview to instruct me as to the terms on which my visa had been granted. I was limited to a small area of New York around the UN building, with boundaries north, south, east and west, marked by streets which I must not cross. I must also leave the USA immediately my business at the UN was completed. I phoned Berlin about the visa and its restrictions, also that I would be on a plane for New York on 21 March. I obtained tickets for Hammarskjöld's London UN meeting on March 20 and for the plane.

I had addressed a letter to Dag Hammarskjöld at the Information Service in London, complaining about the delays of visas for the Status of Women Commission. I did not expect a reply; but I had discovered that the meeting at which he would speak was specially addressed to NGO's. I therefore took the opportunity, at the meeting, of putting a question to him about visa refusals especially to NGO's. This was intended to give warning to the NGO's and I did not expect him to answer.

I found time for a few personal matters; to have lunch with Roddy and my sister Bindy on 19 March, to get to my bank, my accountant and my hairdresser, to see John, 'our Lil' and my friend David Burke, who was much interested in my project.

At 6 p.m. on 21 March we took off from Heathrow. I found the route and stops of the plane journey fascinating. We were at Prestwick by 7.30 p.m. (temperature 43°F and blowy) for a good dinner in a large warm dining room. At 1.30 a.m. we were in Reykjavik, Iceland, in a café full of United States and Canadian flyers drinking Coca Cola, with a girl in a bright green and white coat and black and white wool cap, and another in bright scarlet. Beautiful black and white Canadian Indian sweaters were worn in abundance. A vivid, lively international scene.

Headwinds delayed us; we had to stop at Montreal for re-fuelling and reached Boston at 10.15 a.m., New York time. Here was lovely sunshine and blue water, the atmosphere clear right up to our height. There was no ice or snow. From above, the houses looked so neat and tidy. We landed in an airport that was almost in the harbour.

The glimpse of Boston charmed me.

Leaving Boston at 10.50 a.m. we were at Idlewild airport, New York, at 12 midday, 22 March, again in bright sunshine. Here my odd visa caused me to be delayed. As the other passengers departed, the immigration officers, who seemed both puzzled and amused, said that 'they were expecting me but had not yet got their instructions'. My prompt arrival had apparently taken authority by surprise. Looking at me curiously, they remarked, 'Was there any reason for objection to me?' 'On the contrary,' I replied, 'I have always found that people tend to like me.' Smiles on both sides.

After waiting a short while longer, I decided to end their embarrassment. I pulled out from my handbag the notes I had been given on my visa restriction, and handed it to them, saying, 'Is this what you have been waiting for?' Almost at once instructions came through by phone, the visa rules were taken down and typed out. I went through the barriers to change money and get on the bus to the terminal.

The man at the bank was indignant that my government allowed me to take out only £5. He thought this 'awful mean of the British' and opined, 'How would we get on in Europe if we had such restrictions?' I had the impression that ordinary citizens in the USA did not much trouble to find out what was going on in the world.

The immigration men, frankly intrigued, puzzled and amused, evidently thought it all rather silly. The general atmosphere was so much more loose and casual than I had expected.

On the route to the terminal I passed through extraordinary masses of suburbs. There were winding roads going over bridges and under tunnels to take the vast stream of traffic. There were houses of every kind, with roof tiles of green, blue or red, even blue spotted red. They looked as if made up of prefab tiles, the whole unfinished, torn down and rebuilt – like a child playing with bricks.

When I finally got to the terminal at 2.30 I was tired and starving hungry. I got a taxi to the Hotel Tudor, which fortunately had a room. I washed, did not stop to eat, but went over at once to the United Nations.

This was a bewildering place, which I needed to get used to as soon as possible. On the twenty-ninth floor I found Charles E. Hogan, the official concerned with the Economic and Social Council and specially with NGOs. I have noted that my first impression of him was of a 'tired liberal'. He greeted me with relief, saying that he had been fearing that I had been stopped and was on Ellis Island. He was clearly on our side about the difficulty of visa refusal. He at once made a point of having several copies made of my 'permission', to be sent to all sorts of higher-ups in the United Nations. He asked the United States representative to send him a map for my guidance. Mr Hogan also seemed very greatly impressed by the numbers and deliberations of the recent WIDF conference in Copenhagen.

In this 'permission' was a phrase saying that if the UN invitation was 'withdrawn', then I must leave at once. It was evident that everything turned on the result of a resolution that would come before the ECOSOC (Economic and Social Council). Hogan made a point of open welcome, showing me all the office rooms and introducing me to the women staff, notably Mrs Tennison-Woods, Chief of Section, and Mrs Grinberg-Vinaver, both of whom were concerned with the Status of Women Commission. He gave me tea in the canteen and a load of documents, which I returned to the hotel to read, the commission having adjourned till the next day.

On Tuesday 23 March, I went to the bank to obtain access to the dollars which WIDF had arranged to finance my visit. I then cabled to Roddy, at home in our flat, of my safe arrival and my address.

I now had my first experience of the meeting of the Women's Commission. It was in conference room 2: it seemed enormous and was fully carpeted, which deadened sound. It was equipped with earphones and mikes: my notes say that I felt all this no doubt necessary equipment muted discussion. However, the first incident was a skirmish roused by Mme Novikova (Bielorussia) as to whether they were going to have a separate committee to deal with resolutions, which was not the practice in other commissions. A decision on the point was deferred.

In the weeks of my attendance at that commission I was to learn how the immense complications of national customs regarding the status of women roused continuous intense argument, for here were so many voices, languages, temperaments. To be a delegate seeking to improve the status of women world-wide was no sinecure.

My first action was to make my arrival known to the chairman and members of the commission. I did not at first communicate the terms of my visa. Since it was the first of such visas imposed, it should appear here in full.

155

I sent a letter in the following terms both to Miss Minerva Bernardino, Chairman 8th Session – Status of Women Commission, and to the Chairman and Members of the Non-governmental Organizations Committee.

With your permission I wish to bring to your notice facts regarding my visa of entry to the United States as representative of the Women's International Democratic Federation.

The terms of this visa are as follows:

(1) That such alien shall proceed directly from the port of entry to New York City and shall remain continuously in that city during her sojourn in the United States within a certain area on Manhattan Island, to wit:

On Manhattan Island, bounded on the north by E 97th St. and transverse road No. 4; bounded on the west by 9th Avenue, between 28th and 49th Streets; 8th Ave. from 49th St. to Columbus circle; Central Park West from Columbus Circle to transverse road No. 4; bounded on the south by 28th Street, from 9th Avenue to First Avenue; by 26th St. from First Avenue to East River Drive; bounded on the East by East River Drive;

(2) that such alien shall be in possession of a valid visa or other form of valid authority assuring her entry into the country whence she came or to some other foreign country following her sojourn in the United Nations Headquarters District;

(3) that upon the expiration or cancellation of any invitation by the United Nations she will depart forthwith from the United States; and

(4) that she will not engage in any activities in the United States outside of her official duties with the United Nations District Headquarters.

So far as I am aware, never before in the history of the United Nations has any visa in such terms been issued. I think that you, and the distinguished members of this Committee will share the view taken by the Women's International Democratic Federation that this procedure has no other object but to harass and obstruct us in our work as a non-governmental organization of Status B category and is contrary to the spirit of the agreement under which visas to the United States are granted.

If I may express a personal feeling in this matter, I would like to say that, were it not for the importance of presenting at the United Nations the views of the WIDF's 140 million members, I would have declined to accept a visa in such incredible terms.

This is not the first time that obstacles have been placed in the way of the WIDF – an organization which has held Category B status since March 28, 1947 and has been a loyal supporter of the work of the Commission on the Status of Women from its inception.

At the 5th Session of this Commission in April-May 1951 a visa was refused to Laura Diaz. Miss Betty Millard came in her place only on the last day of the Commission's proceedings. At the conference of Non-governmental Organizations held in New York October 6-10, 1952, Mrs Rae Luckock was unable to be present because her visa was refused.

At the Seventh Session of the Commission on the Status of Women in March, 1953, as is well known, Mrs Rae Luckock's visa was again refused, and the Commission sent to the Economic and Social Council a resolution of protest requesting the Council 'To examine this question at its 15th Session with a view to taking the necessary steps.'

A copy of the resolution is attached.

In view of the terms of my visa for this 8th Session, the WIDF has no alternative but to make emphatic and formal protest against the abnormal discrimination exercised against it.

> Dora W. Grace
> (Women's International
> Democratic Federation)

This is the March 1953 resolution:

COMMISSION ON THE STATUS OF WOMEN, 7TH SESSION

MARCH 1953

Resolution of protest against exclusion of WIDF representatives

'The Commission on the Status of Women, having been informed that the entry into the United States of the representative of the Women's International Democratic Federation, which would enable this representative to take part in the work of the 7th session of the Commission on the Status of Women, has been delayed; considering the 114th section of the agreement relating to the headquarters concerning the admission of the representatives of non-governmental organizations with consultative status,

(1) is sorry that the representative of the Women's International Democratic Federation has not yet received the entry visa which would enable her to go to the headquarters of the United Nations Organization and take part in the work of the 7th session of the Commission,

(2) calls this abnormal situation to the attention of the Social and Economic Council, and begs the Social and Economic Council to examine this question at its 15th session, with a view to taking all necessary steps.'

The countries that voted for the resolution were as follows:

For:- Burma, Bielorussia, Chile, Cuba, Dominican Republic, France, Haiti, Lebanon, Holland, New Zealand, Pakistan, Poland, USSR, Venezuela.

Against:- USA:

Abstentions:- United Kingdom, Nationalist China.

Whilst still on the subject of the visa, I will add that Mr Hogan, within the next day or so, summoned a Press conference to present me and the map which had been obtained. I have no exact details of the Press coverage except that, notably, there was a very considerable article in the *New York Times*. After the debate about WIDF in the ECOSOC I was also interviewed by Cedric Belfrage of the *Guardian*, a left-wing journal which he was running.

The Status of Women Commission at the UN is composed of two representatives from each country in attendance at a session; not all countries are present, they take turns – as do other UN bodies. Delegates are chosen in whatever way their governments devise. In effect this means that they are chosen, not by ballot, but by decision at high level by the government in power. It must therefore be taken for granted that, apart from specific women's demands (open for debate possibly world-wide), the views expressed at the commission represent in general those of the governments of their countries. This can on occasion be a matter of some importance and argument. Consequently governments, more especially their foreign departments, pay careful attention to the selection of delegates. Some evidently consider their women too naive, or politically uneducated, to be trusted. They therefore present a delegation composed of one woman and one man. When I was there the delegation from the United Kingdom, to my anger and dismay, had appointed a man, Mr Attlee, as joint delegate. But some communist countries also displayed similar mistrust and male chauvinism.

A world-wide meeting of women always fasinates me by the greater variety that it affords than a similar gathering of men. Dress, of course, is one of the first things. With some exceptions, men tend to adopt some sort of male uniform, and seem to want to make themselves all appear alike. Women, on the contrary, vary so much, not only according to current fashions, but to the social and economic background from which they come, and the traditional 'image' of women, their character and status in their environment and country. In the company of women, there is delight in a sense of common identity and sisterhood, accompanied by a feeling of being set free from living day-by-day entirely in a male-dominated world; here is a world belonging to all women, which, as yet, is not valued or understood by men.

Here I was able to sit back and watch women from Sweden, France, the USSR, Poland, Yugoslavia; Pakistan, Lebanon and Iran; Cuba, Haiti, the Dominican Republic, Venezuela; the United States and the United Kingdom, in their characteristic dress, pose, voice and gesture, deliberating detail upon detail of their complicated lives. The women of the South American republics surprised me most by the high fashion they assumed; the tinted, perfectly permed hair, the smart hat stylishly poised, jewellery; tight corset and high bosom; small feet balanced on high heels, so that they seemed like pouter pigeons as they walked – so great a contrast to the soft falling saris of the sandalled Far East, or the neat coat and skirt and shirt blouses or afternoon dresses of the women of Europe.

Minerva Bernardino of the Dominican Republic, by now an astute and experienced politician, was in the chair. As I listened to their well-phrased arguments, and at times, the passionate pleas for freedoms, human rights, education, reform of the marriage laws, they absorbed me heart and soul and conveyed to me their message that 'something women have to say was being left out of everything in the world'.

The United Nations' building soared skyward like the old steeples of cathedrals, but oblong, box-like and severe in shape; in shining glass, with its moving stairways, its huge assembly rooms for communication, it seemed to me like a re-birth of the old Utopian dreams of *man*kind, but unhappily already clouded and cracked by ill will and wrong doing.

I knew nothing about procedure at the UN and I would have been very lost, but for the help of those with experience already at work there. I knew, of course, that the fate of WIDF lay with the imminent meeting of the ECOSOC. I met with and was impressed by the ability of Elinor Kahn, who was concerned with the affairs of the World Federation of Trade Unions. They also had recently had some difficulty over a visa for their representative.

A representative of an NGO had the right to address a written communication to the ECOSOC, but no right to speak there. Decisions by ECOSOC about NGOs were usually taken on the recommendations from the Council Committee on NGOs to which I would have to put my case. Not all of the meetings of this committee, it seemed, were open; some were also in closed session.

I set to work to study more carefully the documents with which WIDF had provided me, and to marshal my arguments. In the meantime I noted that another women's organisation, the Women's International League for Peace and Freedom (WILPF) had been permitted by the chairman to make a statement at the Women's Commission. Presently she also gave me my turn. I gave information on the changes in the status of women in China and, as I spoke, I noticed how the United States and United Kingdom delegates listened, since they knew very little of what had been happening in China since Mao Tse Tung took power. The United States was still supporting the Chiang Kai Shek representative in China's place at the UN.

On 31 March at 4.30 p.m. began the session of the Hundred and Thirty First meeting of the Council Committee on Non-governmental Organisations, at which I was to put my case (ref E/C 2/SR. 139). At the UN it is almost impossible to open one's mouth to speak without due reference to the file number of the topic under consideration. I have the documents both of the open discussion at the Council Committee, 31 March 1954, and of the subsequent debate of ECOSOC on 6 April 1954 on the recommendations made by the committee. I will try to describe briefly the arguments of the various representatives who spoke. The documents E/2525 item 20 (b) and E/2551 were the topic.

Mr FENAUX (Belgium) in the Chair, asked me to speak.

I asked the Committee to reconsider its decision, taken in closed session on February 26 1954, to recommend to ECOSOC to deprive WIDF of consultative status, first on the ground that WIDF had only been informed of this decision on March 3 with no reasons given.

I then suggested that this raised a constitutional question which must concern not one, but all NGO's, who were already, as I instanced from their statements, uncertain of their position and were asking for a clearer definition of that position and their rights. Was it not inadvisable to take an arbitrary decision on one NGO without hearing its defence, pending what should be a discussion that concerned them all. A postponement till the next ECOSOC meeting was possible.

If the Committee would not postpone, then I asked for a statement of the objections to WIDF and for the right to reply on their behalf at the Committee or ECOSOC. Further, for the right to circulate a written statement to ECOSOC and other UN organs when the discussion took place during the current session.

Mr FOMIN (USSR) confirmed that the decision had been taken in closed session without all the necessary information. Mrs Grace should be allowed to consult the records and make a statement on which the Committee would surely reconsider its decision.

Mr KOTSCHNIG (United States) then accused me of saying that the Committee had taken an 'arbitrary', in other words irresponsible decision, without examining the facts.

Such a declaration from a NGO was 'quite unacceptable'. He was not prepared to reconsider without hearing from me as to why, in my opinion, the Organisation should retain consultative status.

161

The CHAIRMAN said the Committee could not create a precedent by turning itself into a Court of Appeal, before the Council had considered the report. He then called on me.

Mrs GRACE. I replied that I was put in a very difficult position, since the Committee had taken a decision without hearing my organisation.

I had never accused the Committee of 'irresponsibility'. The word 'arbitrary', which I had used, came from the 1953 conference of NGO's, which had urged the importance of avoiding arbitrary decisions. I would only continue my statement, as the Committee desired, under protest. It was contrary to the legal practice of the United Kingdom, of which I was a citizen, to reply to charges without knowing their exact scope.

The Federation could not reply to an attack when it had no indication of the reasons that occasioned it. It did not have to defend itself since it had always respected the UN Charter and could not be reproached on that score.

The Committee's decision constituted a highly dangerous precedent which might compromise the position of all the NGO's.

I then mentioned that just recently at a meeting in London, the Secretary General had stated that NGO's 'formed a bridge between the UN and the peoples of the world'. I gave details of how WIDF in its work brought the UN to the notice of women in many countries, which were not in the UN.

In mentioning refusal of visas, I remarked ironically that possibly depriving WIDF of status might be a useful way of evading that visa dilemma.

I did not dwell on the restrictions imposed on the liberty of my movements in New York, but I had to draw attention to the statement of Mr Henry Cabot Lodge, the United States representative at the ECOSOC, who alleged that 'certain organisations called NGO's were actually dominated by the Soviet Union'. I would be failing in my duty if I did not ask for proof in support of such a statement. How could the Soviet Union dominate 140 million women scattered throughout the countries of the world, more particularly in Western Europe, where in Italy WIDF had 4 million members, and about the same number in France. It was accused of having members in communist countries, but that was true when it had received status in 1947. I had agreed to represent WIDF at the current session of the Commission on the Status of Women, because women in all countries of the world wanted to prevent the division of the world into two hostile camps. They wanted to see one world only and all human beings working in harmony for the welfare of humanity.

The ECOSOC would not prevent the organisation of 140 million women from existing and continuing its work by banishing it from the UN. But it might cause women to turn their eyes away from the UN to which at present WIDF encouraged them to look as a champion of their rights.
The CHAIRMAN regretted that I had criticised the Committee.
Mr FOMIN said I had not exceeded my rights but had made true and sensible remarks on the Committee's policy.
Mr KOTSCHNIG then became very eloquent about the political nature of WIDF and alleged that it had attacked the UN.
Mr TSAO (Nationalist China) thought the discussion had been long enough and made an attempt to move 'next business'.
Mr FOMIN then replied very eloquently to Mr Kotschnig. He urged postponement and delay to give me an opportunity to reply to accusations.
Mr GORSE (France) (temporising) repeated that the Committee was not a Court but had heard the statement of WIDF with interest. The Council could decide its report at a closed meeting; after this there would be no objections to further open discussion.

Asked by Mr Fomin if I would make a supplementary statement after studying documents, I repeated that I wished first of all to know the reasons which had prompted the Committee to draft its present recommendation, which was contrary to the provision of the resolutions adopted at the Third General Conference of NGO's which the Council had accepted.

The position of the French representative taking part in the discussion was delicate. WIDF had originated in Paris; its president

163

was a distinguished French woman scientist, Madame Cotton; its secretary was Marie Claude Vaillant-Couturier, widow of Paul Vaillant-Couturier, who had been seriously wounded in the 1914 war and was a member of the celebrated group, Anciens Combattants, founded by Henri Barbusse. Marie Claude herself had survived a Nazi concentration camp – and carried the mark of its number on her wrist. She became an eminent communist member of the French Parlement. In the 1930s, when her husband was Mayor of Ville Juif, a left-wing suburb of Paris, I had visited him there because he had known my friend Paul Gillard, but also to see the new school built by Corbusier.

Mr Gorse, on that committee, must have felt that he ought to vote for WIDF. In fact, he probably abstained.

The committee, at its next (closed) session, produced document E/2551 with its recommendations on WIDF and sent it to the ECOSOC which was to hold its Seven Hundred and Sixty Third meeting on 6 April 1954. In accord with the committee's decision and request I wrote my statement for their information and that of the ECOSOC (E/C 2/382). It was circulated on 2 April. Between 31 March and 6 April I had not much time to lobby, in person, doubtful members of governments on the ECOSOC who might support us. Nonetheless, I did try. I had success with Egypt and India, and felt that I had some with Pakistan.

I have my full statement, but obviously can afford space only for points of the argument. One fact which I mentioned was the remarkable growth of WIDF at that time in Western countries – France, Italy and Scandinavia. In both France and Italy women were only then achieving political rights, and the 'simple approach in drawing all women together has a great appeal. This expansion in the West is specially noteworthy, as an organisation does not grow in this manner unless responding to a definite need felt by the women who join it.'

In Italy one of the first tasks facing women after the war was, for instance, the case of war orphans, undertaken by our members. To the accusation that WIDF 'had engaged in political propaganda unrelated to the economic and social objectives of the United Nations' I pointed out that, on the contrary, our conferences revealed great concern with those very issues.

The American representative had also objected to our activities *outside* the United Nations as being, 'confined to political actions unrelated to the Council's work and inconsistent with consultative status with the United Nations'.

This struck me as particularly silly, because, as I pointed out, every NGO was formed for some purpose outside the work of the United Nations. 'A religious organisation for instance, furthers a special religion without specific reference to its consultative status; an organisation interested in travel, does not further its objects at all times in relation to its consultative status.'

The value of a NGO to the UN lay precisely in this dual position. Our work and collection of signatures for peace, it was alleged, 'had not helped the Council'. Indeed? Had it not? On the accusation of a 'sustained campaign of vicious propaganda against the United Nations', with all respect, I asked for documentary proof. In none of the federation documents would such propaganda be found. We had at times appealed to the United Nations for help in cases where action against human rights might need the United Nations' attention, but there was no attack on the United Nations itself.

The representative of the United Kingdom made only one accusation against WIDF – that it had opposed the work of the United Nations in Korea. On this key question I said I was at a disadvantage in having to deal with this briefly. But a perusal of WIDF documents showed that here also, it was an appeal to the United Nations, not opposition to its work.

Why is this objection put forward in 1954 when it was in 1951 that the Federation drew the attention of the United Nations to the terrible devastation and plight of women and children due to the war in Korea? Why does the Committee wish to withdraw consultative status from the WIDF for this event now and not then? The WIDF has never disguised its earnest desire to save human beings from the appalling sufferings of modern war. It is contending for its position here at the United Nations because it believes its work to be a reconciling force. Has peace no social and economic implications, especially for the lives of women, their husbands, sons and young children?

I concluded with an appeal to the ECOSOC not to take a hasty decision to cut the federation off from the deliberations of the council and its Commission. We had so much to learn by being here, and an important contribution to make to its work.

As the ECOSOC debate began at 10.30 a.m., I was sitting in a gallery above, anxious and not very hopeful of success.

Mr FENAUX (Belgium) opened the proceedings by saying that the Committee had resolved to recommend withdrawal of status. Mr HOTCHKIS (USA) led the attack with the usual insults. 'WIDF was a propaganda machine which cynically exploited women for political purposes.'

In its attacks on the United Nations WIDF had even gone so far as to allege that the Status of Women Commission had, in six years, done very little to implement the equal rights of women.

(I had to laugh at this, because our complaint on this was so obviously true.)

Mr MEADE (United Kingdom): His delegation had voted for the withdrawal, but it 'had taken that action only after very careful consideration'. (Of course, in true Foreign Office style and language.)

Action about Korea was clearly seen as the real crime. His assertion that WIDF had gone along with the Chinese accusation of attempts at germ warfare was certainly true. (But this, if mistaken, was no more than prophetic.)

Mr PSCOLKA (Czechoslovakia) then came in with a vigorous and well informed defence of our cause and WIDF's contribution to United Nations' activities, urging that my statement, only just circulated, should be further studied and decision postponed.

Now came Cuba (not yet under the rule of Castro).

Mr NUNEZ-PORTUONDO had come to the Council's session without any preconceived ideas. But for him the mere fact of questioning United Nations' action in Korea was sufficient condemnation of what he certainly seemed to regard as impudence on the part of a mere NGO.

Mr TSARAPKIN (USSR) did his utmost to help both by humane pleading and good documentation.

'If the WIDF were all communists, it must be proof of the strength of communism in the world. Except in the United States of America, it was not considered a crime to be a communist.

'An attempt has been made to isolate the United Nations from the currents of world public opinion; a political campaign to turn the organisation into the preserve of countries which shared the United States' views.'

Debate in the NGO Council Committee had been purely formal, with mere statements. Opinion had been divided; four votes out of seven for withdrawal of status – those four votes obtained only under United States' pressure.

He supported Czechoslovakia and suggested that the council should obtain more data, by a special committee.

Mr HOTCHKIS implied that there had been enough discussion, and that a majority vote of this committee sufficed; unanimity was not required.

Mr MEADE thought the council had had time enough to read the WIDF statement and saw no reason to postpone a vote.

But the indefatigable Mr TSARAPKIN persisted.

'A new principle was being introduced into the council and that a crusade was being organised against bodies which upheld peace and the legitimate rights of women. Other victimisations would occur.'

The views of the Chairman of the Commission on the Status of Women should be sought. The WIDF representative should be allowed to make a statement to the council.

I sat there, as he called out, 'she is here, let her come down and speak', as one might say in 'fear and trembling'. The proposal to consult Minerva Bernadino (which I am sure, must have been made with knowledge of her support for me behind the scenes) was defeated by twelve votes to three with three abstentions.

Czechoslovakia then came to the rescue by proposing an

adjournment. This was carried by seven votes to four, with six abstentions. This was quite an achievement.

At 2.40 p.m. the discussion (on E/2551) was resumed. In the luncheon interval I had been pleading for speeches in support, with the result that, after Mr Tsarapkin had again rebutted and refuted Mr Hotchkis, India was heard.

Mr SAKSENA thought that credentials must have been thoroughly considered when status was given. Withdrawal could bring bitterness and even discredit on the United Nations.

No doubt the outspoken reports of WIDF might have displeased some member states but 'indulgence must be shown' to some violence of language since 'the occasional impulsive nature of women was known to all'.

He advised postponement of decision for a year.

Mr KOS (Yugoslavia) did not agree with WIDF but supported the principle of universality, bringing together nations of different ideologies.

Mr ADIL (Pakistan) appeared favourable but WIDF had been mistaken about rights of women under the Koran. They could own property and men and women were equal.

Mr EL TANAMLI (Egypt) agreed on these points. But he would vote against withdrawal on the principle of universality.

Mr TSARAPKIN in his final plea pointed out that the United States' diversionary tactics were illustrated in an attempt to influence Egypt and Pakistan. WIDF's reports about women's rights were not directed against Pakistan or Egypt, but those countries where women did not enjoy equal rights.

The only just decision for the council was to keep the WIDF in status.

Eighteen nations were present at the session of the ECOSOC which decided the fate of WIDF. Of these several did not speak. In the voting, five – the USSR, Czechoslovakia, Yugoslavia, India and Egypt – kept their promise to support us; six – which included the USA, Cuba, Britain and Nationalist China – voted for exclusion. But there were seven abstentions. It is significant that the United States did not receive more positive support.

The entire speech of Mr Hotchkis, US representative, does not appear in the summary report. I have it in full. It contains a final paragraph marked as to be inserted in his speech to ECOSOC, 6 April 1954.

This was his peroration:

> And in conclusion, Mr President, I am impressed with what historians tell us, that several million years ago, a giant animal known as the dinosaur dominated the world. He was so large that he felt reasonably secure in his size, just as this wonderful group in the United Nations, bound together by the common hope and desire for peace, is likewise a kind of dinosaur in this world today. But what happened to the dinosaur? The paleontologists tell us that a few rats came across the eggs of the dinosaur, devoured the eggs, and the dinosaur, as large as he was, as strong as he was, perished from the earth. We as the United Nations should not allow any rats to devour the eggs of our perpetuation and our success as the United Nations.

Hearing this, I went like a rocket up the flights of moving stairs in search of Dag Hammarskjöld, to protest against this insult to the women of WIDF. I got as far as Mr Humphries, of whose official duties I am uncertain. But to him, in my almost incoherent anger of protest, I remember saying that it was time the United Nations learned from the British that there was something called parliamentary language which made it possible to conduct controversial debate without gross insults.

Mr Hotchkis gave a handle to the Press for their comical comment, which cannot have enhanced his reputation, though it did not bring much help to WIDF, smeared as it was with communism.

Cedric Belfrage, interviewing me, made points about the dinosaur in the topical slang of the day. This defined the expression 'to lay an egg' as committing a gross blunder. An august and wise body like the United Nations might be large, powerful, but it does not resemble a dinosaur, and it does not 'lay eggs'. I was most grateful to Cedric for his gallant support, as I was to the handful of other friends that I was able to find in my short stay.

Being the WIDF delegate was not very pleasant; it led to some obvious ostracism, several people showed clearly in the lounge that they were not on speaking terms with me, or avoided sitting near me in the canteen. On the other hand, Elinor Kahn did all she could to help on practical matters and procedure. And Paul Robeson's wife was constantly at my side, full of fun, and not the least intimidated by authority. She arranged for me to meet women whose political views might bring them into trouble, so that at least I might know that I was not without support in the country.

I think it was customary for some embassies to take some note of their women delegates to the commission – the British authorities entirely ignored my existence. But there was one unexpected recognition and welcome. It came from my daughter Kate. I had written to her saying that, with my present political errand, I was persona non grata, and that she and her husband would be wise to take no notice of me. He was in the State Department; they were in Washington, with their eldest son, David, just out of babyhood. Highly indignant that owing to my restricted movements she could not receive her mother in her own home, Kate rang me up and proposed that they come to New York to visit me. So there was a family party at the Tudor Hotel, which, apart from being a bit disturbed by unfamiliar surroundings, David also enjoyed. For quite a time he would refer to me as his 'green Grandma' (I happened to wear a green dress), and he treasured a cheap picture book that I found time to buy for him.

Within the United Nations building one had a sense of complete absence of secrecy and a freedom that were at variance with many of the ideologies preached within it. Elinor Kahn took me down, for instance, to the basement where masses of UN archives were recorded on discs. It was possible, on payment, to obtain recordings of speeches. (This could be an advantage to some representatives who had to be responsible at home to their governments for what they had been saying.) I did get a gramophone disc of my constitutional argument to the NGO Committee. I am not sure if I still have it. Is my voice still in the archives?

That sense of liberty at the UN once you are 'in', seemed to me to be the general atmosphere of the country, once visa and permission to enter had been granted.

Taxi drivers in New York are famous for chatting to their clients. One asked me, 'Was I enjoying my visit to the United States? Would I like to stay here?' 'Well,' I said, 'perhaps visitors are not so welcome, they are not allowed to stay long.' To this he replied, 'I'll hide yer, if yer want to stay.' He had no idea of the identity of the dangerous person to whom he had made the offer.

Among the Soviet women there for the Women's Commission, who were very kind to me, was Nadia Chimach, whom I had met in Russia, and already counted as a friend. NGOs did not eat with government delegates, but a general place of meeting to talk – or to lobby – was the delegates' lounge. On one occasion I was introduced to Vyshinsky there. We spoke only briefly but, thinking of my own experience, I did say to him that he must find it, at times, disagreeable to be working at United Nations. Throwing his hands apart in an expansive gesture, he replied, 'Madame, c'est mon sort.' ('It is my fate.')

Chairman Madame Minerva Bernardino gave her cocktail party for members of the Women's Commission. I talked there with the tall, impressive delegate from Haiti, and others. More significant was a short conversation with the French delegate, Madame Marie-Hélène Lefaucheux, who signed to me, and stepped into the bathroom, where, sitting on the edge of the bath, she secretly explained to me that large numbers of French women had great sympathy with the efforts of WIDF but, as was evident, they did not have government support. She was a remarkable woman, who became, I think, owner of Renault cars. She died in a plane accident on what may well have been one of the many official journeys which she made.

The most comical incident was my encounter at that party with the British male delegate, Mr Attlee, whose presence I resented both because of his sex and the support given by our government to the expulsion of WIDF. Glass in hand, I approached him. 'Mr Attlee, do you enjoy being here in New York, acting jackal to the American lion?' He was, naturally, a bit taken aback. Precisely at that moment a Press flash photograph was taken. I had never thought of the presence of photographers. However, there we both are still, among my photo archives, in that dramatic pose.

When I knew that I would have to leave New York, Mrs Robeson and I had the idea of giving a farewell party from WIDF to those connected with the commission. Such parties were permitted in the delegates' lounge. We asked some official, who seemed to give consent. So the invitations were sent out with a message from me to the effect that WIDF regretted its departure, but would, in due course, return. On the day and time of the reception, Mr Fomin came to meet me in the corridor and said, 'Madame Grace, the security guards are at the doors of the delegates' lounge. If you intend to go in there, the Soviet women will go with you.'

I burst out laughing. 'Mr Fomin,' I said, 'honour is satisfied – I have many friends who will entertain my guests for me in the delegates' lounge.' I do not know if he was relieved or disappointed. I had no wish to cause embarrassment to the Soviet women or to be myself involved in undignified scuffles at the door.

I made my preparations for departure. Quite a large posse of press men accompanied me right up to the plane. I heard cheerful remarks about 'giving her a good send off – whether from friends or enemies, I did not care to find out. At heart I felt the men were treating an affair concerning women with indifference and contempt.

I was disappointed, but I thought that even with greater experience and skill, I would still not have succeeded for WIDF against such relentless and callous opposition.

I arrived home to find little interest in my doings in the press, except in *Tribune*, which printed a whole column explaining what my visa restrictions would mean, if similar restrictions were imposed in London. There was also a story of the debates on the fate of WIDF and the disgraceful support given by our government representative to its exclusion. I did write something about the romantic glass skyscraper of the United Nations for the *New Statesman* but I am not sure if it appeared.

When I met some of my women colleagues to report, I found that their chairman, Mrs Mollie Pritt, wife of D.N. Pritt, the famous left-wing barrister, who was their chairman, had been invited to go to an important congress of Indian women in Calcutta. She had not been too well and felt that the heat at that time in India would be too much for her. Would I go instead? She was even able to offer me some loose-fitting cotton seersucker dresses suitable for the climate that would almost certainly fit me. Attending the congress meant only a short visit, but it did mean leaving almost at once. My passport was in order. I was free to go. I said that I would probably accept.

Now I found there were family troubles. John's marriage had not been going well. They had, as young people began to do in those days, spent money they could ill afford on consulting psychiatrists. Russell had wanted a place to live, in or near London. His wife Peter had left him; a divorce was contemplated. He had bought a house in Richmond not far from the small flat in which John and his family were living. They had, as he wished, seen to all the adaptations of the house and moved in to share and run it, and also to give him some care.

The three daughters, away at school, were home only in holidays. This seemed an arrangement that pleased everyone. John, especially, was proud of his family's main part of the house and the garden that he had created: it seemed to him that he now had a real home. John had begun writing; in this his father encouraged him and gave him and Susan to understand that they need not worry about money; what he, Russell himself earned, would be shared with them 'rather than give it all to the Tax Collector'. John's first book, *Abandon Spa Hot Springs*, published by the Gabberbocker Press was favourably received. His *Pursuit of the Pearl*, a longer book, had been written but has never seen publication.

John and Susan were closely involved in helping Bertie get through the turmoil of feeling and finance over the divorce. When, in 1952, he married Edith Finch, they were surprised, like most of Russell's friends, but they were, as John has insisted, glad, because this would lift some responsibility for his ageing father from them. All seemed to be going well in the household, until I heard that Susan, followed by John, had left the house, and they had moved to a flat in Bloomsbury belonging to a friend.

When I saw John just before leaving for New York, I knew he was unhappy and undecided about work and a place to live. He had never fully explained to me just why they had left the house in Richmond. Now his father had been worrying him to remove his furniture from the house if he did not mean to return to it. At this time I knew that John had no place to put it nor money to pay for the removal. When they had spent some time with me in Cornwall, where I was taking in summer visitors, in 1953, I urged them to get a home of their own and they had a cottage in mind. But I could see then that there was little of the marriage partnership remaining to provide the will and energy to achieve this. I still had a faint hope that return to Richmond might be possible, as I was making only a bare living and could not finance the whole family.

Early in 1954 John's problem was temporarily solved by the offer of a cottage at Portmeirion in Wales, together with work for the Clough

Williams-Ellises in connection with their hotel and other projects.

Russell's solicitors now asked me to come and see them. They put to me a proposal from Russell that I should join with him in a Chancery action to obtain the right to undertake the care of John's children. It seemed that he considered the parents, especially their mother, irresponsible. I was deeply shocked. The proposal recalled all my distress about the Chancery action over John and Kate, in which, lacking money to fight, I had been obliged to give way. I knew that I could not act with Russell in the use of the law to do to John's children what it had been able to do to mine. I told the lawyers that I did not agree that there was any cause for anxiety about the children; at present their nursery governess was always in the house to look after them in holidays, and see to clothes and everything for them. On the contrary, I said that there was far more cause to worry about John, who was unhappy, overwrought and faced with a situation which he did not know how to resolve. I explained that I had just promised to go to India, but when I came back, I would like to meet Russell and see what we could do to help him. I thought that this suggestion and reassurance about the children would prevent any hasty action being taken.

As so often happens in life (and most disastrously in political affairs) the truth about events only comes to light too late to affect action or decision. Only now, for the first time, have I learned from John what really happened about his leaving the joint home at Richmond, which had seemed to promise happiness and opportunity for all concerned.

A couple formerly on the staff at Dartington, who had left there and since become exceedingly fervent converts to Christianity, proceeded to explain to John and Susan that it was not proper for them to live in the paternal home. The right course for all, when adult, was to set up a home of their own. This interfering, dogmatic advice had no relation whatever to the true family situation and the rightness, in the circumstances, of what had been done. John and his father, both at a difficult moment in their lives, had been in need of support that they had been able mutually to give and receive. Susan had a pleasant home with the children and for them there was a very agreeable nurse-governess, and a lively grandfather upstairs. However, Susan was a restless spirit; she was already quite often away. She appears also to have been afflicted with religion, and influenced by her fellow sufferers' curious, irrelevant interpretation of conscience.

When I asked John now why he did not oppose Susan but concurred with a decision against his will and judgement, he replied that if he had not, Susan would have left him. Hearing this, actually now, so far off from the event, I saw once again that agonised, distraught young man in whom, though he told me nothing, I had sensed a smouldering anger at having been let down by all those closest to him. And I myself felt – virtually physically – the heartache brought by that memory. In that departure was the key to the sequence of his tragically unfulfilled life.

In 1954, ignorant of the full story, I carried on with my political obligations and was by May in India for my first and only visit to that country. I flew by Indian plane, with a brief stop-over in Cairo. At the airport stall for gifts and souvenirs, not having much to spend and more taste for literary material, I picked up a pamphlet that cost very little. My purchase, to my surprise, delighted the man behind the counter. It proved to be Nasser's statement to his people on his first taking power. I still possess it.

I recall the dreamy heat in the plane as blinds were closed against the sun. And, either on this trip, or returning, I was briefly in Beirut – which seemed to me then a blissful place of beauty and charm, created by nature itself for lazy, luxurious, sea-bathing holidays. Now it is destroyed by that same religious fervour which, to me, far from being men's highest aspiration, is the curse which stands between humanity and peace on earth.

In Bombay, the eastern sun pervaded me from shoe soles upwards as I stepped on to the tarmac and met the typical, garlanded, Indian welcome from some energetic, remarkable Indian women. Serious in politics, they also had feminine fun in showing me how they fold and tuck a sari, while their hospitality taught me the pleasures of Indian food.

The congress was to be in Calcutta, where I was hospitably received by a professor and his wife. He astounded me by bringing my book *Hypatia* from the shelf and then, saluting me in the courteous Indian fashion, said, 'You have an undying place in the history of feminism.' I simply did not know how to express my thanks for such a compliment. In the face of Indian warmth in expression of feeling and grace of their approach, the inhibited Northerner feels inadequate.

When I looked out of my bedroom window I saw a breadfruit tree, a raven and other birds. With the cattle and other livestock mingling with the traffic in the streets, my first impression of India was of a place teeming with all forms of life. Calcutta seemed not a city, almost part of wild country bordering on the jungle.

Besides the main streets of Calcutta, I visited also the shanty towns, where people lived in rough huts with muddy tracks between them, lacking water supply and sewage disposal. At night, as we walked back from sessions of the congress we passed, or stepped over, the sleeping bodies of the homeless.

The congress itself was remarkable. Women from all kinds of occupations and environments were there – some had come many miles on foot. There were other women from civil service departments in the towns, such as Bombay. The arrangements for feeding all these women were impressive, not only in the numbers catered for, but in the simplicity of it all: according to their custom, they sat crosslegged on the floor of a courtyard eating their modest meals, without the sophistication of chairs and tables, knives and forks. It was surprising too, to see a conference directed from a platform of similarly seated women. There were, of course, plenty of chairs in the hall.

The congress opened early in June with fraternal greetings read by Betty Healey of Australia for WIDF and others from Pakistan and Nepal. The object of the conference was to set up an all-India Women's Organisation which would co-ordinate the groups of women working for the cause of the rights of women and children; it would also be able to co-operate with such organisations overseas. Mrs Hajrah Begum was the secretary of the National Co-ordinating Committee. She had put in immense hard work for this event. So also had Mrs Charusheela Gupta of the Bombay Co-ordinating Committee. Delegates from the Civil Supplies and Staff Association from Bombay were Miss M.M. Kothare, Miss S.R. Khale, and Miss A.M. Mukerji. All these, like so many other delegates in other regions who were aware of the need for women to organise, had been stimulating interest and discussion and raising money for delegates' expenses for the forthcoming congress.

One of the first items on the agenda was to decide on a name for the new organisation. After lively discussion, the title, National Federation of Indian Women, was accepted with applause. The language of the conference was English. With more discussion it was decided that English and Hindi should be the only two languages of the organisation. The abundance of languages in India might otherwise cause separatist sections of the movement; the use of two languages only would signify a national unity. This decision was also applauded and the organisers were asked to see to it that reports and documents in Hindi should be accurate and dependable.

The enthusiasm and business-like approach of this gathering was very encouraging. Some women did not want all the work left to their leaders and asked for definite counsel as to what ordinary members should do. Women from Nepal protested to me with burning anger that my government was still recruiting men from their areas to serve in the British army. A resolution of protest was also passed about the refusal of visas by the Indian government to women from communist organisations or countries, as also for the difficulty many had had to get to the great congress of WIDF in Copenhagen. There were, of course, resolutions on all aspects of women's rights; about marriage, divorce, the virtual sale of daughters, the poverty of widows. And, as we, on the organising committee, sorted out the resolutions sent in by groups of ordinary members, one clear impression emerged – how very many of them, even on torn scaps of paper, by-passed all concern with women's rights and concentrated on protest against the Hiroshima bomb.

In my speech to the congress I explained that I was there on behalf of WIDF, that, like my colleague from Australia, I had come because, with passports of the Commonwealth, we could not be refused visas.

> On this my first visit to India I bring greetings from the women of the National Assembly in Britain to their friends and sisters – the Indian women who are working for progress and women's rights.
>
> I come chiefly as a representative of the Women's International Democratic Federation, whom I represented also recently at the Commission on the Status of Women at the United Nations.
>
> I want to make clear here in India the work of this important women's organisation. WIDF was founded in Paris in 1945, its president is Madame Eugenie Cotton, a distinguished French woman, and its general secretary Marie Claude Vaillant-

Couturier, another French woman who was imprisoned by the Germans.

United States spokesmen have so frequently stated that the WIDF is a Communist organisation. But I want to make clear that this is not true. The federation has members in more than sixty countries, stretching from Canada and South America, to France, Italy, India, Russia and China.

It will be seen that it bridges the Iron Curtain and this is one reason why I support it, because I believe as Mrs Pandit said in the early days of the United Nations, that women want a whole world, not a world split in two by the Cold War.

The federation has done and is doing magnificent work in encouraging women to fight for better status – especially in the non-self governing territories of the world. But just because the federation tries to help and encourage the women of these countries, it incurs the enmity of some other governments who control colonial territories and who do little or nothing to improve the lives of the women in those countries.

I went on to explain what had happened on my visit to the United Nations in New York, remarking that the Indian representative on the ECOSOC had both spoken and voted against expelling WIDF, saying that it had done great work for women and children and had never departed from the principles of the United Nations Charter. I emphasised that WIDF had over two million members in Italy, it did not exclude on grounds of race or creed any who were 'united in demanding peace, a better status for women, and schools and healthy homes for all the children of the world'.

A march to publicise the congress was planned. Tentatively, I asked if I, though a foreign guest, could take part. They were delighted. 'Oh, oh, England will take a pole,' they said. Long and impressive, the procession of really beautiful women made its way through the streets; the entire tramway service stopped to honour, and, no doubt, to admire them.

It was astonishing when sharing the enthusiasm and excitement of those moments how little one felt the fatigue and oppression of the great heat. Two energetic young women, who took some care of me, remarked that in their political work they found so much to do and interest them that they no longer took the midday rests in which their mothers usually indulged. For myself, I did find the climate trying – I got prickly heat, for which these resourceful young women at once procured soothing calamine powder.

The great outdoor meeting in the evening, at which I had to speak, was a strange experience. We stood on a slightly raised platform with a loud-speaker and some lights. I became conscious of a vast crowd extending in the half dark, who would hear my voice, but whose faces, except those quite near, I could not see. Yet actors on a proscenium stage have to meet this test and communicate the quality and feeling of their performance to their audience. I did my best, as clouds of moths and flying insects attracted by the glowing light, whizzed about my head – and I spoke from the depth and sincerity of my beliefs. I do remember one sentence, recalling how pioneers of the women's fight for the vote had inspired me: 'To follow in their footsteps, you have set your feet on a very hard road, a task in which I wish for you the courage not to falter and lose heart.'

In my short stay in India I was able to visit Delhi, where Dr Suyata Chauduri gave me hospitality and took me to see a village nearby where she was doing work among the mothers and children. She came later to England and to the Mothers Committee which we formed.

I asked if I might see Nehru and, to my surprise, this was arranged. With him I talked briefly of socialism in England and regretted the hostility to contacts with communism. I did not forget to raise with him the question of refusal of visas adopted so foolishly by many governments. I was not aggressive, the talk was pleasant and friendly. He was most courteous.

One very practical custom I noticed as I entered the building – over the door hung a great heavy mat, soaked and constantly dripping in water, which was lifted, then readjusted, to exclude the burning heat from the outer air. No doubt better means of controlling temperature in Government buildings have now been installed.

In Delhi I visited also homes and institutions of women and young girls. I went east from Calcutta by plane into Bengal. My visit to Agartala remains a landmark in my memory, though I cannot remember the names of the friends who received me there. It was a small place, the streets were rough and rutted with mud. I was greeted by two lovely young women, daughters of the local doctor. I slept in a simple flat (I think that possibly its occupant had vacated it for my visit). The two girls sang to me, telling me that in India there was special music for night-time, and for the morning. In the morning with them came one or two men to greet me. They wrapped about me a scarlet sari, and as I sat in a chair, they greeted me with ceremony, as if I were a guru. I still have that sari! I had soon to go back to Calcutta, but there was still some time to talk with the girls. Telling me of their life, they spoke of actually going into the jungle on tiger hunts. Embracing me in farewell they said many times, 'I pray God that you will come again to Agartala.' As I stir the memory of those times, it is that word Agartala which ever recurs and with it the music and appeal of those voices; my conscience reproaches me that I never did return.

I was able to enjoy seeing how the Indian people travel casually and make themselves at home on their trains. Friends conducted me to the Punjab, where I was able to stand and watch how in the Golden Temple the old holy men sit ceaselessly reading and turning the pages of the scriptures. This is never allowed to stop. Down below, people were bathing in the sacred river. We visited the simple mud cottages of the poorer people, in which, as it was explained to me, a room could be kept clean by covering its walls – if desired, each day – with fresh clay-like mud that would dry almost like a coating of distemper. On this visit I felt the heat of the sun too severely on my head so they offered me a topee. But, laughing, I said that I could not put on a symbol of the British Raj.

It was important not to omit a visit to Amritsar and place a wreath on the memorial to those protesters who, caught in a confined space, had been killed by the reckless firing of a high British officer. As I went to the memorial and stood before it, I was aware of the big brown watchful eyes of the crowd that accompanied us. The thought came to me that when those similar reproachful brown eyes, thus fixed upon their overlords, had multiplied into millions throughout the great continent, no government would have had the nerve to do otherwise than ashamedly withdraw and set the people free.

The story of my visit to India is inadequate because I do not have a proper record of the names of those lovable and capable women who did so much for me. To those who still live and remember those days in 1954, I offer once more my thanks. In all events, the congress itself and the contacts made bore fruit, as will be seen, for the growth of our efforts in the future.

Hardly had I got back from India when it became necessary for me to go to Geneva. ECOSOC, as was the custom, was having one of its sessions in the United Nations building there, alternating as it did with New York. A report on the events of the Women's Commission was likely; we could have opportunities to lobby about our exclusion. In addition, a conference of NGOs was taking place. Jessie Street, an Australian, who did an immense amount of work on behalf of women and their efforts for peace, had NGO status on behalf of the Anti-Slavery Society. She raised with Dr Gerhart Riegner, chairman of the NGOs Committee, the position of WIDF and the possibility of my attendance at the conference.

He wrote to me on 17 June from Geneva to say that, since we had lost status, we could attend as observers, but not as members, and only if the Bureau agreed to grant this. He could not guarantee that they would do so, or that I would be allowed to speak.

I replied on 20 June and on 24 June I was in Geneva, armed with various documents, addresses and phone numbers. I saw Dr Riegner and attended the conference, whose members and discussions I found both interesting and pleasant. Dr John A.F. Ennals, representing the NGO of the United Nations Association, was the treasurer of the NGOs committee. He was most helpful to me. A statement on behalf of WIDF was presented to the conference. In the light of our experience, the right of NGOs to criticise actions of the United Nations and its members was discussed, and a decision taken that NGOs should demand and uphold that right.

The ECOSOC session began on 29 June. As I was walking along one of the great corridors of the United Nations building, I met Mr Humphries, the official in New York whom I had reached and to whom I addressed my furious protest against WIDF women being called 'rats'. He came and shook hands and remarked how pleased he was to see me here again. Minerva Bernadino was of course in Geneva and invited me to come and see her at her hotel. She gave me good advice about how to prepare documents for United Nations' sessions. I had some difficulty with my mentors in Berlin about this. They would always write long argumentative scripts, putting *everything* in. I tried to persuade them that at times brevity, and some tact, might be more helpful to our cause.

Minerva was a delight. She chatted to me about her opponents in debate. The US and UK tactics and policies were her *bêtes noires* and favourite targets. She also discussed how men approached women in politics. They would ask her if she was acting as a politician or as a woman. She thought this nonsense. 'What does this mean? After all, I say to men – I am woman,' and she exhaled to the full, an expansive femininity. I said I had the impression that men of the Latin races always tended, rather more than English and Americans, to look on women with sexy eyes. At the same time it was said that 'Latins were lousy lovers'. On this she did not deliver a verdict! Minerva and I enjoyed this little interlude in our exacting and, at times, excruciatingly boring work with commissions and debates, amid the jungle of United Nations files. Later, for some days, I had the great enjoyment of watching her manoeuvring her skilful way through that ECOSOC session. I became absorbed, excited as crucial points were made. I took copious notes, not relevant in these times, and now very difficult to read.

Some success was achieved in establishing the relevance of the continuous presence of WIDF, and the rights of NGOs under the constitution. After all, they are still the only form of access of the general public to United Nations' procedure.

I returned home in time to accept some bookings from summer visitors to Cornwall. As regards my family, Kate was settled in the United States, John and his wife had that cottage in Wales in return for some temporary work, while he hoped to go on writing. Harriet and Roderick had both shown an independent spirit. Roderick was still at the polytechnic; he still earned and pursued his studies while doing an easygoing night watch job at the premises of a firm of some friends. This was certainly better for him than merely keeping house in our flat when I was away. He had many friends and we had not been able to see much of each other. Harriet, I believe, quite enjoyed the job she had on the youth side of the United Nations Association in London. But this was coming to an end, and it must have been at this time or a little later that she asked me for some advice as to what to look for next. She could get responsible secretarial posts with private employers. It occurred to me that some sort of Civil Service job would offer greater security and freedom from the risk of the sack at the whim of the boss. There was work in the Civil Service which did not involve devotion to politics or war. We discovered that the government needed more factory

Left: Dora Russell's daughter, Harriet, sent this photo of herself 'To darling old Lil, Merry Christmas from Harry' when she was twelve or thirteen

Right: Her son, Roddy, and his father, St Stephen's Green, Dublin, 1946. Harriet's caption to the photo was, 'Daddy is standing on that little fence so as not to appear shorter than his fourteen-year-old son (which, of course, he is!)'

Roddy as a promising young cricketer, 1949

БРИТАНСКИЙ СОЮЗНИК

№ 34 (415)   20 августа 1950   Цена 3 рубля

The front page of a 1950 copy of *British Ally*

ПРОЕКТ СОЗДАНИЯ ЕВРОПЕЙСКОЙ АРМИИ

ЗАПАДНЫЕ ДЕРЖАВЫ ОДОБРЯЮТ СОЗДАНИЕ ОБОРОНИТЕЛЬНОГО ФРОНТА

НОВЫЙ МОРСКОЙ ВОКЗАЛ

СОЗЫВ ПАРЛАМЕНТА

ОБОРОНИТЕЛЬНЫЙ ФРОНТ

ЕВРОПЕЙСКАЯ АРМИЯ И АТЛАНТИЧЕСКИЙ ПАКТ

АНГЛО-АМЕРИКАНСКИЕ ОБЫЧНЫЕ ВИЗИТЫ

РОЛЬ БРИТАНИИ В ЕВРОПЕ

ОБЪЕДИНЕНИЕ СУВЕРЕННЫХ ПРАВ

«УГО» И ВОПРОС ПАРТИЙНОЙ ПОЛИТИКИ

НОВАЯ МАГНЕТРОН

ГОРНЯКИ ПОДДЕРЖИВАЮТ ООН

КОНГРЕСС МОЛОДЕЖИ 40 СТРАН В ЛОНДОНЕ

РЕАКТИВНЫЕ ПАССАЖИРСКИЕ САМОЛЕТЫ

ПЕРВЫЕ ЗАКАЗЫ БРИТАНИИ

ЦЕННОСТЬ ЛАГЕРЕЙ

The visit of the women's delegation to the USSR in August 1951 included a boat trip on an Armenian lake. Dora Russell (left) links arms with two other delegates

John Russell, about 1954

During Dora's visit to the UN Status of Women Commission in March 1954, she asked Mr Attlee, British delegate to the Commission, 'Do you enjoy being here in New York, acting jackal to the American lion?'

A march of women to publicise the Women's Congress, Calcutta, 1954

Dora addressing the Congress

Above: Dora and other delegates taking time off to dance at the Women's Congress in Peking, April 1956 *Below:* An exchange of greetings in Shanghai

Delegates to the Seminar of Women, USSR 1956, with a man from the battleship *Aurora*

Delegates on a visit to Leningrad, 1956

The send-off from Edinburgh of the Women's Caravan of Peace on 20 May 1958

The bus crossing the frontier from Yugoslavia into Albania

One of the peace caravaners with the two Albanian drivers

The Aldermaston March, 1959

Carn Voel, 1962

'Our Lil' with Harriet's son, Tom, 1964

inspectors. This could be dull, but *might* prove interesting, and certainly useful. Though she was dubious of success, Harriet decided to apply. While a civil servant I had myself several times been one of a board interviewing applicants. I had seen what types made good impressions and I was convinced that my Harriet, with her modest self assurance and capable air, was one of these. I guessed right. She was accepted and went in to the service at the precise moment when the salary was going up and lengths of leave being extended. The only snag was that her first assignment took her north to Manchester.

I was glad to be back in my home in Cornwall but I was constantly worried about money. Not much could be made out of summer visitors without improving the accommodation I could provide there. My marriage, the school then the Ministry had taken me out of the running for ordinary jobs in education. My work for Marks & Spencer had only been temporary. Eric Estorick had left there and made a good marriage into a commercial family. I still did some ghost writing for him and we had been writing quite a good spy thriller together. I had applied for many post-war official jobs for which my good French and German would have been useful. I did well in interview, but never got the job. I think the embargo on either communist or fascist sympathisers ruled me out. I was assured by kind official friends that this was not so, but watching political trends, I did not believe them. I saw no way to write a book which might not lead to some kind of public argument about Russell's differences with me. I did try to get Victor Gollancz to finance me to go and write about China – it was a very good idea but he would not take the risk.

For the political work which I had undertaken I took nothing but my expenses; I did it because I believed these contacts were important and had to be made by someone, and above all by a free agent, not official or hired by either side in the controversies.

Thus in August 1954 I was ending the summer season with a holiday for John's three girls and Miss Griffiths who looked after them. John came from Wales to enjoy Cornwall and their company with me until they had to go back to boarding school. When finally John and I were alone, he told me that Susan had left him for a young poet. He had left their cottage to stay with friends, but did not wish to return to Wales. Longmans had offered him to write a history of the Russell family. He set about it there and then. He was bitter and lonely, estranged from his father over his departure from the Richmond house. Despondent and uncertain of the future, we prepared to go up to my flat in Hampstead, where I had let a room to my friend Roxanne Arnold and her mother. It was a pleasure and comfort to have them there. John was so depressed that whenever he went out I began to worry that he might kill himself. He had once, when unhappy, become terrified when he felt a sudden urge to throw himself out of a train.

One morning early he had disappeared. I got frightened and consulted Roxanne, wondering what to do to find him. 'We will first make a cup of tea,' she said. And while we had our cuppa, to our relief John walked in. Roxanne, with due presence of mind, did not say 'Where on earth have you been?' but simply, 'Just in time for a cup of tea, John.' I think he had been down to Richmond to see his children, home for the holidays, as it was near Christmas.

Not so long after this incident, when John was out, a call came from Richmond to tell me that he had been put into the psychiatric section of Guy's Hospital near London Bridge. Would I go there and take him pyjamas and anything else that he might need?

With that shock, which came without any previous consultation, began the long saga of anxiety about John's state of mind; medical advice, discussion and dispute; sojourns in and out of hospital, finally ending by John sharing my home with me whether in London or Cornwall, thus far, and for the rest of my life.

Notes

1. *Listener* 3.6.83, p. 2.
2. The BBC Russian Service 9.11.50, Anatole Goldberg.
3. European Service, General News Talk 31.10.50, Walter Kolanz.
4. Notes by our observer, Anatole Goldberg. Russian section 26.11.50.

9

SCIENCE SUCCUMBS TO THE COLD WAR

'In tragic life, God wot,
No villain need be! Passions spin the plot:
We are betrayed by what is false within.'
George Meredith

The fear and anxiety aroused by Hiroshima did not go away, but in those countries not themselves affected, life after the war had offered new interests in considerable variety. What is more, the imagination of ordinary people, including politicians, had not – could not – fully absorb the horror and danger for the future which now faced humanity.

Only scientists, or those in association with their work, could really understand what was involved. Bertrand Russell's speech to the Lords (1945) had said it all. But, as he later remarked, politicians then regarded scientists as peculiar people remote from life, whose utterances were irrelevant to politics, however useful might be their inventions in time of war. Scientists, on the other hand, even when faced with so alarming a fact and so severe a test as the atom bomb, still adhered to their traditional faith that scientific knowledge must be shared. And now this was not only right, but expedient, because soon the Russians would know the secret and be able to make a bomb themselves. Some form of international control and co-operation with the Soviet Union must be sought.

185

This was scarcely a matter for deliberation and decision at the United Nations because basically the subject of negotiation lay only between the makers and potential users of the bomb, the United States and the Soviet Union, and to a lesser extent Great Britain and France. These former allies had now, by fostering the bitter hostility of the renewed Cold War, rendered the atmosphere for negotiation exceedingly unpropitious. Nonetheless, politicians hastily began the attempt in the hope that some agreement with Russia might be reached while the Western powers still held the monopoly of the bomb.

The Baruch proposals put forward from the American government at the first meeting of the Atomic Energy Commission in New York on 13 June 1946, were summarily rejected by the Russians. In that same year the inner Cabinet, about three people, of the British Labour government had, in great secrecy, set in motion the making of the bomb for British defence. They also sought advice as to how to cajole or put pressure on the Soviet government to acquiesce in some form of international control. Their attitude was both ignorant and irrational. They wanted the bomb because they could not endure the humiliation of dependence on the Americans both for the making and possession of the first bombs, but also for the economic aid accepted to rehabilitate Europe. As regards the Russians, the power of their armies' advance and first arrival in Berlin roused fury and fear, rather than gratitude for help. These Western statesmen never used their imagination, or sought to find out what was the true economic state of the devastated Russian territories, or the post-war mood of her war-torn people. They conjured up visions of those cohorts that had crossed rivers and swept in triumph into East Germany embarking on an unstoppable advance to the Channel coast.

One of Britain's leading nuclear physicists, P.M.S. (later Lord) Blackett gave the Labour government, in great secrecy, the soundest advice, to this effect: 'That the USSR would capitulate before a threat alone can be excluded as not remotely possible.' On the contrary, he pointed out that the Russian reaction would be to speed up her nuclear research, consolidate her influence in the semi-satellite countries and strengthen her defence.[1]

This view was in tune with the balanced judgement which I had observed when he discussed with his colleagues of the Association of Scientific Workers whether the United Nations Security Council should work by democratic vote or, as he felt right, permit of a veto. Julian Huxley and others had been surprised at his view. But it seems to indicate that Blackett, knowing even before Hiroshima about the bomb and the secrecy on all new technology being preserved towards Russia, foresaw something like the situation the governments were now facing; what is more, he had less prejudice and better insight into what might be expected of Russian character and achievement.

Russell's speech to the Lords on the bomb had shown that he too was aware of the imbalance in the Security Council, on which, he said, the Soviet Union almost invariably found itself in a minority of one, and that therefore, in negotiation with the Soviet Union, the utmost delicacy was required.

Unhappily Blackett's foresight, both scientific and political, seems to have been ignored. At this point of crucial debate on the bomb Russell began to play a prominent and, in my view, a tragic role, in the attitude of the government and public opinion in Britain both to the bomb and the Soviet people. Blackett and Russell were both brilliant men, each outstanding in the academic discipline which he followed; not dissimilar in political outlook, but differing widely in temperament. Historically they were never, so far as I know, in active opposition. It is only in my own mind, as I look back, that I see them in contrast and wish that Blackett rather than Russell had been more listened to in these early stages of the nuclear debate.

Russell's distinction made him the first of the BBC Reith lecturers in 1948-9. In broadcasts both on the home and overseas services he became, in spite of Conservative press and party opposition, something like a Voice of Britain. And his broadcasts, given between 1945 and 1952, and about eighty-two in number, are on a great variety of topics, and do not contain attacks on the Soviet Union. But his political theory was constantly at variance with theirs. He was, naturally, much concerned with the influence and destiny of his own country. Mainly – as shown in the Reith lectures – he was upholding the position of the individual in relation to State power. And he had begun to adopt the view that some form of world government could ultimately be the only way to avoid war. The Soviet critics who picked on him as a 'howling wolf of capitalism' did him, on his expressed opinions, an injustice; but they could not be mistaken in discerning his underlying growing hatred and fear of communism, expressed, and now revealed by Clark's book,[2] in his correspondence with all his friends and colleagues.

The argument as to whether Russell favoured the 'preventive war', even dropping a bomb on Russia, his denials or forgetfulness as he grew old, has continued. To discuss this is a waste of time because it has been most clearly set out by Clark, and ends with Russell's own statement, in March 1959, to John Freeman on a BBC interview. In that he said he had definitely been in favour of such a threat and did not repent of it, because it appeared to him that the Baruch proposal of the Americans to internationalise the bomb when they still held the monopoly, was 'an extremely generous proposal and one which it would be very desirable that the world should accept'.[2]

His ambivalence about the Soviet government and people has always been to me a source of personal sorrow. At the outbreak of the Revolution he had felt, with most workers and intellectuals, in Wordsworth's famous words on the French Revolution, that it 'was bliss to be alive', and though Russell was not an adolescent, 'to be young was very heaven'. His standing with socialists greatly increased at that time. When socialists fell out with him for professing disillusion after his visit to Russia in 1920, I defended him then because, like him, I disliked the Marxist hold on Russian thinking. Nonetheless, I admired the courage and idealism of the Bolshevik leaders and their people and in that respect I have never changed. The rise of Stalin, his dominance and the period of his cruel persecutions did alter the image of Soviet Russia for those who had admired those ideals. But Stalin as warlord and post-war diplomatic chess player was no different from any of his rivals – the powerful supremos of State, West or East, American or British, who sought to move the pieces (populations, in fact) on the board.

As Blackett had predicted, Stalin, aware of enemies with the power to inflict a Hiroshima tragedy on his people, manoeuvred to strengthen his defences through control of potentially satellite states, meanwhile desperately speeding up atomic research so that Russia might equalise by possessing an atomic bomb herself. Equally predictable was the reaction of the terror-struck Western statesmen to Stalin's unwise move to control the whole of Berlin.

But how could Stalin ever have been persuaded that the Baruch proposals were, as Russell suggested, 'generous', in the face of the bitter propaganda, threats, actual invasions which his country had endured ever since 1917, on account of the political doctrine and principles on which, by that very revolution, the constitution of his country had been founded? Western diplomats were angered at his determination to control Poland; but, in 1920, Polish armies, with their encouragement, had been advancing on Moscow. International control, world government at this stage would mean nothing less than Anglo–American, and ultimately, American capitalist hegemony. However stained Stalin's record in destroying his colleagues or those considered subversives, it later appeared that unshaken loyalty to the principles of the 1917 Revolution was the dominant faith of his life.

In 1949, Russia, having equalised in the nuclear bomb race, and acquired an ally in Mao Tse Tung's communist China, the two powers began what I have described as their peace initiative. This was met, as we saw, with hostile misrepresentation and attempts by the West deliberately to undermine the faith of the Soviet peoples in communism and their own government. Western statesmen made no moves for peace; into the bargain they attempted to suppress all initiatives for peace with the Soviets made by individuals or groups among their own populations. The Iron Curtain had split Europe in half. The politicians' policy of intimidation appeared to have reached a dead end.

It would seem that most men of science, while secretly offering advice to the politicians, were beginning to accept that nuclear policy was a matter for governments. Accused by the lay public of having devised and instigated the dropping of the bomb, they were not sorry to divest themselves of responsibility. At a meeting of the British Association for the Advancement of Science, Sir Edward Appleton, FRS, of the Government Scientific Research Department, had maintained that a scientist could not be held responsible for the results outside his laboratory of the discoveries made within it. I had then challenged him from the floor, asserting that a teacher had responsibility for the results of his or her teaching outside the classroom.

The stalemate of the politicians was broken and the hope of a possible 'preventive war' revived by the outbreak on 25 June 1950, of the Korean war. The swift action of the United States in calling a meeting of the Security Council and elevating the hostilities to a United Nations' war has already been related. This involved the sending of troops by all United Nations' members.

189

From the Soviet side came no admission of guilt, but at the Warsaw Conference in 1950 came a plea for peace, specifically in Korea. In 1951, after a year of hostilities, the World Council of Peace, representing the Soviet and communist supporters, issued from a meeting in Helsinki (20-23 July) a plea for an armistice in Korea where 'the year of frightful struggle had demonstrated the futility of attempting to resolve international conflicts by the use of force'. It called for negotiation to lead to a pact of peace by the Five Great Powers, which would be 'open to all'.

> It is because the United Nations has failed to fulfil its prime
> object, the maintenance of peace by peaceful means, that
> negotiation between the Big Five is today the only method of
> adjusting the present disputes. The first result of a Pact of Peace
> between the Big Five would be to restore its original mission to
> the United Nations.

It called for 'progressive, simultaneous and controlled disarmament' and the 'absolute and likewise strictly controlled prohibition of atomic weapons and other engines of mass destruction.'

Thus far, in an effort to probe the secrecy surrounding the war in Korea, the views and efforts of both sides have appeared repeatedly in my pages. I leave them as written. Only now have I learned of research by an American which vindicates both our disbelief in the official version and our desperate attempts to bring the war to an end.

Professor Bruce Cumings of the University of Washington is the author of *The Origins of the Korean War*. His letter to the *Guardian* (9 August 1983) fully justifies those of us who, in 1950, maintained that the atrocities of Syngman Rhee in South Korea led him to start the war to avoid the loss of United States' subsidy and support. Professor Cumings also corroborates Jon Halliday's account (*Guardian*, 25 July 1983) of the 1950 contemporary actions in South Korea and Britain. What is more, he is able to supplement his views from documents of our own Foreign Office[3] as to the 'brutality' and 'black reaction' of Syngman Rhee's regime, of the 'more disciplined' and 'less atrocious' behaviour of the northerners; and the statement of the first British representative to arrive after the war began: 'It appears from here that this war is being fought to make Korea safe for Syngman Rhee and his entourage.'

What is surprising is, first of all, the concealment in 1950 of the plain truth from the British public and those who had to fight the war, and the still stranger fact of the present apparent unwillingness to admit and publicise that truth to the American, British and European public and thus redress the false and unjust version of history.

The Korean war made its tragic mark on the contemporary condition, the future of nations, and on individuals involved. Its most important result was to rouse the scientists, at long last, to take some action about the nuclear threat of both the hydrogen and atom bombs.

There is no mention of Korea in Clark's life of Russell. My son John tells me that he and his then wife, Susan, argued repeatedly against his father's continued belief that only some powerful intimidation, or 'preventive war' would avail in the face of the Soviet refusal of the basis offered for negotiation. Aware of the danger, Russell went on with his speaking and writing for peace and continued his association with movements aspiring to world government.

The death of Stalin in 1953, the end of hostilities in Korea (though no peace), made no difference to the situation. Both sides began to accept what is now called the balance of terror.

Russell's almost hysterical utterances against communism and Russia in the early stages of the debate may have had some relation to the disturbed state of his own life. In 1949 his wife Peter had left him, taking their son; in the same year Colette[4] finally put an end to what, in her feeling, had been a long and patient utter devotion to a man who, professing love, had never been willing to show it by breaking ties with other women for a marriage with her. When, in 1952, Peter was divorcing Russell, according to John his father was in acute mental disturbance, desperately pacing the room and in need of companionship – even advice – which John and his wife sought to give. They were as astonished as everyone else when, aged eighty, he married once more, not Colette, but Edith Finch. Feeling some relief from responsibility, John and Susan were on a brief visit to me in Cornwall when Russell became ill, possibly with his old enemy bronchitis. Edith was seriously alarmed. At her request John and Susan immediately returned to Richmond. This last marriage proved stable and, almost certainly, coloured much of Russell's work until his death.

The passions that spin the plot do not all derive from the fervour of the patriot.

It is worth noting that 1952 was the date of the Vienna and Peking World Peace Congresses, to whose messages nobody but communists and a few left wingers paid any attention.

The attitude of equal vulnerability, but no surrender, continued to dominate the minds of statesmen both sides of the Iron Curtain. Whatever may have been the inspiration that prompted him, in June 1954 Russell moved to end the deadlock by suggesting to the BBC that he should do a broadcast to arouse people to the gravity of the issue of the H bomb.[5] How little the lay mind could grasp this is shown by Clark's account of how the BBC proposed to use his suggestion as a message, on the eve of Christmas, by Three Generations – Sally Graves, journalist, Roger Bannister, young sportsman, ancient intellectual Russell.

Russell replied angrily that their proposal was frivolous. What he had in mind was 'an appeal to mankind to turn back from universal suicide before it was too late'. For the Three Generations broadcast they could find 'some other old man'. This broadcast on 23 December, 'Man's Peril', in which Russell urged that he spoke neither as a Briton nor a European, but as a member of the human species, became the basis of the famous joint Einstein-Russell appeal. It stirred the consciences of anxious people world-wide; shoals of letters came in. Here are some of the words of this very famous broadcast:

> Was the human race so destitute of wisdom, so incapable of impartial love, so blind even to the simplest dictates of self preservation, that the last proof of its silly cleverness is to be the extermination of all life on our planet?
>
> I appeal to you as human beings – remember your humanity and forget the rest.
>
> Even the animals, whom no one could accuse of communism, or anti-communism, would perish with the rest.

Russell sought the help of a commission of neutral nations, of a world-wide meeting of scientists. A letter came from Joliot-Curie on the communist side. He was now President of the World Federation of Scientific Workers, who had already sought such an international meeting, so far without success.

Russell approached Einstein for support, which he hoped and expected to receive from some American scientists. While on his way to Paris to consult Joliot-Curie, he learned of Einstein's death – but fortunately a letter of acceptance from Einstein had arrived. An apparently interminable wrangle followed as to which men of science would, or would not sign the manifesto; as well as the exact wording of the manifesto itself. To sign might mean branding oneself as either pro- or anti-communist. Russell himself was chary of any association with Bernal, but knowing that East and West must show some sort of agreement, he did his best to meet points made by Joliot Curie.

Disappointed that he had no more than a mere dozen signatures, Russell nonetheless went ahead with a public meeting at the Caxton Hall with Joseph Rotblat, Professor of Physics at St Bartholomew's Hospital Medical College, in the chair, to launch the manifesto in Britain. This first definite, united, international action by scientists on a burning political issue, due mainly to Russell's determination and eloquence, met with popular attention and success. The quest which was to lead to the Pugwash Conferences and the start of the Campaign for Nuclear Disarmament was under way. This was 1955, ten years after Hiroshima, yet according to Clark's estimate 'the idea that scientists should concern themselves with world affairs was still discussed seriously only within a very small circle. Outside this it was considered certainly presumptive, possibly ill-informed, and probably Communist inspired.'[6]

For me, although after 1949 I met Russell only once again, there was naturally always some feeling of interest and sympathy in what he was doing, the more so when I felt we were, even if temporarily, on the same wave length.

For my son Roderick, the Korean war – a war actually in progress in which his country was pledged to take part and young men were being killed – presented a dilemma, because compulsory military service was still in force. He was not a pacifist, but he believed neither in this particular war, nor in the use of nuclear weapons. His position differed from that of the scientists; he could not take refuge in procrastination. He had to make a decision. He felt that his only course was to go to the Tribunal and make a conscientious objection, based on nuclear weapons, which, from statements made by Field Marshal Montgomery, were to be at the disposal of the British forces in NATO. Both he and

I believed that his objection had not the least chance of success, but he was anxious above all to give publicity to opposition to the bomb and incidentally, the Korean war. He needed two sponsors at the Tribunal to vouch for his sincerity. The Einstein Manifesto was receiving publicity. I suggested to him that he should approach Russell to be one of his sponsors. A potential soldier basing his objection on the bomb, and sponsored by the eminent co-author, with Einstein, of the manifesto, could at least obtain publicity which might impress and awaken public opinion.

Russell refused on the grounds that Roddy was a communist. I think at the time, Roddy was no longer a member of the Young Communist League, but at any rate, in making conscientious objection he was in direct opposition to Communist Party policy. I believed Russell had other motives. His refusal made me angry because, as publicity, the idea was superb. In the end, my own friend and former colleague Lena Jeger acted as one sponsor, and a friend of Roddy, John Lyons, a trade union official, was the other.

The statement covered only two short paragraphs on quarto paper. As far as I remember, it said quite simply that he was neither religious nor a pacifist; he believed war to be the worst evil for mankind but would nonetheless not refuse to fight. Nuclear weapons, however, were in a different category, aimed at entire peoples. He could not take service in any army that would use them.

The proceedings were very brief. To his surprise, and mine, and I suppose many others, the objection was granted. Roddy and his friends then sought to do publicity for the fact that refusal of 'the bomb' implied refusal of military service. But, as was expected, editors were not inclined to print such suggestions.

Roddy next had the option of choosing some form of alternative two-year service which the authorities would accept. This could be service such as agricultural work or helping in hospitals and institutions. With his strong feeling for the workers, and no doubt, with thoughts of the young men who had faced death in Korea, he decided to go down the mines. Accordingly, he went early in 1955 to Wakefield in Yorkshire to work in a nearby mine. He chose Yorkshire because, he told me, he hoped he might play cricket for the county.

After the Russell-Einstein Manifesto in 1955, some scientists, by creating the Pugwash Conferences, and other groups, endeavoured to keep the spirit of international scientific co-operation alive. There were those, like Professor Rotblat and Russell himself, who never gave up; but, for the most part, scientists now found themselves obliged to pursue researches which prepared for war, especially in the nuclear field, and to which vast amounts of money were devoted by bellicose governments intoxicated with their Cold War. The scientists obligingly found a word for their surrender – the gospel of 'nuclear deterrence' rules, OK? This is as far as the most brilliant masculine minds of the world scientists have ever been able to reach.

Notes

1. *Life of Bertrand Russell*, R.W. Clark, p. 250, Jonathan Cape and Weidenfeld & Nicolson, 1975.
2. Clark, *op cit*, pp. 522–528.
3. Foreign Office FK 1022/249 9.7.50; FK 1015/202 17.8.50; FK 1022/143 17.7.50.
4. Colette O'Neil, formerly wife of Miles Malleson, who had loved Russell since their first meeting in connection with support for conscientious objectors in 1918.
5. Clark, *op cit*, pp. 536, 537.
6. Clark, *op cit*, p. 543.

10

WOMEN MAKE
THE MOVES:
THE PEOPLE WAKE UP

_____

In spite of the warning of the Russell-Einstein manifesto of 1955, the public had continued hypnotised by the 'superior wisdom' of science and the incessant propaganda of the military. Current belief in the West held that all communists, whether inside or outside Russia, were desperately wicked and likely to embark on an aggressive war. Expressions of hatred left little scope for moves towards peace. The communist countries, on the other hand, were convinced by these expressions of hatred that the armies of the West were poised for attack as soon as they were satisfied that their weapons were adequate.

At this point the indefatigable WIDF called a World Conference of Mothers, 'for the defence of their children against war, for disarmament and friendship between the peoples'. It took place in Lausanne on 5–10 July 1955. Although I kept in touch with the movement, I now had John with me, and could not go away without getting some capable person, usually our good friend, 'our Lil', to come and look after him. There were also many complications about his affairs. I was therefore not able to be present at this new effort by WIDF.

The Mothers' Congress received remarkable support and messages from women and women's groups in very many countries. Women seemed to become aware that the nuclear bombs heralded much more than the usual threats of war, of which they were traditionally afraid. This was also the prelude to the awakening of the peoples of the world to the threat of annihilation.

Messages to the Mothers' Congress were received from many countries, groups and individuals. The original invitations to take part were sent out in an appeal translated into thirty-two languages! To this appeal seventy-nine countries responded. Every European country was there with twenty-four delegates; from the United States came sixteen. Other countries with delegates were: nine countries from Africa, eight from the Middle East, ten from the Far East. In some countries large meetings were organised to publicise the congress. In South Africa a massive demonstration of 2,000 women, that the police could not control, virtually took over Pretoria.

As regards the professions of the women delegates: there were thirty-two members of Parliament, nine lawyers, 150 factory workers, peasants and other wage-earners, 398 housewives, ninety-seven educators, fifty-five doctors, forty-one writers and journalists, eleven students and twenty-three workers in cultural and scientific fields.

Messages came from Queen Elizabeth of Belgium; Madame Irene Joliot-Curie, French scientist; Madame Olga Lepechinskaya, Academy of Sciences USSR; Dr Dorothy Needham, Fellow of the Royal Society, England; Sybil Thorndike; Agnes Stapledon and Phoebe Cusden of the Women's International League for Peace and Freedom; Thea Arnold, former member of the West German Bundestag; Anna Seghers, East German writer; Charlotte Bass, Progressive Party Candidate for Vice-President of the United States in 1952; Florence Gowgiel, Chairman of the 'Save Our Sons' Committee, USA; Idell Umbles, President of the Chicago 'Women for Peace' and Mrs Paul Robeson. From the Far East, Soong Ching Ling, Vice-President of the Permanent Committee of the National People's Congress of China; Amrit Kaur, Minister of Health for India; Rameshwari Nehru, Deputy Minister for Rehabilitation and Uma Nehru, Ganga Devi, Mrs Khongman – all three members of the Indian Parliament; also Mrs Arudji Kartawinata, Vice-President of the Indonesian Parliament.

Here I quote extracts from the important message of Amrit Kaur:

I have often felt during my long career of social service that women have not played the part which, by reason of their innate qualities they are fitted to play in the matter of friendly relations between man and man, between communities and between nations . . .

197

Gandhiji taught us that the best way – by no means the easiest – to combat evil, was to non-co-operate with it. Will the women of the world be strong enough to carry this message to and practise it in their own countries? I hope it may be given to us all to act peace, talk peace and think peace so that our influence may permeate into the general warp and woof of life in our various countries.

Madame Eugenie Cotton (President of WIDF) opened the session. The congress adopted a manifesto and addressed its appeal to the United Nations and the heads of governments of the Four Great Powers. An important initiative was taken by Madame Cotton in her closing speech. This was a proposal to set up an International Committee of Mothers that would be wide open and world-wide, 'comprised of mothers nominated by the different national organisations, whether they were members of WIDF or not.' The composition of this committee could only be settled after the return of the delegates to their countries. But the Presiding Committee and leaders of delegations already proposed that Andrea Andrean, of Sweden, be elected as its chairman. Madame Griesemann, member of the West German Women's Peace Movement, would give the committee her co-operation.

Later, when I was proposed as its possible secretary, I visited Andrea in Stockholm to assist in the preparation of information for her opening speech, in correspondence, and other duties concerned with the first meeting of the committee, which took place in Lausanne on 2 February 1956. I thought that, even while caring for John, I could undertake the secretaryship of this committee because its meetings would not be frequent and a great deal of the correspondence would be conducted from my flat. What is more, the clear aim of the Mothers' Committee, as outlined by Eugenie Cotton, was that the mothers of the world, irrespective of party, country or religion, should unite to make known their demands as to the lives and welfare of their children, and for the sake of all humanity. This was the unity and purpose which I also sought.

John and I went by air to Lausanne for that first meeting. He agreed to come and take a look at the town as a tourist while I was busy. I thought this might be of interest and distraction for him.

The delegates of the Mothers' Congress had been very active on their return home. The list of members appointed to our committee comprised already forty countries, each with two or more delegates. Not all were at this first meeting, because of lack of money for travel and some political hindrances. But the distribution was widespread. Delegates from Lebanon and Iraq, Indonesia, Africa, China, and Japan were present. It was a remarkable meeting of remarkable women.

Andrea Andrean, in her opening speech, limited herself to some explanation of the Mothers' Congress, and mention of the many women's organisations which had recently passed resolutions urging governments towards peace. She remarked that the United Nations had recently accepted the admission of several new member states, irrespective of differences of race, religion or ideology. At the Mothers' Congress, Roman Catholic women from Italy had spoken passionately of the need of mothers to protect their children. Andrea continued,

> As a result of the congress decisions, we meet here today as a committee, charged with the solemn responsibility of realising the unity of the mothers of the world, and of helping them to understand the dangers which threaten them and their children and to act swiftly and effectively before it is too late.
>
> Accordingly, as your president, I am asking you all, not so much for eloquence, as for concrete and practical suggestions as to how we should work, what should be our first aims . . . how we shall co-operate with every kind of national and international organisation of women, on what principles we shall base united action, and what that united action shall be.

I remember little of the comments that followed Andrea's speech, except the remark addressed to me by the delightful young Soviet representative, Zoya Ivanova: 'Well Dora, now we have this Committee, what shall we do with it?'

'I would have thought,' I said, 'that we should say what are the demands which all mothers make for their children.'

Our first day thus ended with a request to me and Maria Madelena Rossi, a member of the Italian Parliament, to draft a Mothers' Declaration. Like Zoya, she was young and lively; we became great friends in the course of our work for the committee. She and I started to draft the declaration in English. In the end, laughing, she said, 'Oh Dora, you finish,' and leaving me to do the last paragraph, she went up to bed. Almost at once the lights in lounge and passages of the frugal hotel went out. I groped my way to bed with the draft in my hands. This is not to suggest that our committee was frivolous, only that we were not stuffy and old.

The next day our draft was carefully considered and amended. Because of the additions that came from so many countries, it was not as concise or well arranged as one might wish. The German comrades, West and East, were useful, especially Professor Maria Fassbinder, a Catholic from the Federal Republic, and Wilhelmina Schirmer-Praescher of the German Democratic Republic. The committee also decided that when the declaration had been translated and distributed we should endeavour to send a delegation with it to the United Nations.

My massive card index, covering all the countries participating, with Britain itself classified by districts and counties, all our women MPs and all organisations contacted, is evidence of the time and effort that went into our work. Over the next three years I came to know personally, and by contact through correspondence, so many women of character, courage and determination.

Of the women I specially recall at that first committee, there is of course Andrea, one of those who, over the years – like so many Swedish people today – tried to check the insensate quarrels of other nations; Zoya, with that balance and effective action that so many Soviet women possess; Phoebe Cusden of Britain, for a similiar persistence and courage in joining us; Madelena Rossi, of course; Ceza Nabaraoui, already famous Egyptian feminist; Birgit Schiotz from Norway; Dr Tomi Kara from Japan; the practical, ever active Dr Fassbinder, and the buxom yet almost masculine Wilhelmina Schirmer-Praescher from East Germany, who showed me special friendship for my efforts.

John and I left Lausanne for Geneva, but the cold was so intense, with a wind that cut like a knife, that neither he nor I had any pleasure from this visit. We were only too glad to be back in London. Immediately began the work of publicising the Mothers' Declaration and our plans to present it in New York to the UN. The English version was in my hands; I had it duplicated and began to send it out to likely people.

A copy of it is in Appendix 9.

A letter from me about the Mothers' Committee in the London *Observer* brought a response from five hundred women within a few days. At once, our enemies responded with an attack on our organisation as 'communist'. As we were aiming so sincerely for universality, I had hoped against hope that this would not happen. I replied with a letter; the argument continued, there was some cartoon in the *Observer*. But the damage was done.

This perpetual Cold War on communism, which included the expulsion from the Labour Party of all members attempting friendship with communist countries or organisations, was the main cause of the slowness of public opinion in the West to show an initiative against the threat of nuclear war. People simply had not understood that the legacy of Hitler to all nations was *total* war, which meant that governments now had a powerful vested interest in preventing even the genesis of any friendship and understanding between nations and peoples. But there was growing disquiet, mainly focused on the dangers of radiation from the atom bomb tests that were being carried out both by East and West. On this issue the various organisations concerned with peace were beginning to stir. But such protest as there was aimed at persuading the governments to stop the tests, because of the fear of radiation. Likewise, pleas for disarmament still accepted the doctrines of war and did not envisage the encouragement of peace and fraternisation.

In this connection my records, my voluminous correspondence with Andrea, my journeys in the next few years, show just how desperately 'we few, we happy few, we band of *sisters*' strove with reams of documents, argument, lobbying, marching on demos, to break the ice that had frozen both hearts and minds of the peoples of the West against even a tentative approach to the peoples of the communist East. I had been to the UN in New York; was in India, Geneva, Lausanne, Stockholm, Bulgaria, Moscow and China. As today I read Andrea's and my letters, there emerges between us a growing aim to lift our Mothers' Committee out of the morass of ideologies and the chessboard moves of international power politics, into a universal voice of the women who bear children, demanding those children's rights to love and care. We did not want our committee entangled only in mediation between unchanging power drives, or involved in co-operation with feminism and other worthy causes. Our cause, the peace and harmony universally needed to bear and nurture children, transcended all these and was the voice of human life itself.

In some countries this mood showed itself in spontaneous Mothers' Congresses. During 1956 we had no difficulty in obtaining and organising a delegation of twelve members to go to New York in January 1957. For me, 1956 was both a hectic and tragic year. In between work for the committee in my London flat – typing, drafting, phoning – combined with seeing people and some journeys, I had to go down to Cornwall to cook for a batch of Easter or summer visitors, or to arrange a summer let for the house, to try and make some money. John was with me in London and Cornwall, but if I left him I had to find someone (preferably, the doctors said, someone he knew, or a motherly woman) to take my place. To go for consultations to East Berlin was necessary from time to time. Once when I was there, my mother died suddenly and I returned at once; my brother and his wife arrived from Canada for the funeral. Although I had not been able to see my mother often, we had usually had Christmas together with my sister Bindy, who lived with her. I missed her badly, she had always taken a lively interest in her children and grandchildren, and I felt still more lonely.

After the committee meeting on 2 February, Andrea and I undertook some journeys to make our committee known. On 22 March she wrote to me about a projected trip to China which she felt unable to undertake and asked me to go instead. From Cornwall where, John with me, I was actually cooking for Easter visitors, I replied that I had been to Berlin, and again to Geneva to lobby a meeting of the Status of Women Commission for WIDF; that I would now be in London on 14 April, leaving again on 18 April for the ECOSOC meeting in Geneva once more to lobby for the restoration of status to WIDF.

But China meant a great deal to me. Soon I was on my way there via East Berlin, Moscow and Siberia, in time for a Women's Congress in the great hall, and to view the May Day celebrations from the beautiful temples of the central 'Forbidden City'.

Crossing Siberia by air in two-engined planes, we went up for about three hours, then came down in Irkutsk, or other Siberian towns, to partake of a meal and rest or sleep and then again into the air. It became difficult to remember whether one was eating breakfast, lunch or supper, but no matter which, it was always Siberian chicken, with very tough legs. But hospitality was never lacking.

At the Peking airport came warm greetings and then the comfortable Peking hotel. My first and lasting impression of those liberated Chinese women whom I now met, was of their happiness, quick lively movements, and an energy and efficiency which seemed to me (perhaps as a prejudiced observer) to rival that of the men whom we also met. Nor have I ever been at a May Day celebration to surpass that one in Peking. To begin with, there was not a military vehicle or weapon in sight, in fact nothing on wheels except, I think, a few bicycles. But the Chinese taste and artistic gifts made their banners and the floral tributes, carried by the masses of marching men and dancing women, a feast of light and colour. People in native costume represented the countries which are different, but part of China's dominion.

One incident at this demonstration stays firmly in my memory. A flight of doves for peace was loosed and flew up across the great square and over the marvellous tiled roofs of the temples where we stood. One bird failed to take flight and fell into the water of a narrow ditch between us and the edge of the square. I began to worry, not wanting it to drown. Spectators, not marchers, felt likewise. I saw them trying to reach the bird as it fluttered helplessly. And then, suddenly, along the narrow canal came a small boat marked with a Red Cross, and, in a moment, the little creature was rescued and in safe hands. In the midst of all these rejoicing thousands, it had not been forgotten, but noted and cared for. This sounds like a fairy tale, but every word of it is true.

I was able to meet a number of guests from several countries who were there for the festival. To my surprise, they included Monica Felton with whom I had a useful talk. I found Bertie's and my old house in Sue An Bo Hutang still much the same; the family occupying it kindly showed me over. With other guests, I saw factories in which the Russians, at that time, were helping the Chinese with their development of large-scale industry; though it was not long after this that differences arose and the Russians withdrew their help, thus, as the Chinese felt, letting them down.

Visiting a hospital in Peking mid-morning, I found all the doctors and nurses doing their exercises in the courtyard, according to Chinese custom. I remember creches of children with scrupulously clean cots and nurses. We visited a tea plantation. While there I had a severe digestive upset. Brought back to the hotel at once, I was attended by a doctor.

A dinner was given for the May Day celebrations and congress in Peking at which Chou en Lai was the host, receiving and shaking hands. 'We Chinese,' said one of the women who sat at my table, 'take great pleasure in entertaining guests.' The guests were encouraged to step to the microphone, not to make speeches, but to sing or recite poems. I was tempted to take part, but shyness overcame me. Talking to those present about parenthood revealed that most had not had more than one or two children.

There was a concert of Chinese music played entirely on Chinese instruments; this was not the music of the Chinese theatre which is raucous and loud. I remember sitting in the raised balcony of the hall, entranced as I have not been by some Western orchestral music, in which the see-sawing of the string instruments has an unpleasant roughness. This Chinese music stole into my ear and my heart with a subtle rhythm and a delicacy of sound that I can describe only as the very soul of pure music. Writing this has brought back to me the gentle emotion of that experience.

We went down to Shanghai in a well-equipped train whose only defect for me was the less agreeable constant muzak. One of my companions was a Bulgarian woman of some eminence. We talked women's politics, of course, and of the Mothers' Committee. 'Dora,' she said to me, 'where there is woman, there is child.' In spite of my maternal mission, I put on my feminist Status of Women Committee 'hat' and insisted to her that this view was not axiomatic for all women in England, or indeed elsewhere.

In the environs of Shanghai I was impressed by some new buildings for workers' families; even more so by the way women had made special efforts to help in what were really still slums, by installing a central pump to give facilities for water supply. There also, in a room off the street, we saw women being taught to read, who were so concentrated that they barely lifted their heads when we came in.

In the Museum of the Revolution in Shanghai I found an account of the demonstrations we had made in London in 1927 in which I had personally insisted against the use of British troops to hound the alleged communist subversives who, at the time, were under attack from the Kuomintang. In the library in Peking University I also found Russell's and my books. There was a great garden party in Shanghai given by Soong Ching Ling, at which I was delighted to meet and talk with her.

Now once again I was able to visit the Western Lake at Hangchow, which had so delighted Bertie and me by its 'enjoying rain' pavilion and which, for its peace and beauty, was frequented by Chinese poets. A modern hotel had been built on the lake shore. To my relief and pleasure it was in Chinese style and accorded with its surroundings. We went boating on the lake.

I came back from this renewal of my love for China full of happiness and hope for the work of our committee. Not long after my return came, on 9 July, the terrible news of a disastrous accident to Roddy in the mine. The first year of his service was nearing its end and he had been looking forward to a brief holiday. While they were taking out pit props the unsafe roof fell, Roddy's spine was injured and he was, aged twenty-four, condemned to a wheelchair for the rest of his life.

I went to him in hospital immediately and, in my grief, I said that I feared the influence of my own politics had brought this disaster on him. 'Mama, you must never say that,' he said, 'you helped to make me.' I knew he had his own convictions and had shown a gift for leadership among fellow students. Would he be able to surmount this terrible handicap?

His father, who for some time had been living in London to see something of his son, came with me. We could do no more than try and comfort Roddy. For some time after hospital, he would have to exercise in how to use his arms to compensate for his now useless legs. Details of the accident, claims for compensation would arise. I have a poignant memory of how he put into my hands his wallet with the money he had saved for the planned summer holiday and asked me to bank it for him.

Since he died recently when he was just fifty, I feel able to give some account of what his life meant to me and to his friends. But I will reserve that for later and include here only what Lena has written to me about his Tribunal.

How clearly I remember Roddy and the Tribunal! Honestly I was nervous for him that morning at Hammersmith, mainly because I was not very experienced in the ways of tribunals and I did not know Roddy very well. He put a case which the old gentlemen could seldom – if ever – have heard explained so clearly and unequivocally. In fact I feared it might have been above their heads and that they would find against him. So at the end I gave full marks to both sides!

But what an irony was the outcome! You and he have been marvellous in coping with the cruelty of the accident. I suppose we shall never be able to measure whether his influence has been stronger because of it. But that's no comfort. In a way it's marvellous that he carried on so long. I remember him coming on a peace lobby to the House of Commons years ago and I was anxious about the strain then.

Roddy's action is topical now after thirty years. In West Germany the strong movement against nuclear weapons is now saying that military service must be refused because nuclear weapons mean genocide and therefore the complete destruction of the Germany which, in theory, the army would defend. What is virtually 'nuclear service' should be refused.

While, with hindsight, I can now feel that Roddy, by his example, truly did his part in the great struggle for peace and survival which, with increasing vehemence, continues unabated, I also recall the many adjustments that at the time resulted from his accident. Roddy was already independent of maternal care; he would not want to be obliged to live with me, nor could he do so in a flat two floors up without a lift. Some family argument went on. He might share a flat with friends. When I considered that a handicapped person would always need at least some attention and care, I felt that friends might be casual; and that he needed someone responsible who would realise that there are 365 days in a year. He needed also a ground-floor flat, at a time when to find any accommodation, furnished or unfurnished, was not easy. After wandering through Hampstead looking for 'To Let' boards, I had the luck to find just what we wanted in Broadhurst Gardens, and with access to a shared open field in the rear. Harriet was able to obtain a transfer from the north on compassionate grounds to live with her brother, and Lily and Walter agreed to move in to share and help in what was really better accommodation than they had been able to get after we had left the house in Willesden. Walter's job at the Central Office of Information continued. I could at least feel that Harriet and Roddy had independence, a place of their own, some comfort and security.

John continued to live with me. I had never been free of anxiety about him since the moment, just before Christmas in 1954, when I was informed that he had been placed in the Guy's Hospital psychiatric unit near to London Bridge where he remained for a considerable time. I had visited him regularly and was with him there when he signed the papers, divorcing Susan. He looked sad but said no more than that she desired this. I could not tell whether this was also what he wanted. The hospital suggested that I should not come so often, and then, one day, phoned that I should come. It seemed that John was going to be moved to a hospital out of London. The attendant brought him in to see me, warning me to go gently with him. After greeting him I said that I understood he was going away to the country. He looked up at the attendant then at me and said, 'I am not going away, I am going home with my mother.' Nonetheless, after this John was often hospitalised by the psychiatrists advising his father. Even Roddy and I persuaded him to try hospital once. But he invariably escaped or signed himself out and came back to me. I decided that he must have one person whom he could look on as ally and friend, and that I would therefore support him in whatever he wanted to do.

As with very many people diagnosed as 'mentally disturbed' or schizophrenic, psychiatrists and doctors have no explanation of the illness, its causes or cure. Electric shock therapy became used for depression; it was only once used on John. At that time a cure was also attempted by the use of insulin, which carried certain risks. Many people have a great fear of anything approaching madness. John's father was no exception. He did want John to stay in hospital, hoping I suppose, for some treatment that would enable him to manage a normal life. Bertie had undertaken the care and education of the three girls; they were still living in the house at Richmond during their holidays, with their 'Griffie', a very good woman, in charge. I went to see them in Richmond from time to time and took them some gifts from 'abroad'.

I went on with my work for the Mothers' Committee. I was able to make sure that when John lived in the flat he was not left alone if I had to go away. A young French girl, Jacqueline Giroux, came for a time, mainly to help me with correspondence and to improve

207

her English. She was understanding and quite untroubled by giving John the minimum attention which he required. For a long period he would only emerge from his small bedroom to cross the narrow corridor into the bathroom, and would allow nothing in his room to be disturbed.

Vera (now Mrs Woods), a young teacher I knew – we had worked together in Cornwall on holidays or camping abroad – came to lodge with us. Later she was actually married from my flat. She is now a head mistress, and John and I have been fast friends with her these many years.

John wandered about London. I felt that he still grieved for the loss of his wife. Once when I said to him that one did not love only one person for the whole of life, he answered that 'he did not see why not'. Presently he began to occupy himself with writing – a great deal about the gods of mythology, especially of Egypt. He also crocheted, mainly articles in string. He had an accordion on which he played extremely well and fortunately the neighbours did not object.

I consulted Dr Joan Malleson, an old friend, and John came with me to see her. She had experience of mental disturbances and thought she could help John when she came back from a visit to Australia which she had undertaken. Soon came the tragic news of her death by drowning on the barrier reef.

Worry about John reached a climax in 1956, when he was in the mental hospital at Holloway, Egham in Surrey. I do not now remember just why he had been put there. I had visited him there, shut in with a number of senile old men about twice his age. On one visit I happened to go by train and met on the station near the hospital, an elderly man who, in talking to me, revealed that he was living in the hospital still. He told me his story. He had been a doctor with a practice in Liverpool in a working-class area. A bomb had destroyed his surgery and left him in such a state of shock that he had been put in a mental hospital. Presently his wife died; there was no relative to give him a home. It seemed that he had two sons, now grown up and married, but, he implied, either they had not offered to receive him, or he did not wish to impose on them. The thought that a man or woman certified mentally ill, neglected and forgotten, might be marooned in hospital for the rest of his or her days appalled me. Nothing like this must happen to John.

One day he escaped and, as usual, arrived at my flat. The hospital rang to ask if he was with me. I understood them to say that he was having insulin treatment, and it was therefore important what he had to eat. I said that he wanted to see his father, which was not possible till the next day. First thing next morning, he had gone out. Sure that he had gone to Richmond to see his father, I took a train there myself. As I came out of Richmond station to climb the hill, I met him. 'What does your father say?' I asked. 'He says, "No".' 'That's not good enough,' I said and I took his arm and we went back up the hill.

I was convinced that John really wanted to be back in that house where he could at least be with his children part of the time. I rang the bell and Bertie came to the door. Seeing John, he said: 'He can't come in here,' and looked frightened. 'I can't see why not,' I said. 'I want to talk to you and he can sit in another room and wait.' So this was agreed. Bertie then insisted to me that John was ill and should be in hospital. I said that I knew he needed care, but, in helping him to get better it would mean a great deal to him to know that he could come back to live in what he had felt to be his home, together with his children. He was no trouble, he did not need to be in hospital to get some medical or psychiatric care. Then a woman who must have been Edith came in, intimating that some message had come for Bertie, who then said to me that John might stay to lunch. Thinking that I had made some headway, I said that if John would ring me when he was ready to return, I would come and meet him as he was inclined to be vague wandering about London. I had not thought it odd that, in the circumstances, I had not been invited to lunch, but when no call came, after a time I rang up and asked for John. 'When are you coming back?' I said. 'My father says I must go back to the hospital.' 'Never mind, don't worry, I will come and see you.' I guessed that the lunch invitation had been given to allow time for the psychiatrist who had been summoned to arrive.

I now became really anxious that an application to certify John might be made. I consulted my solicitor, who assured me that, as John's mother, I had equal rights. I had no psychiatric adviser, or money to pay one, but I had met a man up in Wakefield, liberal-minded and interesting about cases he had dealt with. I knew from experience of other hospitals that they would usually not want to keep a patient who wrote himself out. I rang the hospital and said that I trusted John would be all right, as I had to be away for a day or so, but would be back to see him. I went at once to Wakefield to ask this psychiatrist friend if he would come to court, if necessary.

As soon as I arrived home I rang the hospital again, and was informed that John was, at that very moment, being examined by two doctors and a magistrate with a view to certification. If I had anything to say I had better come at once. I took a taxi straight to the hospital where I immediately made clear that I had not sanctioned any application for John's certification, and was opposed to it. There was nothing to do, at the moment, but sit and wait for the present result.

Under the rules then existing, certification required the presence of a magistrate and two doctors, who had not been in attendance on the patient. But certified patients with all their resources, finance included together with responsibility for all their care, came under the Board of Control. It was extremely difficult to obtain their release, nor could independent doctors attend them.

The time seemed very long before the two doctors reappeared. 'We find no grounds for certifying your son,' they said. 'I never thought you would,' I replied. 'He is, however, very ill,' they said. I then asked if he could stay in the hospital and I received the expected reply that he should not. I then suggested that they should communicate with his father. Whoever it was who went to the phone returned with what seemed to me a shocked impression. John would not, as I knew, be received at Richmond. What was I now to do about him, I asked. It seemed that some other place from which he had not already escaped should be found. In their opinion, he needed care and 'treatment'.

'Well, gentlemen,' I said, 'well or ill, my son shall find a place in my home. Shall I take him now?'

It seemed that John could not be released until the next day, since certain formalities would be required. So I asked to see him. In his little room John asked me at once, could he come home.

'You give me a lot of trouble,' I said. 'What have you been saying to these doctors?' 'I asked them,' he said, 'to give me a definition of insanity and they could not do so.'

The next morning I came again to the hospital and John was given into my care.

Not long after this, the house in Richmond, without consultation or even information to John, was vacated and practically everything in John's part of the house either disposed of or moved to Wales, where Bertie and Edith now took a house. They also began making arrangements to move the girls to a different boarding school. Some parcels of John's books, mostly old and perhaps valuable, began to arrive unexplained at our flat.

The tragedies and burdens of personal life have somehow to be met and endured. So also do those of the political world by those of us who become involved. As if I had not had enough to contend with, this happened to be the year in which the United Nations, in connection with the Status of Women Committee, had decided that it would be a good idea for member states to help the cause of women by holding seminars to illustrate what their governments had done, or were prepared to do for women's education and advance. Consequently, the Soviet Union in September 1956 held such a seminar, which was open to all nations and to any of the non-governmental organisations attached to the UN. This had more to do with feminism than with our Mothers' Committee, but in my capacity as representative for WIDF in New York in 1954, I had virtually a duty to attend. At this moment this was an arduous assignment, but it did something to force me to turn my mind from personal grief.

At the same time, grief, disappointment and frustration in the field of international politics were for me associated with this seminar. It was held in accord with a decision of the United Nations; it was financed and organised with the utmost generosity and skill by the Soviet government. Yet reports and knowledge of its procedures were almost entirely absent from the Press or institutions and individuals of the West. I have a notice of a meeting organised by the energetic Jessie Street to report on the seminar in October of that year at Caxton Hall in London. I do not know what the attendance was. In any case, this very honourable and remarkable action of the Soviet Union was largely ignored.

To give an adequate account of this 'Seminar on equality of Women in the USSR for representatives of the member countries of the Commission on the Status of Women, UN Economic and Social Council, and for representatives of Non-Governmental bodies' would require a book in itself. I can only give some indications of its scope, the participants and its achievements in stimulating discussion and imparting information. Among those who could be reckoned official representatives of their governments were those currently on the Status of Women Commission: Israel, Poland, Yugoslavia, Bielorussia USSR,

211

Czechoslovakia and Bulgaria. It is to be noted that the commission must have included representatives of the UK, France and USA, but these were not there. Nor does the name of any government member of the ECOSOC appear. But the officials of the UN connected with the ECOSOC and specific women's questions, were present; Mary Cecil Tenisson-Woods, and Sophia Grinberg-Vinaver, whom I had met in New York. There were also Alice Ehrenfeld, an official of the UN Secretariat, Pippa Harris from UNESCO and Jessie Bierman of the International Health Organisation. There were some women MPs from India, and, notably, from Burma, Daw Saw Shwe, deputy of the Chamber of Nationalists and Daw Mya Si, member of the Chamber of Deputies.

All these names are included in a total list of some eighty-nine participants, representing every variety of profession pertaining to an NGO, most of them international in scope, but others represented the most important women's organisations of their respective nations. It is not easy to ascertain from this list the proportion of women from specific nations who appear as delegates of international bodies, covering for instance, the Red Cross, journalism, co-operatives, lawyers and so forth. But there are a certain number of the groups that were definitely national: France, Belgium, Italy, Australia, New Zealand, Austria, Norway, Finland, and others. From the UK, Monica Whately represented the Six Point Group; Edith Adlam, the Women's League for Peace and Freedom; Margaret Airey, the Assembly of Women. Like others, I was there for an international body. No participation by American women is shown and that from Britain was small. The lists of Soviet women participating contain eighty-nine names. These are divided into groups according to professional status or function.

The programme provided that we should spend from 15–20 September in Moscow and on each day meet in a great hall to hear the speech of an eminent woman representative in her particular sphere of activity. This was followed by questions and open discussion. 15 September was given mainly to women in government positions; 17 September to Ministers of Justice and the law; 18 September to factories, trade unions, economics, social security and medical care; 19 September to medicine and health; 20 September to education, training, culture and the arts. I have several booklets, which contain the speeches made on all these aspects of women's status. I have rarely been at public meetings which afforded so much lively and open discussion. I remember especially the exchange of views between the representative of the Open Door Council and Soviet women on the question of how far women should be 'protected' in factory work.

Nor were we merely informed by speeches. There were visits to factories, to hospitals, to the law courts, to schools, on which I have copious notes. I was among those who listened, for instance, to the very interesting exchanges between the judge and the petitioners in a divorce case.

There was a reception at the Kremlin on 15 September, opened by Deputy V.T. Lacis, who introduced the members of the Supreme Soviet as well as the members of the Supreme Soviet of the Russian Federation (RFSSR). He explained to us the Soviet Constitution and the two chambers, the second being that of the Federation of Independent Republics. He gave us also the numbers of women deputies, amounting, in the various Soviets, to something like 32 per cent to 35 per cent. Mr Lacis referred to the prejudices that existed abroad about the life and aims of the Soviet people. They wanted to live in peace with all and he urged that we should 'get closer together, learn to know each other better'. For this reason he welcomed the seminar. P.P. Lebanov, chairman of the Soviet of the Union of the Supreme Soviet, then spoke.

The entire programme for the seminar was in the hands of the Soviet Women's Committee, whose very efficient chairman at that time was Nina Popova, Deputy also of the Supreme Soviet. She was the speaker at the meeting on economic equality for women. It was her function also to explain to us the extension of our opportunities beyond Moscow. The numerous visits to observe the Soviet people of all ages in their life, work and entertainment in the city, ended on 21 September, a Friday. For the weekend the delegates had a choice between two groups: one would go by train to Leningrad, the other fly to Stalingrad. On Monday, the Stalingrad group would fly to Tashkent, whilst the Leningrad group would divide into four and visit either Kiev, capital of the Ukraine, Minsk, capital of Bielorussia, Tbilisi, capital of Georgia, or Erevan, capital of Armenia. After two days of these visits, all groups would fly, on 27 September, to Sochi on the Black Sea until 29 September. Then all would fly from there to Moscow to arrive on Sunday 30 September where they would be met by the active women in Moscow. On

1 October at 8 p.m., there was to be a final reception in the Kremlin.

It had been a long while since I had visited Leningrad, so I chose to join that group. With me, among others, were Madelena Rossi from Italy and Tomi Kora from Japan. Of course we visited all the historic sites – the Smolny School with the room which Lenin and his wife had occupied for a time in the exciting first months of the revolution; the Hermitage Palace with its art and archaeological treasures. We saw too the famous statue of Peter the Great – the Bronze Horseman – about which a very moving ballet has been made whose performance in Moscow we had also seen. The small battleship *Aurora* still lay moored there near the Hermitage. According to legend, it had fired the first shots in 1917. We were taken there and shown over it by an elderly guide, in the uniform of a naval officer. We saw downstairs on a wall photographs of some of the naval heroes of 1917, and one was quite certainly our guide. When he admitted it, laughing, I said: 'Well, you were here in 1917, but I was here at least in 1920.' So we embraced in celebration of both having memorable associations with a great event.

When we divided, my section went to Armenia, beautiful and fruitful, and agreeable in the harvest season. There in Erevan is an opera house, where we saw a performance. At Sochi, on the Black Sea, where all of us travellers forgathered again, there was a constant buzz of exchanges of experience, opinions and impressions in many languages. And there were also excursions in motorboats on the sea. Nearby, at the airport, stood what looked like half the fleet of Aeroflot planes, ready to lift us back to Moscow.

At the final reception, the Kremlin was brightly lit with its chandeliers, adorned, and thronged by many women and men of eminence; among them was Molotov, credited by Western diplomats with his capacity for glum silence or 'No' saying. This was a very different Molotov, part host in his own country, and happy to greet many women, who were equally happy to request his autograph.

This seminar was, for all who took part, a very great occasion. It also illustrated features of the Russian character, so little understood by the West, for instance, their love of open and even ostentatious hospitality, coupled with a reckless disregard of its expense. But there was also their attachment to intellectual pursuits, and a meticulous demand for

214

excellence in these coupled with, as it was then at any rate, an idealist regard for the health and care of their own peoples and all those they took under their wing.

I doubt if any of the women from the NGOs who were there failed to come away with a very profound impression of what Russia could and might achieve and how much the linking of this achievement with peoples now hostile might mean for the world. But, like me, I fear that many of those women must have returned to their homelands sick at heart with the knowledge of the futility of our efforts, thus far, to bring about any such fusion and understanding.

The first task facing the Mothers' Committee in the new year was the presentation of the Mothers' Declaration at the UN in New York by the delegation of twelve representatives who were ready to go there in January. Immediately, we had one more bitter experience of the malevolence and hostility of the West. On the excuse that we were not a sponsored organisation (an NGO), visas were refused to all but three, including the widow of one of the Japanese fishermen whose boat had been overwhelmed by fall-out from the Bikini nuclear test. The American women of the Women's International League for Peace and Freedom intervened to try and help about this one, but not in time. The delegation, led by the indefatigable Professor Fassbinder, and supplemented by friends who were actually in New York, reached by means of frantic messages and phone calls, did a patient and thorough round of all the delegations, presenting the declaration and giving it all possible publicity.

The second session of our committee for 1957 had, after complex negotiation about dates, received the permission of the Swiss government (as well as the requisite Swiss canton) to be held on 27–29 April at Lausanne in the Hotel Central Belle Vue, Place St Francis, as before.

It was very difficult to collect news from our representatives in time to translate and prepare it for the committee. We especially needed Professor Fassbinder's report. I even planned to go down to Southampton to see her when her ship docked there en route, but found that visits 'in transit' were not permitted.

Our efforts in New York met with greater success and publicity than at first appeared. The Japanese widow was in the end allowed a visa and, with help from our supporters in Canada, also visited that country. The

Observer opened its columns again to correspondence from me about our committee's attempt at the UN. It was again attacked as communist propaganda by a Catholic woman, Mrs Bower, who was specially insulting to Andrea for her association with Soviet institutions; so that Andrea suggested to me that she had better resign since her name seemed to harm us. I urged her to take no notice of such tactics by our opponents. In fact, I was greatly encouraged by the editorial attitude of the *Observer*. It gave each side a strict number of words, which was rather comical, but it also held up publication when I was away for me to get my letter to them in time to appear with the opposition. I was desperately busy working, up till 2 a.m.; people wanted to know the results of the effort at the UN. I had 200 women in Britain interested in the committee and asking how they could help. We issued a regular bulletin in which I wrote editorials. This had to contain a report in readiness for the committee in April. Andrea and I achieved some correspondence at top level with Hammarskjöld. She wrote to ask why our delegation had not been allowed to see him. He replied to her, and his secretary to me, that they represented governments, public access was through the NGOs. This was precisely what Andrea and I objected to, that 'the people' had not sufficient access, and this bore hardest on women who were represented, even in NGOs, already in smaller numbers than men.

Questions were being asked in Parliament about the atomic tests being carried out by both sides. I sent a letter to every MP and urged our supporters to do the same. The Labour Party objected to the tests, but, as I explained to Andrea, did nothing more, whilst the Liberals waited for a report promised from the UN on the effect of the tests on health. Dr Haddow, who was eminent for work on cancer, gave an excellent speech to the MPs about the genetic effects of radiation. He annoyed me by adding that the Soviet Union had made 'nauseating statements' regarding the relative hazards of the tests; 'their explosions have been in essence no different from others'. It seemed that the Russians had claimed that their explosions had been from the air, whereas the Bikini test had been a 'fireball close to the ground'.

Professor Blackett published his book, *Atomic Energy and East-West Relations* (1956), in which he said he thought the Russian atomic bomb of 1955 was probably like that of the Americans in 1954, a very deadly 'fission-fusion-fission'. He does not doubt the Russian bomb was launched from a plane: 'the immense amount of radio-active dust is carried around if the bomb is exploded so low that the fireball touches the earth', as at Bikini. But Blackett was more worried about the fact that the use of 'tactical' atomic bombs might hurt the enemy so much as to cause him in desperation to launch the strategic H-bomb. I thought that launching the bomb from the air, while no doubt carrying much radio-active dust, would at least have avoided the killing of the Japanese fishermen.

I felt angry that even people protesting on our side found it necessary to add insults to the Russians, who after all had not invented or launched the first bomb. I wrote to Dr Haddow and sent him the declaration and other documents from our committee and remarked that the Russians offered to stop testing if others would also do so.

The press in Britain began to be full even of leading articles against the tests. The *Observer* carried a cartoon of a small naked child carrying a paper marked 'question on nuclear tests' and facing a row of MPs half asleep on their benches. Over the heads of the sleeping MPs was written 'world statesmen'. I wrote to Andrea that I felt sure this was inspired by our work. I said also that I thought my 'breakthrough' with the *Observer* had resulted in other papers – the *News Chronicle*, *Sunday Pictorial* and *Manchester Guardian* – following suit. Now some Quakers had stated that they would sail into the affected areas of the Pacific in protest.

The younger generation, stunned at first by the Hiroshima bomb, had been accused of taking little interest in politics. They were hemmed in by the ban imposed by the Cold War and the proscription by the Labour Party of any contact with communist countries or organisations. Now, in the newer universities, student discussion brought about the New Left, with the New Left Club in London. Hundreds flocked to its now open discussions.

Due to an initiative in Hampstead, in part from the local newspaper, Labour Party members – mainly the women – supported by the Friends Peace Movement, the Council for the Abolition of Nuclear Weapons was born. The exact date of birth was 6 February 1957, and, having been invited, I attended its first meeting on 7 February when Dr Burhop was present and gave us an account of the risks of strontium in our bones. A march of women supporting its aims was really the first action of the council. This took place in May, in pouring rain, with Diana Collins (wife of Canon Collins) as leader, along with Joyce Butler, MP, Dr Edith Summerskill and Vera Brittain, all speaking in Trafalgar Square. Women in black picketed the lobby of the House of Commons. The committee then began to seek eminent names in support. I would have preferred to see it carry on with those committee members who had taken the first initiative, with a view to recruiting more and more ordinary women and men from the general public. I think I hoped that it might then in due course see the advantage and strength of some co-operation with the still disregarded World Council and Peace Petition efforts. In the event, with the joining of J.B. Priestley, Sir Julian Huxley, Bertrand Russell as president and Canon Collins as chairman, this became a 'Campaign Committee for Nuclear Disarmament' – CND – whose slogan was not peace and disarmament but the banning of the H-bomb.

There was already also a direct action committee with Hugh Brock, Allen Skinner, the Rev. Michael Scott and Pat Arrowsmith, associated, I think, with *Peace News*. A small group of pacifists had already gone to protest at Aldermaston, and this group now had the idea of a march there at Easter, 1958. The new Campaign Committee, CND, decided to support this effort. In March 1958 the National Assembly of Women organised in London the first Women's conference against the H-bomb. Our Mothers' Committee, of course, had been at the UN in January 1957. The people were at last waking up and demanding to be heard.

With the experience I had gained of the feelings of women on an international scale, I regretted to see the restriction of the movement within national limits, and to the nuclear threat. So doing it disregarded also the prominence of women in their world-wide cry for peace and disarmament in the interests of the entire human race.

After failing in an attempt to induce the UN Disarmament Sub-Commission, whose section was meeting in London, to receive a deputation of our Mothers' Committee, I went down to Cornwall with John for the fresh air which always invigorated me and to write and send out hundreds more documents in preparation for our Mothers' Committee in April. I was unable to go to Berlin to consult about the agenda for April, because our friend Vera had got married, and would no longer lodge with us. We thus lost the immense help that she had given us both. I was, however, present at the committee in Lausanne and once back in London, was busy getting out the next bulletin with the speeches and reports of activity in different countries. There were good women at this committee but what to do next was not clear. The awakening of the people to the nuclear threat had brought a new, and in many ways, complex element to our activities. In June there was a second march in London, of women and men, with a vigorous lobby of Parliament, in which I took part. To take part in this and at the same time run, almost single-handed, an organisation that really now needed a fully staffed office, began to be more than I could endure. But what was more disturbing to me was my analysis of the varying interests and purposes of the many organisations.

Every women's organisation had a different scale of demands that it made on behalf of the female sex, and these demands, whether national or international, tended to be linked with current political purposes. I respected the Women's International Democratic Federation, although communist-inspired, because its demands regarding women were wider and more international than others. Though linked with it, our Mothers' Committee was only a small offshoot and had to contend with numerous other interests of women, as well as the drive for communism, which it sponsored, and the national viewpoints of the really excellent women of many nations who composed its secretariat in East Berlin.

The new CND in Britain, campaigning only for nuclear disarmament, soon made clear that they did not want any association with pacifists who sought understanding or had any connection with communist organisations or countries. Those who had been doing the most work for peace were now required to 'keep away' to avoid CND being smeared! The broadly based 'Assembly of Women' did not quite know how to carry on its work. When I was asked to speak for CND to some schoolchildren, I realised that they, feeling themselves part of a fine new peace movement, were too young to know of the strenuous work done by the 'proscribed' since 1950, while they were growing up.

Andrea and I, fully aware of how our committee would get 'smeared', had endeavoured from the start to avoid its being used for other purposes. We took no part in protests about Suez or Hungary. We wanted the universal voice of mothers to be heard above wars and political strife. On 3 July 1957 I wrote a despairing letter to Andrea about these problems. I had been talking to Mme Renu Chakravarty about how some Indian women felt that our special effort as mothers could draw away women's energies from the new Indian National Federation. I felt this might be true. In England and many countries, it seemed that the movement for women's liberation laid stress on women's rights and equality with men as workers. What was missing here were the old traditional values for which women and mothers must stand. This would not be so true in India, where the movement would still be primarily maternal for some time. I did not feel that WIDF stood in the right way for *women's* values. This in fact expressed my deeply felt conviction which had brought me to the fight for birth control – that the mother was the most neglected and oppressed of her sex; liberation must begin with and for her. In my mind, almost unconsciously, this had now become associated with all that went with the new nuclear threat, including the results of radiation and strontium on our species.

I felt that humanity must awake to this danger. To Andrea I wrote that I was 'tired of all these party politicians' who in Britain and other countries were

> in their old blinkers, missing all chances of drawing people together. [In England] the pressure about the H tests has had some effect, but it did not come from the party leaders. The *people* here are in an interesting mood, waiting for a lead which no one is giving them.

I went on to complain bitterly of a right-wing research section of the Labour Party which had just issued a pamphlet called the 'Communist Solar System'

> which listed all friendship and peace organisations proscribed by the Labour Party, with names, histories, affiliations etc, much of it inaccurate. Our committee is in it and you and me, with the usual statement that we operate from Berlin and are subservient to WIDF.

I recognised that all this was done 'to warn people off us', but it was damaging because it was totally impossible to get publicity to reply. Andrea had been trying to get a group of women scientists of several nations to meet, perhaps in Geneva, and express their views. The response showed that it was unlikely to succeed under the threat of seeing Andrea as 'untouchable', 'communist inspired'. 'I have come to feel,' I wrote 'that there is no room for any sincere efforts to run an organisation which really tries to do for people what it sets out to do. Both sides in the cold war twist and distort it for their own ends.' I expressed the wish that we had been able to start our Committee 'as something entirely new and away from all existing organisations and party people who want to twist everything their own way.' I continue

> I feel I cannot go on doing this job. I have too many
> commitments with family, house and home to do singlehanded
> work that needs a full office and staff. And I feel terribly lonely,
> as maybe you do too. For 37 years now I have spent a great deal
> of my time trying to build a bridge between communist
> countries and the west and the wreckers win every time. I must
> go away and rest and try to write a book about all this. When I
> look at all my friends of the Labour movement of the twenties
> now, I just have to weep. By the way, their booklet refers to me
> as secretary of the PICM as 'our own Dora Russell'. I wonder
> who they mean I belong to? Personally I want to belong to
> myself, and unless I can say what I mean and think I want then
> to be silent.

My family responsibilities had, indeed, increased. After the attempt to certify John had failed and what had been his home at Richmond disposed of, John had no access to his three daughters, Sarah, Lucy, and Anne (Anne, Susan's daughter, had been adopted by him). During term-time they had now been placed in Morton Hall, a young ladies' boarding school, while their holidays were spent in Wales at the Russell home, Plas Penrhyn, Penrhyn-dendraeth.

Bertie had taken action in the courts for full custody of the girls by him and his wife Edith. If John was not to lose his children altogether I had to fight this action on his behalf. There were affidavits and argument on both sides; I did not have to go to court. I was fortunate in having the support of a statement by George Morgan, a psychiatrist who had been giving me advice and help about John. With money, title and great reputation on one side, and only John and me, with slender resources on the other,

I scarcely hoped for our success. When our solicitor, Mr Derek Taylor, rang to say that the case was lost, I replied, 'I never thought we would win.' He thanked me for accepting the result so calmly, remarking that most clients on receipt of bad news were usually very angry. In fact, all was *not* lost. Whether it was my urgent plea, or George's, or Mr Taylor's skill, the Judge gave me, for the first time, some legal status by saying that the girls should visit their father and grandmother for half of their holidays.

In the spring, therefore, the girls had been with John and me in Cornwall. After their visit I had regretfully let the house for the summer to make some money. I had also acquired an old but quite serviceable coach, which was adapted for camping holidays abroad. From 22 July to 11 August and 17 August to 1 September that summer (1957), I took two tours to France, with groups of friends, who enjoyed co-operating on such excursions, and who also paid reasonably for the holiday. I had served my own apprenticeship in such co-operative camping (not the highly professional organised camping to highly organised professional sites which came later) with the enterprising David Burke and friends whom he collected. I saw David now from time to time when I went about by car or coach to speak against the atom bomb tests.

On this issue, some of us women did get to the UN Disarmament Committee in London and had been told by the Soviet delegate, Dr Profitch, that all five powers were nearing agreement and sought only a formula. In the end they broke up without agreement. The next thing was to be the Indian resolution to the UN Assembly, once more demanding that the tests end.

Meantime Andrea and Molly were out in Japan at a Mothers' Congress; and Andrea learned of a similar mothers' movement in Indonesia, and Portugal. It did seem as if in countries where women were still segregated, their movement began naturally in this way. Just before leaving for Japan Andrea wrote to me about the International Congress of the Co-operative Women's Guild. She was impressed by the fact that this (also an NGO) was acceptable to UN agencies and both sides of the Iron Curtain. Could not our Mothers' Committee ally with them for our purposes? The Co-operative movement in Britain had originally been one of the first organisations to concern itself with mothers. But almost from the start it had been closely allied with the Labour Party and anti-communist feeling now pervaded all sections of the movement. I had little response to my approaches from the Co-op women.

In September and October I had taken my coach with a banner along its sides saying, 'Women of All Lands Want Peace' and, with a few helpers, we had distributed leaflets outside both the Labour and the Conservative Party conferences. In talking to a group of young technical men students whom I met casually in Brighton, boys who grew up during the war, I became very worried about the general state of opinion in the country. The only idea of Soviet Russia which had been planted in these young men's minds was that Russia intended to conquer the world for communism, and we had to have nuclear weapons to frighten her off. They also said that Russia had 'kept out of the last war' and let us fight alone, so that we would get exhausted and then they would walk into Europe and take half of Germany. The Russians were ignorant and barbarous peasants. When I asked them how, in that case, the Russian technical education was so good that they had launched the first satellite, they simply repeated that the Russians were not civilised, educated people, but barbarians, always murdering each other and Hungarians. When I suggested that we had murdered people in Cyprus, and mentioned the German gas chambers they did not want to listen. I met much the same attitude among young men at a factory gate meeting in Rochester. Women were different – the older ones. The young ones were enjoying a higher standard of living than they had ever known, dressing up like film stars. Even some communist women who came back from a holiday in Russia said that Russian women were all frumps. 'When you think,' I wrote to Andrea, 'of the lovely intelligent faces of Russian women and their devotion, and compare it with the false values our women seem to have.'

The Russians had, in fact, to the dismay of the Americans, just put up the famous sputnik, and were giving it full publicity by organising a special celebration on 7 November of the fortieth anniversary of the Revolution. In September, I had received a telegram inviting me, as of the Mothers' Committee, to attend. I wrote to Andrea saying that, as our committee avoided political and national issues, we should not really attend, the more so as it gave a handle to the accusation of a close link with the Soviet government. She urged me, nonetheless, to come, because it was useful that representatives from the West should be there. In the end I agreed to go 'in my own right' as it were, since by going via Berlin, I could have some discussion about the next meeting of our committee.

I don't remember how I made arrangements for John at this stage. I think others of the family helped, but I did mention to Andrea the help that I had from George Morgan, who had advised me not to give up all my own work and devote myself to caring for John, as I was now inclined to do. John himself, if seems, said I ought to be at the anniversary, whereas, formerly, he had never much liked my absence for any reason.

For me it was a great pleasure to be in Moscow; to talk with my friends and colleagues on the Women's Committee, and to laugh with them as we listened to the constant 'bleep bleep' emerging from that contraption of triumphant technology overhead. In a great hall, where I sat in an upper gallery, the delegates from one country after another paid their compliments to Soviet achievements. As I knew was customary on these occasions, most of these tended to be long-winded.

Khrushchev's report on forty years of achievement, which I possess, runs to ninety pages of typescript. It is a fascinating account of progress in all fields of activity: agriculture, mining, industry, engineering, and comparisons with American and European achievements in similar fields. The sense of rivalry between the two growing industrial empires is lamentably present throughout. As always, this foolish and unnecessary schism depressed me. Many pages were, of course, given to greeting the foreign visitors and delegates. Then began the history of the long struggle of revolution up to what the Soviet leader felt was the justified victory of the working class.

The conditions of capitalist encirclement, ceaselessly combating the machinations of international imperialism and overcoming the frantic resistance of the enemy classes, the working people of the Soviet Union, led by the Communist Party, succeeded in establishing socialism in an historically brief space of time. They demonstrated to the whole world the tremendous creative energies of the people when emancipated from the shackles of capitalism, energies which were channelled into vast constructive labour.

Further on was his tribute to his country's latest triumph of science.

The crowning scientific and technical achievement was the creation and launching on October 4, 1957, of the world's first earth satellite. Less than a month later another Soviet sputnik, equipped with better and more varied scientific instruments and carrying an experimental animal on board, was sent into the heavens. Our first sputnik no longer feels alone in the universe. Two messengers of the Soviet Union, two stars of Peace are circling the globe. Our scientists, designers, engineers, technicians and workers gave Soviet people a really fine present for the fortieth anniversary of the October Revolution by bringing the most daring of human dreams to life. These achievements of the Land of Socialism, which mark the beginning of a new era in science and technology, have stirred virtually the whole world.

The demeanour of the speakers gave some indication of their feelings. I did not like Harry Pollitt's[1] speech, it had a patronising note. And Mao Tse Tung seemed to me as if he did not feel entirely at ease or at home. There were receptions and the usual Red Square demonstrations where we had places of privilege quite close to the marching battalions.

I spent much time with Madelena Rossi, Italian member of WIDF and already my friend. She said many things about the Russian character – a people, she felt, who had a great capacity for suffering and endurance.

The talk in Berlin about the next meeting of our committee was concerned in part with finance. Local groups might finance Mothers' Conferences, but for the committee to meet there was the problem of where and when, and the cost of fares. We had been approaching the Bulgarian women, who seemed likely to receive us. As to action, I talked of the Aldermaston March which had taken place at Easter – according to its custom, a real march on foot, and beds on the floor at sundry halls provided en route. I had taken my coach, not to carry people, but to make tea and even cook sausages. I began to think of a similar trek by women across Europe. I remember that Zoya was intrigued by the idea: we even talked of progressing from Europe to China! I came back to England, in time for John's birthday on 16 November, with some such plan germinating in my mind.

Returning from the enthusiasm of the Soviet celebrations, stimulated by these and the fun of chatting with lively Soviet women about new initiatives for peace, I arrived back refreshed and hopeful, to be immediately discouraged by the atmosphere at home. Our Mothers' Committee had always been regarded by us (and also so regarded by WIDF) as a body that could act independently of WIDF's other activities. The hope was for co-operation with other similar groups of women active for peace, and specially against nuclear war. When I was out of England this idea of co-operation looked so much simpler than it really was. Back at home, plunged into the implacable hostility to co-operation with anything from the East, the difficulties became more obvious, the prospect not at all rosy.

As I reflected on Andrea's idea of the extent of the Co-op's influence and money, I knew that we might certainly get individual Co-op women to join our efforts, but this would not win the whole movement; on the contrary, it tended to make those women ineffective in their own organisations. Phoebe Cusden's support of us had lost her the Vice-Presidency of her own group, the WILPF. I even pointed out to Andrea that I might do better for our cause myself if I gave up all association with proscribed groups and worked with the Labour Party. The Co-operative party had adopted a definite policy against the H-bomb and might feel that it was ploughing its own furrow and had no need to work with any others in the field. The only effective thing seemed to be to try and push the Labour Party (and thus a potential Labour government) into direct negotiations with the Soviet Union. Meantime, it was being said widely in the West that the Russians refused to work with the Disarmament Commission of the UN because they now felt strong enough not to need to disarm!

Attention was focused on these arguments and negotiations, whilst protest continued to centre solely on opposition to nuclear tests and weapons. This was coupled with a firm resolve to keep clear of any association with Soviet influence, and the implanted conviction that Russia was the enemy whose policies were totally unacceptable and whose proposals could never be trusted – an attitude which, as the Russians perceived, clearly rendered all negotiation futile.

I went on dutifully preparing and sending letters to the UN as well as corresponding about the third meeting of our committee, which was now definitely to be in Sofia on 20-22 February 1958. My idea of a Women's Caravan of Peace, which had been so favourably received by the women with whom I discussed it in Moscow and East Berlin, was to be on the agenda, coming as a proposal from the 'Mothers of Great Britain' asking the Mothers' Committees, especially in Europe, to study the possibility of welcoming this caravan and giving it all possible publicity.

I had taken new courage, but both Andrea and I were still despondent about results. We were so tired of seeing how, in everything that we touched, the opinions of women counted for so little. Andrea thought of resigning as president. I still wanted to retire to Cornwall and begin to write a book stating women's position more clearly. I complained that women were always 'on the outside looking in'. My link with the Soviet peace initiative was keeping me out of print. An article which I wrote urging that there should be more women MPs was rejected by *Reynolds News*, which was, in most respects, a left-wing paper. *Peace News* agreed to print a statement from me, whilst telling me that they did not agree with it. Its content was quite simply that I believed an attempt to create friendly relations and meetings between the peoples of East and West was as important, perhaps even more so, than merely marching against nuclear weapons and tests.

Nonetheless the enthusiasm of my women colleagues in Moscow and Berlin encouraged me to pursue our two aims – the next Mothers' Committee and the Women's Caravan of Peace.

In my annoyance at the failure of the pacifists to accept my plea for approaches across the Iron Curtain, I was unfair to those fundamental pacifists – the advocates of disarmament. While the anti-nuclear agitation, stimulated by fears of radio-active fall-out, hostility to Russia, and the argument now beginning about the morality of Britain's possession of her own bomb, held the centre of the stage, the total disarmers had never ceased their activities. Their protest was directed mainly against the war-like acts of their own government, and can now, in hindsight, be seen as having gone direct to the heart of the matter.

Members of the uncompromising Peace Pledge Union, already in 1952, led by Michael Randle, had trespassed on the United States air

227

base at Mildenhall, Suffolk, in protest against the presence there of the two US nuclear-armed bombing planes. The existence of these planes was unknown to the public; only the voice of John Platts Mills MP had been raised in Parliament about their presence – and put down with vague, soothing reassurances by a rather conscience-stricken government. It is hardly necessary to stress the strength and relevance of American bases on the soil of Britain and Europe here and now, thirty-three years later.

The trespassers had been brought to trial at the Old Bailey; their eager supporters maintained a presence in the visitors' gallery by queuing outside and taking turns for a short time within. I was one of these and, by sheer accident, was there when Bertrand Russell came to give evidence for the defendants. The judge gave Russell a warning against 'incriminating himself' which he cheerfully proceeded to disregard, and then did what he could in support of the intentions and characters of the accused, who were all sent to prison. I heard little more of the proceedings, owing to my brief allotment of time. But this was an early and courageous example of the rising popular protest; it also signifies the beginning of Russell's stand, not as a member of the élite scientific clique, but of the mass of ordinary people. He continued to be anti-Soviet, to favour the 'both sides nuclear' balance, and did not accept the unilateral position until some time in 1958 when he concluded that America was likely to drag Britain into a war with Russia.

What is significant in this history of the nuclear protest is that it seems as if that bleeping sputnik of 1957 was the main cause of the committee meetings between eminent persons, aided and abetted by Kingsley Martin, Editor of the *New Statesman*, that led to the absorption of the other anti-nuclear committees into CND. Was it also the sputnik that prompted Russell's impulse in November 1957, in a moment of desperation about the US–USSR confrontation, during those anniversary celebrations in Moscow, to write those letters to both the 'Most Potent Sirs' – Khrushchev and Eisenhower? It is an intriguing but tragic reflection that, while I in Moscow was finding some light-hearted amusement in those sputnik bleeps, to Russell at his desk in Plas Penrhyn they spelt a warning to which he must respond. If we had only achieved a united policy about Russia in 1917, what might we not, together, have achieved? The contact which Russell established that November with

Khrushchev bore fruit later in the matter of the missiles in Cuba, when Russell was in fact a potent instrument in averting world war. My own conscience moved me to persevere in our efforts to make those in power listen to the voices of mothers, now being raised in all corners of the world. The third meeting of the Mothers' Committee in Sofia was impressive. Twenty-seven countries from East and West, from Albania, right through the alphabet, were represented, including Britain, France, Denmark, Switzerland, Germany, both East and West, Israel, Indonesia, Mongolia, and many more.

Andrea, as president, opened the meeting; Jessie Street (Australia) followed on the subject of disarmament; Tzvetana Kiranova (Bulgaria) was next on the education of youth in a spirit of peace and friendship among the peoples. I was then able to explain our ideas for the Peace Caravan and ask for the help of our members throughout Europe. On all issues on the agenda there was discussion, twenty-nine speeches from the delegates working in two commissions, and in commissions for editing the reports. These were a large number of messages from all kinds of international bodies, as well as from individuals, including Mme Amrit Kaur from India, Tomi Kora from Japan, and Mme Simone de Beauvoir from France. The Bulgarian women took a deep interest in the conference, many delegations came to bring greetings – co-operative women, school girls, medical workers, teachers. I recall specially the presence and address of Dr Sujata Chauduri, with whom I had stayed in Delhi and visited with her the mothers' and children's clinics in the neighbourhood which she had sponsored and regularly attended. There was only one untoward event at this congress, when the Israeli and Arab women refused to sit down with one another. I do not now remember who began this dispute, but it was ended by Andrea's flat refusal from the chair to continue, and threat to disband the whole meeting, if these advocates of peace would not display that quality themselves.

Personally, I took a very great liking to our hostesses, the Bulgarian women, and also to their city, Sofia. There was a charm about its size, compactness and the main buildings. I was also reminded of their hero, Dimitrov, who had won the admiration of socialist Europe for his outfacing of the Nazis in the Reichstag fire trial. His tomb in Sofia is regularly honoured.

When I got back from our very successful time in Sofia, we had barely three months to organise the Caravan of Peace if it was to set out in the early summer. The Aldermaston March at Easter would intervene both to attract and to draw away interest from our project. We planned for a group of women leaving from Britain to cross Europe, reach Moscow and return. Our hope that women from other countries might join us as we passed through proved too difficult. But, travelling by road, our vehicles would stop, we would meet and talk to people. We expected that members of our committee would help to organise our reception as we passed.

We prepared a letter making clear the non-party policy of the caravan. It said (in part):

> Women especially are impatient at the absence of any initiative
> by the statesmen, and many of us feel that the time has come for
> us to act and to make a practical gesture of goodwill from the
> West to the people of the East . . .
>
> Women want an end to these intolerable anxieties which
> haunt them. We cannot wait for our politicians, we ourselves
> must act. We need trade and peace and a secure future for our
> children. Do not the mothers in all countries feel the same?
> Those who join the Women's Caravan of Peace can find out for
> themselves.

This letter was sent out in thousands to every organisation likely to be interested; political parties and all the trade unions. It was handed out at meetings and on the Aldermaston March. Information about the caravan was published in *Tribune*, *Reynolds News*, the *Daily Worker*, the *Co-operative Press*, and their bulletins. Publicity in the national press failed entirely; the *Observer* went so far as to refuse a paid advertisement.

A great moment came when Mrs Ridealgh, secretary of the Women's Co-operative of England and Wales, rang me to say that her committee was 'with us'. They showed at first great enthusiasm, suggesting that the Caravan could set out from the forthcoming Women's Co-operative Congress in Blackpool, then have a big send-off meeting in London. This gave me great hope of financial help in obtaining the women who would travel, and still more, with the Co-operative women's aid, of getting from the trade unions the loan of good coaches for transport. But the enthusiasm did not result in practical concrete promises or financial support. They offered only one Co-operative woman delegate.

Alone in my flat I faced responsibility for the whole project. I had discussed it with David Burke; I now called on him for help, knowing that he was resourceful and a good organiser. He was also Irish, with their characteristic impudent intransigence, and carelessness of risks in undertaking doubtful projects. He was the kind of colleague needed for this adventure. I knew, from the letters that came in, that many women would want to undertake such a journey. What would they be like? How much could they afford for the cost? Transport was the first problem; the second, financial support for subsistence. We made efforts to interest some trade unions and trade union representatives, for we thought that, if we could obtain a vehicle which showed British workmanship, this would symbolise our demand for freer trade relations. The Secretary of the Confederation of Shipbuilding and Engineering Unions refused even to see me to discuss the project. Some manufacturers were approached without result.

We were obliged to fall back on the vehicles which we already possessed, my coach, which carried eighteen passengers and a driver, and which had been adapted and used for holiday camping tours abroad, and a Ford truck belonging to David Burke which could carry luggage and also passengers if desired. Both vehicles were thoroughly overhauled and provided with tents, cooking facilities and a considerable quantity of food. We knew that it would be necessary, so far as possible, to be self-supporting and independent. We were unlikely to have enough money to stay at hotels, though we were prepared to accept hospitality if offered.

Meantime, our group of travellers was forming. Lack of official support in finance, or transport, limited the numbers we could take. To this day I have no doubt that, given just the help we needed, our Caravan could have been of a very considerable size and such as to make an extremely important impression. As it was, our achievement on so little was remarkable. Each traveller had to be asked to find £100 for the whole journey, and lesser amounts for a part of it. As we expected to be away for three months this was not a large sum for travel and subsistence. Nor were the women who decided to come well-to-do.

They were fine people and, as it turned out, representative of different organisations, different generations and points of view. In addition they came from several districts of the country.

Of the full-time travellers, Jane Wyatt, of Bristol, professionally a teacher, had been a militant suffragette; she celebrated her seventy-ninth birthday during the journey. Mrs Hilda Lettice, officially delegated by the Women's Co-operative Guild, was a local Councillor, a JP, whose home town was Worcester. Edith Adlam, a Quaker, was well-known for her work in the pacifist movement in Somerset. Doris Adams, from Plymouth, is a speaker and worker in psychosomatic healing. There were six young women: Rosaleen and Paula Popp, two Irish girls working in London; Jill Vasey, a designer from Rochester; Josephine Warren, trained as a nurse, from Essex; Helga Ginige, Swiss, working in London; Julia James, an Australian working in film production. She in fact made the greater part of the film. The youngest of these was just twenty-one; most were in their early twenties.

Others who undertook a part of the journey were Mrs Sybil Cookson, from Sussex; Mrs Jane Saxby, from Liverpool; Miss Wynne Marshall, from New Zealand; Mrs Diamond, Mrs Allen, Miss Gall, Mrs Grant, from London; Mrs Fynn from Birmingham.

Important members of our party were the two men who undertook to drive, David Burke with his truck, and Alex Piper, who had driven my coach for me. Their invaluable help was given free, as were also the two vehicles.

It was, I think, the spirit of adventure inspired by the Aldermaston marches in this political field, that helped to make the Caravan possible. One of my hopes had been that the CND people might see the advantage of extending their action to a Europe that was already taking note of their existence as a force. Their anti-Soviet prejudices stood in their way. But the really delightful young women who joined us were more open-minded; happy in their independence to represent themselves, with a strength of character which became increasingly apparent on the journey. And the older women, in whom there always lurks that spirit which Sybil Thorndike appropriately called 'the young woman inside', did not lack the sense of adventure both to think and to go outside the confines of family and home.

David Burke and I were up to our eyes in work. Only those who have some experience of organising tours on the Continent will be able to appreciate some of the hard and complicated work which had to be put into this journey. Without the facilities of a commercial tourist agency the two organisers had to cope with the innumerable visa forms, photographs, passenger lists for many frontiers in duplicate, triplicate or even worse! Then there were the petrol coupons and regulations. Distances and times had to be calculated, in the absence of the planned schedule of a holiday tour, for we had no idea what our exact stopping places would be, nor precisely how long we would be in each of the countries which we hoped to visit. While David was immersed in passport photos and visas, I conducted a correspondence in English, French and German, trying to establish a rough time-table of dates. What precisely would be the programme in each country was left in the hands of our friends.

Encouraging support from Edinburgh, helped by the energy of Eileen Mayes, decided us to make this the official starting point. We had been invited to visit the Co-operative Guild Congress at Blackpool: the Guild tried also to arrange for an outdoor demonstration there as a part of the send-off. As this seemed to be against local regulations, we concentrated on a meeting in London. To David Burke must go the credit for the idea of a service at St Paul's. This was supported by the Guild and, by the courtesy and kindness of Canon Collins, the necessary arrangements were made. We received an invitation from Mrs Nowell Hewlett Johnson to spend the night at the Deanery in Canterbury on the way to embark, with the expectation that a meeting might be planned for the evening. But we were given to understand that to accept this invitation would rule out the St Paul's service. So we reluctantly gave up this idea and resigned ourselves to a night on the floor of the Co-operative Hall in Dover instead.

This outlawing of the Red Dean on account of his attachment to Soviet countries, reveals once again the absurd schism in the peace movement with which we had to contend.

It was evidently necessary that the basic principles of the Caravan should be clearly stated. Accordingly, a leaflet was prepared in agreement with the Co-operative Guild. This statement, printed in English, French and German, was distributed widely throughout the tour. It said:

This is a mission of Peace and Friendship among all nations!

Women of the West are on this mission of peace and goodwill to the women of the East.

We PROTEST against the manufacture, testing and stockpiling of nuclear weapons and the building of rocket sites.

We DEMAND that planes carrying nuclear bombs shall not fly overhead.

We PLEDGE ourselves to urge our Governments to negotiate immediately for TOTAL Disarmament.

We call upon the UNITED NATIONS to ACT energetically for peace and disarmament.

We APPEAL to women of all lands to join with us!

WOMEN must help to create a united world at PEACE!

We prepared banners, carrying in English, French and German the straightforward words, 'Women of all Lands Want Peace', expressly avoiding any criticism or comment on the nature and governments of East and West and of all the countries which we visited.

On 26 May, Whitsun weekend, we left London. During that three-month journey there was not one day when we were not speaking, meeting people or travelling; we were never more than three nights in one place, at times travelling all night to keep appointments. Since to tell the story of the Caravan required both a book and a film, it is clearly not possible to relate the whole of it here. It seems best to select some outstanding events, moments of emotion or special atmosphere.

Masses of Co-operative women in Blackpool, cheering and singing, saw us off. Not far away in Morecambe the men's electrical trade union was also meeting. Not only did they ask me to speak and took up a collection, but they organised, at a moment's notice, a surprising, unusual demonstration of men with their banner, marching behind an enterprise undertaken by women. The congregation within St Paul's, the meeting and speeches outside on the steps, were also remarkable.

The start of the journey was less propitious. Our landing at Boulogne was dogged with uncertainties. France was in a crisis over General de Gaulle's bid for power. All street demonstrations were forbidden. Expecting a general strike, all the miners of the district were already 'out'. We drove to a point near the Town Hall where, we understood, someone would meet us. There, in the square within the walls of the old town, were a group of women and children, with the young Deputy Mayor Monsieur Desmoins. We ought, he said, to have been received by the Mayor with 'plush and champagne' and full mayoral honours; there would have been a march by the trade unions. But we should, nonetheless, enter the Town Hall, and there we went, children clinging to us with flowers in their hands. They had taken up a collection for us, offered for petrol expenses, but we insisted that they use it for the miners on strike.

Next day in Belgium, we learned of the fall of the French Government and of great demonstrations, despite the ban. Baron Alard had arranged a reception at the International Club to meet members of the Resistance. Brussels was, by contrast, cheerful and full of tourists to a great International Exhibition with pavilions of some of the countries we would visit. We were able to spend a short time there.

A great ball, symbol of the atom, was poised above all. There it shone brilliant and golden in the sunshine, like an immense question mark over Europe – for peace or war?

In spite of other commitments, radio and television found time to greet us outside the International Club. And beds were found in private homes for all of our party.

We were due in Paris next for two days at a conference of French, German and other European women on Women's Responsibility in the Atomic Age. Our Belgian friends were a little apprehensive about our reception, no one could quite tell what might happen in that troubled city. But when we drove, with our banners up, to a reception offered by the Mayor and municipality of the borough of St Denis, we were cheered at first sight of us in the streets. The Mayor, Monsieur Auguste Gillot, made of this quite a celebration. It was the first among very many such mayoral occasions which we had scarcely expected to receive.

Anxiety about the political situation led to some cancellations by women due at the conference. Marie Claude Vaillant-Couturier, in the chair, was glad to see us arrive, more especially the lively young women. Three women scientists spoke – Simone Laborde from France, Kate Kuperfle from Germany and Antoinette Pirie from England.

I record two significant 'moments' in Paris. On 15 June we parked our vehicles behind Les Invalides. Taking our lunch, prepared in the coach, we gave leaflets to interested passers-by. Suddenly the whole square was alive with police on motor cycles, rows of armed trucks full of St Cyr cadets in plumed hats. Two gendarmes enquired of us: 'Après de déjeuner, quoi, madame?' I intimated that we were, in any case, about to leave Paris. They advised us not to stay just where we were. Asked why not, they replied that there would be demonstrations. 'Oh', said I, 'for, or against General de Gaulle?' 'Both' – and their smiles grew broader. The French political situation was not for us a laughing matter. Paris had spoken already on a great march for democracy. No mob was there from whom these cohorts need protect the General.

At 3 p.m. the General was to try his luck with the Parliament. At precisely two minutes to the hour, we passed the Chambre des Députées. Army, police and Press photographers were all that could be seen.

That evening, just short of Rheims, we camped in a field and open barn at Varenne par Courtements, where we spent the evening dancing with the local people outdoors. Views about de Gaulle were mixed, but no one had a good word for war or atom bombs. Next morning at 11 a.m., we learned that the General had won supreme power.

Our friends in West Germany had fixed 4 June for us to cross the frontier; we had another rendez-vous with our Belgian friends in Liège, a tight schedule which meant that we should be on our way. But suddenly we were surrounded by a group of lively women and conducted to a hall close by. They had planned a demonstration with decorated coaches filled with women and children from the surrounding districts. This could not take place because of the ban. So here they were – nearly all of them, with a long table spread with refreshments, and with champagne – the wine of the country, as they said. The children danced, councillors made speeches, as also did Nelly Maigret, mother of nine, young and good-looking with her smooth dark hair, making the first speech of her life. We had to respond; Mrs Lettice spoke of the Co-operative Women's campaign with the white poppies of peace on Armistice Days.

Our route to Liège was hard-going, by winding roads through the Ardennes. The coach engine over-heated and we broke down about nine miles short of our destination. Before this disaster, we had sent the truck ahead with two of our party. I had neither address nor phone number; by the time, with police help, we had a phone number, it was too late to make contact that night. We slept in the coach. Next day, repairs to the coach, more serious than expected, were undertaken through the generosity of Baron Alard. Somehow the Caravan must keep its appointments. We decided that as many as could get into the truck would go on; the others would wait till the coach was roadworthy. Luggage was unpacked, and repacked, half was stored in a friend's garage. We did not forget to put our banners along the sides of the truck.

The tremendous importance of the supporters of the Mothers' Committee was demonstrated. For the generous help and resourcefulness of Jacqueline Valkenes, Georgette Michot, and other women of Liège, as of Baron Alard, I shall be eternally grateful.

The strength of the anti-nuclear movement in Liège province surprised us; 350 local councils, whose constitutions did not permit of their pronouncing on international affairs, had, nonetheless, gone on record against the bomb.

After four hours of a cool, rainy night, eleven of us, packed in with luggage, round, under and above us, crossed the German frontier near dawn. Outside the main station of Duisburg, I got through on the phone and heard the desperate cry of our Committee member, Milly Bauer, 'Ach, meine liebe, wo wart Ihr? Ich habe die ganze nacht nicht geschlafen.' (Oh my dear, where are you? I haven't slept all night.) Recalling our three sleepless nights, I exploded with laughter.

A good thing we were on time, for we were the guests of the local authorities, who were a bit surprised to find the Peace Caravan arrive in an old military truck, though they agreed with us that it was a better use for it than battling with Rommel in the desert. After some taking of photographs we were ushered on to a launch where the deputy Mayor received us and we cruised up and down the Rhine answering questions from journalists. Around were all the rather sombre evidences of a big industrial town in the heart of the Ruhr. They showed us some fine modern buildings, notably some old people's homes of which they are proud. In the afternoon we took tea at the local Co-operative establishment.

These visits, and some other parts of our time in West Germany, are on our film. But, because so much was in halls, or could not get filmed,

I will give some account of meetings and the contacts we made. The first days in the German Federal Republic brought a remarkable impression of the Germany which had arisen out of the rubble of the bombed spaces. There was evidence of modernity, cleanliness, prosperity in buildings, trains, restaurants and dress. The German zeal for correctness and order is well-known, they would not long tolerate the dirt and shabbiness of our post-war towns.

But what would be their attitude to the anti-nuclear protest? Whoever hankers after respectability or fears ridicule will not make an effective demonstrator for unpopular views. For me, who had known and loved the German people of pre-Hitler days, it was a delight to rediscover them as they used to be, sturdy, warm-hearted and practical, but no longer acquiescent, overcoming their strong bias towards correct behaviour. Unavoidably the bitter memories of the war with Hitler had prevented most people in Britain and other allied nations from recognising that, in spite of brutal Nazi oppression, and the exodus of refugees, there still existed, and among ordinary people and scientists, an undercurrent of resistance and sabotage of Nazi tyranny. Heroes and heroines of the open resistance, as well as the Jewish population, died in the concentration camps. But this was not the only means of resistance. On our journey in Germany we met men and women who had held on to hope throughout the war, refused to escape, but did what they could to preserve humane thought and bided their time for the rebuilding of their country. These, like those who died, were betrayed by the post-war policies of the Allies, who demanded of their former enemies a German army to unite against a 'communist menace' from the East.

We found that, shattered as they were by war and under foreign occupation, condemned with their whole nation as responsible for the atrocities under Hitler, isolated too and lacking encouragement from outside, masses of these Germans of the Federal Republic had been building a strong movement against rearmament, nuclear weapons and war. And this movement was now faced with repression and persecution by their own government, which was directed by NATO. The vigour of this anti-nuclear movement at that date of our visit astonished us. Thousands of professional people – professors, doctors, scientists – also trade unionists and housewives had given it their support. The medical profession already had taken a far more vigorous stand than with us. The German Medical Council at its sixty-first meeting issued a very strong statement, addressed to all world statesmen, categorically condemning nuclear weapons and tests, biological and chemical warfare. In Bavaria medical men and women had underlined this statement by appending their personal signatures.

Though with us medical men and scientists made protest as individuals, their institutions were silent. I had got no response from the Royal Society, nor the British Association for the Advancement of Science. Our Medical Women's Association replied to me that their constitution precluded political action. And when I urged that the bomb was, after all, a matter of health, they replied that they had nothing to add to their previous letter.

At Duisburg that evening women of differing political views came to hear us at a meeting presided over by a local woman Councillor, Anna Hegemann. Our Milly Bauer spoke eloquently, urging that, since the statesmen did nothing, women must act. We learned that local councils and even States were demanding a referendum against nuclear weapons, but the High Court at Karlsruhe, on the application of the Federal government, had ruled that this was against the constitution.

We found that our friends in Germany, as also in other countries that we visited, wanted to commemorate those who had died in the war, not for military reasons, but as a pledge to a future of peace and reconciliation. Our film shows us going to the Reichswald cemetery near Cleves, where, beside the German dead, 10,800 British soldiers and airmen are buried. With us came Charlotte Kugel and Gertrude Lagermann to lay a wreath inscribed 'Deutsche Frauen gedenkenshich aller Muttersöhne' (German women commemorate all mothers' sons). After a ceremony of brief speeches, David sounded the last post. We signed the visitor's book with our pledge against war. Nearly all the gravestones showed that the young men who died were between the ages of nineteen and twenty-five; many were unidentified, inscribed 'known to God only'. One epitaph to an airman read:

From sky to earth
For liberty I fell.
I fought. I won
my wings again
Farewell.

Next day we were in Dortmund, once more received with full

mayoral authority, backed by the big steel firm Holsch, who showed us the evidence of welfare under benevolent capitalism – nursery school and paddling pool. With our guide we lunched with the workers in the canteen. Nowhere in this region could one forget the significance of heavy industry. A broad round chimney belched orange smoke, shaped like an atom bomb mushroom, against the blue sky.

We were grateful for the courteous hospitality, even though capitalist. In the afternoon we viewed a large co-operative establishment, where we took tea with women representatives. In the evening it was the Trade Union Hall that received us, in the German style of public meeting – *gemütlich* – cosy and convivial; no rows of seats, but small tables so that the audience could refresh themselves with coffee or beer. It was a packed meeting and the proceedings were long. Mrs Lettice, Edith Adlam and I were asked to speak, followed by a lecture on the atomic danger with telling lantern slides by Dr Schmidt.

The call for the meeting had been issued by Professor Karl Jaspers, and two women, Frau Clare Kleinert and Frau Muebe. Karl Jaspers also spoke and to him we owed the night spent at very small cost, at a conference and holiday house for 'young Protestant women'. Only just completed, this building, with its lighting, colours, and design, was one more example of modern German architecture.

At that meeting in 1958 Karl Jaspers was to me simply a good friend who helped us on our way in a mission of peace. But in the summer of 1983 I received from a German friend visiting Cornwall, a book which she had just published of the exchange of letters, 1945–1968, between Karl Jaspers, philosopher, and K.H. Bauer, a very eminent surgeon, both connected with Heidelberg University. These two men had been among those who sought to restore their country and its universities to their old brilliance as centres of learning.

In the Federal Republic, Paula Karkutt, our Mothers' Committee member, the wife of a miner, had arranged for us to stay at what were really youth hostels. She accompanied us as we journeyed on down the Rhine to Wiesbaden, where we had the usual mayoral welcome, met the wife of Pastor Niemöller, famed for his stand against the Nazis. In a coach provided by friends we made a useful publicity tour, especially through the streets of the section newly-built by and for the American occupation.

Crossing the frontier from Lörrach, on arrival in Basle we were met by friends who told us that the Swiss Parliament had just been discussing a motion put forward by thirty-five members, demanding nuclear weapons for the Swiss armed forces and that it should be regarded as treason to speak against this plan. The local women were holding a demonstration against nuclear war in the Barfussplatz. It would not be possible for us to speak there. We therefore decided to support them by driving through with our banners up. As we came in we saw the police breaking the women's banners, but before we got through the police were upon us, seizing David by the shirt and conducting us to a police station. Behind formidable closed doors, we protested that the visit of our Caravan had been arranged and expected. The two Irish girls had plenty to say. Speaking in English, thus suggesting my ignorance of German, I listened to what the police said to one another. They did not know quite what to do about us. I told them we had to await the arrival of our coach with the rest of our party before leaving the country. 'Oh,' they said, 'will they do like you?' 'Oh yes,' put in David, 'they are very determined old ladies.' After some hours we were let out but admonished that we must not make speeches. Switzerland was a peaceful country, they said, not in need of people talking about peace.

Outside, friends who had waited, ran beside the truck telling us where next to go. Protest meetings, which we could not attend, were held by our supporters. Bed and food were there for us all. Then a message came that the coach and occupants had gone on to Milan. And so, travelling by night, over mountains, at dawn we were descending the slopes into Italy. We took a surpassingly beautiful road to Turin where we met the Turin Women's Committee and, over lunch, some Co-operative women, photographers and reporters. By evening in Milan we rejoined the others, who had attended some meetings there. The coach was now with us; by the next evening we were in Bologna. Here in the medieval Town Hall with crimson and gold chairs, and beneath crystal chandeliers and ornate painted ceiling, the President of the province and colleagues received us with cocktails, the town's Mayor showed us copies of his council's minutes against nuclear weapons, and paid tribute to the 'gentile Caravana'. A packed meeting of women supporting us was addressed by Camellia Lorenzini, a distinguished doctor of philosophy. Near Bologna we visited the village of Marzobotto, where two thousand men and women partisans together with their children had been slaughtered by the Germans. Here we

241

spoke to honour their memory.

In Verona we found some fifty of the representative men and women of the town and province waiting for us at a cocktail reception, Signor Luigi Bertoldi and the socialist senator Dr Giuseppe di Prisco taking the lead. Later, in the women's office, we danced with the women, embraced, drank vermouth, then settled to sleep on the floor.

On to Trieste and surroundings, where we again met mayors, and the people came from their cottages to offer hospitality and cleared the local communal club to accommodate us.

In the countries on the other side of the Iron Curtain there are national committees organised to put forward the views of citizens on peace. There are also national women's committees forming one body, with local branches which deal with all questions with which women are concerned. We thus naturally had the support of the peace and women's committees. Hospitality and help with transport were given. There were pleasant little ceremonies of symbolic crossings of frontiers when the welcome Caravan visitors were handed over to the care of the next country, the Caravan receiving the national flag to place beside our own Union Jack on our vehicles.

As we travelled by the open road women from the villages would hurry to greet us with flowers or cakes. In the towns, crowds appeared outside the restaurants where we were seen eating, asking that each one come out to speak and be greeted. There were some huge indoor meetings, and also impromptu speech-making outdoors, when crowds collected. In Albania we spoke at one meeting from the centre of a four road crossing where the far-off edge of the crowd was barely visible.

We visited, of course, the main cities: Tirana, Sofia, Bucharest, Budapest, Prague, Warsaw, Krakow, Kattowice and finally Moscow. But in between we covered vast areas of the countryside and some smaller towns. When we drove into Zagreb, into the square outside the main railway station, for some reason our local women friends did not find us. At the central post office nearby I tried unsuccessfully to get to a number we had in Belgrade. We were there all day, parked with our vehicles, talking to people and giving out leaflets. There was no sign that the authorities were displeased at our presence. The police did not appear. We found a camping place outside the town.

The motor road to Belgrade was dull, white and dazzling to the eyes. It seemed endless. Two peasant women thumbed a lift. After we had set them down, we decided to turn back and follow where they had gone. Motorways lead nowhere. We realised that we would need to camp another night. Up the country road we found the village of Novi Varos, near Starogradiska. It was like a fairy tale, with goose girl and flock, storks on the roofs, men returning from work shouldering shovel and pick. An old woman brought a free can of milk to the coach door. For some of our older travellers a huge family bed was vacated. There was singing and imbibing of slivovitz. Next day our friends in Belgrade were relieved to see us arrive. We learned about the heroism of the partisans, saw their women's work in factories and a children's country home.

We had to press on to Albania. On the way, at Hilda Lettice's request, we stopped at a co-op farm which turned out to be a vineyard. After drinking toasts for peace, under our comrade Edith Adlam's disapproving eye, we came away clasping bottles of wine. We were urged not to believe what the Albanians would say about our Yugoslav friends – the countries were not on good terms. As we left the Yugoslav frontier the guards on motorcycles accompanied us up to the entry into Albania. We were not expected to arrive at this frontier post; the amazing way in which a huge crowd of the local people greeted us, is on our film. In Kukes, rooms in a small hotel, damp from scrubbing out, were quickly made ready for us. Next day cars came from Tirana to escort us over the mountains. We were at a Peace Conference, and we took part also in a moving ceremony of tribute at the monument to the partisans. Women and children sang and danced for us. Vita Kapo, leader of the women, and Liri Tashko, with her fluent English, were delightful companions. Unfortunately our coach was badly damaged by the rough driving at Kukes. Mechanics worked hard to repair it, but in the end had not some necessary parts. We went on in a coach provided for us with two Albanian drivers and David driving his truck. A mountain route edged with precipices daunted even the Albanians. All three men achieved a feat of skill and courage. David deserves special tribute for his skill and nerve throughout the tour. At the Bulgarian frontier we were met, as often on this journey, with the ceremony of partaking of the bread of hospitality, then conducted into a coach which was in readiness. Kiranova, President of the Bulgarian Committee of Mothers, insisted that we must stay a week. Mr Volko Chervanko, Deputy Prime Minister, assured us of the government's support of our mission. But there was nothing official about our visit in the kaleidoscope of the next few days, travelling under the constant sun through a countryside rich in crops and fruit, sunflowers and roses, met everywhere by women who held up their babies for kisses, touched our dresses to see if we were real; had we really come all this way to bring them messages of peace? Mr Petko, our interpreter, spoke better English than we did!

From Bulgaria to Rumania we crossed the Danube by the friendship bridge, built by both countries. In the centre of the bridge we all played a game of Rumania's eager welcome against Bulgaria's wish to detain us. As we danced and laughed, the Rumanian women, lovely in national dress, pulled one way, Bulgarians the other, in the midst was the mayor of the frontier town giving us his greetings. Rumania differs greatly from Bulgaria; in language and culture it reveals French rather than Russian influence. Bucharest has an arch resembling the Arc de Triomphe in Paris.

Our visit took in the industrial and literary side, including the great skyscraper printing works, Scanteia, as well as maternity hospitals. The central point was a mass meeting in the huge open-air amphitheatre where seven thousand women applauded us. All day a brilliant sun beamed down on us as Madame Gabrielle Bernacki, of the Mothers' Committee, and other Rumanian women, one an MP, spoke. One of our young members, Jo Warren, and I responded. The audience were not passive, they took every point, waved, shouted greetings and demands that America and Britain stop intervention in the Middle East. We had learned already in Bulgaria that a revolution in Iraq had caused a fear of war and United States' intervention. With no detailed information we did not feel able to do more publicly that hold firmly to our pleas for peace. Our Rumanian friends understood this. But we sent a telegram to our government saying, 'British Women's Caravan of Peace touring fifteen countries West to East, and aware of great tension over Middle East, strongly urges summit meeting reach agreement resolve situation and withdraw troops.' After the meeting Hilda Lettice and I were driven at breakneck speed to broadcast on television. To fulfil all engagements we had to divide into two sections. Everywhere official speeches were interspersed with gaiety, gypsy orchestras and dancing. Gentlemen who had never met an Englishwoman were loth to let us go.

Urgent messages had come from the Hungarian women. Darkness

fell as we progressed, but there was not a town or village without a crowd to greet us, often with cakes and large jugs of hot tea. At a town halfway we were due for dinner; we reached it at 1 a.m. Some of us, including myself, had reached the utmost limit of fatigue. To move, to eat, seemed impossible. But response to such loyal hospitality was imperative. As the serving began a woman teacher rose to speak of the function and duties of women in political life. This unknown ally in the heart of a troubled and unknown land was voicing the hopes and beliefs underlying most of my adult life. Such moments of psychic fusion are like bright jewels, almost mystically illuming the past, the present and the future. As I stood up to give her an answer in almost her own words, it seemed to me as if there were present in the room with us a great company of women who had set themselves free and would make their impact on the world.

At length we reached Budapest at 5 a.m. By 11 a.m. we faced a Press conference and the cameras. One of our hostesses, greeting me in the morning, after my brief sleep, did not recognise me as the haggard individual overnight. The Hungarian women gave us a badly needed rest and talk while they showed us the city. They had themselves been through the agony of the rising in which many of their youth had fled the country.

A telegram had come urging us to spend a week in Czechoslovakia. On the Danube bridge we performed our ceremony of exchanging flags at the frontier and, in the care of Czech women, drove into the square at Komarov where the high balcony of the Town Hall carried the legend, 'Welcome to the Caravan of Peace'. From there to Bratislava onwards our film tells the story of the gifts, the pages full of signatures for peace, the children dancing in costume. This country suffered bitterly from the Germans; at Lidice we visited the rose garden that was planted in memory of the whole of the male population who were shot. We were at Teresin, the dreaded concentration camp, where Madame Hodinova spoke to a vast assembly. I did not know how to reply, but suddenly realised that the date was 4 August, so I began to speak of how my first knowledge of war had come to me in my childhood on that day. From that, with a lump in my throat, I managed to go on and speak, specially to soldiers who were there, about our fears and hopes for the future.

We moved on to Tesin to a farewell meeting. The next morning we crossed to the Polish frontier where a reception committee could be seen waiting. Madame Kralova, international secretary of the Czech women, in her farewell speech said that, with our journey, we had done a great work for peace. It was one thing to dream of such an enterprise, but another to make that dream become real, as our group of women had done.

In Poland there was so much of tragedy to commemorate. There was also the joy of seeing so much reconstruction already undertaken. Here I will record only one special visit. This was to Auschwitz, the death camp where whole families had been incinerated. We saw the sheds in which women lay crowded on mere shelves until they were too weak to work and were taken out to die. We laid a wreath at a memorial stone. I knew that I must speak. It was almost impossible to express our sympathy and horror, for which there were no words.

Time was short. In Moscow our Soviet friends were waiting. They contributed three days of hospitality and an open meeting in Gorky Park in Moscow, at which three of us spoke. We met there Madame Kosmedemyanskaya, whose daughter Zoya, working with the partisans, had been hanged by the Germans. Her son, a partisan, had also died. She had come to our meeting as the appropriate person from the Soviet Women's Committee to receive from us a book carried on our journey and signed by anyone who wanted to record having greeted us. We carried an identical book to bring back to London.

Returning via East Germany, we insisted that we go to Dresden, because of the very severe bombing of that city by the Allied forces towards the end of the war. In Wiesbaden and Liège, on our way home, our faithful friends again welcomed us with hospitality and asked for news of our travels. We were indeed tired and not sorry to be near the end of our strenuous labours. We had left London on 26 May and now it was September. During all that journey there had not been one day when we were not speaking, meeting people or travelling; we were never more than three nights in one place, at times driving all night to keep appointments.

To tell the story of the Caravan has required both a book and a film. I have been able here to give only a record of facts and significant details.

Although we were tired, we were still exalted, carrying back with us the memory of so many different friendly faces; courteous speeches from many men; and from women words that moved us so deeply because they fully echoed the aspirations and hopes within our own hearts.

At the invitation of the Ex-Service Men's Movement for Peace in London, some of us appeared briefly on their platform in Hyde Park, to be greeted, as our film shows, by the sneering faces and hoots of disbelief that it was customary to bestow on anything about the Soviet Union – another of those 'far-off countries' of which the British both know, and desire to know, very little. We were indeed back home.

Our fellow travellers prepared to seek opportunities to speak to organisations in various parts of the country. Meantime I had to take steps about having a film made fit for showing. I also thought I should write an account of our experiences. I had not kept a full diary, but I had notes. I sat at my typewriter and wrote while it was all fresh in my mind. In Drayton Film Productions' Ken Daley and John Ward, we found skilled and interested help in putting the film together. But money was the trouble. I had only so little of my own, but with this, and some help, I managed to get enough. My son Roddy gave £300 out of the compensation which he had, by now, received for his accident in the mines. Even so, we could not afford to record a commentary.

Our communist women friends had loaded us with gifts which we really could not carry home. To my surprise, there arrived for me a large packing-case containing them. Alas, it took £30 customs duty. But I arranged a small exhibition in my flat; I did manage to sell some of these gifts, others I still possess.

I was able to deal with all this work, and had been able to go off on the Caravan, because I had now, in Gena Ingram, a wonderful housekeeper who had come in answer to an advertisement. She became for John and myself a dear and valued friend, with whom we still correspond.

I sent the Caravan book to several publishers who turned it down. And presently we found that the very success of our enterprise, shown by the welcome from the crowds of people in Eastern Europe, began to militate against the showing of the film. Governments, and some political parties of the West did not want known the strong feelings of the peoples of Europe against nuclear weapons and war, more especially those in communist countries. How else could they continue to deceive the people with the story that Soviet Russia was about to attack them?

I persevered. We carried our Women's Caravan banner in 1959 on the Aldermaston March, and some of our friends from Germany joined us, amazed at the way we marched, and casually slept on bare floors. But the CND and the Left remained blindly parochial. It was Macmillen, in 1959, who emulated us, by putting on a white fur hat as a symbol of peace, and crossing the Cold War barrier to Moscow in preparation for the summit of May 1960 in Paris.

The summit was ruined by the spy flight of the American U2, inopportunely brought down by the Russians! David Burke and I, with the truck, took a party of women representing the Caravan of Peace to Paris to lobby the embassies with a written appeal. We were well received, though not at top level, by both Americans and British, and would have been really welcomed by Khrushchev, I felt sure, but the U2 story broke and all the diplomats suddenly began seething with rage and the summit was in pieces. We happened to be near the British Embassy when Macmillen drove by and I remember his anxious face.

The climate of opinion in America, hostile as ever to the Soviet Union, was encroaching more and more on the build up of military defences of Western Europe; equally, it was influencing public opinion and social customs, thus preventing any move towards recognition or friendly overtures to Russia. All the knowledge we had gained on our journey went for nothing. No one wanted to hear us.

Andrea had resigned as President of the Mothers' Committee and I had been appointed in her place. But we took no steps to call a further meeting of the committee. I felt that our committee members throughout Europe had done all that they could, and that our friends and colleagues, the women behind the Iron Curtain, had used every effort and probably dug deeply into their resources, to welcome and support our rather limited and not very efficient attempt to bridge the gulf. They could see that, on our return, we continued to be ostracised and frustrated. As I remembered those peasant women who had embraced us and thanked us for 'coming all this way' to bring a message of peace, I felt like a fraudulent saleswoman offering goods that I could not deliver. I do not think that our colleagues in the communist women's movement as a whole blamed us for failure. With us they too had tried, and they knew, as well as we did, just what we were up against. After all these years, I want to thank all my colleagues once again for their faith and confidence in the integrity of our purpose to unite women for disarmament and peace in the interest of our children and the future of life on earth.

What I felt to be a political failure was not the only cause for concern. The climate of opinion in our country was changing; the era of 'you've never had it so good' and 'I'm all right, Jack', as well as the heyday for the teenager, was upon us. Young people were employed, getting good money. They seemed to require incessant pop music, and radios in full play were carried everywhere, even on holiday beaches. Television as an influence rapidly overtook radio.

Teachers in the schools, who felt that they were required to educate their pupils in the ethical and cultural standards laid down by the traditional consensus of established authority, were alarmed at the prospect of alternative views and values being presented outside school hours in increasingly attractive ways. So on 26–28 October 1960, the National Union of Teachers organised a conference, held at Church House, Westminster, under the title of Popular Culture and Personal Responsibilty. This conference I regard as the watershed, the mountain range dividing the traditional way of life in our country and the social structure, customs, habits, ethical and cultural values that moved in to succeed it and now increasingly prevail. The teaching profession, in contact day after day with the next generation as it grew up, and aware of the problem presented by the growth and changing character of methods of mass communication, called the conference:

> Of those engaged in education together with parents, those
> directly or indirectly concerned with the welfare of children and
> young people, and people involved in the mass media
> themselves, to examine the impact of the media of mass
> communications on present day moral and cultural standards.

Except that it centred on only one nation, this conference, in some respects for me, resembled the world conferences organised by the Soviet Union, in which people of widely differing views and backgrounds searched their consciences in efforts at mutual understanding. I do not think that ever before in Britain – certainly not since – has there been a conference of such wide appeal called to examine the ethical and cultural values shaping the purposes of our nation. It resembled too the efforts of the conference of the World League for Sex Reform which I had helped to organise in

Britain in 1929, in that the participants were all people of creative and progressive intentions who hoped for a consensus of improvement in standards and ideals.

The conference was opened by the president of the National Union of Teachers, Mr S.W. Exworthy, followed with an address by the then Home Secretary, the Rt. Hon. R.A. Butler. The closing speech was by Sir Ronald Gould, NUT General Secretary. A verbatim report of the conference was prepared by Fred Jarvis, then NUT publicity officer. This covers all the eight sessions, which surveyed a wide field: the growth of communications; should we be concerned with its moral and cultural standards; what is the effect of the media, especially on the young; the cinema and recorded music; the arts and design; television and radio; the Press, magazines and advertising; the theatre; the responsibility of providers of the mass media; the restrictions or difficulties of creative persons working in the media; and finally, what if anything, should be done.

I had no doubt that Sir Ronald Gould was the moving spirit behind this enterprise, and when I went to attend every one of its sessions, I remembered his conversation with me at the opening session of UNESCO in Paris, about the futility of editing history and geography books for schools in the face of the new instruments capable of letting loose floods of propaganda and ideologies on communities the world over.

A few sentences from the NUT President's speech indicate how, at that date, they defined the functions of their profession.

Ours is not a narrow view of the teacher's role; the great range of 'out of school activities' involve contact with the world outside the classroom ...

We are conscious too, that young people do not live and work in a vacuum, but that the home, the street, the community and the culture of our society are all vital factors impinging on the education and development of each and every child ...

We believe that ideally the child, the school, the church and the community should all work in harmony with each other, and when these uphold a widely held standard of values then we should have the ideal state. We believe that there must be co-operation and a common sense of responsibility to children and young people shared by teachers, parents and those in positions of authority in the tremendously powerful instruments of mass communication which we now call 'the mass media'.

I cannot possibly enter into details of what, hour after hour, was an utterly absorbing conference, in which every effort was made to give all opinions a voice, even to illustrate by sessions on the influence of films. Education was represented by teachers, men and women, from nursery right up to university; directors of education from local authorities; research workers; parent-teachers organisations. Present were also the chief representatives of heads of television and radio; editors of papers, publishers, advertisers, authors, playwrights, artists, film producers. And, of course, the public was there from the varied organisations which took part, and some came as individuals.

The speaker who opened the very first session is one who still holds a foremost place in our present discussions about culture and social purpose – Raymond Williams. Other well-known persons who appeared were Hugh Weldon, Sir Herbert Read, Arnold Wesker, Norman Collins, Dr Hilde Himmelweit, John Freeman, Karl Reisz, Francis Williams, Jack Longland, Cecil King (at that time the controversial proprietor of the *Daily Mirror*, he was much quizzed about his paper). The exchanges between the 'floor' and the speakers are among the best parts of the verbatim report. Anyone interested in cultural research with an afternoon or day to spare for sheer entertainment, should somehow get hold of Fred Jarvis' splendid book. I take it from the shelf for my own amusement at times and am so grateful to him for it. I wonder what he thinks – or feels – about it now?

I have found just one or two points I made in intervention, drawing attention to the relevance of communication with other countries, notably a recent meeting at UNESCO of the heads of television in twelve countries, 'considering their obligation to seek the truth for their programmes without distortion' and a possible 'code of honour' for themselves. In another discussion I accuse our Press of telling plain lies, especially of falsifying views about other countries, as Lord Silkin had recently complained in the Lords. I said that censorship during the war had led to a deterioration of our Press, from which it had not recovered. I became aware of this on a visit to India, where I had noted the contrast between the Indian English language papers and our own. Our Press, now increasingly under the control of one or two big interests and of advertising, was cynical in tone. I also had something to say about the women's magazines. I mention these remarks because they indicate the extent to which I was always worried by the parochial nature of so much of the thought and comment in our own country.

Marghanita Laski, representing the PEN Club, moved a vote of thanks to the NUT for organising the conference. Sir Ronald Gould concluded with a summing up that was extremely moving in its sincerity and genuine concern. He pointed out that for the first time the teaching profession and multiple other professionals influencing the social life and culture of our people had met in frank and open discussion. He did not consider that concern for the welfare and values of children should be left only to the parents and the schools. One speaker, Jack Longland, had said that the school was an oasis constantly threatened by the surrounding desert. Sir Ronald also did believe that there was a threat. Accordingly, although he was aware that teachers in the public service had an opportunity for direct influence on values, and in the mass media motives of profit determined and limited action, nonetheless, he put the question – are the mass media on the side of the school, or in the desert; upholding or debasing the best of what the schools believe in, or standing on the side, washing their hands of the whole affair?

As to the values which he thought teachers should try to transmit,

> They are simple things, nothing exciting about them at all: truth, honesty, tolerance, a sense of duty, courtesy to others and, not least, kindness to others. These are all values which ought to be inculcated in school, and if our way of life means anything I think too that children ought to know something of the meaning of liberty under law, which is after all a very great element in our sort of civilisation. For what does this mean in practice? It means that quarrels ought to be settled by negotiation and by discussion, and, if that fails, by recourse to a third party and not to force. This indeed is a value which we ought to seek to inculcate.

These values might be given lip servce but they were threatened by the society of the day. As to the schools themselves, they were certainly open to criticism, but their classes were over-large, attention and money should be given to education.

Some participants in the conference queried the fact that no resolutions had been proposed. The organisers had thought it better that the discussion should promote its own answers. Conference agreed on a very mild and general statement:

> That this Conference on Popular Culture and Personal Responsibility records its anxiety at the present results of the mass media on the life and development of children and young people, and urges that the providers of these mass media and those who work for them should adopt a greater sense of responsibility in relation to programmes
> 1) that inculcate hatred and violence,
> 2) that play upon greed and excessive competition.
> It further calls upon teachers, parents and educationists to study these media at first hand and themselves take all possible steps where necessary to protect children against harmful effects and to assist them in critical appreciation of these media.

What shocked me at the time, and still does, was the hostile reception of that conference by most of the national Press. Their attitude to the teachers was one of contempt, as people who had no business to interfere with anything outside their class and examination rooms. The teachers were not asking for censorship, merely for recognition of the problems and some sense of personal responsibility.

In a letter to *Reynolds News* on 2 November 1960, I took this up. A suggestion had been made that the fuss was all about nothing.

> If there were no problem about the mass media and the young, then why did 274 organisations think it worth while to send delegates and why have there been three well considered reports by committees on children and television. Teachers took this splendid initiative just because they know that 'children feel that what goes on in school to-day has nothing to do with the world they know outside.' Teachers are not stuffy old squares, nor by

'defending standards' do they mean boycotting the cinema, telly, or radio, or censorship. They are talking about responsibility for moral values. Nobody can deny that the telly brings the whole 'I'm all right, Jack' outlook, slick advertising, money for jam, and violence right into every home. Certainly adults create those values by their support of a materialistic society geared to total war. Blame those who prefer to spend on rockets rather than on education and care nothing for the future or the young. The teacher does what he can with classes too large, inadequate equipment, an out of date curriculum, determined by examinations. I say 'Bravo NUT' who brought the apostles of mass culture in a constructive encounter. Sorry to see a Co-operative journal in the role of Pontius Pilate.

I shared the anxiety of the teachers, but for many years I had not been directly concerned with education. I had in fact, after my job at the Ministry of Information ended, applied for some educational posts without success. I had no base from which I could do anything to help, but I was now, with adolescent granddaughters, becoming aware of the problem.

As a grandmother, my expanding family had claims on my attention. By 1962 I returned to Cornwall with John. From then on visits from friends and family occupied us. The crisis of the missiles in Cuba, in which Russell played so vital a part, came and went; the war in Vietnam was going on.

In what some of us women had oddly begun to call the 'fight' for peace, there had also been little success in the ten years which I had given to it. I saw that the peace and nuclear disarmers of both East and West were content to remain prisoners of their own ideologies, and had not, any more than the statesmen, really abandoned the chessboard moves of power politics and faced the problem of laying the foundation of a world disarmed, which could only come about by ending the Cold War with its propaganda of hate and suspicion that alone maintained it and alone made possible the 'balance of terror'.

I made one excursion from my base to go to a World Congress of Women in Moscow in 1963. The Soviet Women's Committee were the hostesses, but participants had to pay their own fares. The group that went from Britain consisted only in part of those who had long been politically engaged; quite a number came out of curiosity, almost as tourists.

Hungary was host to us for one night on the journey, and here I met once more my old pupil Tibor Szamuely, who brought his wife to the hotel, and expressed regret that he could not entertain me in his own home, but to have some talk with him reassured me that he and his family existed.

For me personally the congress had some moments of pleasure, others of disappointment and grief. It was a pleasure as always, to talk with Russian friends. There were many younger women now; they showed an appreciation of a speech of greeting from me in which I gave some account of the Soviet Union as I had known it on my first visit in 1920 in contrast with the way things were now. Some of the women who were on our delegation said to me that they would like to meet women from the German Democratic Republic – East Germany, and hear their views on peace. I said, 'What about the peace movement of the women in the German Federal Republic – the West?' 'Is there one?' they asked. 'Of course,' I said and promised to introduce them to its representatives.

The conference was in that splendid new building and hall built within the Kremlin enclosure, and which astonishingly fits in with the traditional medieval structures. At the opening session when the delegates had assembled and virtually all taken their places, I asked some of our delegation to come with me. We crossed the floor and I led them to where a large group of German women were sitting. Here I introduced them to the German women from both East and West, all sitting together, Moscow being the *only* place in the world where they could do so!

There was, unhappily, not the same harmony between the Soviet and Chinese women. The disagreement of their governments, which I had somehow felt to be pending when I was at the celebrations in 1957, had happened, and we were feeling the effects. The Chinese women were obstructed in moving resolutions in the open conference, a procedure that reminded me of my anger when the ILP women at our Labour Women's Conference were similarly treated, and we had replied by walking out. Here in Moscow I was on one of the commissions which, at such Soviet conferences, try by open discussion to conclude by delivering a consensus. I do not now recall what all the resolutions were about, but I tried, over and over again, to find a form of words in which they would be accepted by the Chinese delegates. On such commissions it was customary to take votes. I remember some brightly intelligent Sri Lankan women who also tried to help in the quest for unity. It was not successful. But it is not for me to judge which side was right and which wrong. The Chinese delegates invited us to some celebration at their embassy; I had been known to them in Peking, and our English delegates could see no reason why we should not enjoy Chinese hospitality for a short space of time. Our Soviet hostesses were deeply hurt. They, and soon we also, were in tears. I pleaded with both sides, urging that we loved both, and could not comprehend why they would not love one another. When I got back to London, I found in the *Observer* a brief but unfair account of what took place. The editor accepted a protest from me, limited, as was their wont, to about one hundred words.

Women from Vietnam were at this conference. They spoke with anger and distress about what the Americans were doing in their country. They showed me a photograph of a Vietcong lying on the ground and being brutally treated by American soldiers. At the time I felt hardly able to believe that this could be true; subsequent revelations have, I fear, shown that it was. Russell, at this time, had been trying to get publicity for the Americans' use of dangerous chemicals for the defoliation of trees and crops. He succeeded in getting a letter into the *New York Times*. The Vietnamese women showed me a cutting from that paper and asked me, on my return, to thank Russell for his efforts on their behalf. I said that I would do so and I kept my promise. Meantime, a young woman neighbour of mine near Penzance in Cornwall, Judith Cook, independently acquired fame, a congratulatory letter from Russell, and a foothold in a successful journalistic career by getting a letter on the subject into the *Guardian*. Both she and I took part in some CND demonstrations in St Ives. I tried to persuade a very eminent doctor in London to support Russell in this matter. His reply was, 'Oh, Russell believes that, of course he will believe anything.' Russell's effort to put America on trial for war crimes in Vietnam is known.

I was glad to have been able to attend that conference, but my general impression was of little hope of improvement in international affairs. On the contrary, fresh points of disagreement, even among allies, were increasing the atmosphere of tension and hostility. But through it all I admired the constancy of the efforts of those Soviet women.

Though I lived in Cornwall and presently gave up the London flat, I did not lose touch with the causes which I tried to serve. It was a relief to be free of perpetual attendance at committees and conferences, and to be able to reflect on politics in some peace and quiet. We had not had television in London; down in Cornwall I acquired it, as much for John's entertainment as my own. I began to find that with journals, radio and television, I was able to know more about politics than in the midst of the struggle. But, I also felt that elderly persons retiring to country seclusion ought not to be indifferent to the lives and welfare of their neighbours. Thus presently I found myself on the Parish Council, and one of the managers of the three local primary schools. I continued my inveterate passion for writing letters to the papers. And it was in fact I who alerted local people and our movement to the poisonous work, in connection with Porton Down, which had been going on at Nancekuke. About this, supported by the then keen Liberal candidate for the constituency, we made publicity and caused some demonstrations to take place. A peace movement was active.

My own house and garden, too long only half cared for, needed my attention, but most of all did my family, whose visits became frequent, and with whose lives and interests I had managed never to lose touch.

Notes

1. Harry Pollitt was the leading figure in the British Communist Party.

11

CORNWALL
AND FAMILY LIFE

Very many busy and active people need, now more than ever, to seek some quiet and relaxation from the strain of the endless noise of traffic and the bondage to time of city life. More than many other places, Cornwall seems to have acquired a romantic appeal. Its seas have fantastic changes of colour, and, like its skies, swift changes of mood from storm to gentle radiance. Its great cliffs evoke thoughts of eternity, whilst in their crevices nestle the most fragile evanescence of flowers. Small wonder that many would dream and sing of that 'little grey home in the west'.

For John, as for me, Cornwall gives breathing space, a room for himself where he can type, play the accordion, or idly compose on the piano, giving, as we found, pleasure not annoyance to passing neighbours. And for me to be at home in far Cornwall and my hands in its soil has ever been a source of renewal and a refuge from despair.

From now on, living mainly in Cornwall, I was able to keep open house for my growing family, and in contact with their varied, changing, eventful lives. I had always to provide for the holiday visits of John's three – Ann, Sarah and Lucy. I took pains to try and give them what they might otherwise not have at those times. When in London I took them to their first opera, and to theatres, and Sarah and Lucy once for ten days to Paris and Versailles, paid for by making this coincide with my saving on not smoking for a year, for which I had wanted to find a

258

strong incentive. It worked: I have never smoked since. For other holiday visits, there was always Cornwall.

Harriet, while living and working from the flat in Hampstead, married her cousin Chris Unwin and went to live with him just outside Sheffield, where he was part of the management of a steel firm. Shortly after their first son Barney was born they returned to a new flat in London because Chris was to deal mainly now with Eastern Europe. While Harriet was in hospital in London giving birth to their second son Tom, I remember helping Chris to put down the lino in what was to be the nursery in their new flat. Chris went out to South America for his firm and on his return he and Harriet were the hosts for the first Christmas which John's girls (after the court ruling) were able to share with us, and thus meet 'Uncle' Chris and 'Aunt' Harriet.

Then tragedy struck. Chris, never known to have a day's illness, died suddenly of a coronary in the middle of the night, with no possibility of help. It was on the eve of a planned visit by us all to a theatre. So that the girls should not be involved in the family grief, a friend had them to stay for the remnant of their holiday.

After little more than two years of marriage, Harriet was left with two small boys. On marrying she had resigned from work as factory inspector. Now she turned to the possibility of work in 'further education' for which grants for training could be obtained. As her mother, I felt love and admiration for her steadfast courage under such a burden of grief and anxiety, and also that – unlike so many young people – she did not exclude her mother from sharing in her troubles and discussion of her difficulties. And it was 'our Lil', with that Lancashire sturdiness always at hand, that helped us all to get through.

Later, through the training course, Harriet's meeting with Colin Ward, her second husband, was, I have always believed, a very fortunate chance for them both. At first meeting my new son-in-law and I became friends. The partnership of these two was such as to invite friendship, as many will know who found lively conversation and a welcome at their home in Putney, where both of them worked hard to bring up three boys (Harriet and Colin had a son). Colin's work at Town and Country Planning, and his writing and some television appearances on social and environmental questions are a part of the leaven, or the salt whose savour quietly helps to shape our society. So too was Harriet's subject for a further education syllabus, 'Great Powers of the 20th Century', to which she gave years of work for what has become a text-book now in constant use.

For some years Colin, Harriet, Barney and Tom were a fixture with me in Cornwall for their summer holidays, and I was welcomed by the family on my rare visits to town. As the boys grew and plans changed, Ben only came much later to Cornwall.

Harriet and her brother Roderick had shared with me all the changes and hardships of our lives after Russell left me in 1932, when Roddy was being born. Until the time when I was fully employed at the Ministry and the bombing in London was severe, and I was able to send the two into Bill Curry's care at Dartington School, we were virtually never parted. Love and understanding between us was never broken. Roddy's death last year leaves a void in my life that will last till I, too, die. That Harriet, lovable, capable, dependable, and very much a personality, is still there and in spite of all the cares of family and the horrible political times in which we now live, still finds some happiness herself and imparts it to others, is a joy. She and her brother developed their own friendships and independent way of living, never making demands on me, but not shutting me out. When their father came to live in England (he died here), they both came to understand something of his Irish American nature and the good and bad in our relation to each other.

Their feeling for Cornwall was lasting. Only last summer Harriet and some of her family were here. Roddy and his wife also visited, in the first years of his disability, but there were other places more suitable where access to the sea was simpler. He was able to go by air to spend summers and bathe from the island of Formentera in the Mediterranean. Travel became difficult for him. Nonetheless, recently he planned to come again to the house and the Cornish landscape. On the day he would have arrived, he told John and me on the phone that he would postpone it for a few days. That evening his heart failed and he died. He had lived just fifty years.

Any parent mourning the death of a deeply loved son or daughter whose whole life has been changed and marred by an irrevocable disaster such as came upon Roddy, will hark back to memories of the promise of the early years; to the thoughts of all that might have been, to the agonising doubts of when and how parental care might have failed to

260

prevent, or to mitigate disaster.

Should I have tried to warn my son against the hindrance to a conventional career of left-wing politics? Should I have argued with him that conscientious objection did not require the deliberate choice of two years' service in a coal mine? Had his upbringing and education been wrong? Was this another story of a wasted life?

As a baby, the home to which Roddy came straight from hospital was Beacon Hill School. He often said to me that he was glad to have been brought up in a community without narrow family life, because it left him free of some of what he called the 'hang-ups' from which so many of his friends suffered. He would also add, with a smile and note of pride, that he had two mothers, myself and 'our Lil'. Both of us were there to care for him in sickness and in health and watch over his early development, and both of us continued to do so, serving very different purposes, all through his life. I am in no way belittling the love that came from Harriet, wives, or friends; these and all human contacts were the core, the essence, of his existence.

In the freedom of our school I observed him as physically very active and plucky; climbing, jumping, bathing, showing signs of leadership with his friends; we had no organised games. He was quick to contribute with words in class and making plays, but he was not interested in reading, and was actually nine or ten before he could really read. But then he began to read books both easy and difficult. He later developed a marvellous skill at picking out essential books, and was never addicted to trash or detective thrillers. When the school was in Cornwall for a few years during the war, Roddy fetched the milk on his bike, planted broccoli with me, cared for goats, rabbits and the pony which he and others rode. He and the boys once insisted on watching by night for a prowling badger. His one short experience of a proper boys' school taught him only two things, a loathing of corporal punishment, and a love for cricket, which, when he went to Dartington, he began to introduce into that also no-orthodox-games school! It was there, rather than in Beacon Hill I think on the games side, that Roddy first showed interest in communism.

He was happy enough at Dartington, I believe, but he wanted to leave because he felt he was not doing much on the academic side. So together we went through the difficult years of his balancing between professional cricket and a degree in economics at a polytechnic. I was

261

still earning at the Ministry, but with long hours. In 1949, Roddy was made captain of the young professionals at Lords and was photographed as a promising young cricketer. I think he was chosen rather for his gift of leadership than for special batting skill. This was also the year when my husband Pat died. Roddy felt this death because from childhood he had known Pat at the school, and they had mutual affection and respect.

By 1950 both Roddy and I were trying to arrest the Labour government's mounting hostility to the Soviet Union and the left in general. By then I had no job, it became a struggle to keep Roddy at the polytechnic. We were closely united both in that financial struggle and in politics. I, who had inner knowledge from my work on *British Ally*, as to what had been going on between our Foreign Office and Moscow, could not have brought myself to advise my son to be diligent in economic studies and keep off left-wing politics. He had been brought up in freedom to think for himself and had shown originality and a gift for leadership.

The economics degree achieved, then came the Korean war and the political choices which it forced upon him. I have often thought that, specially in his case, the most tragic loss in being condemned to a wheelchair was that zest for physical activity. The early showings indicate that his adventurous spirit was made for movement and action. Perhaps he should have been a cricketer. It is fine to be a handsome young man standing before your wicket to pit your skill against the bowling, to win the plaudits of the crowd. Why, passionate in politics, did he not stand for Parliament? Some disillusion that came to him was, perhaps, not the real reason. He went on demonstrations and deputations in a wheelchair, but I believe that he would have felt that a politician must be an upstanding, commanding figure on his feet to address and inspire a crowd; he must be able to be among them on foot in a demonstration in the true character of a leader. On the other hand, a wheelchair man is not feeble, his weapons can be negotiation, writing, persuasion.

This was the course that Roddy took. He hoped to write plays for television. *Pay Day*, about a mining accident was a success. As well as the risks, it voiced also some of the political views of the miners. As I recall it, the central figure, a miner played by Barry Foster, was indignant about the death through lack of foresight of his comrades, of an Italian working in the mine. The central character leaves mining and, with a final angry gesture, he takes his heavy boots and thrusts them into the fire of the railway station waiting room – the fury perhaps with which Roddy parted with his legs. Roddy wrote other plays, which were political, and were not accepted. For a time with some friends he tried his hand at film scenarios and scripts. Writing did matter to him. When we talked about work and politics, he would urge me, long before his accident, to write my book on *The Religion of the Machine Age*, teasing me by saying that this was my one really original idea. It is dedicated to him. He did not seem inclined to try for any ordinary jobs; he was, I believe, disappointed at his lack of writing success. The experience of a severe setback, such as that accident, for an energetic, enterprising young man, can long affect him with disorientation and confusion as to what to do next. In some respects Roddy's mood began to resemble that of his father, to whom also a setback to a promising career had occurred, though not so cruel as that which his son endured. Barry was an up-and-coming young journalist at the Peace Congress in Paris, popular and meeting everyone, it is said. His visit to the Soviet Union with John Reed inflicted a damage to his career and his temperament from which he never fully recovered. The arrow in full flight must speed to its mark or fall.

With handsome looks and charm of voice and manner, Roddy had never lacked friends nor love affairs. But we were both worried as to whether his handicap would prevent his marrying. He had appeared serious about one girlfriend. He talked to me frankly, saying ruefully that he was just getting nicely adjusted to sex. In fact he married three times; first a fellow student who came from Israel, then a Swiss girl; his third wife was Spanish. Neither he nor, I think, these girls, really believed in formal marriage, but as they were not English, visas and attitudes of immigration bureaucrats tended to limit the exercise of true freedom.

Once in fun I asked Roddy how it came about that a man in a wheelchair could prove so attractive to women. 'Well you know, Mama,' he said, 'women really like to have a life-size doll.' It was characteristic of him to make a joke of his condition, but I know that there was real love on both sides in those partnerships. I do not think that there was any special reason why he did not marry an Englishwoman. The two later marriages came about partly because he took to living abroad.

He had his first sea bathing as a paraplegic when he came on one of my trips with the coach down to Hendaye on the Spanish border. In the sea, when the legs are borne up, paraplegics can feel their bodies whole, a pleasant experience which can matter to them a great deal. He enjoyed that tour, and Alex Piper, who drove, helped him in and out and with the wheelchair, doing quite a lot for him. I remember Alex saying to me that helping him was no trouble, because, 'he is never sorry for himself'. Similarly, later one of his male friends whom I thanked for something he did for Roddy, said to me, 'Never thank me for anything I do for your son, I love him.'

Roddy went to the Spanish islands for love of the sea bathing and the simple, primitive life, as also for the company of the bohemian young people who congregated there. Among them he met his second wife Claire and later Pilar, the Spanish girl who was a trained nurse and had a local health visiting job. I did not see much of Susie, his first wife. When they married I was working hard and, before long, I was in Cornwall. She did not come down there with him; Claire, and later Pilar, did come. I have seen a great deal of these two, and I love them both. Harriet has remained in touch with Susie, who was very good to John's daughter Lucy when in trouble, and recently also to his other daughter, Sarah. Our family have always intermingled, Roddy and Harriet ready to give brotherly and sisterly help to Sarah and Lucy and likewise even to John at times of need. It was no business of mine as to why Roddy's marriages ended, but I do know that, though there was grief, there was very little recrimination or bitterness.

Claire was very young when they met. He insisted on her coming over so that I might meet her in his flat in London. They had begun living together in Italy. He became ill, developed septicaemia and for weeks in University College Hospital, London they vainly sought the right antibiotic to administer and thought that he would die. Claire barely left him, day or night, and undoubtedly helped to save his life. A friend who had done well in the film world, Lukas Heller, invited them to California. As Roddy told me, he flew there in a half-dead state, but fell straight into the swimming pool to revive.

The narrow confines of party politics ceased to interest Roddy, but his revolutionary stand never changed. He saw, with regret, the move of former comrades towards 'moderate' or right-wing views. His reading must have been intensive; it included the whole of Carr's *History of the Soviet Revolution*. The last time I saw him he was wanting the final volume and complaining that it was so expensive.

Between Formentera and a flat in Hampstead he appeared to settle for a life of intelligent discussion and dispute, often late into the night, with a growing circle of friends. When I, on occasion, occupied the only spare bed in the lounge, at three in the morning I had to suggest that the visitors leave and all of us retire to sleep.

Roddy's Spanish became quite good; to my surprise he suddenly decided to get a grant for language study in Spanish and Chinese. It seemed that there was need for these two languages; in fact the study course would lead to the possibility of going to South America or China. He had always had a love for China, and to find that this language offered a grant and a study course, delighted him. He had no desperate need for money. He had received compensation payment and had invalid benefit, but living was not cheap. He worked with enthusiasm, plastering the walls of his lounge with Chinese characters, fascinated by the way they were put together to create a word with new meaning. Working with Chinese students, he found that there was in them a tradition of the sharing of ideas and knowledge rather than competition. Chairman Mao's advice to students on sharing was thus quite in the tradition.

Because Pilar and he were not married, she was with him only by means of tourist visas. For periods of time he was much alone doing everything for himself, driving his three-wheeled vehicle to classes, and out in the evening for a restaurant meal, doing all the toilet and domestic things that his condition required. I have often thought that all this taxed him beyond his strength. Just as some of his class in Chinese were due to go to Peking, he had to go into hospital for what seemed quite minor attention to the abrasions of the skin that come of too much sitting.

On arrival he had two heart attacks, severe enough to fear that he would not survive or might suffer brain damage. He recovered, clarity of thought fully returned. But the fates seemed determined to play their tricks for his frustration. Now it seemed that the bones of the legs were brittle, could not be mended, and one should be amputated. When I heard the news about a probable amputation, I left John and everything in Cornwall and went up to Pilar in their Hampstead flat. We took consultation from many sources as to whether this surgery was really necessary. Pilar and I talked at some length with the surgeon himself. In those weeks, day after day, Pilar and I set out on the long trek to the hospital in Northwood while this terrible decision was under discussion. Roddy's friends and ours came too, and there was, as ever, lively talk around his bed.

When the day came he surprised the doctors by refusing anaesthesia. Since he could not feel pain in the leg, he said he preferred to remain conscious. Moreover, with the device indicating the state of his heart in view nearby, he declared that if he died under the operation he would at least know the moment of his end. Because of those two previous heart attacks, there was reason to fear that he might not survive. Pilar and I got to the hospital in time to await the result. As we came along the passage leading to his ward, we learned that he was just being moved back there. 'Oh Pilar,' I cried, throwing my arms round her, 'he is alive.' That evening his friends came too, to find him, as usual, mocking fate. 'Where's the champagne to celebrate?' he demanded. So it was fetched and brought, his health was drunk. As Shakespeare said:

> Men are fools that wish to die
> Is't not fine to dance and sing
> While the bells of death do ring?

After this I urged Pilar and Roddy to get married without delay. Their devotion to each other was obvious, and Pilar must have the right to be with him as much as she desired. So they made enquiries about marrying then and there while he was in hospital. I found them laughing because it transpired that marriage in hospital was only permitted when a patient was actually at the point of death! Thus, after making enquiries and correct arrangements, Roddy went in an ambulance to the Hampstead registry office, and the deed was done.

Roddy's life, unfortunately, continued to be beset by periods in hospital due to his condition, but, as one of his friends said after his death, he had found the secret of a happy life.

I last saw him in February 1983 when he was temporarily in the Royal Free Hospital at Hampstead, and I kept a day free to spend with him. It was typical of such occasions – friends arriving, talk both serious and entertaining. Visitors were turned out briefly by a surgeon arriving with a whole army of students. I thought to myself how much Roddy might be enjoying describing to them all the details of his case.

He was reading about the Chinese way of the Tao. He gave me what he said was his non-filial estimate of the Machine Age book; he approved it, and described it as an ideological thriller. I had sent a typescript of the book to him at Christmas. When he died before it was published I added an epilogue to the dedication. He said to me, 'You and I have got to have two days' talk before we both die.' It was for this that he planned the journey to Cornwall once more, which he was not able to accomplish. It is tragic that we did not have that last exchange of views between us two small comrades in arms in the age-long struggle for life, love, beauty, happiness, liberty for men and women on this earth, against the dark forces of hatred, tyranny, destruction and death.

Roddy's funeral at the Hampstead Cemetery on 25 April 1983 was more like a festival occasion than one of mourning. Harriet and her husband Colin notified his circle of friends. There was standing room only at the secular ceremony in the chapel, where those who had known him at different stages paid tribute. Colin wrote of how he would sit with his guitar and sing the Irish lament for his namesake Kevin Barry, and the American workers' songs, of Woody Guthrie's 'Hard Travellin'. Hard travelling, which he took with incredible good humour, had been Roddy's own experience.

He was, automatically, and without thinking about it, a world citizen. If he fell in love with a person, or even with an idea, he fell in love with a whole culture and its history and aspirations. He was a self-appointed stateless person, an honorary citizen of everywhere. Roddy was, for example, an honorary Jew. He was instantly at home in a world of wry humour, disputatiousness and instinctive human warmth. And by the same token, he was an honorary Arab, an honorary American, Russian, Swiss, Italian, Spaniard.

Roddy's life was a continuous love affair with people and ideas, nothing at all to do with states, frontiers and governments. He was always making new discoveries and was anxious to share them.

I have given this space to Roddy in this account of my relation to my family because, while he meant so much to those who knew him, his life also has a wider relevance. Praise and glory are copiously given to those who die in battle in the pursuit of wars. The 'patriots and lovers' who go forth in the quest for peace are likewise 'comrades of danger' but far too often also of 'poverty and scorn', like the Greenham women of today. There are very many who have died and suffered for human aspirations far more than did my son. But I am one of those who knew intimately what was the cost to one such comrade, and those who loved him. Therefore in honour of all those scorned and unsung millions like him, his story should be told.

My close relations to my other two children, John and Kate, were broken by the divorce proceedings between their father and myself. It is not always understood that the divorce took place at Russell's request, I would have wished our partnership to continue.

I knew that since Russell had an hereditary title, personal distinction and money, their life with him would now be very different from any time they would spend with me. It was evident from the start that Peter attached importance to titles and names of distinction. When she became Countess Russell she also changed her names to Patricia Helen. The feelings of the children followed the correct Freudian line: Kate was devoted to her father, John to his mother. John once told me that he never forgave his father for leaving me.

My relation with Kate troubled me over the years of separation. I have told in *Tamarisk Tree 1* of the very close link between us, when she was four, and for the first time I left her for a lecture tour in the United States. We were both affected by that parting. In the school before the divorce, Kate followed her own bent in work and play, she liked to wear shorts and was rather boyish. When Peter came as holiday governess she gave her attention to Kate more than to John. After the separation Kate was encouraged to take an interest in feminine delights, in clothes and style and dressing for dinner. As she grew, feminine interests would have come in any case, but these she related to her stepmother, and for a long while Kate preferred her to me, who was regarded as rather casual and dowdy, and of course, not so well off. But we did have some good holiday times. They were not with us for Christmas, so once Pat and I went to Gamages with them later to buy presents. Their choice was a little capuchin monkey for John, and a furry little grey kitten for Kate; we took care of these and tolerated as well a wheezy pet rat that Kate was sorry for and cherished.

Their departure in 1938 on the eve of the war for America broke contact. Though both were over during the war for a time, they were back there as the war ended, and both married Americans. I accepted these in-laws, there were no quarrels. Kate had two sons and a daughter when her husband Charlie gave up his rewarding work under the US government. They had decided to become Christian missionaries. Charlie was attached as a deacon to St Andrew's Church in Plymouth, England. I visited them there; there their son Andrew was born, and it was Harriet who came to stay with her half-sister when the event took place. They did a period of missionary service in Uganda, fortunately before the later outbreak of savagery there. Kate wrote to me of the warm welcome from fellow members of their church given to them on their return home. But Charlie spoke, or preached against the Vietnam war and his connection with the church was arbitrarily severed. For both it was a difficult time. Charlie found temporary work with the Quaker Peace Committee in New York while Kate coped with the problem of children and the city streets. Presently, Charlie obtained a post teaching in an independent school. Rearing and educating four boys and one girl occupied them both. Outside her home duties Kate has also worked, but though qualified with degree and doctorate, she has never, in my opinion, been given the status and opportunity which her intellectual ability deserved. For what intelligence tests are worth, her IQ was one of the very highest of those we tested at Beacon Hill School.

Kate and members of her adolescent family either together or separately have made frequent visits to Carn Voel. Once, when I was showing Kate some family correspondence, I asked her if she remembered the trauma of our parting in 1928, when she was four. She had not forgotten, was conscious of it still. That moment stirred deeply in me all the maternal tenderness for her that had always existed. J.B. Priestley once wrote about 'these moments' – flashes of insight and feeling that may connect two people, or an individual with a scene, a sound, a familiar scent. Such memory intuitions can keep members of a family in contact in spite of separations in space and time.

For Kate, her father continued to be the finest man she had ever known, her love and admiration unchanged even by the realisation that, though a supporter of votes for women, he was not a true feminist. When he died in 1970, she wrote that she needed me and wanted me to come to America. She and Charlie had separated – she felt very much alone. It was difficult either to leave John or arrange for him to come with me. Also Russell's death automatically put an end to my alimony (£500 a year subject to tax). I had to earn. I began to write my autobiography and to prospect for advances from publishers. By 1972 I could afford to organise what became a family reunion. Kate, with her daughter Annie (then studying medicine), and her sons Andrew and Ben, were able to book on a charter flight to Paris. John and I came there to meet them, via Southampton to Le Havre. Kate's son Jonathan was already in Spain and joined us later in Cornwall. Only David, her eldest, was absent. My friend Jacqueline Giroux booked a hotel for us in Paris on the Rive Gauche. I booked the rest of our Continental tour – hotels and transport. I found that the usual choice for tourists was between travelling with your own car, for which there were easy facilities, or a fixed route organised by a professional operator. Thus I had to act as operator and courier on my own.

From Paris we went to Geneva by a train at such speed that the scenery flashed past before we could see it. In Geneva we were entertained by my old friend, Thérèse Nicod. But Mont Blanc disappointed us by being shrouded in mist. From Basle the tour by coach through the Black Forest was marvellous, and at Rudenheim we skimmed over the vineyards by cable cars, thence by Rhine steamer past the Lorelei rock to Cologne. I had promised John he should eat cream cakes and drink coffee *mit schlagsahne* (with whipped cream) in the shadow of Cologne Cathedral. One anxiety of this tour was the phobia of train travel which he had developed. With us all there surrounding him this was overcome and on the cable car trip I, and not John, was the one to feel nervous. The Russells (John and I, plump and mature, excepted) never missed an opportunity of mounting skywards up buildings – the Eiffel Tower, Notre Dame, Cologne Cathedral, and in London, St Paul's. Their tourist energy was untiring and helped by Kate's fluent German first learned at Beacon Hill. We travelled to Wiesbaden and Frankfurt, and home via Belgium. Annie later produced a book of photographs of the 'Grand Continental Tour'. In London, Colin and Harriet housed the family indoors and out. John, Annie and I queued for hours to see the Tutankhamen exhibition at the British Museum, then got a taxi and just caught the train for Penzance to prepare for the final part of the reunion of both families at Carn Voel.

Kate and Harriet had the memory of the four years of Harriet's college days in America; but for some it was a first meeting. We enjoyed ourselves wholeheartedly and were rather proud of our achievement. Everything had gone well and without a hitch. This reunion of 1972, though two years after her father's death, was designed to reassure Kate in her lonely endeavours that others of her family were there in case of need.

Before this, in the 1960s, as John's three daughters grew up, they began to present the problems that belonged with that generation's outlook and needs. Ann, the eldest, always rather managed, but also took care of, the younger two. She showed her independence by her choices in holidays and activities. But she could share everything, no difference was made because she was adopted. All three had been at a young ladies' boarding school with good intellectual standards, though, by persuasion, Lucy got to Dartington for a period. Ann's taste was for the Arts, Sarah obtained a scholarship to Lady Margaret College, Oxford, and Lucy reached university standard at Kent University in Canterbury. Like thousands of their generation they went holiday hitch-hiking in Europe, through Spain and even to the borders of Africa. But they had been brought up in a rather unusual and very sheltered environment, and without the advice and guidance that adolescents, whatever their adventurous spirit, do sometimes need. Even Kate had found her much-loved father inadequate at this stage. Now he and his wife Edith were more than ever immersed in politics.

It fell to Harriet and Colin, Roddy and his wife Susie, in London, and to me either there or in Cornwall, to become involved in the love affairs, aspirations, and consequent escapades of these three.

Some part of what they did and felt must, I think, be related because it illustrates the mood of that generation, a mood of revolt but also of despair, distressing and often angering their elders who failed to understand it, or to learn the lessons which it should have taught. The bomb that those elders loosed over Hiroshima fell upon the hearts of the young. They could not forgive it. Its shadow haunts, and has never gone away.

The hysteria of pop festivals, agonised screechings at the microphone, expressed the need to find a sense of community and belonging that had departed from the autocracy of the religious and national loyalties in which they had been reared. There was flower power, which said 'make

271

love not war', then the fellowship of the 'drop-outs' and the turning to meditation and the Indian religions of mysticism, quietism and the relaxation of yoga.

Ann, more extrovert than Sarah and Lucy, though concerned about their affairs, got married, divorced, then was involved with a young American pop singer with whom she went to America. In a third marriage, she lives now with husband and daughter in New Mexico. Colin and Harriet saw much of her in the years before she left England, and Kate visited her recently.

Sarah and Lucy, both introvert in character, though not inactive, became 'drop-outs'. 'Drop-outs', it seemed, were a sort of fellowship, repudiating and refusing to serve the abhorred social system, moving about like mendicant friars, seeking their food and bed (or pad) wherever these might be found. Meantime their thoughts were bent on what sort of world nuclear disaster would bring and how best to prepare for it. I think in some way this disaster loomed like the prophesied second coming of Christ, it was expected to come very soon.

My home was open to Sarah and Lucy, who came with their friends for short or longer stays. Most of the time they were wandering about. My anxiety was in trying to find out where they were and what might happen to them. Now and then other wanderers would knock on my door, disappointed to learn that Lucy had just gone away!

After a term or two Sarah gave up her university career and scholarship. I spent hours when she came to Carn Voel vainly imploring her not to do this. The traditional teaching of school and university seemed to have lost all meaning for these young people. It was a waste of time and bore no relation to what they called 'real life'. How they proposed to live 'real life' was not so clear. Surely, as I argued with Sarah, three years in which to think about life and your future in peace and quiet were worth having? Her subject was history; she complained that because she had a scholarship 'they' wanted to drive her too hard, she would have no leisure. History, anyway, was past and not real life.

Every sensitive young person goes through a period of asking what is the meaning of the universe. It is a time that may be critical, when emotions stirred by questioning and speculation can cause breakdown or disaster. Once over this hurdle, young minds relax and can mature at ease.

272

In what does 'real life' consist? For some, the answer may be to find god. Most people presently find their answers in the changing and chances, the fullness and abundance of mere ordinary living, and the recognition that the universe will not yield up its secrets in one lifetime and, whatever our hopes, probably not even after death.

Sarah's quest for god and the meaning of life was individual, pertaining to herself. It has led her to wander about and travel in many places – twice to India in search of the teaching of a guru. She is still young enough, and also old enough, to find her own way to the solution of her own problems.

Neither of the two girls was interested in the passionate campaign of their grandfather for nuclear disarmament. But Lucy's quest was the more social and even political in aim. Those who taught her at school and university thought highly of her intelligence. She herself worked hard to secure entry to university. Through some funds in a Trust which Russell had established for the girls, she was, in the summer of 1968, on a course at the Sorbonne. From there she wrote to me that 'this is a place where I can really study'. But halfway through she gave up and came back to England, thus missing the outbreak of the near-revolution which the students, backed by the French workers, provoked.

Yet in her was a revolutionary spirit active on too many fronts, willing to experiment in too many directions. A love affair with a young Arab, whom she met while hitch-hiking in Spain, raised the colour question and consequent involvement in the attitudes of lodging keepers to such partnerships. Once she consulted Roddy in confidence about taking LSD. There was so much about Lucy's life and contacts of which I knew very little. It was when she spent long summer months at Carn Voel that we talked. I knew that when, after various escapades, her young man had left England, she went out to find him again, only to learn that he had lost interest and was back amongst his family and their traditions. She told me something about discussions among students, about which she contemplated (and even began) a novel. Class seemed to come in a great deal; she complained of young men accusing her of her aristocratic descent. Like others of her generation she had the idea of finding a cottage and some land on which to set up a commune. She talked happily of some days spent camping like primitive people sharing food and labour, seeking an example of what would follow the breakdown of our industrial society. The turning point for her was a visit to Katmandu to learn meditation and its religious observance. She then became a Buddhist and planned her diet accordingly.

Though I believe in tolerance, and raised no objections to her religious views, this choice distressed me. I knew something of her ability. We had frequent, though never acrimonious, arguments. I urged against 'dropping out', arguing that it was not really possible while living within, on and by, our social system, to follow the beliefs, customs and habits of one totally different. I too – I would say – hated our worship of the machine, and the invention and threat of nuclear weapons, but, however much we might learn from other civilisations, our job was to struggle against the iniquities and abuses of our own. I did indeed feel that all this movement of young people towards cults and new religions was for some in the nature of an escape from dilemmas they did not care to face. Apart from that, it was drawing away the youthful energy so greatly needed to contend with those very dangers and evils of our times.

The Vietnam war was going on, our Labour government did not support it, but would not oppose it; it preyed on the minds of all of us who were constantly seeking a way to a peaceful world.

Lucy, so bright and lively in her schooldays, had become intently serious. Looking back, it does seem strange to me that neither she nor Sarah ever seems to have had much use – well, just at times – for fun.

Lucy was mentally disturbed and, for a time, in hospital. Later, when better, she was, characteristically, active with some people in quite a well known 'squatting' incident in London.

On what was to be the last of our frequent discussions, Lucy told me that she would like to go to India and become a Buddhist nun, but needed money. I began to think of how I might help in that. The next thing I heard of her was that, emulating the monks and nuns of Vietnam, she had burnt herself to death. The Americans were then just bombing Cambodia.

It is unbearable for me to write about that death, which I felt should have been prevented. It seemed to me that not only I, but all those who had been responsible in some way for the care and guidance of Lucy, had failed in understanding and the help that we owed her at this critical adolescent stage.

I did see that her Buddhist faith had become the centre of her being, and I think that perhaps she really believed that her soul or spirit would live again in some other body or shape. She seemed to me also to suggest that she had not done enough, or served sufficiently or rightly the social and political causes which she had followed. From this had come the idea of devoting herself as a Buddhist nun in India. To advise against or oppose such religious vocations is almost futile, if not ethically wrong. Lucy was to me a lovely young woman, brave, gifted in mind and spirit and on the threshold of life in which for herself and others there was so much that she could have achieved. I could not follow her faith. I had hoped to help her to its wider application in a world or society unbearable to both of us, but in which there might still be something our actions or beliefs might alter.

It was only after her death that I heard from several who had known her about some events and fears in her life. Roddy told me then that when consulted in confidence about 'trips with LSD', he had advised anyone with fears against taking it. And he, who had himself made a choice, out of a sense of a compelling human obligation, which had brought tragedy in his own life, once said that if Lucy could not tolerate the life which our system compelled her to live, she had a right to take herself out of it.

For me both Lucy and Roddy belong to those whom we honour without medals, that band of 'patriots and lovers, comrades of danger, poverty and scorn' who are now the only hope of human survival.

12

THE GIFTS OF LOVE
AND FRIENDSHIP:
JOHN BECOMES A LORD

———————

Those of us who settle for a permanent home in Cornwall soon become aware of the consequences: that summer invasion of friends and even bare acquaintances who find themselves in the neighbourhood and knock upon our doors. They may seek only to exchange a few words and a casual cup of tea. Others hope for an invitation for a longer stay. I do not say that such people are unwelcome, merely that, in my case, with members of my family of all ages occupying the holiday months, it was not easy for me to entertain my personal friends, most of whom, like them, only had the holiday months of freedom.

Philippa Burrell, a writer, Jane Wyatt, Suffragette and eldest of the Peace Caravan women, and Dolly Farrelly, Jane's friend, once came for a brief holiday. I had met Dolly in Bristol when we showed the Caravan film. She lived on her own, separated from her husband, and we became very close friends. She came to stay with me, not permanently but for long periods; thus we were together through the comings and goings of my numerous family, every member of which she came to know with affection and understanding. I had no domestic help and did most of the cooking. But together, for whole afternoons, we worked in the garden. Dolly was not physically strong but she had a passionate love of flowers, sowing, planting, caring; indeed, a love of the whole of nature. She would listen for the call of birds and watch them. For her, plants were not just things that grew, each had its own individual personality, almost a soul. I thought of Dolly as Irish, I don't think that she really was, but she had been in Ireland a good deal, especially at the time of 'the troubles', which meant the Black and Tans.

Dolly was the most intimate friend of my life. We were in harmony in our political views. It was her presence and care of John that made possible my visit to the Moscow Conference of 1962, and other occasional absences from Cornwall. But though we met through politics, our love and friendship were not on that basis. Our relationship was entirely personal, belonging only to us. I felt happy at her presence in the house, loved her comments and flashes of wit; her sensitive affection entered into every aspect of my life. It may be that our friendship was, for both of us, a remedy for loneliness.

While writing about Lucy I remember how, when she was at Dartington, Dolly and I, to please her, fitted out an old bicycle of mine for her to take back to school; how Dolly had also talked with Lucy, knew her value, shared my grief and anger at her loss.

One marvellous thing that Dolly did for me was to turn one room into a study in which to write what became the first volume of my autobiography, *Tamarisk Tree 1*. She papered the walls with the bright coloured, artistically very good, covers of a Polish magazine which used to arrive. There I could sit by a window that gave me a view, not only of the back entrance gate, but of the distant hill of Chapel Carn Brae. Dolly was proud of her own home which she retained in Bristol, where occasionally, when I could get away, I was able to visit her. Her son Denis, who loved and admired her, came to visit when she was with us. I remember how he liked and quoted some of my poems from my autobiography (many reviewers despised them). As Dolly's health declined, Denis took an early retirement and went to Bristol to take care of her. He brought Dolly down by car on what he and I both felt would be her last visit. John was temporarily in hospital in Bodmin; Denis drove Dolly and me there because she wanted to see him. At Carn Voel, she was delighted by the old familiar views from our windows and, of course, it was she who, in the early hours, spotted young foxes in the coppice at the bottom of the field. During the following year came the expected phone call from Denis to tell me of her death.

Those years of the sixties and seventies up to and after Russell's death, filled with anxiety about money, worry from family matters, more especially about John and what was happening with his daughters, writing day after day, keeping open house, seeing to house repairs, catering, were I think the unhappiest years of my life. Every human being lives alone in the face of the universe. Merely to survive we need fellowship and co-operation. But what keeps each solitary individual going is that he or she has someone who believes in and cares just for that person and what for him or her is the meaning of life. It is in this that true friendship consists. Dolly helped me to live through those years and to believe in continuing to pursue, with what ability I had, the purposes that I thought worthwhile.

There was also some fellowship to be found among those involved in local politics. Among the local councillors, I met in Robin Ball someone whose public spirit I noted and admired, especially during an enquiry about preventing the tearing up of our beloved Chapel Carn Brae and turning it into a clay mountain like those that bring prosperity but so greatly disfigure the Cornish landscape. He began to talk about technology which was his work and interest, and I about the machine age. Because of those discussions and his continuing interest in the theme, though I had been working on *Tamarisk Tree 2*, I started, and did finally complete, the arduous task of *The Religion of the Machine Age*, on which Roddy constantly insisted. But Roddy was not, like Robin Ball, at hand to encourage me from time to time to keep going. I owe the book to both of them.

About John I have already written much, as is natural, since from 1954 onwards he has shared my home. About his own activities there is also more to be said. Here I want to mention some things about his relation to his father because, in many ways, they are characteristic of the relations of most fathers and sons which I feel to be unfortunate and harmful to both. It is well known that virtually all men hope that their first born will be a son, that sons are requisite to follow in their fathers' footsteps and inherit their wealth, if such exists. In some cases there is, as with John, an hereditary title.

I was never under any illusion that if I had deprived John of his nobility by refusing to marry, Bertie would have forgiven me. He might even have broken our partnership and disowned our son. Though he did not entirely approve of his brother Frank, the Earl, one only had to see them chatting together to recognise in both the characteristics, good and bad, of a long line of ancestors deemed superior to ordinary men, born to attain distinction and to rule.

Bertie loved his young son, delighted to play with him, but showed the usual parental ambitions to rear sons whose intelligence, courage and ability would do them credit. John was not beaten or punished by his father like many sons, but being handled with logical and elaborate explanations may have produced, as Kate and others have suggested, a sense of guilt and awe similar to those evoked by punishment and severity. How could a child reach the high standard required? This dilemma has faced other children educated in schools directed by a parent.

It is clear that from the time Bertie left me, John fell into disfavour, which did not help him to make the best of himself over the ensuing years. When Bertie set up the joint household at Richmond he had at the time as much need of John as John of him. John had done some good writing, he had felt able to leave the Civil Service and rely on his father's promise of a home and support, in return for the care which John was able to give. John would never have left that real home for himself and his children which he cherished, if he had not felt so much less welcome and needed once a new wife was installed. Bertie could have helped him, very much too, to find openings for his writing, much of which was remarkably good. Some father–son jealousy appears to have entered in, totally unnecessary one would have thought in this case. This reciprocal father-son, son-father antagonism is one tradition that may perhaps fade out, if the patriarchal system can be diminished and overcome. Did Bertie not realise that he was himself breaking a compact in letting his son go away without a job, home or security, and in addition with three dependent children and an unstable wife? Nor do I doubt that, after his wife left him, John could have been persuaded to return to what was still, in the holidays, his children's home. John had little alternative but to break down – which, significantly enough, occurred near to that Christmas when he left my flat to visit his children. John says his father would not have him back to live because he thought he was mad. But John could certainly not have been so described until that Christmas when I was informed that the doctors had put him in hospital.

This was all past history when, in 1970, Bertie died. John had by then been receiving a small sum from his father. Under the will he was left an annuity of £300 a year. (My alimony, as already explained, ended at

279

once.) It seemed that John would have barely enough even to live in National Health hospitals. I decided to apply for an increase in his annuity, and on legal advice put him and his finances into the Court of Protection. They accepted me as his Receiver.

The Russell 'Estate' – quite large, though all in royalties – was shared mainly between the Russell Foundation and his widow Edith. The administration of his copyrights and documents was in the hands of literary executors, not, as is usually the case, the concern of his heirs Kate, John and Conrad.

By my own earnings, and two applications to the courts on each of which John's allowance was slightly increased, it was possible for John to continue to live out of hospital with me. He had in fact been persuaded by me to accept a brief stay in hospital and treatment by a drug. In his own continued opinion, this drug makes not the slightest difference to his state of mind, but, in the opinion of others does, while diminishing 'fantasies', help an individual to live life on what is considered a more normal basis, and even to earn a living.

John was now more rational and attuned to ordinary life, but a job was still not very likely, nor was it easy to publish his work. It seemed to me that he had one right of his own to participate in what was considered part of our society and constitution – the House of Lords itself. So one day John and I went to the door by which the public have access to Parliament. We told the police on duty there that we wished to go and find out how a Lord could take his seat. 'What Lord?' they said, 'This Lord,' I replied pointing to John. John then told them in detail which Lord he was, and they looked him up carefully in their book. Thereupon they said we should go right through the Commons lobby and thence to the Lords lobby and put our question to an Usher there. In the lobby the Ushers brought to us a very pleasant and knowledgeable lady who gave us much information, which we then took to John's solicitor, Mr Derek Taylor. We found that unless proper procedure on the part of some elder member of his family was taken in time, John might lose his right to sit. Mr Taylor and I then set about the necessary procedures.

Meantime, I took steps about some accommodation for John in London during sessions of the Lords. We went to see Miss Jansen, who had already done so much in establishing hostels for mentally disturbed people who had left hospital fit to take jobs. She was about to take a delightful house at Twickenham with a garden down to the river. John liked this and we arranged for him to have there a very pleasant room. The rate for board and lodging was £40 a week which had to be paid all year except for three weeks. For out-of-London peers there was, of course, an allowance of first-class return fare plus a certain settled sum per day of attendance to pay for nights at hotel or club. Knowing John's fears of rail travel, I thought this plan would, at first, be better than a weekly rail journey and that he would of course be home in the Lords' vacations. His total income was then only £40 a week, and we had to accept some help for him as a patient from the Cornwall County Council. On means testing he had about £10 a week pocket money when in London, the council recognising that he did contribute to the rates of our home in Cornwall. We believed, as did Miss Jansen, that when John took his seat in the Lords, his out of town allowances, then about £13 a day, would help out to just meet the deficiency.

Everything went well. I received letters from him full of joy and pride. He at last felt himself to be taking part in what was held to be the work life of our society. Whatever he might feel about the House of Lords, he, born to be a peer, could at least contribute something. He attended the Lords about two to three days a week, had company at the hostel, and on Sundays lunched with my daughter Harriet and her husband and played bridge with his nephews there.

John made his maiden speech on 21 July 1976 in a debate initiated by Lord Brockway about feeding the world, in which he was complimented by Lord Richie Calder as well as by the Black peer, Lord Pitt of Hampstead, who, I felt, understood best what he said. Lord Brockway was happy to see and hear the son of his honoured friend Bertrand Russell.

Then came the bombshell. The Court of Protection ordered me, without a word of explanation, immediately to repay the Lords' expenses grants which I had banked in good faith in John's account. I refused to do this without any reason given. I was told that John was now permanently resident in London, and thus could not claim out of town peers' rights. Furthermore, they repudiated that he had any obligation to the house in which he had been living for at least sixteen years, sharing with me our resources. Nor was he, in any sense, 'permanently resident in London', and in fact, had he been taking all his rights, return weekly first-class travel, he would have cost the country considerably more than on the arrangements we had made.

To my amazement, John's solicitor, Derek Taylor supported the demand of the court; all the bureaucrats seemed to be in a state of terror as if we had committed a crime. Other Lords said I was right, but such is the discretion that surrounds these grants that an argument about them can be dangerous! I briefed Michael Rubinstein and a meeting was arranged for him and me with the deputy master of the court; I could not convince him that the court had misunderstood the arrangements I had made, nor make him understand just why in the interests of John's own psychical welfare I had made them. I warned him that I could predict what my son would do if our action was not accepted as correct. Threatened with being deprived of my Receivership I had to give way. The money was repaid. This made the financial situation impossible for both John and myself. As I expected, John, in great anger, packed his belongings, returned home and thereupon refused to accept the medication that I did think had helped him.

Lord Brockway, when he later heard what had happened, assured me that I had been right in supposing that the basic motive of expenses grants is to assist a peer's attendance. He wanted to take some action but John's solicitors' adherence to the court's decision proved an obstruction, and by then, it seemed to me that any action was useless. I did try, through the Parliamentary Commissioner, to criticise the court's action, but it seemed that he had no jurisdiction, the court being answerable only to the Chancellor or High Courts. My own view is that the Court of Protection, having been instituted mainly to protect minors and others in need of such care over their finances, was concerned primarily only with money; they had neither the staff and hence not the understanding to deal with the needs of the increasing numbers of the mentally disturbed who come under their care. I do not know whether they have as yet been able to increase and extend this important feature of their care.

John himself, in a mood of anger against the severity of police action about cannabis and other matters, in July 1978 went to London and placed a speech in a forthcoming debate on crime initiated by Lord Longford. In delivering it, he was interrupted and left the chamber without continuing. Several young people, reading part of the speech in Hansard, wrote to John. I learned that the page in Hansard had been circulated as a leaflet in Camden Town. Consequently, when I happened to be in London, I arranged to meet Heathcote Williams and

Richard Adams of the Open Head Press. I gave them the speech in full to be printed: 'The Full and True Text of a Notorious, Remarkable and Visionary Speech made by John, Viscount Amberley, Earl Russell, on the 18th of July 1978 at 9.8 p.m. in the House of Lords.'[1]

It received a very considerable circulation and has been declaimed dramatically at the ICA in London, also I understand in New York. It is not in the measured academic terms which apparently noble Lords demand. But it has a rhythm and vocabulary such as ordinary people use and thus a meaning which expressed what many young people thought and felt and wanted to hear someone say. John was thus right in his demands that Parliament should listen to all those under thirty.

Owing to other financial battles fought, and this time won, on John's behalf, he can now afford to attend the Lords without needing grants in aid. I regret that he now says that since what he might say will fall on deaf ears, to attend would be boring and a waste of time.

When I wrote of the death of Pat, my second husband, I indicated that I would reserve for later what he had meant in my life, and what we had meant to each other. Paul Gillard's image barred the way to any man who might approach me in love; for Pat that image, impeding a new relation, was there too. Since all three of us had shared political beliefs and hopes, the urge to continue in our labours, not in memory or adulation of a comrade, but in sheer fellowship of all hands to the task, was enough to bind us together.

We dealt with and made plans about the school. I think that Pat was able soon to transfer some of his affection and loyalty to the children and myself. For me it was quite some time before I saw him as anything but a helper and one in need of comfort like myself. I remember my surprise when the touch of Pat's hand in mine one day roused sexual feelings.

Pat was an Irishman, with all the intransigence, pride, loyalty, swiftness to take offence, indifference to risks, characteristic of his people. He had also a loyalty to his class, and, as a communist, to all peoples of the world who must be delivered, if need be by revolution, from poverty and repression for a life of equality, happiness and freedom. Pat's faith in all this was real; he would insist that he owed allegiance to the IRA and chant their song, as he did other revolutionary songs, much to my enjoyment. We might have had a child, but he would not, insisting that I had enough troubles already. Those whom he loved he cherished and was as much concerned about my four as if they had been his own. He was not an intellectual, though he listened obediently to – as he said – 'Old Tommy Jackson on Marx'. His own political judgement, prompted by feeling, was sound enough for his purposes. It was the sincerity, warmth and humanity which issued from him that mattered.

E.M. Forster and Naomi Mitchison, as I remember, once exchanged views as to whether barbarians or civilised men were more to be trusted for loyalty. I think they both opted for barbarians. Perhaps some similar doubts prompt the uncertainty with which committed proletarians regard intellectuals who support their cause. Undeniably, ambitious members of the working class may sell out, but the motivation of the middle-class intellectual who, when faced with choice, votes anti-trade unionist, represents a more complex betrayal. This contrast often occurred to me when I considered the very different characteristics of Bertie Russell and Pat Grace in such matters. Pat could be dogmatic and infuriating, we could quarrel, almost come to blows, but you knew where you were with him. With Bertie I was never able to have a quarrel, I felt that for him any difference of opinion could put an end to our relations. He would just not be there, as in fact proved to be the case. But tiresome though he was, and annoying as he must have found me, this fellow Pat would never go away. I do not suggest that there was anything saintly about his character; but he was not selfish or ambitious. In any case, neither of us had much to gain except to stay alive during those terrible years when we had only each other to rely on.

I like to look back on Pat telling the school children tales about his grandfather with his pet alligator; of the fun we all had over taming the jackdaw, and the way Pat's whistle would fetch him from far away; of how Pat would create a little circus by getting John's capuchin monkey – Litiman, Raspy the Mad Monk – whom we also tamed, to ride upon the back of Rover, the school dog; of the night drives without lights over the moors to Cornwall to save the house from requisition and again with our nanny goat and her two kids. The years we worked in London were hard on us both. The hours in the Ministry of Information, where Pat also worked as an accountant, were long. Pat was wiry, but always subject to bronchial troubles. Nonetheless he used to tell me not to worry about my old age, he would take care of me. When he died we had for fifteen years persevered together in what we both saw as the task of those striving for peace and hope for humanity.

After Paul Gillard's death I had found copied by him lines from a favourite poem:

Allez fades ritournelles
La vie est vraie et criminelle.

So indeed was life criminal, so indeed it is now, even more so than when both Pat and he died. I hope perhaps one day to publish the novel Paul wrote. Now I feel glad that they were both there to help me live my life, and also that they are not here to be disillusioned by the world that they would find. To Pat an apology, because I still feel with remorse that I did not give him all the love that he deserved.

To return to my first and famous husband, Bertrand Russell. Most interviewers insist on asking me whether I did not feel overshadowed by him. Though I know that, to most people, in relation to his greatness I was a nonentity, I have repeatedly tried to make clear that it was not Russell the peer, brilliant mathematician, philosopher, logician, that I loved. To begin with we both, with Victorian or Edwardian romanticism, saw one another as beings out of fairy tales. I said he was like the Mad Hatter, or a leprechaun; he described me as a nymph dancing barefoot in the dewy grass. In the real world he was and remained for me 'Our Bert' as the students called him, someone who had stood up for the young men being slaughtered in a war that was only about commerce and colonies.

He became for me the knight errant who would challenge all the destructive forces in the world, but was in himself a man persecuted, much in need of someone to cherish and reassure him. I laughed with others at his jokes and wit, but I soon saw that, as with Shaw, they were a sensitive man's armour against attack. When I learned about his upbringing I realised that he had really never had any family life, nor been helped to understand or know anything about women, or even sex. I have said many hard things about his defects as father and husband. They are nearly all traceable to the inadequacy of his unusual upbringing, to the traditional view of woman, and also to the traditions of knowledge and education learned at Cambridge University. What he needed of a woman was first of all a mother. His mother died when he was quite small and he had no substitute. Like most Victorian men he looked for a woman who would, if possible, be beautiful, but in any case, would want and care for children, and be the background and organiser of a pleasant domestic life. She would manage the servants and leave him free to do his work and entertain his friends. She must have sufficient cultured education and intelligence not to be boring at the dinner table or in the drawing room.

Unfortunately, many intelligent women growing up in the days of the Suffragettes were no longer quite like that. They wanted votes, and independent jobs, were not quite sure that they wanted babies, and greatly resented being told to get back to the kitchen when they voiced their demands. Bertie did his utmost to keep up with these modern trends; it is not surprising that he felt overstrained and reverted to type. I often think that he would have so much preferred it if I had delicately languished with smelling salts on a sofa and drawn out in him the solicitous, strongly protective male. In fact, because of his need for mothering, he was intensely dependent on the woman he was in love with and indecisive and liable to errors of judgement if he feared being left alone. But indeed, there are very few men or women who, from a solitary position, continue to act with decision and sound judgement.

There were plenty of women about, who would have been proud to make a good wife to Bertie, devoted only to his service. Yet such women do not seem to have attracted him. It may be that those of us women who did love him ought to have educated him about sex and the way a woman thinks and feels. Unfortunately we ourselves were not sufficiently informed or proficient, and also too much in awe of him, to make the attempt. Ottoline Morrell, I think, had the social standing and dignity to help him a great deal.

I do not know how people feel in these days about the ending of love affairs or broken marriages. With divorce possible after one year, marriage seems trivial and nonsensical. It is best to end without bitterness if possible – but if not, when the bitterness fades then everything about the good times should remain.

For me there came first the blissful – again almost fairy tale –

atmosphere of the adventure in China, exploring relations with a fascinating lover, amid an unfamiliar background of sights and sounds and dress, and unfamiliar people whom we had come to meet and learn to understand. I had burnt my boats, taken the risks. I would have been less happy had I known that I was very much on trial and might have been discarded as unsuitable on our return, if I had not produced the son and heir.

Then the halcyon days of family life in Cornwall, the house, the sea, visits and talks with friends. And in London some active partnership in politics. The twelve years of that marriage were fruitful in both of our lives.

In reviewing the past it is folly to harbour regrets and brood about possible mistakes. As the song says:

What's gone 'tis but in vain
To wish for back again.

Like all human beings Bertie and I did not always stand by our principles. But I believe that, though we parted, we did in many ways measure up to what we hoped of one another. In true love there is even more than this, there is a very deep experience, the gift of a vision that carries and sustains you on through life.

Something of this is expressed in a poem which I wrote in China. It was inspired by our visit to the beautiful lake at Changsha, honoured by the Chinese as almost magical, where we sat by the lakeside in the 'enjoying rain pavilion', warm and dry under its tiled roof, on which were perched small effigies of such birds and other creatures who do indeed enjoy the rain. On arrival in Peking I wrote the poem. I include it here with its vision of that love and concern for humanity which, to those of whom I have written, and many others, brought inspiration, grief and suffering, but also always great hope.

Love Song From China

Here by the fire you read me poetry:
And I remember
Nights when love gleamed divine delirious passion,
Long lonely days of mourning when love fled.

287

Such rainbow cataracts for me spelled love.

But so to sit and like the lotus cup
Stretch forth my quivering petals to the moon,
And slowly yield my shimmering incense up,
Nor dread mine ecstasy will perish soon;
While you, a calm and silver scented lake
Do softly stir and kiss my trembling leaves
And nourish with white fire my supple root,
That fearlessly your depth mysterious cleaves,
And spread your flowing mirror to the stars;
To sway and shine and sing until we wake
The birds that slumber on the painted eaves
And each begins to tune his drowsy throat
To join the nightingale, whose golden flute
Tells forth their praise who wear love's honoured scars;

This love I knew not. But this love once known,
Let me proclaim it to an aching world.

O fling your blue and silver mantle wide,
To garner sorrows on the mountain shores,
And bear the tumult and the noise of wars,
Red lust and pestilence and tyrant laws,
And gaunt-eyed Famine with her festered sores
On your bright surface to your lily bride.
My golden heart on all Earth's crimes shall sup,
Joy to distil within my crystal cup
And with my lover's incense offer up
To soothe the startled denizens of the skies,
Earth's barren hopes, her fears,
Brave griefs, and noble tears;
While music of the spheres
Descends to greet my offerings as they rise.
So betwixt Earth and Heaven there sways and sings
A misty Peace compounded of these things.

Ah Love, this must be Love that dares to pluck
The poisoned weeds that choke a tortured world,
And from their treacherous hearts the venom suck,

And yield them chastened, roses, dewy pearled;

And they are knit in Love, whose passions shed
This mystic radiance; who dare lay their head
'Neath Heaven their canopy, the Universe their bed.

Notes

1. Published by Open Head Press, London, 1978.

13

THE POLITICAL WORLD
1906–1984

I was born in 1894, ninety years ago, but first became aware of the world of politics seventy-eight years ago, when, at the age of twelve, I stood with my father in Trafalgar Square watching the screening of the results of the famous Liberal election victory of 1906. In spite of his faithful adherence to his duties as a civil servant, my father, Frederick William Black, was a very keen Liberal.

That packed square, the cheers and groans that went up as the results appeared high on the lantern screens by St Martin's-in-the-Field, is vivid in my memory, as also the laughter and jokes around me as people teased each other with the paper joke contrivances of the fairs – one a bunch of coloured paper streamers in a handle that was flourished in your face, another that blew out with a pop and was launched at your cheek. How mild seem those amusements of the good-tempered democrats at play in their election, contrasted with the political climate of today. There were of course all the elements of politics – wars, national antagonisms, poverty, labour troubles, but at first nothing like the shock that came upon a surprised Europe in 1914.

My progressive father favoured education, he was very active at Morley College for working men and women. He believed in a university education for his daughters as well as his son. It is not surprising therefore that I raised the issue of votes for women in the French conversation class at school, admired the Suffragettes and was very early convinced of the need and right of women to take part in political life.

Other very early influences which show how a child will pick up clues to what is going on were the holidays abroad, when we took part in the way the Belgians and French amused themselves. Russia first appeared on my political horizon when, as we played throwing or shooting games in the fairgrounds of France, the women in the booths would shout, 'La France et la Russie gagnent *deux* barres de nougat.' Russia then, as friend and ally was early planted in my mind, and, as is evident by the present recall, never went away.

I have described in *Tamarisk Tree 1*, how, during the vacation from the University, helping the Women's Emergency Corps with Belgian refugees taught me the lesson of war for civilians, above all women, old and young, and the children. Though involved with conscientious objection and admiring Russell at Cambridge, party politics did not appeal to me. My subject was modern history and literature, not only English but German and French. In this I took a first-class degree with distinction. My interest lay in the sheer act of writing, in plays, in dramatic criticism. I still nourished a faint hope one day of leaving the academic world for the theatre. I did however obtain a postgraduate grant for some research which had begun to interest me in the small books of the 'philosophes' in eighteenth century France. I had begun pursuing this, attached to University College, in the British Museum, when, in 1917, came the suggestion from my father that I, together with a former school friend, should go with him as joint secretaries to the British War Mission in New York.

This was work for the war, and I had a growing feeling that the conscientious objectors were right. I went to consult Bertrand Russell, on his advice I agreed to go. To my friend, Dot Wrinch, who objected, he said that if I went I would be able to find out what I really thought. My father was then Director of the Ministry of Munitions. Earlier, at the Admiralty as Director of Navy Contracts, he had been very closely concerned with supplies of oil to replace coal in ships; he had advised the government purchase of Anglo-Iranian oil to ensure supplies and hence was the true originator of British Petroleum (BP). But the shape of tankers bringing oil was not difficult for the German submarine commanders to identify; very many were being sunk. If there were a naval battle after Jutland, would there be enough oil to bunker our ships for battle? America had just come into the war. My father was sent to ask them to help, if need be, by using their tankers. My school friend Gladys and I went with him because his secretary, in middle years, I think, did not care to risk the submarines. In fact women were not being allowed to cross the Atlantic unless on serious business. I was twenty-three, young enough not to think too much about danger.

In New York one met in the streets the full blast of enthusiastic recruiting for war, with flags and singing of 'Over There'. I did not relish the thought of the slaughter of more young men and already felt misgivings about the entry of America. Years later I learned of the desperate attempts of Lella Secor (later Mrs Sargent Florence[1]) to prevent this at the very time when I was in New York.

Our requests to the American government having been repeatedly referred to the Petroleum Executive, a body which we found to consist entirely of Standard Oil and other wealthy commercial oil companies, it was not long before I decided what I thought about the war. Observing to my father that the socialist claim that capitalist firms controlled governments was true, I became, almost overnight, a pacifist and socialist. My father was asked to replace Lord Northcliffe as Head of the British War Mission, thus in charge of staff requirements. In due course I was able to return home.

I carried with me my firm conviction that the United States, with its advanced technology, passionate devotion to profit and industrial expansion, was likely to embark on imperialist domination of the world. If I had expressed this view to any officials, or indeed to almost anyone of my acquaintance, at that time, it would have been thought crazy, or even treasonable. As regards the American entry in the war, I refer to this with hindsight in my book on the machine age. I note that researches into the nature of conflict among animals have shown that they do not fight to the death against one of their own species. I suggest that when the British and German armies were stuck in the Flanders mud, they had reached a stalemate. Had they then made a truce Europe might have reached some unity and thus avoided the second war. By calling in the Americans and demanding total surrender, the warlords of the time showed themselves inferior to animals in that they by-passed, or had already lost, an important instinct in their animal inheritance vital to self preservation and survival of their species.

Back in Europe, I was in time to see Russell go to prison for his articles against government policy. The Soviet Revolution happened, the war ended, I went back to my researches, and was not much inclined to pursue politics as an interest or career. But Russell, who had urged me to marry him, wanted us to make a joint visit to Russia to learn about the Revolution. As is known, we made separate journeys, differing in route and circumstances.

In 1920, in Leningrad and Moscow, politics re-entered my life. Though at no time a professional politician, I have never been able to escape its clutches since. Very many times I have tried to get myself free in thought and action to pursue other less demanding and harrowing occupations, but there was always some human problem, need, injustice, from which in conscience, one could not turn aside. The Soviet Revolution was, for my generation, what the French Revolution had been for the young of that generation.

The end of the war had left widespread starvation in Germany, the need for massive reconstruction in all Europe. The flower of our youth had died, the older generation were still in control. The political future in England was uncertain; after two elections the Labour Party was in power but without a decisive majority, and surprisingly with a leader, Ramsay MacDonald, who was a conscientious objector. On the left wing there began to stir some hope of reforms; women were to get the vote. But it was the news coming from Russia that aroused the greatest hope, curiosity and speculation. Here was a nation, the mass of whose people were poor and illiterate, who had overthrown despotic power, repudiated debts to all capitalist concerns, and were prepared to stake their future on comradely equality, and the communal sharing of goods and labour. Here was an example to the aspiring socialists of the West, and equally a warning to its capitalist forces, of which they were not slow to take heed.

I had not been ignorant of the great names in Russian literature, and of the movement among Russian intellectuals who, in seeking to abolish serfdom, prepared the way for revolution. In 1920 I found in Soviet Russia two strands of the Revolution: the one which named and admired Chicago as the great centre of American technology, the other a nearly religious aspiration towards human brotherhood that, in essence, had belonged traditionally with devotion to the orthodox church. Religion might be, in the words of revolutionary leaders, 'the opium of the people' but the Russian temperament was religious in the sense of seeking the ideal, the other wordly, which transcends the limit of human powers, though not the limit of human imagination. Many of the revolutionaries had been in exile for years, actually working in industry in Britain and America. They returned in 1917 imbued with Marxist dogma to join their comrades who, unless exiled to Siberia, had remained at home. The home-bred Soviet revolution – the Russian temperament that inspired it – was what I came to admire and to love on that first visit. And from this love of their human quality, added to respect for the high degree of their intelligence, I have never departed, no matter what their style of government.

This is what I sought to explain in the 'Soul of Russia and Body of America', hoping that the Russians would purge themselves of Marx. I wrote this in 1921-22 after my visit to China; I did try to get it into weekly journals such as *The Listener* but it was never published until 1982, then as a pamphlet by the Open Head Press, and included in *The Religion of the Machine Age* in 1983. The genesis of that book was also my Russian visit of 1920. I became aware that in the Soviet vision of industrial society, the machine, until then considered by the industrial worker – the proletariat – as a means of lightening labour and speeding up production, now began to be seen as the means, with a centralised state, of organising the basis of society itself. Industrial civilisation, whether run by socialism or capitalism, would not be human but mechanised, and as such, I feared, dictatorial and inimical to democracy. Since Hitler we now have the word totalitarian.

Why did I not say all this as soon as I returned from Russia in 1920? No one would have noticed or believed it, and Bertie wanted us to go to China. My arguments did induce Bertie, very generously, to include a chapter by me in his book on Bolshevism, written in Paris when we were on our way to China, where my political education continued. Meanwhile began already in 1920 that isolation of Soviet Russia, making actual war on her and encircling her on all frontiers with enemies, as has virtually been the case ever since. To me, the refusal to recognise the Soviet government in 1917 and the subsequent Cold War represent the greatest blunder of human history. Here, awakening to a new life was a people already rich in imagination and intelligence, likely, as its education developed and expanded, to contribute much to the skills, culture, scientific knowledge and ability of the world. Western capitalism, in its envy and greed, shut that people out from potential civilised colleagues in the West, with a barrier of hatred and misrepresentation that none dared cross in friendship.

In Russia I had learnt the recipe for revolutions according to Karl Marx. What did China teach me about politics? Bertie and I arrived there the year after the May 4th Movement, 1919, in which the students had actually succeeded in forcing their government to alter its pro-Japanese policies at the Paris Peace Conference. This is considered to have been the start of the Chinese Communist Revolution. At Peking University some of the students who came to study Russell's philosophy were certainly among that number, or their friends. Besides learning to love – by that I mean really to care about – the Chinese, and respect their ability, as I did that of the Russians, I was fascinated by the immense difference of temperament of the two peoples in their approach to life. The Chinese had a Temple of Heaven, but did not care for transcendental religions, and had no doctrine of original sin. As their wise elders are reputed to have said to Jesuit missionaries – 'religions are many, but reason is one'. In their traditional philosophy and social structure the Chinese seem to me to have found the nearest approach to civilised life on this planet.

It seemed probable that China, shocked by the European war that had resulted from trade and colonial rivalry, would follow the Soviet example and see in communism the best way to combine people's ownership with people's labour. There was no point in going through the period of private capitalist ownership with resultant exploitation and conflict with labour.

Bertie and I told this to our Foreign Office on our return; our impression was that they did not believe us. I was not surprised, but greatly shocked at the hostility which Stalin developed to the Chinese communists. They were accused of heresy in that they did not follow the Marxist doctrine of 'dictatorship by the proletariat'. Not having much industry, China had to rely on forming her cadres from the peasantry. The Chinese felt that Russia was developing a bourgeoisie. In any case, Stalin sided with Chiang Kai Shek and the Kuomintang which led to the attack on the communists in the Shanghai area in 1927, in which Chou en Lai barely escaped with his life. I helped to raise a protest in Britain about the use of British troops against them, at which George Lansbury and I both spoke. But there was a long way to go yet in China before Mao Tse Tung and the Long March.

Back in Britain Bertie and I now had a home in Chelsea where our son John was born in 1921. Though Bertie had not fully recovered from his pneumonia, from which he very nearly died in Peking, he was the Labour candidate for Chelsea in the elections of 1922 and '23. Ramsay MacDonald was Prime Minister as well as in charge of Foreign Affairs. Without a full majority his position could depend on which way the six Liberal members voted. With an able colleague in Arthur Henderson, Ramsay had in mind to ease the situation in Europe by modifying the terms of the German peace treaty, and take steps to recognise the Soviet government. The Tories saw an opportunity to daub Labour as Bolshevik by representing the withdrawal of their Solicitor General from prosecuting a communist – Campbell, for something considered subversive which he had written – as an action taken for political reasons. It is held that the law requires in all cases that prosecution must depend solely on whether a crime, or offence, has been committed.

In the Campbell case the Liberals voted with the Tories and the Labour government fell. The result of the election of 1924, which followed, was vital not only for Britain but for the future of Europe. It so happens that, because of his health, I took Bertie's place as the Labour candidate for Chelsea, the only time I ever stood for Parliament. I have told the story in *Tamarisk Tree 1* but its details are relevant here, and, even now, not fully known. MacDonald's constituency was in Wales, in those days not rapidly accessible from London. On the Friday of the weekend preceding the poll, the *Daily Mail* carried a story of a letter said to have been sent by Zinovieff to his comrades in the British Labour Party, encouraging and advising them how to vote. It had come to the Foreign Office. For every Labour candidate the question arose – what was the truth of this, what had the Prime Minister to say? Many of the Labour candidates were in fact not at all pro-Soviet, but whether or not, this supposed link was appallingly damaging. It was well timed to arouse all the weekend press. Rumour has it that Ramsay himself, taken aback and uncertain, sent for an aide from the Foreign Office who did not reach him before he had delivered his eve of the poll speech.

I went out to the customary site for Chelsea's soap box meetings outside the old World's End pub and delivered a stinging speech to the effect that this Red Letter was nothing but a forgery. Among the comrades in Russia I had met Zinovieff and was sure that he would not have been such a fool. I did not, however, think it wise to advertise my own acquaintance with Bolshevism.

The smear did its work. Labour lost the election. Unrest in Germany followed; in Britain in 1926 came the General Strike to support the miners, in which Baldwin quelled the trade unions by telling them that it was unconstitutional. The miners were left isolated and their wages actually reduced. Presently followed Ramsay MacDonald's betrayal of his party, the ins and outs of British elections, the Spanish Civil War, the rise of Hitler and the Nazis to power and the continued failure of Britain to make approaches for understanding with Russia.

All this time, right up to the outbreak of war in 1939, the truth or falsity of the Zinovieff letter remained unknown, until finally the Conservative Central Office cheerfully admitted that the whole thing had been engineered by their dirty tricks department. Defeating Labour in that 1924 election by these devices, they had prevented MacDonald from pursuing his pacifying policies which might have averted the Second World War.

The war in which Soviet Russia, fighting with the Allies against Hitler, suffered extensive invasion and destruction, brought also the invention of jet planes and rockets, and the atomic (later also hydrogen) bomb which was now part of the armaments of both sides of the Iron Curtain divide.

From 1924 onwards Labour had been in opposition or coalition. In 1945 at last came the decisive Labour victory. What occurred then to the relations between the British government and the Soviet Union we have already seen in the early part of this book. The political events of importance from 1948 till this year, 1984, have mostly been chronicled. Following the stationing of United States bombers in East Anglia, Britain became ever more subservient to the United States. With the setting up of NATO and the creation – against the wishes of its people – of the German Army, America increased its hold upon Europe. The Soviet Union's reply in self defence, was, six years after NATO, the Warsaw Pact.

Unlike the British government, General de Gaulle became aware of the dangers of encroaching American power. In 1959 he ordered the withdrawal of American bases from French soil and began preparations for France's own defence. He did not withdraw from NATO but maintained his connection. Owing to the withdrawal of the American presence, there has not been a strong nuclear opposition in France.

There has been a sense of national unity in self defence which the French communists recognised in de Gaulle's action. They were not as hostile to him as might otherwise have been expected. A movement against *peaceful* nuclear power is now active in France.

The United States not only instigated the Korean war and forced their allies into it, they took over from the French opposition to Vietnam's hope of independence, and the Vietnam war began. This was not supported, but not opposed, by Harold Wilson's government in Britain.

In the near East, with influence in Israel, the United States was also active. When our Peace Caravan was in Bulgaria in 1958, a revolution in Iraq brought the over-flight of US planes and the fears of open war. A Bulgarian MP expressed to us his anxiety. Since then, there have come the fall of the Shah in Iran, the horrors of events in Lebanon, the desperate, unceasing war between Iran and Iraq. This is virtually 'holy war' between Moslem religions, but it is also holy war against the whole technologically based system of the United States. The Soviet Union, with millions of Moslems within its borders and an exposed frontier, moved into Afghanistan, thereby causing an angry reaction from the United States and leading to propaganda amongst its allies against Russia's 'act of aggression' which led to countries refusing to attend the Olympics in Moscow in 1980.

Then and now, the United States has had far more of its troops stationed on foreign soil than have the Russians. So the war dance and brandishing of fists continue, and again the Olympics are the victim in that Russia refused to attend in California in 1984. Following the re-election of President Reagan the dialogue between Soviet Russia and the United States is still in abeyance, constituting a nuclear stalemate, and, it may be, a pause in the application of science to nuclear war. At the time that I write there are signs that negotiations may be resumed.

This may be a good moment to consider the position of science today as compared with its traditions and purposes as defined in its origins. The governments of the world are facing economic crisis in the continued slump, unemployment, lack of foresight and misuse of capital. It would seem as if industrialism – the machine age – is near collapse. Some philosophers and commentators have been speculating as to what may be the political development in these two spheres of action, science and economics. To take first industrialism: here the basic element has been the studies of Karl Marx, supplemented by Engels, out of which revolutionary ideology developed. Exiled from Germany, significantly, Marx pursued his work entirely in Britain. His picture of the classes in society is that which prevailed in Britain in his day. In his theory of history based on the means of production, the industrial working class – the proletariat – would rise to supersede the capitalist bourgeoisie and create an egalitarian communism served by the machine. This procedure became a dogma to be applied wherever revolution was contemplated, regardless of whether it actually fitted the circumstances of the particular country or people.

I wonder if it ever occurs to the savage opponents of communism – especially among Americans – that the system they seek to destroy, by every murderous means, is nothing but the pattern of what actually happened in Britain as the trade unions developed in number and power? If those Brits had not embarked on industrialism there would not have been any Karl Marx. Britain, with her Tolpuddle Martyrs, her demanding trade unionists, is the mother of the revolutionary proletariats throughout the world. The British capitalist class still know this full well and are in hot pursuit of the enemy within their own borders!

In the Marxist reading of history, industrialism was the obvious next development of society. Essential to it was man's 'conquest of nature' and the exploitation of natural resources, in which may be included the human species itself! Industrialism was, moreover, a system created, like the machine, by a purely male consciousness. The labours natural to females were drawn into the growing factory system.

Waste of time and pages of bitter controversy have centred on the marxists' claim that their interpretation of history was 'scientific'. This would have to mean that it was determinist – destined to take place. A scientific truth is one on which there is consensus of agreement by scientists after intensive experiment and study of the object or process, with results that appear invariably to occur. Even a truth thought to be established in science may be changed by fresh discoveries. Interpretation of history may employ many methods, the study of kings and queens, wars, conditions of peoples, it cannot lay down that such and such events will invariably take place. Marxism has been so dogmatic with regard to the 'economic determination of history' that many marxists have had great difficulty in liberating themselves from Marx in order to think afresh about social planning.

The 'dictatorship of the proletariat' was not very clear as to what would be the form and meaning of the hoped for communist utopia. It began to resolve itself into what may be called the Chicago pattern – obeying the smooth running of the machine and the development of technological skills which led to totalitarianism.

When did science begin? What were its origins? One may describe the astronomers' observation of the stars, the invention of mathematics, as the first elements of scientific thinking. But science, as we describe it today, dates rather from the Middle Ages, when the alchemists and inquisitive minds in the monasteries of the eleven and twelfth centuries were active, and, into the bargain, repressed by the Church. Grosseteste, Roger Bacon, Peter of Maricourt, were concerned with the power and direction of light, the rainbow and its curve and prisms, magnifying, and the power of magnets. Later there was the inventive and artistic genius of Leonardo da Vinci, the important voice and advocacy of science by Francis Bacon. In *The Machine Age* I described how men began to single out the powerful and important functioning of the intellect, how curiosity about matter in movement brought the clockwork measurement of time and the machine.

Not until under Charles II was a consensus about all this new knowledge established by his founding of the Royal Society, whose principles were to follow and make widely known what was called the New Philosophy. This principle, that scientific knowledge should be shared by all scientists the world over, continued up to the 1939 war when it was destroyed by the manufacture of the atomic and hydrogen bombs. Though scientific knowledge was viewed as a source of benefit to humanity, men in power never hesitated to call the scientist from his desk or bench to take part, either in person, or by his inventions, in the acts of war. There may have been secrecy about some devices, but intense secrecy became important only because of the increase and variety of deadly weapons, culminating in the bomb.

The vain attempt of Sir Henry Dale, President of the Royal Society, to escape from the secrecy surrounding the bomb has been noted, as also the declaration of Russell and others that, even with the bomb, the principle of sharing scientific knowledge must somehow be maintained and established. We saw how the scientists betrayed their trust in succumbing to the Cold War. We hear no more of science as a great

300

uniting force, of the Universal Philosophy of Scientific Humanism which Julian Huxley hoped to promote by the work of UNESCO, and the United Nations. Though we have the use of science for human welfare, science itself has become incorporated into the military industrial complex. Mathematicians of high skill spend their time scratching on to silicon chips the hieroglyphs for the computers that will trigger off weapons – untouched by human hand – in the murderous acts of our ships, planes, tanks, or whatever vehicle bears these weapons. For this use of science the governments of nations find money; the production and sale of armaments is the chief business and profit of governments throughout the world, selling to one another the means to perpetuate the conduct of wars.

Not content with the power which male consciousness evolved by the cultivation of the intellect, man has now programmed these instruments with what is called 'artificial intelligence' that can think and act with lightning speed, beyond that of the human brain. The technology of electronics using the waves of the air, the rays of light itself, the positioning of satellites, has ushered in what is called the 'information revolution', bringing, we are told, immediacy of communication to serve news, business, entertainment. Above all, the warlords have seen in this the vast possibilities for exchanging rapid coded views with allies, giving orders during battles, spying on enemy communications.

We live today in a world full of secret noises, fit for the magic of Prospero: the cloud-capped towers flash their momentous messages across the ether, within electronically slender tubes, rays of light itself speed masses of doom-laden information from one Lord High Executioner to another. Devoted fingers tap computer buttons exchanging communications in their peculiar language through the air. No word, no moment of these potentially death-dealing dialogues must be missed. Shining great dishes catch the precious coded sounds, palaces are built to house high priests who will record them, green flickering, on their screens. There are secret high altitudes – the old Brocken mountain, once haunt of the witches on their Walpurgis Nacht, now dispenses this modern-style witchcraft.

What does all this mean for those of us who just walk the earth, while the Great Powers use our work and our substance for this colossal enterprise of arrant nonsense? 'We are such stuff as dreams are made on.' Is there still time to rouse ourselves and others from this ultimate human fantasy before, as Prospero warned us, it is ended and 'leaves not a wrack behind'?

It is possible now to see how disastrous and lacking in foresight was the outlawing of Soviet Russia in 1917. Thereby was created that rift, now grown to an appalling gulf of hatred, fear and secrecy between two great states, both now possessed of highly skilled technology. So they stand, poised for war, while the whole world, immobilised in terror, awaits the moment when one or the other makes that first strike which ends us all.

Two Great Powers through whom, united for peace, the discoveries of science and the labours of men and women might have heralded for all on our planet a glorious future.

Notes

1. She had come over on the Ford Peace Ship. As Mrs Sargent Florence in Cambridge she became well known as a feminist and supporter of birth control.

14

MAN, WOMAN
AND THEIR PLANET

———————

Suppose we set aside fear of our immediate dangers and see our world as if it were a jigsaw puzzle of innumerable pieces scattered far and wide. There is the landscape, hills, valleys, the seas. Existing on and by these are the living creatures – the bewildering, astounding variety of what we call the natural world of which we gradually begin to learn something when we take the trouble to study it. All creatures have their span of life, seek their food to reproduce themselves so that their species will survive. Among these is the species spread across geographic areas and climates, which, though differing enormously in colour, size, degree of consciousness, we recognise as human beings. We now believe them to have changed and evolved through millions of years and that they have thus become the supreme dominant species, predators on others, and even on themselves. To create a human being by natural means requires a male and a female. The nature and relation of these two sexes is thus the beginning of all social life and therefore of all politics.

When in the Soviet Union in 1920 to find out about the Revolution, my first question was, 'What's in it for women?' The men looked surprised as they remarked that they supposed women would go on as usual. Then I met Alexandra Kollantai who told me that in her view, despite war conditions, more concern should be shown about the exploitation of children. She took me to her exhibition designed to help and advise mothers about childcare, and to the Bolshoi theatre which was filled to overflowing with a conference of women from all over the country. This was only three years after the Revolution, and at this time the mass of the population in the Soviet Union were still illiterate.

Kollantai saw that a revolution meant much more than machines and economics; it would, and should, affect human relations – between wives and husbands, parents and children. She became for me the pattern and the inspiration of the part women should play in our own political life, and indeed the world. Since then the voice of women, as we know, has been heard more than often on the rights and liberties of women – and others – and on peace, but women still remain stifled and powerless. It is a 'man-made world'. When I wrote *The Religion of the Machine Age* I tried to find out what that meant in terms of developing male consciousness and the horrors it has consequently imposed on us today.

It is a mere platitude to say that men, since they were not involved in the constant nurture of children, had time and opportunity for independent activities. Repudiating their animal origins, they declared themselves possessors of souls but denied these to women, leaving them in the category of animal existence. Then also came gods, still mostly male, and religions – a prime source of wars and the consequent slaughter of young humans. Ultimately came the growth of the thrusting male intellect that produced mathematics, machines and science. In past times, though the birth of children was welcomed by fathers, they were seen as there to be used for whatever might be the purposes of the dominant males. Until the theory of evolution was advanced there could be no sense of children, by reason of their nurture and care, being envisaged as the 'future of humanity'. Females have perforce been obliged to accept their world and themselves as designed and described mainly by men. Female consciousness and activity in past times has been observed as directed towards food gathering and agriculture and must have concerned itself with the welfare of children, though without any power as to how children were treated or used.

This is a very bare outline of the relations of conscious purpose as between men and women. It deliberately leaves out what might be written about the passions and romance of heterosexual love, as well as the skilful manoeuvres of women to get their way within male politics and employ their subtle power over men.

There is much talk today about defining the nature of the sexes. We hear about 'gender'; about learning 'roles'; the avoidance of sex discrimination in the work performed for our society by individuals. Secrecy about sex has decreased, with the result of great lenience in the marriage laws, and the legal acceptance of homosexuality. Briefly one might say that when the male sex is in love with itself it is homosexual, the female sex loving itself is lesbian. There is much talk now about these descriptions and a tendency for the sexes to think about themselves in these terms, thus making clearer dividing lines between them. And since sexual intimacy is used for pleasure and for a means of close friendship and temperamental understanding, rather than for procreation, it may be said, by some in jest, and by others with seriousness, that for each sex to enjoy pleasure within itself will at least limit the population and avoid the problems of rearing children.

Excessive individualism prevails in the advanced countries of the mechanistic industrial revolution, based as it is on material comfort and gain. Against this divisive tendency it becomes difficult to see how the directives of consciousness in men and in women can be brought together, as they must be to form a coherent and integrated society. The current stress on homosexual and lesbian practice is relevant in a society which gives priority to the self-satisfaction of the individual. Such expressions of love and friendship issue from the feelings and desires inherent in every human being. Though emotions, to a very large extent, influence our conscious thought and purpose, it is the social directives of consciousness as expressed by men and women which determine the policies of communities and nations.

Since women began to rebel against their low status and subjection and demand their rights, very many changes have been brought about by legislation and reforms that were also supported by progressive-minded men. But we are apt to forget how long and arduous has been this continuing struggle for the liberties of women and children. In 1920, when I was admiring Kollantai in action, I was one of the relatively small number of English women permitted a university education; nor had we yet got the vote. When we finally had it, there was talk of creating a women's party. But the general view was that exercise of the vote by either sex was a matter of rational thought and choice between the programmes of the existing parties – created by men. Accordingly, these parties set up women's sections and conferences for discussion, but without power. Battles on sex matters

305

loomed – marriage and divorce, birth control, abortion law reform. When I put forward a resolution on birth control in the Conference of Labour Women in 1924, the party Woman Organiser sharply admonished me not to 'drag sex into politics'. Today, I believe, most people closely associated with politics and public affairs would admit that both men and women are not temples of pure reason but, for the most part, indulge in sexual thinking.

What then in our orderly, mechanised society becomes of anti-discrimination at the workplace? Are we not saying that defining women as equal with men, means that they are identical? Of course not. Skills in work are learned and depend not on the sex but the quality of the learner. But there can be, and are, issues on which the views of the sexes are in bitter opposition.

Let us now return to the state of affairs in the man-made industrial technological social system under which we now live and by which we are governed. This machine civilisation, external in content, has afforded immense advantages in that aspect of our lives – comfort and appliances within individual homes; fast and convenient travel in our own private cars and also by road, rail and air; advances of discovery in science and technology, in medicine and other fields. There is a massive accumulation of knowledge – in my view, more than human organisms in our present state of ethical and emotional judgement can assimilate. And individuals in advanced societies tend to believe that whatever they suffer from or think to be wrong, science will find a way to put it right. At the same time, there are indications that science and industrialisation will not be able to continue on their present apparently unstoppable course.

Economic and scientific determinism are falling out of favour. Human minds seem to be turning to introspection, and some individuals and societies, to religions. It is in this context that I am thinking of changes in the directives of consciousness, whether male or female. The human organism has evolved many faculties. Of these we have for centuries tended to over-value the intellect, stifling and under-valuing not only the emotions of love and fellowship, but the greatest, the most creative of all, the human imagination. We are aware of creative life in other organisms surrounding us on our planet. We know and feel creative life within ourselves. It is the source of sex and procreation, but, in the human being, of so much, much more. We do not know the cause of this living element of creation, which the imagination of many has ascribed to gods, or to one omnipotent deity.

Though I pay tribute to the infinite variety, beauty and attributes of the many gods and goddesses (also devils) devised by human imaginative ingenuity, and then worshipped, I do not believe in them nor in an omnipotent god as creator and arbiter of our fate. Not only do I not accept such a belief, I do not *want* to accept it. We do not need to invent gods. The destiny of the human race lies in what we are and can make of ourselves, in the faculties we ourselves create and which of these we choose to employ. How frequently our wiseacres tell us 'You can't change human nature' and again 'You can't stop science'. Both these statements are false. If human nature had not changed, however long this has taken, we should not be what we are today. And science will cease to dominate our lives when we envisage, or imagination proposes, new modes of thought and action.

The need to commune within ourselves is salutary, but it may be observed that such introspection, in revolt against machine technology, tends at present to focus on old religious beliefs and practices. This revival can be seen already producing, as in the past, savage persecution and devastating war. By this upsurge, the danger of our predicament is greatly increased. The omnipotent god imagined by man is interpreted by each sect in its own peculiar way. What then of the gentler religions of love and compassion? These are a vital part of the human psyche, of that aspiration towards the skies, that reaching for perfection, which can, if we hold on to it, further our evolution by subduing our desire to kill and destroy. With what dignity and beauty these aspirations speak in the music, dance, poetry, song, hymns of so many peoples.

When those whose goal is power step in with their dogmas and regulations, religion becomes a state institution, armed for suppression and conquest.

> The glories of our blood and state
> Are shadows, not substantial things.

wrote a seventeenth-century pacifist. And here is one hymn whose simple message has appealed to many socialists, believers or unbelievers.

> When wilt thou save the people

307

O Lord of mercy, when?
The people, Lord, the people
Not Kings and Crowns, but men.

When comes the blessed time
When war shall be no more,
When lust, oppression, crime
Shall flee thy face before?

It is only the face of the people, men and women together, that can be turned against evil, it is their voice that will answer that prayer.

Since the revival of traditional religions has not, so far, shown itself in purity of aspirations, but on the contrary, in the traditional savagery of war, it offers no help. And as I indicated, there are signs that, for many minds, even economic and scientific determinism are falling out of favour.

Jurgen Habermas (*Theory and Practice*, 1963) asserts that human beings cannot be handled by determinism, they have personal desires and choices. His statement that human beings cannot feel loyalty to a whole mass of technologies, resembles my argument about the danger of the 'state' seen as a machine, served by individuals as cogs. He also remarks that science is not the only kind of valuable knowledge. Rudolf Bahro (*Socialism and Survival*, 1982) is very definite about the need to liberate thinking from Marx, and practice from the machine, in favour of ecology.

Raymond Williams mentions ecology and feminism, and is also greatly concerned with the effect of the massive developments in technology on human communication (*Technology and Cultural Form*, 1974).

John Rawls (*Theory of Justice*, 1971), held to be influential especially in America, places liberty of *all* kinds above that of economics, though economic justice greatly concerns him. He is even prepared to admit the right, by disobedience, to challenge unjust laws.

More universal now than books, world-wide television tends towards everyone accepting the same impressions and opinions, yet at the same time the movement of peoples by immigration and the consequent mixture of cultures produces a confusion and insecurity in each one of us as to what are our basic beliefs. Men have clung on to intellect – human reason – or to scientific 'truths' as a lifebelt in a sea of turbulent myths and visions. Indeed, Don Cupitt uses the symbolism of the sea of faith on which to float a non-supernatural version of Christianity which apparently accepts the philosophic contributions of Copernicus, Galileo, Descartes and others, all formerly oppressed by the Church. He creates what appears to be a religious humanism, that would not, however, be acceptable to those humanists who insist on faith in the stated 'truths' of science.

There is no sign of any change in the preoccupation of the scientists with the power of the intellect. The recipe is still the same – to use the machine to replace human labour, and the skills that program computers to fashion more robots; to continue to disregard the effect of unstoppable industrialism on the environment. Profits are made by the introduction of computers into school and home, with games for young children, keeping their minds tuned to numbers and to the information revolution, concealing the fact that this, together with AI, artificial intelligence, will spell, for them, unemployment. Human beings, redundant, may find themselves being taught, or advised, about their ills or states of mind by these modern Frankensteins! The discovery of DNA – the hereditary genes – may lead to the artificial manufacture of human beings themselves. Computers, source of ingenious robots, are programmed by minds, devoted to the intellect and artificial intelligence, that have become an élite detached from their fellow travellers on this planet. What is their purpose? It would seem to be intense delight in their intellectual achievements, but beyond that can be perceived the goal of immense profits for themselves.

We learn that companies are investing in the 'life power' gifts of microbiology; that the minerals of Antarctica, of the deep oceans, of the derelict moon, are to be the subject of ruthless competition by the commercial corporations. Perhaps this élite of disembodied spirits are already transformed into space travellers and should seek their natural habitat on the planets, rather than our humble earth, whose products they despise until they have either picked them to pieces or transformed them into something manufactured by man.

As this book goes to press comes the news, which I feel obliged to insert, of an example of precisely that savage, competitive greed of large-scale corporations. In Bhopal, India, literally thousands of men, women and children have been dying, choked and blinded, many even as they slept, due to the escape of the gas from the American plant of Union Carbide. Such chemical insecticides, or fertilisers, issue from the test tubes of scientists; huge factories are built to make the products for use, sited in areas where labour is cheap but unfamiliar with the methods of such production. The commercial promoters assert that agriculture needs these products to increase the world supply of food. In fact they are useless, being dangerous to life when applied, as well as harmful in their ultimate effects on crops and soil. Their entire purpose is the profit of the commercial corporations, whose operations, in the interest of humankind, should be terminated by law.

H.G. Wells was the true prophet of the Machine Age, perceiving both the good and the bad that science and technology might bring, not forgetting, as others did, that in the human body beats the human heart. He warned men of science and imagination against acting as obsequious courtiers to men of power. He predicted the moon journeys, watched the machine enter warfare, foretold the very date of the outbreak of war in 1939. In one prediction of the future he imagined the proletariat living underground with an idle, luxurious aristocracy above, the aristocrats devoured one by one by predators from the underworld.

Later, in *Mind at the End of Its Tether* (1945), he reached different but no less depressing conclusions. Accepting the 'slowing down of terrestrial vitality' he sees that all life on earth must ultimately cease. He doubts 'whether contemporary mankind is sufficiently accessible to fresh ideas', and fears that

hard imaginative thinking has not increased so as to keep pace with the expansion and complication of human societies and organisations. That is the darkest shadow upon the hopes of mankind.

In the past he has liked to think that Man could pull out of his entanglements and start a new creative phase of human living. In the face of our universal inadequacy, that optimism has given place to a stoical cynicism. The old men behave for the most part meanly and disgustingly, and the young are spasmodic, foolish and all too easily misled. Man must go steeply up or down and the odds seem to be all in favour of his going down and out. If he goes up, then so great is the adaptation demanded of him that he must cease to be a man. Ordinary man is at the end of his tether. Only a small, highly adaptable minority of the species can possibly survive. The rest will not trouble about it, finding such opiates and consolations as they have a mind for.[1]

Equally true perhaps of the 1984 state of mind? It would seem therefore that Wells eventually foresaw the autocracy of the intellectual élite rather than their defeat by the proletariat. Nonetheless, throughout his writing ran the optimist theme of creative idealists, and of the 'samurai' (men, one may note, but not women) whose exploits were inspired by care and concern for a human race which, by improving its ethical and aesthetic values, would live out its final span of life on earth not in conflict, but with dignity, in mutual help and peace.

Today I look back, as did Wells, to the days of Pure Science, the honoured learning issuing from the universities, seen as deriving its purity from serving knowledge for itself alone, not for gain, or even specifically for human welfare. Its devotees led us to accept that this pursuit of knowledge had as much nobility as the spiritual aspirations of the religious although, within the psyche, the two faculties were at variance – scientists might well be, mostly were, unbelievers. So ordinary people believed that science was a Good Thing and, as such, good things would come of it.

When scientists split the atom in the Rutherford Laboratory at Cambridge, they were acclaimed, not so much by pride in the achievement, as respect for the intellects of the men prominent in mathematics and physics who began to congregate in that university (much loved by its students of whom I was one), spreading their knowledge and their great reputations world-wide. No one then expected what came of the atom splitting – the atom and hydrogen bombs, spreading anxiety and protest, equally world-wide. It should be noted, however, that after the bombs had fallen their creators took pains to weather the shock by reassuring us that nuclear power, now come, could be used to produce energy for light, heat and mechanical power.

During the making of the bomb the men of science, contrary to Wells' hopes, continued to kow-tow to the men of power. Such protests as they made were feeble. Only one, Joseph Rotblat, from

311

Liverpool, withdrew from the group working on the bomb project. In consequence he was at Russell's side, much later, in effective protest, and was founder of the Pugwash Conferences of international scientists which still survive. As the years have gone by these men of science have made no attempt to solve the nuclear stalemate and thus lift our burden of fear. Could not men of such brilliance offer something better than a 'balance of terror' between two power blocks of nuclear protagonists? There was nothing to prevent men of science from uniting and proclaiming to the world that they would make no more instruments of genocide. On the contrary, their chief pursuit has been the perfection and proliferation of war weapons. Pride in their achievement comes before survival, even of themselves. Like our well devised myth of the Daleks, they join in with the warlords in screaming delightedly, 'Exterminate, exterminate'. In the meantime, ironically, together with this madness, the application of the intellect to the sciences continues to be the goal. Physicists pursue their quest for the particles within the atom; biologists and medical men make contributions to problems in antibiotics and procreation. Electronics, microbiology, silicon chips, computers, all inventions of the human intellect, are acclaimed and rewarded with prizes in diverse countries and places. Nowhere more than in Cambridge, where the zeal for devotion to the intellect has become traditional and where today are to be found the main centres for the production of silicon chips to make computers. These highest of the high, the supremely intelligent élite, have shown little realisation or concern for the effects, or ultimate consequences, of the accumulation of all this knowledge. They babble of technology for everything. Profit and competition are their watchwords. They appear to claim the right to rank with, even take their seats beside, those 'men of power'.

Their protective screen is autocratic government using repression by laws, police and injunction by judges, apparently with the aim of obstructing those who still seek to do the work of the world by intensive human labour and the sharing of its products, or to protect the natural world from pollution and desolation. Government authority has punished those who opposed atom tests, not those who made them; those who resisted having nuclear weapons on their land, not those who impose them; the efforts of Greenpeace to stop nuclear pollution, not its perpetrators; those who defend young seals, not the profiteers in their skins; the miners who would keep pits open, avoiding the sacrifice of more agricultural land; those whose devices increase automation, without care for unemployment, get knighthoods.

In the light of these experiences we may ask again, what are the purposes of those who seek and obtain power to rule over us? As the whole world knows, the massive and growing anti-nuclear protest has been intensified by the continued proliferation of nuclear weapons and the refusal of the perpetrators to reach any solution as to their abolition. But, besides this dominant issue, almost all matters concerning life on earth are now, among ordinary human beings, a source of anxiety and protest. There is concern and conflict about the incursion into what are called developing countries, of the industrial revolution, whether by capitalist enterprises, or by the efforts of local people themselves – it may be on Marxist terms – seeking to preserve their independence. Problems of the destruction of resources, forests and land, pollution, and mechanisation, demand solution. In the industrialised countries, the incursion of technology into medicine and surgery has arisen; there are risks through the proliferation of innumerable drugs that bring profit to their makers, but doubtful benefit to their users.

Among people in Western societies, even now, there are those who find the pace of modern life too hectic, who would like to assemble a few pioneers and establish, outside current altercations and conflict, some simple peaceful utopia on a small remote island. Today no such island is safe from the planes, rockets and tanks of some powerful predator, prepared to suppress the inhabitants and take over their land with bulldozers. Small wonder that one hears of young Maoris in New Zealand, who, in spite of having received a modern education, call upon their people to return to their old gods, since the white race, with their greedy technologies, are oppressors. Then one reads of the rape of Indian women and the murder of their children in Guatemala, their bodies left fly-blown, urinated upon by their aggressors.

What can we do? Cruelty has always existed. And times of natural disasters, drought and famine call constantly on our compassion. Ironically, it is by one of our modern technologies – television – that we are aware of the state of affairs in almost every corner of our planet.

Precisely this awareness faces us with the stirring of conscience and the dilemma of choice.

By whom, by what, do we want ourselves and our world to be governed? Active politicians have persuaded themselves and others that in democracy, by one man, one woman, one vote, human reason has found the best method to establish the general will, and, for individuals, 'human rights'. To those peoples deemed 'backward' this method of government is taught, or it may be imposed on them. What democracy or human rights are there in the autocracy of the super intellectual élite who hold power through their refusal to divest themselves of nuclear weapons? Could not, will not, these oligarchs continue to rule and hold us all hostage merely by refraining from use of that threat of the 'final solution' which remains in their hands? With their computerised weapons they can kill as and when they choose. Might not this super race of accomplished technologists presently make room for itself on the planet by clearing out of the way those masses of unskilled unemployables? Some para-styled troops such as we see pictured on television, heavily armoured top to toe, computer on the brow, equipped against poison gases, could make short work of all those nature lovers, poets, artists, musicians, writers, philosophers, sportsmen, footballers, cricketers, who are cluttering the earth and eating up even the latest processed food. A few, scientifically nurtured and trained, might be kept to entertain spectators in the arena, as was done, it is believed, by the ancient Romans. Why not? The massacre of tribes is not new in human history.

The crisis of our times may be for our parochial politicans a mere trivial matter of politics. But for a growing number of thinking people it is moral, and lies in ourselves and our destiny. So going back to our introspection, we take a look at some very recent pronouncements made by men applying their intellect in varied professions.

Astronomer Fred Hoyle[2] sees his study of the stars as a confrontation between the human brain and the universe. He implies that for men like him, of superior intellect, talking to mere humans is a waste of time. Charles Lecht, of the Advanced Computer Techniques Corporation asserts that he 'really believes that machines can do everything better than people'.[3] Clive Sinclair, recently knighted for his commercial success in the production of silicon chips, sees no harm in massive unemployment rendering the human race redundant, since man's brain is not equal to AI, artificial intelligence.

Not only are computers becoming dominant in mechanising human life, but with their superbly swift reactions they can, it is said, defend man from his enemies better than man himself. What are the ultimate purposes of these arrogant, highly intelligent gentlemen, and to what species do they belong? Whence came that active brain of Fred Hoyle's that plays dice with the universe? Whence, indeed, the brains of all the other computer idolators?

Every single one of them, together with all their ambitions, dreams, affairs of love, hates, fears, nightmares, even those very thoughts invading the mind with mathematical symbols, issued from the *animal body* of the despised human race itself.

Since the species can apparently produce such prodigies of paramount quality, why has man (disregarding his partner, woman) been wasting his offspring in increasingly devastating wars?

What became of the promise that science by its universality would bring international unity and peace? Should not AI now demonstrate its supremacy by advising its devotees that, unless they join the miserable ordinary humans in their demand for abolition of nuclear weapons, they will have no planet as a basis for their future operations?

Such narcissism and self-deception in those who are regarded as at the top levels of our perceptive thought is alarming. The sphere of abstract concepts, the pursuit of the infinity of knowledge, whether intellectual or the 'eternity' of religions has had a long enough innings.

On the other hand Professor Weizenbaum, a computer scientist, is one of those who see that mere logic does not suffice to make human decisions.

> Thus we have very nearly come to the point where every human dilemma is seen as a mere paradox, as a merely apparent contradiction that could be untangled by judicious application of cold logic, arrived at from a higher standpoint.
>
> Even murderous wars have come to be perceived as mere problems to be solved by hoards of professional problem solvers.[4]

Is then the picture of the world given by sense perception more true than that presented by mathematics? Why did mathematical man prefer to think in a straight horizontal or perpendicular line when our planet, and the whole universe it seems, is curved? What chances we may have missed. How we have been wasting our time quarrelling with one another, following false trails and side issues. Why have we not yet found, can we yet find, how best to live on this planet and continue to probe the mysteries of the universe?

At this moment of near collapse of machine civilisation, some wiseacres seek remedies in feminism and ecology. At this any woman will burst out laughing, so abundantly clear is it that these two –women and ecology – are the very factors ignored by male-directed society from the start – the contribution that female thought might have made to human policy, and the necessity of understanding and relating to the organic natural world.

Mary Midgley, in her insistence on the importance of human feeling versus intellect and of the relevance on our social thinking of the practices of animals and the way we regard them, makes an outstanding contribution.

No one who values the quality of abstract and perceptive thought would deny the gifts to the world made by the inventive human intellect. It may be conceded that the intellect, clear and impartial, undisturbed by emotions, is necessary in undertaking accurate and concentrated pursuits such as mathematics and science. But in the use of this intellect men have made a crucial and tragic error. Dissociating it from its biological origin within their own bodies they deny also its relation to the realities of the natural world. Intellect, thus remote and isolated, regarded as a 'special creation' is easily overtaken by cynicism and indifference to creative human values, and may well become the vehicle of lust for power and aggression. I believe that these tendencies of the male consciousness have been one of the causes of wars, and certainly of the intensely high degree of skill and increased inventiveness of both nuclear and non-nuclear armaments of today. As I was writing this, John Searle in the Reith Lectures (1984) punctured the bubble of Cartesian philosophy with his assertion that the mind is no 'special creation' but actually derives direct from the biological brain itself. No male philosopher, as far as I know, has ever before made this statement. It could revolutionise our entire thinking on religions, and reconcile male and female consciousness in their concepts of the natural world. Like other women, I challenged (in my book *The Right to be*

316

Happy) the Cartesian mind-body machine man theories and argued for the natural world as the basis of human life and society.

Side by side with my respect for men's intellectual abilities, I registered, early in life, admiration for the high courage of the suffragettes in the battle for the vote. The women's cause immediately became my own, and has since then inspired my almost every thought and action in a long life. But I did not at first realise the repercussions that it would have in every aspect of human concern and endeavour. Through feminist pressure women made some gains in their own status, but many were apt to evade action on matters associated with motherhood. There was also a tendency for women to emulate men in the type of work they sought, because it was better valued, not only in money, but in estimation, than work considered to belong to women. Similarly, women tended to accept top level decisions by men on the issues of war and peace. For men, conflict and war are an integral and irrevocable element in human consciousness and endeavour. Suddenly came a great change – what I think must be called the women's revolution.

It really began with the bomb – the shock that roused the mass of the peoples into action and mounting protest. What is more, this triggered off, in the consciousness of women, a total distrust and opposition to the way men conducted the affairs of nations and the world. If this could be the result of splitting the atom, what then of all the multifarious activities of men in the sciences of medicine and biology? Women had, with misgivings, been obliged to trust men as husbands and fathers. But now suddenly came enlightenment; why have we let them go on disposing at will of the children that we bear? I remember how, in 1954 in Calcutta, when my women friends and I sat on the floor planning the agenda for their great Women's Congress, incorporating the usual requests for equal status and liberty, we were almost put to shame by the mass of pathetic crumpled bits of paper, from remote rural areas, demanding the banning of the bomb. Mothers had begun to speak out loud and clear. After this, in most countries where a women's movement was new, it almost always took the form of a mothers' congress in defence of their children. I recall now how the motive behind our battle for birth control had not been the commonly held romantic, sentimental view of motherhood, but the reality that both mothers and children were an oppressed class in a society which, by refusing women advice and help, imposed upon them unlimited childbearing without providing adequate means for nurture and care.

It has always been in the nature of a pretence that, in times of peace, men's first concern was for their wives and children, and that they shielded and fought for them in times of war. The genocidal bomb and total war finally exposed the fraud in all its hideousness. So today, from the deepest instincts of women, centred in the womb, comes a colossal wave of indignation at last prepared to challenge the men in power of no matter what country, party, denomination or creed, who dare to persist in their age-long treachery of destruction to their species and the planet which is their home.

Realising that not only the human race is threatened, some have called their protest 'Women for Life on Earth' which does express the emotional drive of very many. But it by no means represents or comprises the many elements and sections that are now fused in a common unity of purpose. Those who treat the present mood of women with contempt should be warned that it is not mere tantrums. Its roots lie far back in the almost universal, age-long subjection of women. This is a fact of history never absent from the thinking of women, and which men would be well advised not to deny but to recognise. It is a fact of history with which men and women must come to terms. Women have continually made demands for their status. The suffrage agitation took years and years but, like all justifiable demands, it did not go away. Nor will, or can, the present upsurge of women's anger and impassioned active protest go away because it is rooted in their determination themselves to undertake, at long last, the defence of their children – all children – the human children, abused and exploited, never really cherished, children to whom women gave birth. The defence of those lives is a symbol of the hope of future for us all.

There has never yet been anything just like this, an ever-rising, mounting, rolling wave of feeling that floods across from country to country, unites women as women, all women, the female sex, half of what goes to create a whole human being. Women of the present generation are embarked upon the hardest struggle ever faced by their sex. They are demanding, because of their biological rights as equal partners with the male sex in the creation of human beings, their rightful share in the purpose and destiny of those human beings born and of the

318

species to which men and women belong. Evidence of the depth and unity of this tide of female purpose can be plainly seen not only in actions, but in the flood of books, pamphlets, manifestoes, now being issued. All kinds of women – professional women, working mothers, welfare workers, feminist and pacifist –contribute their thoughts and feelings to books such as *Keeping the Peace*[5] and *Over Our Dead Bodies*.[6] Individual women explain just how and when they felt summoned to take their part in the one great cause they cannot evade. What use is it to care for the sick, teach the young, comfort the anxiety-ridden or mentally disturbed, even devote ourselves to daily tasks, when the threat of universal death hangs over all?

The one hope is in massive united protest. So women leave their homes and can be seen marching, often with their children, facing opposition and hardship in the streets, in the open country. Opposition comes, of course, from the authority of those who guard, are prepared to use, make and sell the deadly weapons. As in the past, when making demands, the women suffer and endure. Hard to bear is the opposition which comes very widely from men as a sex, and even from those who themselves campaign against the nuclear threat, *but* want men and women to work together and object to women 'going it alone'. Of course women also feel the need for united action and do not deny that vast numbers of men are, with women, in such organisations as CND, playing an important part. But the danger continues to threaten and there are also formidable numbers of men who refuse to consider abandoning the practice of war for methods of reconciliation.

In the present crisis something more is needed to galvanise our whole mode of thought into moving in a different direction. For men it is difficult to do this, since their whole concept of a social system, law and custom, attitude to women, is based on general modes of thought and action that have been established by their sex alone and become traditional. It is also very hard for us women to shake off the fetters of that same masculine mode of thought and action in which we too, perforce, are imprisoned because so far, there is nothing to take its place. We are engaged in the effort of freeing our minds; and thinking for ourselves. Hence our resolve to act independently and, in the matter of anti-nuclear protest, for instance, to avoid violence and confront-ation, and to attack, not people, but the weapons and their hiding places.

As we review the situation, there are other questions which cause us to distrust male judgement and procedure. Seeing what came of the result of scientists splitting the atom of inorganic matter, we are troubled at the onset of male technology in the field of biology and organic life. We have become more aware of the insult of some male attitudes to the equality and dignity of women; the patriarchal system comes under scrutiny and attack.

To men accustomed to their habitual customs and values, these criticisms are apt to be reviled as rampant feminism. Some critics accused me of feminism when, in my book about the machine age, studying the rise and power of the intellect of men, I merely indicated that it tended to leave out consideration of the conscious thought of women. Surely the effect of this long neglect is the very reason why we women are 'going it alone'.

Let us look at the argument honestly in the hope that men will understand and welcome rather than oppose our purposes. In writing that book and this book also, I gradually came to the conclusion that we may now be in one of those periods of history resembling the end of the cultural level reached in the classical world of Greece and Rome. Humanity then began to seek fresh values, new beliefs and ways of life. As people shook off the power of Rome, so now we rebel at the prison of the definitions of space and time, law, work, conduct, in which, by our own imagination and thought we have locked ourselves. A way out must be found into clearer, uncluttered air, into a breath of freedom. That human thought and imagination can bring about such changes is proven by the fact that a whole new era of beliefs, conduct, values, myths, was able to rise over the ruins of the Roman Empire to become Medieval Christian Europe – an astonishing historical feat which we take for granted without realising just how remarkable it was. The change was not all beneficial. For instance, the light of the Greeks' vision of how to live on earth was extinguished by the new religion for fifteen hundred years.

In our day, the minds of men and women are able to take to pieces the whole of our very considerable inheritance of belief and social structure, scrutinising and rejecting much of it with the aid of new knowledge. Women's attack on the continuing male dominance in the spheres of work and politics has had very modest success. In the subtler and more complex area of social relations, sex and parenthood changes

320

have brought discord rather than harmony. The difficulty of dialogue when one partner alone has defined the spoken and written language has been shown very ably by Dale Spender in her remarkable book *Man Made Language*.[7] She encouraged women to air their views and recorded on tapes the lies they had been told about sex and childbirth, adding their own sexual feelings and maternal experience. The derogatory words used to describe sexual matters revealed just how such matters were regarded by men.

The subject has been confused still further by the dogmas of the Church theologians. Aware that the sexual impulse, as the source of procreation, could not be denied, they recognised also its power and quality, and that it could be dangerous and cruel. They sought to subdue sex by monastic abstinence, and to harness it with the laws of wedlock. Love is now admitted as an element in sex by a religion which exhorts men and women to love their god and each other. The mistake is the refusal to admit that human beings are part of the animal kingdom, thus holding sex, as part of the animal body, in contempt and ostracising it from civilised life. The extraordinary feature of the isolation of sex as animal is that the fathers of the Church did not place a similar ban on other human faculties which likewise proceed from the animal body. They were determined to assert the existence of the soul, and to admit reason (by means of which, after all, the theologians conducted their disputes). These were the gifts of God to man as the 'special creation' – but the fathers of the Church did develop hostility to man's searching intellect when it began to give birth to science.

To shut out sex is to shut out life itself. It is as much a part of life as the creative force by which everything lives, moves and has its being, the flowers that bloom, the budding of trees in spring.

Even the admission of love did not enhance the status of women. On the contrary, it degraded them still further by demanding that females should value chastity above passion. Most religions seem to have conspired, in some way or another, to deny sexual pleasure to the female, while admiring sexual prowess and enjoyment in the male. Love as we think of it today can hardly be said to have existed before the development of consciousness of our emotions. But there was always that empathy between one living organism and another, acting like cement to bring about mutual aid, the foundation of social living. And primitive males and females, however little they may have understood

321

the impulse, were irresistibly drawn to one another. Love, homosexual or lesbian, was there in Greece, and sex not ostacised. We know very little of Greek family relations, unless we accept them as exemplified by Greek tragedy.

Because of the considerable freedom in sexual thinking and practice today, surely it is important to examine how these appear in relation to traditions from the past. In my own view, on account of the oppression and consequent silence of women about sex, sex – one of the most vital elements underlying the structure of human society – has been abused, misused, vilified, corrupted. We have thrown into the filth of the gutter what should be honoured as one of the finest sources of inspiration that issues from within the human organism to endow the human psyche. But sex, I hear many say, mere sex is not love. Such a remark dishonours what should be pride in our animal origin. We may like to pretend that we are a separate creation superior to nature; such arrogance is not justified by our parental and marital performance, which is inferior to that of many other species in which mating, courtship and parental care are very much the concern of the two sexes involved. And whatever the quantity or quality of love that we bring forth it comes from within ourselves, from the human heart.

Recently women have been concerning themselves with the problem of rape and the way some cases are handled. The frequency of such attacks, and kerb crawling by men, cause women to fear being out alone at night. There have been abductions, assaults and murder of young girls and boys; quite young vandals attack lonely old women. Women's views should be heard on these questions which relate to the way in which the whole meaning of sex should contribute to love and compassion in spheres of life outside its own. Sex is not an instrument of power and domination. Between any two people it conveys a message of trust, friendship, love and a desire to know and bring pleasure to one another. Any review of the future of human society should contain a serious consideration and re-thinking on this subject. Children should be enabled to grow up in an atmosphere in which sex has its part in their whole way of thinking about life. I do not mean by this what we call sex education. How much we need to re-think occurred to me when I read in a journal about a novel which had been considered for a literary prize that was full of the male proposition that women like being hurt. I read also of a club to which men go for the pleasure of being taunted by women as 'naughty boys'.[8]

In 1926, some pioneers, chiefly in Germany, Austria, Britain and Denmark, started a World League for Sexual Reform, and in 1929, with Dr Norman Haire and Professor Jack Flugel, I was responsible for organising in London an international conference on the subject, amazingly supported by everyone with views on the subject, from Marie Stopes to Bernard Shaw and Bertrand Russell.[9] The suggestion we put forward was that a better understanding both of what sex meant and could be would contribute to happiness and stability, and even to peace. That is still my view. I am sure that creating such a social outlook would greatly diminish the crimes that are attributable to sex, especially within or in relation to family life.

The new thinking of female consciousness in politics can only be carried further if women attain more constitutional status in political parties than they have so far achieved. So long as men refuse this equality, women will not join the parties; their 'going it alone' outside electoral procedure will increase. Even so, just as with language and education, women embarking on a political career have to adopt all the traditional procedures of the parliamentary and legal institutions created by men. Women see these as based upon concepts of conflict and recognise ways in which these processes could be changed, involving less argument and more hope of finding solutions.

However that may be, it is clear that as we live day by day with one another, both sexes are engaged in their own ways of thinking, prompted first by the emotions, then issuing in speech or conscious action. It is suggested by archaeologists that the social structure of a society will depend on what faculty or conscious purpose is uppermost – whether, for instance, a war-like stance or, on the other hand, concern for the construction of family behaviour. In a recent study of the Masai tribe in Africa, now at peace, but harbouring a traditional respect for warriors, initiation of the adolescent continues; but modes of family behaviour and family structure are defined; as also a concern for fertility. Here the female element is not suppressed but plays a significant part.

For the past 300 years, and even earlier, we have lived in a society dominated by the male intellect in science and mechanism, and increasingly fine divisions of time. How real is this world? As I watch millions of men and women in cars speeding up the motorways, eyes and senses alert, ears perhaps cocked to the radio, I wonder what are their thoughts and their purposes. A motorway anyhow, is a road that goes nowhere, you must leave it to find an interesting destination. How much do those people now think for themselves, or take it all from that other product of human imagination and ingenuity, television?

The universe, with its own time, is still going on around us. With our five senses we are aware of the teeming life on our planet. Where do we belong in it now, what do we do about it? Do we go on acting like savage predators? Technology rules OK, and humans can now neither believe, think, nor act except under the direction of what we call science, a science now more than ever the handmaid of war. To restore sanity to our civilisation, a new definition of reality must be sought. How can we revive the human values of our culture now obscured? A generation of fine actors and actresses is dying out; who will replace them? Think of the great beauty of our language, with its rhythm in the verses of our poets; of the music that rises mysteriously within us, and that our voices and instruments make known to our fellow men and women. Think of the grace of the human body, in dance, in balance, in sport, mounting the waves of the sea, skimming on ice; of the good work which designers of fabrics, painters and sculptors can produce given quiet, patience and slow care.

Why do we put up with the ugly, repetitive words and voices of our mentors in a society tuned to admiration of profit, competition, computers, silicon chips, the utmost speed in travel, discotheques, the business efficiency of world-wide telecom, not to mention those nuclear weapons in space? Why go on pretending to be gods, why not assert that we are human animals with the good fortune to live on a well-stocked and beautiful planet. We have become aware of some of our errors, and will need to take steps to avoid their results on our soil, atmosphere and seas. The machine must be tamed to be servant not master; science likewise be held back from vainglory and used for the life and care of ourselves and other living creatures. We should reproduce ourselves by natural methods, not by test tube babies. Spare part surgery should be avoided; the body is not a machine, and should from its earliest years be helped to grow in health, and with opportunity for each to discover and develop his or her talents which, if useful, will be of benefit to all.

We do not need to travel fast and faster. On the contrary, life would be more pleasant and enjoyment of the scenery greater if we slowed down. Even constant tourist travel has many disadvantages. Staying at home and using one's gifts to 'cultivate our garden', and making friends with our neighbours might be preferable. To the modern man or woman this may seem a dull life and a backward step into the past, a retreat from the so-called 'progress' achieved by our present mentors and dictators. They should be warned that such a retreat may well come about through the very decay of that civilisation under the folly of its present administrators. In the Green Movement there is a new faith stirring, though I fear that it may not gather strength in time to save us from the inventiveness of those who prefer Armageddon. Let us face our reality.

We know no forces in nature apart from storm, tempest and earthquake that can change the lot of humanity unless it be by the choices and actions of human beings themselves. This should inspire us with pride rather than with dismay, prompt us to thought and consideration of our resources. In the natural world there are possibilities of beneficial forces, overlooked and by-passed.

But is not our first concern to undertake, like other living species, that duty to survival which we have shamefully neglected by lack of concern for our children, their exploitation and slaughter in wars? If we are to survive, surely it is the care, nurture and quality of our children that will determine our future? And this applies world-wide, since whatever the culture in any region, the lesson of care for the future generation must likewise have priority. As regards the needs and ambitions of adult individuals, for them too any social system should provide what they themselves need, while accepting from them according to what their ability can achieve – a very old socialist dogma but nonetheless pertinent.

Every human being is unique and has within him or her the seeds of life and creation. Thus, when we look at the world threatened with utter destruction by warlords with nuclear weapons, every one of us, man, woman, and child, has the right to protest at the usurping and infringement of the right to life. After centuries of the folly of tribal wars, it is time that humanity declared that no one has the right to destroy the planet that belongs to us all. This human protest must grow and spread to ever more millions, taming as it grows the destructive element within itself and opening the road to the utopian future on which our age-long hopes and dreams are forever set.

There is so far not much sign of hope that the massive protest of those who seek peace can move those governments who, in their idiocy, still imagine that nuclear weapons are a defence. On the contrary, such governments imprison and persecute the peace seekers. But at last the leaders of five governments have associated themselves in their Four Continents Peace Initiative with the people's urgent pleas. They know that the whole planet is in danger. They promise to do all in their power to restrain those who may bring about nuclear war. The names are: Indira Gandhi, who headed the list before her tragic death, Olaf Palme, Prime Minister of Sweden, Julius Nyerere, President of Tanzania, Andreas Papandreou, Prime Minister of Greece, and Raul Alfonsin, President of Argentina. There can be little doubt that Indira Gandhi was one of the originators of this gesture. To the Women's Liaison Committee in Great Britain, she wrote recently what proved to be her last message to us. She said: 'There seems to be an undeclared, unconscious and wishful-thinking assumption that no nation would actually go to the extent of using nuclear weapons on another. *This complacent attitude has to change.* Movements such as yours can contribute a great deal.' The leaders of the Four Continents Peace Initiative say that they are aware of the mass of protest rising all over the world, and conclude their statement:

> We have faith in the capacity of human beings to rise above the current divisions and create a world free from the shadow of nuclear war. The power and ingenuity of the human race must be used, not to perfect weapons of annihilation, but to harness the resources of the earth so that all people may enjoy a life of security and dignity in an international system free of war and based on peace and justice.

This is an important indication of support at the top level. If we can persuade other leaders to join them, survival is possible. They are human beings like ourselves. New Zealand and Australia show signs of following their example.

We, the human race, are the guardians of our planet, the potential builders of its future, men and women, male and female, united by the physical bonds that create human beings and thus by the psychic strength and pervasive ambience that such unity can bestow. Our sexual impulse, which we despised and placed under taboo as sin and shame, thus causing so much hostility between men and women, is the true source of all life and creation within us, of empathy with living things, of the sympathy drawing us together in partnership, giving birth to love. What, after all, then is the quest of humanity? Is it not love? Passionate love for the man or woman we desire; tenderness of husband and wife, protective cherishing of our children; compassion for the old, the sick, the grief-stricken. Do not the highest flights of our religious imagination focus on a god of love and bid us love one another? Love is the theme of our poets, our artists, our singers.

Amor Vincit Omnia

Does love indeed conquer all? How, but for the loving care of our ancestors did we come to be what we now are? How shall our species prosper and grow in beauty, strength and wisdom, unless we emulate our ancestors in care for our young?

That the human organism contains also the ugliest and most brutal of emotions, none know better than our present generation. We know from observation that the need of all creatures for food may render them predators, but have we not in 'nature red in tooth and claw' tended to overstress this instinct in them, as in ourselves, undervaluing the quality and practice of parental care? May it not be that our emotional addition to war springs from a conflict of these two tendencies within ourselves? At least we have begun to come to terms with ourselves and to recognise that sex and the breath of life within us are one with the spirit that animates every living thing.

Can we not begin to shape a philosophy for our future which will begin with the obvious need to seek harmony and reconciliation between the peoples of our earth, side by side with recognition of the care that we owe to the animal and plant life of this planet on which we live. On some such basis of security, humanity may evolve greater skills and powers. There will be room for the release of the human mind and spirit to explore the mysteries of the universe and to embark, if desired, on space travel.

We cannot know what may be the ultimate fate of ourselves, or of so much of that universe towards which, day and night, eternally we gaze, longing with the whole of our being, to know and understand more. So great a thing it is to be alive, to be human.

We do not want our world to perish. But in our quest for knowledge, century by century, we have placed all our trust in a cold, impartial intellect which only brings us nearer to destruction. We have heeded no wisdom offering guidance. Only by learning to love one another can our world be saved. Only love can conquer all.

Notes

1. H.G. Wells, *Mind at the End of Its Tether*, William Heinemann, 1945.
2. *The Listener*, 16 August 1984.
3. *New Waves*, 16 August 1984.
4. Professor Joseph Weizenbaum, *Computer Power and Human Reason*, Penguin, 1984.
5. Lynne Jones (ed.), The Women's Press, 1983.
6. Dorothy Thompson (ed.), Virago, 1983.
7. Routledge & Kegan Paul, 1982.
8. Rosalind Coward, 'D.M. Thomas: Writing as Rape?'; Stuart Weir, 'School Dinners yum yum?', both in *New Socialist*, September 1984.
9. Norman Haire prepared a quite full report, well worth reading and available in libraries.

APPENDIX 1

Some Contributors to British Ally

These are some of the more prominent contributors of articles and messages; many of the articles and all the messages were especially written for *British Ally* (*Britanski Soyuznik*); the rest are reprints.

Abercrombie, Sir Patrick
Agate, James
Aitken, Group Captain Hon. Max
Alanbrook, Field Marshal Viscount
Alexander, Rt. Hon. A.V., MP
Allen, Major General R.H.
Allison, George
Ambler, Eric
Andrade, Professor E.N. da C.
Angwin, Colonel Sir A.S.
Anstey, Brigadier E.C.
Anstey, Edgar
Appleton, Sir Edward
Asquith, Anthony

Barker, Sir Ernest

'Bartimeus'
Barton, Sir William
Bates, H.E.
Bell, Adrian
Bentley, Nicolas
Bentley, Phyllis
Bernal, Professor J.D.
Bevin, Rt. Hon. Ernest, MP
Blake, George
Blom, Eric
Bolitho, Hector
Boult, Sir Adrian
Bowra, C.M.
Bracken, Rt. Hon. Brendan, MP
Brophy, John
Brown, Rt. Hon. Ernest
Browning, Lieut.-Gen. F.A.M.

Bryant, Arthur
Buchan, Charles
Buckley, Christopher

Campbell, Commander A.B.
Canterbury, Archbishop of
Cecil of Chelwood, Viscount
Chase, James Hadley
Cheshire, Wing Commander
   G.L., VC
Chifley, Rt. Hon. J.B.
Christie, Agatha
Church, Richard
Churchill, Rt. Hon.
   Winston S., OM, MP
Churchill, Mrs
Citrine, Sir Walter
Clifford, Alexander
Cockcroft, Prof. J.D.
Cole, G.D.H.
Cole, Margaret
Coningham, Air Marshal
   Sir A.
Cummings, A.J.
Cunningham, Admiral of the
   Fleet, Viscount
Curtin, Rt. Hon. John

Dale, Sir Henry, OM
Dent, E.J.
de Valois, Ninette
Dickens, Sir Henry
Dickinson, Thorold
Dimbleby, Richard
Douglas, Air Chief Marshal Sir
   W. Sholto
Durbin, E.F.M., MP

Durham, Dean of

Eaker, Lieutenant-General Ira
Easterbrook, L.F.
Eden, Rt. Hon. Anthony, MP
Eliot, T.S.
Edwards, W.J., MP
Elton, Oliver
Elliott, Col. Walter
Edwards, Ebby
Ensor, R.C.K.
Epstein, Jacob
Evans, B. Ifor
Evans, Edwin

Falls, Captain Cyril
Fellowes, Dr. E.H.
Field, Mary
Fleming, Sir Alexander
Foot, Dingle
Forester, C.S.
Forster, E.M.

Gardiner, Sir T.
Garrett, Sir Wilfrid
Gibson, Wing Commander
   Guy, V.C.
Gilliat, Sidney
Gillies, Sir Harold
Gordon, John
Gordon-Taylor, Surgeon Rear-
   Admiral
Gossage, Air Marshal Sir Leslie
Greenwood, Robert
Grigson, Geoffrey
Guthrie, Tyrone

Haldane, Professor J.B.S.

Hammond, Professor John
Hankey, Viscount
Hanley, James
Harris, Air Chief Marshal Sir
    Arthur
Haskell, Arnold L.
Hill, Professor A.V.
Hill, Dr. Charles
Hill, Ralph
Hodge, Herbert
Hodson, J.L.
Hopkinson, H.T.
Horner, Arthur
Horrabin, J.F.
Hurd, Sir Archibald
Huxley, Julian

James, Admiral Sir William
Jones, Sir Harold Spencer
Jordan, Philip
Joubert de la Ferte, Air Chief
    Marshal Sir Philip
Jowitt, Lord

Kerr, Sir Archibald Clark
Kimmins, Anthony
Knight, Dame Laura

Langdon, David
Law, Rt. Hon. Richard, MP
Lawther, Will
Lehmann, Beatrix
Lehmann, John
Lewis, Cecil Day
Liddell Hart, Captain B.H.
Lloyd, A.L.
Low, Professor, A.M.
Luke, Sir Harry

McCullogh, Derek
MacNalty, Sir Arthur
Mann, Thomas
Martell, Lt. General
    Sir G. de Q.
Martin, Kingsley
Masefield, John, OM
Medhurst, Air Vice Marshal
    Sir Charles
Megaw, Sir John W.D.
Mills, Freddie
Montgomery, Field Marshal,
    Viscount
Moorehead, Alan
Mortimer, Raymond
Morton, A.L.
Morton, H.V.
Mosley, Leonard
Muir, Edwin
Murray, Gilbert, OM
Murrow, Ed

Needham, Dr. Joseph
Newton, Eric
Nicolson, Harold

O'Casey, Sean
O'Faolain, Sean
Olivier, Laurence
Owen, Frank

Parker, Ralph
Peck, Air Marshal Sir Richard
Petrie, Sir Charles
Pile, General Sir Frederick
Plomer, William
Portal of Laverstoke, Lord
Portal, Marshal of the RAF,

Viscount, OM
Pound, Admiral of the Fleet
    Sir Dudley
Powell, Dilys
Priestley, J.B.
Pudney, John

Quennell, Peter

Read, Herbert
Redmayne, Sir Richard
Rees, C.B.
Reilly, Sir Charles
Robinson, Sir Robert
Rowan-Robinson, Major
    General H.
Rowse, A.L.

Sackville-West, Edward
Saunders, Hilary St.George
Sayers, Dorothy
Selborne, Earl of
Semmern, Sir Alfred
Shaw, G.B.
Shore, Bernard
Shute, Nevil
Simon, Sir E.D.
Slater, Montagu
Southwood, Viscount
Spender, Stephen
Spring, Howard
Stapleton, Sir George
Steed, Wickham
Stephens, James
Stone, Christopher
Strabolgi, Lord

Strachey, John, MP
Strong, L.A.G.
Swinton, Viscount

Tallents, Sir Stephen
Tawney, R.H.
Tedder, Marshal of the RAF,
    Lord
Thorndike, Dame Sybil
Tilsley, Frank
Tomlinson, H.M.
Tovey, Admiral of the Fleet,
    Sir John
Travers, Ben
Trevelyan, Sir Charles

Vevers, Dr. G.M.

Ward, R.M. Barrington
Warner, Sylvia Townsend
Wavell, Field Marshal
    Viscount
Whittle, Air Commodore
    Frank
Wilkinson, Rt. Hon.
    Ellen, MP
Williams, Francis
Willink, Rt. Hon. Henry
Willoughby de Broke, Group
    Captain, Lord
Wilson, Professor Dover
Wood, Sir Henry
Woolf, Leonard
Woolton, Lord

Yorke, F.R.S.

APPENDIX 2

The following table shows how widely *British Ally* penetrated throughout the Soviet Union. It lists, by the districts to which they were sent, some 22,000 postal subscriptions – as distinct from purchases at kiosks. The Moscow region is not included. The position is as at 1946.

Distribution of British Ally

Name of Republic, Region or District	Administrative Centre	No. of Copies by Subscription
Russian Socialist Federal Soviet Republic		
Altai	Barnaul	128
Amur	Blagavyeshchensk	109
Archangel	Archangel	126
Astrakhan	Astrakhan	107
Bashkir ASSR	Ufa	134
Bryansk	Bryansk	68
Buryat-Mongol ASSR	Ulan-Ude	109
Veliki Luki	Veliki Luki	88
Vladimir	Vladimir	152
Vologda	Vologda	123
Voronezh	Voronezh	148
Gorki	Gorki	172
Grozny	Grozny	93
Daghestan ASSR	Makhach-Kala	114

Name of Republic, Region or District	Administrative Centre	No. of Copies by Subscription
Birobidzhan	Birobidzhan	102
Ivanovo	Ivanovo	118
Irkutsk	Irkutsk	122
Kabardino ASSR	Nalchik	101
Kalinin	Kalinin	136
Kaluga	Kaluga	114
Kamohatka	Petropavlovsk	108
Kemerovo	Kemerovo	114
Kirov	Kirov	116
Komi ASSR	Siktivkar	115
Kostroma	Kostroma	111
Krasnodar	Krasnodar	164
Krasnoyarsk	Krasnoyarsk	139
Crimea	Simferopol	115
Kuibyshev	Kuibyshev	146
Kurgan	Kurgan	107
Kursk	Kursk	123
Leningrad	Leningrad	1169
Mari ASSR	Ioshkar-Ola	115
Molotov	Molotov	132
Mordvinian ASSR	Saransk	115
Murmansk	Murmansk	136
Nizhne-Amur	Nikolaevsk	101
Novgorod	Novgorod	107
Novosibirsk	Novosibirsk	151
Omsk	Omsk	119
Stavropol	Stavropol	144
Orlov	Orel	104
Penza	Penza	114
Pskov	Pskov	80
Primorak	Vladivostok	120
Rostov	Rostov	154
Riazan	Riazan	119

Name of Republic, Region or District	Administrative Centre	No. of Copies by Subscription
Saratov	Saratov	154
Sakhalin	Alexandrovsk	102
Sverdlovsk	Sverdlovsk	172
North Osetia ASSR	Dzowdzhikow	110
Smolensk	Smolensk	116
Stalingrad	Stalingrad	113
Tambov	Tambov	138
Tartar ASSR	Kazan	137
Tomsk	Tomsk	97
Tula	Tula	117
Tiumen	Tiumen	108
Udmert ASSR	Ischevsk	117
Ulyanovsk	Ulyanovsk	118
Khabarovsk	Khabarovsk	129
Chelyabinsk	Chelyabinsk	122
Chitin	Chita	119
Chkalov	Chkalov	158
Chuvash ASSR	Cheboksari	124
Yakutsk ASSR	Yakutsk	118
Yaroslav	Yaroslavi	124

Ukraine

Ismail	Ismail	103
Vinnitsa	Vinnitsa	109
Voroshilovgrad	Voroshilovgrad	107
Volinsk	Lutsk	82
Dnepropetrovsk	Dnepropetrovsk	120
Drogobich	Drogobich	111
Zhitomir	Zhitomir	124
Zaporozhe	Zaporozhe	105
Kamenets Podolisk	Proskurov	102
Kiev	Kiev	637

Name of Republic, Region or District	Administrative Centre	No. of Copies by Subscription
Kirivograd	Kirivograd	93
Lvov	Lvov	172
Nikolaev	Nikolaev	103
Odessa	Odessa	182
Poltava	Poltava	78
Rovnoe	Rovnoe	102
Stalino	Stalino	117
Stanislav	Stanislav	104
Sumy	Sumy	105
Tarnopol	Tarnopol	102
Kharkov	Kharkov	173
Kherson	Kherson	99
Chernigov	Chernigov	102
Czernowitz	Czernowitzi	88

Bielorussia

Baranovich	Baranovichi	87
Bobruisk	Bobruisk	190
Brest	Brest	108
Molodechno	Molodechno	81
Vitebak	Vitebak	78
Comel	Comel	108
Grodno	Grodno	38
Minsk	Minsk	495
Mogilev	Mogilev	96
Pinsk	Pinsk	108
Polesie	Mozir	100
Polotsk	Polotsk	31

Uzbekistan

Andijan	Andijan	96

Name of Republic, Region or District	Administrative Centre	No. of Copies by Subscription
Bokhara	Bokhara	103
Kara-Kalpak ASSR	Nukus	113
Namanchan	Namanchan	99
Samarkand	Samarkand	108
Surkhan-Darbin	Termez	87
Tashkent	Tashkent	457
Kashka-Darin	Karshi	102
Fergana	Fergana	104
Khorezem	Urgench	100

Kazakhstan

Akmolinsk	Akmolinsk	115
Aktyubinsk	Aktyubinsk	74
Alma-Ata	Alma-Ata	445
Eastern Kazakhstan	Ust-Kamenogorsk	77
Gurev	Gurev	35
Jambul	Jambul	94
Western Kazakhstan	Uralsk	98
Karaganda	Karaganda	110
Kizil-Orda	Kizil-Orda	101
Kokchestav	Kokchestav	103
Kustanai	Kustanai	94
Pavlodar	Pavlodar	102
Northern Kazakhstan	Petropavlovak	103
Semipalatrinsk	Semipalatinsk	101
Taldi-Kurgan	Taldi-Kurgan	114
Southern Kazakhstan	Chimkent	92

Tajikistan

Garm	Garm	96
Gorno-Badakhshan	Khorog	74

Name of Republic, Region or District	Administrative Centre	No. of Copies by Subscription
Kulyab	Kulyab	95
Kurgan-tube	Kurgan-tube	103
Leninabad	Linenabad	109
Stalinabad	Stalinabad	330
Turkmenistan		
Ashkhabad	Ashkhabad	324
Kerki	Kerki	90
Krasnovodsk	Krasnovodsk	102
Marii	Marii	
Tashauz	Tashauz	94
Chardzhu	Chardzhui	99
Kirghizstan		
Djalal-Abad	Djalal-Abad	81
Issyk Kul	Przhevalsk	96
Osh	Osh	98
Talas	Talas	131
Tien Shan	Narinsk	102
Frunze	Frunze	304
AZERBAIJAN	Baku	359
ARMENIA	Erevan	323
GEORGIA	Tiflis	446
KARELO-FINNISH	Petrozavodsk	250
MOLDAVIA	Kishinev	223
LITHUANIA	Vilno	242
LATVIA	Riga	220
ESTONIA	Tallinn	201

APPENDIX 3

Scientists for Moscow

The scientists who were about to depart were as follows:

Professor N.K. Adam F.R.S. F.R.I.C. M.A. Sc.D. Professor of Chemistry University College, Southampton.

Professor E.D. Adrian F.R.S. M.D. F.R.C.P. O.M. Professor of Physiology, Cambridge University. Representing Cambridge University.

Professor E.N. da C. Andrade F.R.S. D.Sc.F. Inst. P. Quain Professor of Physics and London University.

Professor J.D. Bernal F.R.S. M.A. University Professor of Physics, Birkbeck College, London.

Professor P.M.S. Blackett F.R.S. Professor of Physics, Manchester.

Dr. Max Born F.R.S. F.R.S.E. M.A. Sc.D. Professor of Natural Philosophy, University of Edinburgh.

Professor V. Gordon Childe D.Litt. D.Sc. F.B.A. F.R.A.I. Professor of Prehistoric Archaeology, Edinburgh. Representing the Royal Society, Edinburgh.

Dr. E.M. Crowther, Rothamsted Experimental Station.

Sir Charles Darwin K.B.E. F.R.S. M.C. Sc.D. Director of the National Physical Laboratory. Representing the Institution of Naval Architects.

Professor P.A.M. Dirac F.R.S. B.Sc. Lucasian Professor of Mathematics, University of Cambridge.

Professor S.G. Donnan F.R.S. C.B.E. D.Sc. L.L.D. F.R.I.C. Representing the Chemical Society.

W.N. Edwards B.A. F.G.S. Keeper of the Department of Geology, British Museum.

Professor C.N. Hinshelwood F.R.S. Professor of Chemistry, University of Oxford. Representing Oxford University.

Sir Thomas Holland K.C.S.I. K.C.I.E. F.R.S. F.G.S. P.R.S.A. President of the Geological Society, London.

Professor Julian Huxley F.R.S. D.Sc. F.R.A.S. President Royal Astronomical Society.

Dr. Alex Muir.

Professor N.S. Mott F.R.S. Professor of Theoretical Physics, University of Bristol.

Professor R.G.W. Norrish F.R.S. Sc.D. F.I.C. Professor of Physical Chemistry, Cambridge University.

Dr. W.G. Ogg B.Sc. F.R.S.E. Director Rothamsted Experimental Station.

Sir Robert Robinson Kt. F.R.S. M.A. F.I.C. D.Sc. Professor of Chemistry, University of Oxford, Vice-president of the Royal Society. Representing the Royal Society.

Lord Radnor Forestry Commissioner. Representing Rothamsted Experimental Station.

Professor E.K. Rideal M.B.E. F.R.S. D.Sc. F.I.C. M.R.I. Professor of Colloid Science, University of Cambridge.

Sir Harold Spencer Jones Kt. F.R.S. Sc.D. B.Sc. F.R.A.S. Astronomer Royal.

Sir Arnold Sorsby M.D. F.R.C.S. Surgeon Royal Eye Hospital. Chairman Anglo–Soviet Medical Committee.

Henry Thomas F.B.A. F.S.A. D.Litt. Keeper of the Printed Books British Museum.

Professor R.H. Tawney Professor of Economic History, University of London.

Professor D.M.S. Watson F.R.S., Professor of Zoology and Comparative Anatomy, University College London.

Dr. W.A. Wooster. Representing the Association of Scientific Workers.

APPENDIX 4

List of Delegates to Newton Tercentenary Celebrations

Algeria	Professor Bourion	Professor of Mathematics at the University of Algiers
Argentina	Dr J.B. Collo, Professor B.A. Houssay	For. Mem. RSO Institute of Biology, Buenos Aires
Australia	Dr E.H. Booth	Wool Secretariat London
	Dr A. Maccoll	London University
Belgium	Professor J. Cox	Rector of Lille University, Astronomer
	Professor C. Manneback	Louvain University, Physics
	Professor J. Timmermans	Professor of Chemical Physics at the University of Brussels
Canada	Professor J.S. Foster	FRS Professor of Physics at McGill University
	Dr P. Gagnon	Laval University
	Professor O. Maass	FRS Physical Chemist at McGill University
	Dr E.S. Moore	President of the Royal Society of Canada, Geologist at the University of Toronto
China	Professor Y.R. Chao	Director of Linguistics, Chungking
	Professor P.Y. Chou	Theoretical Physicist
	Professor T.Y. Wu	Spectroscopist, Peiping
Colonial Empire	Mr A.G. Beattie	Director of Agriculture, Nigeria
	Mr R. Daubney	Kenya Veterinary Services

	Lord Hailey	Chairman of Colonial Research Committee
	Professor W.A.E. Karunaratne	Professor of Pathology at Ceylon University
	Dr H. Smith-Bracewell	Geological Survey, British Guiana
	Dr H.H. Storey	East African Agricultural Research Institute
Czechoslovakia	Professor B. Bydzovsky	Professor of Mathematics at Charles University, Prague
	Professor E. Cech	Professor of Mathematics at Masaryk University
	Professor V. Trkal	Professor of Theoretical Physics at Charles University, Prague
Denmark	Professor N. Bohr	For. Mem. RS, Professor of Physics at Copenhagen University
	Professor A. Krogh	For. Mem. RS, Professor of Physiology at Copenhagen University
	Professor J. Nielsen	Secretary of the Royal Danish Academy
	Professor N.E. Norlund	For. Mem. RS, Professor of Mathematics at Copenhagen University
Ecuador	Dr H.V. Lafronte	Minister Plenipotentiary and Envoy Extraordinary of the Republic of Ecuador in Great Britain
Eire	Dr F.E. Hackett	Member of the Royal Irish Academy
	Dr A.J. McConnell	Professor of Natural Philosophy at Trinity College, Dublin
	Dr J.J. Nolan	Professor of Experimental Physics at University College, Dublin
Finland	Professor J. Wasastjerna	President of the Societas Scientiarum Fennica
France	Dr E. Borel	Member of the Academie des Sciences, Paris
	M. le Duc de Broglie	For. Mem. RS, Member of the Academie des Sciences, Paris
	M. J. Chazy	Member of the Academie des Sciences, Paris
	Professor A. Denjoy	Member of the Academie des Sciences, Paris
	M.H. Deslandres	For. Mem. RS, Member of the Academie des Sciences, Paris
	M.E. Esclangon	Member of the Academie des Sciences, Paris

	Professor J. Hadamard	For. Mem. RS, Member of the Academie des Sciences, Paris
	Professor G. Julia	Member of the Academie des Sciences, Paris
	Professor P. Langevin	For. Mem. RS, Member of the Academie des Sciences, Paris
	M.E. de Margerie	For. Mem. RS, Member of the Academie des Sciences, Paris
Greece	M. Th. Aghnides	H.E. The Greek Ambassador
Hungary	Professor L. Feher	Member of the Magyar Tudomanyos Akademia
	Professor R. Ries	Member of the Magyar Tudomanyos Akademia
India	Professor H.J. Bhabha	F.R.S., Director of the Tata Institute of Fundamental Research, Bombay
	Sir Kariamanikkam Krishnan	F.R.S., Professor of Physics at Allahabad University
	Professor M.N. Saha	F.R.S., Professor of Physics at Calcutta University
	Mr D.N. Wadia	President of the National Institute of Sciences of India
Iran	Dr M. Hessaby	Dean of the Faculty of Science, Teheran
Italy	Professor G. Abetti	Member of the Accademia Nazionale dei Lincei
	Professor G. Armellini	Member of the Accademia Nazionale dei Lincei
Netherlands	Professor J. van der Hoeve	President of the Section of Sciences at the Netherlands Academy
	Professor H.R. Kruyt	Vice President of the Netherlands Academy
	Professor F.A. Vening-Meinesz	For. Mem. RS, Member of the Netherlands Academy
	Professor M.W. Woerdeman	Secretary of the Netherlands Academy
	Professor J. Clay	Professor of Physics at the University of Amsterdam
New Zealand	Dr E.M. Marsden	F.R.S.
Norway	Professor V. Bjerknes	For. Mem. RS, Member of the Norwegian Academy
	Professor O. Holtedahl	President of the Norwegian Academy
	Professor H. Solberg	General Secretary of the Norwegian Academy
	Professor C. Stormer	Member of the Norwegian Academy
Palestine	Professor S. Brodetsky	Leeds University
Poland	Dr C. Bialobrzeski	Member of the Polish Academy

343

	Professor M. Kamienski	Professor of Astronomy at Warsaw
Portugal	Professor V.H. Duarte de Lemos	Former Director of the Faculty of Sciences at Lisbon University
Roumania	Dr N. Vasilesco-Karpen	Former Rector of the Polytechnic Bucharest
Scotland	Professor J. Kendall	FRS, Professor of Chemistry at the University of Edinburgh
	Sir Edmund Whittaker	FRS, Professor of Mathematics at the University of Edinburgh
South Africa	Dr J. Jackson	FRS, HM Astronomer at the Cape
	Professor B.F.J. Schonland	FRS, Scientific Adviser to the Prime Minister
	Professor K. Smeath-Thomas	Principal of Rhodes University
Spain	Don Dr J.M. Otero de Navascues	Member of the Spanish Academy
	Don Dr E. Torroja	Professor of the Institute of Civil Engineering, Madrid
Sweden	Professor B. Lindblad	Member of the Swedish Academy
	Professor T. Svedberg	For. Mem. RS, Member of the Swedish Academy
	Professor N.E. Svedelius	For. Mem. RS, Member of the Swedish Academy
	Professor I. Waller	Theoretical Physicist at Uppsala
Switzerland	Professor A. Mercier	Member of the Swiss Academy
	Professor M. Lugeon	For. Mem. RS, Member of the Swiss Academy
	Dr G. Piotrowski	Member Institut National Genevois
	Professor L. Ruzicka	For. Mem. RS, Member of the Swiss Academy
	Professor G. Tiercy	President of the Swiss Academy
United Kingdom	Professor E.N. da C. Andrade	FRS, Professor of Physics at the University of London
	Dr C.H. Andrewes	FRS, National Institute for Medical Research
	Sir Edward Appleton	FRS, Secretary of the D.S.I.R.
	Professor W.T. Astbury	FRS, Professor of Biomolecular Structure at Leeds University
	Professor P.M.S. Blackett	FRS, Professor of Physics at Manchester University
	Professor D. Brunt	FRS, Professor of Meteorology at Imperial College, London
	Professor S. Chapman	FRS, Professor of Natural Philosophy at Queen's College Oxford
	Sir Henry Dale	FRS, Professor of Chemistry at

		the Royal Institute. London
	Sir Alfred Egerton	Secretary of the Royal Society, Professor of Chemical Technology at Imperial College, London
	Professor F.E. Fritsch	FRS, Professor of Botany at the University of London
	Professor S. Goldstein	FRS, Professor of Applied Mathematics at Manchester University
	Professor A.V. Hill	Foreign Secretary of the Royal Society
	Professor W.V.D. Hodge	FRS, Professor of Astronomy and Geometry at Cambridge University
	Dr G.M. Holmes	FRS, Professor of Geology and Mineralogy at Edinburgh University
	Sir Harold Spencer Jones	FRS, The Astronomer Royal
	Professor H.W. Melville	FRS, Professor of Chemistry at the University of Aberdeen
	Sir Thomas Merton	Treasurer of the Royal Society
	Professor R.A. Peters	FRS, Professor of Biochemistry at Oxford University
	Professor H.H. Plaskett	FRS, Professor of Astronomy at Oxford University
	Professor H.C. Plummer	FRS, Professor of Maths, Military College of Science Woolwich
	Dr D.R. Pye	FRS, Provost of University College London
	Lord Rayleigh	FRS
	Sir Robert Robinson	President of the Royal Society
	Sir Edward Salisbury	Secretary of the Royal Society
	Professor H.W. Turnbull	FRS, Professor of Mathematics at St Andrews University
	Professor S. Zuckerman	FRS, Professor of Anatomy at Birmingham University
Uruguay	Senor R. MacEachen	HE The Uruguayan Ambassador
USA	Dr W.S. Adams	Retiring Director Mount Wilson Observatory
	Professor T.M. Bogert	Professor Emeritus of Chemistry at Colombia University
	Dr F.E. Brasch	Library of Congress, Washington
	Mr L. Carmichael	President of Tufts College, Medford
	Professor L.C. Dunn	Professor of Zoology at Columbia University
	Dr J.C. Hunsaker	Chairman of the National Advisory

345

		Committee for Aeronautics
	Mr H.E. Ives	Physicist at Bell Telephone Laboratories
	Dr T. von Karman	For. Mem. RS, Director of the Guggenheim Aeronautical Laboratory, Pasadena
	Professor T.R. Miles	Professor of Physiology at Yale University
	Dr Peyton Rous	For. Mem. RS, Member of the Rockefeller Institute
USSR	Professor V. Ambartsumian	Astronomer, corresponding member of the Academy of Sciences, USSR
	Professor A. Arbusov	Chemist, head of the Kazan Branch of the Academy of Sciences, USSR
	Dr B. Vedenski	Radio Physicist, head of the Technical Sciences Dept at the Academy of Sciences, USSR
	Professor I. Vinogradov	For. Mem. RS, Mathematician, Director of the Institute of Mathematics of the Academy of Sciences, USSR
Venezuela	Dr H.J. Duarte	Member of the Venezuelan Academy of Science
	Dr E. Rohl	Member of the Venezuelan Academy of Science
Yugoslavia	Dr Z. Markovic	Member of the Yugoslavian Academy
	Dr V.V. Michkovitch	Member of the Yugoslavian Academy
Brazil	Senhor Dr J.J. Moniz de Aragao	HE The Brazilian Ambassador

APPENDIX 5

―――――

Minute about British Ally *from Dora Russell to Keith Fowler*

To: Mr Fowler
From: Mrs Russell

I have been reading carefully the paper prepared by EEID, FO on the subject of periodicals published in Eastern Europe, together with the minutes of the joint meeting between EEID and COI. Certain aspects of this statement of policy seem to me to require analysis and comment.

Though the memorandum contains directives as to what type of material should be used in the papers in question, it still does not make clear what is the underlying policy and ultimate objective of these papers. *British Ally* and the *Voice of England* are paid for by their subscribers and readers in the Soviet Union and in Poland, and by the British tax-payers. Is it not important that this fact should be borne in mind in assessing what the effects of these papers may be on the lives of those people who are paying for them?

One might suppose that the primary object of publications financed in this manner would be to promote better understanding of British life among their readers and to evoke mutual good will. If this is not the primary object, one must ask oneself why such papers should be published at all?

Those people in Eastern Europe who buy the papers surely must do so out of a genuine interest in Great Britain – her life, her art, her scientific achievements. The average Briton, on the other hand, speaking through journals with such names as the *Voice of England* and *British Ally* must wish to have his country presented in a straightforward and favourable light, with a view to gaining him friends and good will in Eastern Europe. Such a presentation of Great Britain and her Commonwealth is not only vitally important but far from difficult.

Britain has played and is playing a great creative role in the world: her culture is rich, her achievements magnificent. There is no need for apology, humility, or undue self-critical analysis, though modesty is not out of place. It seems to me that belief in our Country and the positive achievements and greatness of our people suffices as a fundamental directive to those who serve the British public.

Yet this quality is, on the whole, absent from the *Voice of England* and *British Ally*. On the other hand, it is amply apparent in such papers as *Soviet Weekly*, however crude its approach. Though I wish to make quite clear that I in no way suggest *Soviet Weekly* as a model, it is instructive to consider why our papers lack the 'punch' which *Soviet Weekly* undoubtedly possesses.

I believe the reason for lack of 'punch' to be that these papers are no longer projecting Britain and the British people as a whole, but have become bogged down in the directives of government departments with their own axes to grind, and more especially in the confused animosities of diplomacy. Diplomacy and the projection of Britain through information services are very distinct activities and have little in common either in method or ultimate aim. Nor does the fact that the FO is the department ultimately responsible for overseas publicity invalidate this contention.

EEID's memorandum seems to imply that, so far as the FO is concerned, the main purpose of *British Ally* and the *Voice of England* is to 'publish official statements of British policy in relation to the Eastern bloc' and explicitly states that if such statements are no longer permitted by the censor in Poland it will be necessary to 'consider whether the continued publication of the *Voice of England* is worth while'.

Elsewhere the memorandum speaks of using the *Voice of England* as a 'channel for the new anti-Communist line of publicity adopted in 1948', and, as regards *British Ally* 'using the paper to foment the uneasiness of

Soviet intellectuals in regard to the propaganda put over by Soviet Government'. In addition there is the suggestion of projecting Britain's military and economic strength. The final paragraph proposes that in the absence of 'untoward results' every occasion should be seized to level criticism of Soviet institutions and their conduct if this can be done 'under the pretext of an expression of British and Western opinion'.

In my view the policy suggested by these statements oversteps the legitimate bounds of information services to countries which extend them hospitality and enters the field of political warfare, which is neither morally justifiable nor politically effective in publications whose apparent aim is something quite different. Further, it is a negative and destructive policy in a situation which calls above all things for a creative purpose.

Undoubtedly there is an imperative need to acquaint the peoples of Eastern Europe with the truth about the way of life and aspirations of the British people and the false statements put out by Soviet propaganda are very hard to endure. The answer, however, lies, not in recrimination and sneers but in a positive attitude which gives dignity to our people as individuals and a society.

I consider that the publication of Sir Henry Dale's letter to the Soviet Academy of Sciences has already had 'untoward results' in that it led to the estrangement of some of our fair-minded readers, and the lampooning and ridiculing of Sir Henry – one of our great figures – in *Krokodil* and elsewhere in the Soviet press. One must note that in the main Soviet propaganda of this type goes out in their own papers and on the radio and is not retailed in their official publication in this country.

I think that the tempers of those responsible for the publication of British papers may be too much affected by the volume of Soviet propaganda which they read in the course of official duty. A similar study of the British and American press for home consumption and of the radio broadcast reveals an equal volume of criticism and abuse on the other side. This, no doubt, has its effect in goading the Soviet propagandists to still more extravagant efforts. This virulent propaganda ends in stalemate, as possibly those responsible on both sides may ultimately realise.

In the meantime I wish to plead most earnestly that our publications

349

should take as their task the bridging of this gulf, and the healing of this quarrel, rather than widening and intensifying them. For I cannot agree that the Eastern European peoples and our own should be paying for methods of publicity whose ultimate result must be to set them at enmity with one another.

It may be argued that, if our methods of publicity are regarded as subversive by E. European governments they have it in their power to require discontinuance of the papers. I think this is not likely to happen, and for reasons which may also be worth considering.

First: these governments may well believe that the psychological effect of our journals on their people will be quite contrary to that which our government may hope and desire.

Second: the material which appears in the papers provides a constant and useful clue to what is in the minds of those who control policy.

Third: certain obvious propaganda lines afford the governments excellent opportunities for counter-attack.

Fourth: the necessity of working with Soviet or Polish staff affords them opportunities for picking up information of all kinds and for internal intrigue. These opportunities are greatly increased when the policy of the papers is obscure, indirect, or covertly hostile. Though an atmosphere of suspicion may well be unavoidable, a straightforward job done in a straightforward manner would greatly diminish the trouble and improve internal relations.

Finally, while we may regard the press departments as providing us with good 'nuisance value' in the anti-Soviet campaign initiated in 1948, E. European governments, as events have shown, do not find it difficult to turn the tables and use the departments as 'nuisance value' on their own side.

For all these reasons the new policy would appear to have little strategical value. It is unlikely to produce disaffection in the countries concerned, it can only produce resentment and ill will towards this country and bring discredit upon us. Even on the assumption that we regard the Eastern bloc as an enemy, these methods are likely to strengthen the 'enemy's' resolution and solidarity. I can, in fact, see no purpose which this policy serves other than emotional satisfaction to those who promote it.

27 May 1949

APPENDIX 6

Executive Committee of the Six Point Group

Miss Roxanne Arnold
Miss Sybil Morrison
Miss Gertrude Lieben
Mrs Hazel Hunkins Hallinan
Miss Marion Baker
Miss Clare Campbell
Miss Harriet Campbell
Mrs Diffley
Miss Lyndal Evans

Mrs Clifford Jones
Miss Claire Madden
Miss Elsie Maitland
Miss Charlotte Marsh
Mrs Joan Mineau
Mrs Dora Russell
Miss Myrtle Solomon
Mrs Phyllis Vallance
Miss Muriel Winter

APPENDIX 7

'2000 A.D.' – Six Point Group Pamphlet

2000 A.D. . . . Can the human race survive until then?

Is there a hope that twentieth-century civilization, embodying at least the germ of happiness and prosperity for the modern world, can last out another fifty years?

Has the child born to-day the ghost of a chance of living the 'allotted span' of three score years and ten?

What in fact is the prospect?

Since Hiroshima and Nagasaki these have become the fearful questionings of men and women.

Of men . . . AND WOMEN.

The most urgent need of our time is for constructive, realistic management of world affairs so that war is banished and peaceful co-operation between the nations is assured. From whom will the lead come? From statesmen? Along the years, political man has shown an infinite capacity for making bigger and bigger wars. This may be due to the so-called 'masculine attitude', to tradition, or to mere stupidity; whatever it is, it seems to make it easy, if not inevitable, for the average man to accept the policies that lead to war. Nor can the average woman deny her share of responsibility for the chaos of the world since she has failed to use to the full her political power.

To-day, a lead must come from women whose concern for the

preservation of society must be developed speedily and positively into a great wave of practical enthusiasm for creating the peaceful society in which war can have no place.

How can this be achieved? Ideals and policies have been stated and re-stated but the road to international harmony is still to be found.

Can we find the way?

Women must demand — and accept — a greater share in responsible government. Several generations of men and women have struggled for an equality of the sexes that would give to women their rightful share in government, in social and in economic affairs. The principle of equality is now widely accepted but equal power and responsibility are still denied to women *for no other reason than that they are women*, and every small advance has been won only by determined and often bitter agitation.

Three points should be considered in relation to the problem of sex inequality.

First. A sound society must rest upon the expression within the community of man's view of life, and woman's view of life. A balance and a synthesis is required for society's general welfare and the common good.

But in our society to-day masculine values still predominate. As a result the woman seeking equality has found herself too often obliged to imitate men, too often swayed by values and judgements that are not her own.

Second. It is still necessary to combat some mistaken notions of woman's physical powers. History supplies ample evidence that women did more than their share of heavy work in primitive communities, and in present-day society a high proportion of women carry the double task of home and a full-time job. In fact, the bearing and rearing of children and the duties of a housewife call for powers of physical endurance at least equal, and often superior, to those of men.

Third. In the last few decades many scientific advances in the care of mothers and children have been made, but modern war makes a mockery of this creative effort, for scientific genius is equally vigorous in devising new ways to destroy the life it has fostered with so much care.

Society to-day is like a car running on two cylinders instead of four,

353

and until the capacities of women are accorded the fullest possible expression in our social philosophy, and in the life, plans, and work of the nations, no real advance will be made towards the peaceful society in which men and women, nation and nation, race and race, can live in harmony.

THE SIX POINT GROUP, therefore, proposes to work for the following aims.

1. Peace

The creation of a society in which war can have no place should be the first objective of women, in whom there is a deep biological need to safeguard the future of the human race.

2. International Co-operation

As an essential preliminary to a peaceful society women in all countries must co-operate on a basis unrelated to creed or party.

3. Equal Status

The fight for equality of opportunity and status must continue until occupational, moral, social, economic, legal and political equality has been fully achieved.

4. Equal Power

No government or assembly is fully representative unless it is composed of men and women in equal numbers. Women should, therefore, participate at all levels of government, local, national and international. There cannot be a balanced society without the expression in government of both man's and woman's point of view.

5. Status of the Mother

The status of the wife and the mother must be raised, and society must be so shaped that motherhood does not preclude women from gainful employment and participation in government.

6. *Education of Children*

All children should be given the same educational opportunities and encouraged to develop in accordance with their individual tastes and abilities irrespective of sex. Their education should be directed towards diminishing aggressiveness and encouraging co-operation since competitive aggression is proving so disastrous a factor in international affairs.

THIS POLICY MUST FIND ITS EXPRESSION IN THE CO-OPERATION OF WOMEN'S GROUPS ALL OVER THE WORLD, WHOSE AIM WILL BE TO AWAKEN PEOPLES TO AN UNDERSTANDING OF THE VITAL NECESSITY FOR MEN AND WOMEN TO DISCARD FOR EVER THE PRIMITIVE PURSUITS OF WAR AND SEEK TOGETHER, AND IN FULL EQUALITY, A CREATIVE WAY OF LIFE.

APPENDIX 8

Women's Delegation to Russia, 1951

Members of the Delegation:

Mrs Dora Russell
: International Women's Day Committee, Chairman

Mrs Mollie Mandell
: International Women's Day Manchester Committee, Secretary

Mrs Doughty
: Golders Green Women's Co-operative Guild

Mrs Porter
: Guildswoman, President of Birkenhead, Wallasey and Wirral District Committee of Co-op Women's Guilds, Member of Labour Party

Mrs Chappell
: Cardiff International Women's Day Committee

Dr Mary Barber
: Bacteriologist, St. Thomas's Hospital

Mrs Walker
: Newcastle BSFS, Ex-Teacher, worker for International Women's Day, Tyneside

Mrs O. Davies
: Watford Co-op Education Committee, BSFS Women's Committee

Mrs M. Martin
: Teacher, peace worker

Mrs Margaret Davies
: Clothing worker, elected by factory Dreedner, Manchester

Mrs Sweby	Member of USDAW, Delegate to USDAW Divisional Conference
Mrs Dallamore	Shepherds Bush Co-operative Guild
Mrs Nancy Silverman	Wife of Sidney Silverman, MP for Nelson and Colne
Mrs Allen	Former Councillor, endorsed by Carpenders Park Co-operative Guild
Mrs E. Smith	Guildswoman for many years, Secretary of local Parent Teacher Association
Mrs Molly Keith	International Women's Day National Committee
Miss Rosamund Hayes	Clothing worker, Secretary to Leeds Forum, former delegate to Trades Council
Dr B. Ibbotson	Clinical Assistant, Temperance Hospital, National Committee of International Women's Day
Mrs M. Evans	Chairman, Bishopstone Ward Labour Party Bristol, housewife
Mrs Pecker	Member of Intenational Women's Day North-west London Committee

APPENDIX 9

Mothers' Declaration

APPEAL OF MOTHERS
FOR THE DEFENCE OF CHILDREN AND YOUNG PEOPLE AND FOR
THEIR EDUCATION IN THE SPIRIT OF PEACE

The Permanent International Committee of Mothers, considering the question of peace in relation to the present condition of children observes with regret that, at a time when all people should reap the benefit of the outstanding discoveries of science two-thirds of the world's children, according to a UNICEF report, live in deplorable conditions, harmful to their physical, moral and mental development.

Atomic energy, which could bring prosperity and well-being to all mankind, but now in fact used for purposes of war, constitutes an unprecedented danger to all those children affected by harmful radiation.

Further, in the field of education, it is clear that hundreds of millions of children, especially girls, are still illiterate. Large numbers of children, although they receive instruction, can scarcely be called educated. Many are subjected to the pernicious influence of bad radio and television broadcasts, to unwholesome literature and films, which predispose them to violence and feelings of hatred inimical to co-operation with other peoples.

Moreover, the atmosphere of the cold war fosters suspicion among young people, parents and educators; it hinders mutual understanding at the very moment when the world so greatly needs a fruitful exchange of ideas on the problems of peace, education and the care of children. Military service interrupts the harmonious development, the forming of the intellect and the professional training of young men. In many countries, increasing numbers of parents and educators are becoming concerned and feel that the moral standards of youth are in danger.

This state of affairs demands on the part of the adults that they themselves should shake off the prejudices which they derive from the cold war, in order that they may educate young people in a brotherly and co-operative spirit. It requires also a closer contact between parents and educators on the methods and principles of bringing up children.

The Permanent International Committee of Mothers calls upon parents, educators, churches and religious bodies, writers, journalists, on all those responsible for radio and television programmes and for the production of films, to use their best endeavours to bring the peoples closer together for the creation of a better world.

It urges Governments and Members of Parliaments to concern themselves more seriously with the needs of youth, and requests them to re-examine the conception of education in accordance with the principles set forth above.

It calls for free compulsory primary education in all countries of the world.

The Permanent International Committee of Mothers declares its support for the activities of the United Nations Commissions and Specialised Agencies — such as UNICEF and UNESCO. In accordance with the principle of co-operation, we would request a close working relationship within the UN agencies based on equality of all States.

It proposes that member States of the United Nations, instead of increasing their military budgets, should allocate far greater financial assistance to the various Specialised Agencies, for the express purpose of improving the condition of children, more especially of those in under-developed countries, with regard to differences of race and religion.

The Committee regrets the insufficient publicity given to the activities of the various United Nations Commissions and Agencies, which, because of lack of information, do not receive more effective support from the public.

The Permanent International Committee of Mothers supports the Declaration of the Rights of Children and asks that it should be approved by the General Assembly of the United Nations.

The Committee expresses its desire to co-operate with all organisations and institutions which work for the protection of children and for peace.

INDEX

Mayes, Eileen, 233
Mayhew, Christopher (Baron Mayhew), 102
Meade, James Edward, 165, 167
Medical Women's Association, 239
Midgely, Mary, 316
Mikardo, Ian, 132
Mildenhall, Suffolk, 228
Milk Marketing Board, 84
Miller, Wright, 56, 82, 101
Mills, John Platt, 126, 228
Milne, Professor E.A., 29, 33–4
Ministry of Information, x, 4–9, 10–24, 27–8, 30, 41, 42, 48, 50, 100, 126, 183, 254, 260, 262, 284; see also British Ally, Britansky Soyuznik and Central Office of Information
Molotov, Vyacheslav, 10–11, 12, 23, 39, 76, 98, 214
Montagu, Ivor, 131, 132, 133
Morgan, George, 221, 222, 224
Morley, Iris, 36–7
Morrell, Lady Ottoline, 286
Morrison, Herbert, 106, 131, 136
Morrison, Sybil, 114, 116, 118, 128, 130
Mortimer, Jim, 127
Moscow Conference see World Congress of Women
Mothers' Committee, 179, 198–205, 207, 211, 215–17, 218–21, 222, 223, 225, 226, 227, 229, 237, 240, 242, 243, 246, 248
Mothers' Congresses, 196–8, 202, 222, 225
Mothers' Declaration (1956), 199, 200–201, 215, 217
Mott, Professor N.F., 29, 33
Murray, Marris, 13
Murray, Thomas, 97

Nansen, Fridtjof, 98
National Assembly of Women, 46, 123–4, 151, 177, 212, 218, 219
National Federation of Indian Women, 176–81, 220
National Union of Teachers, 64, 65, 70, 249–54
National Union of Women Teachers, 116
NATO (North Atlantic Treaty Organisation), 99, 193, 238, 297
Needham, Professor Joseph, 23, 28, 100, 126, 127, 149
Nehru, Jawaharlal, 179
Neruda, Pablo, 150
New Left, 108, 217
Newton, Isaac, tercentenary, 45, 46, 51–5
NGO's (non-governmental organisations), 8, 152–72, 181–2, 211–15, 216, 222
Nicholson, Max, 61
Nicod, Thérèse, 270
Normanton, Helena, 122
Norrish, Professor R.G.W., 28, 29, 33
Nutting, Lady Helen, 100, 119, 121
Nyerere, Julius, 326

OEEC (Organisation for European Economic Co-operation), 77, 95
Oliphant, Professor Marcus L.E., 71
Olympic Games, 298
O'Neil, Colette, 191
Open Door Council, 213
Open Head Press, 283, 294
Orwell, George, 109
Oshinsky, Lydia, 56, 60, 80

Palme, Olaf, 326
Pan-American Union, 7, 27

371